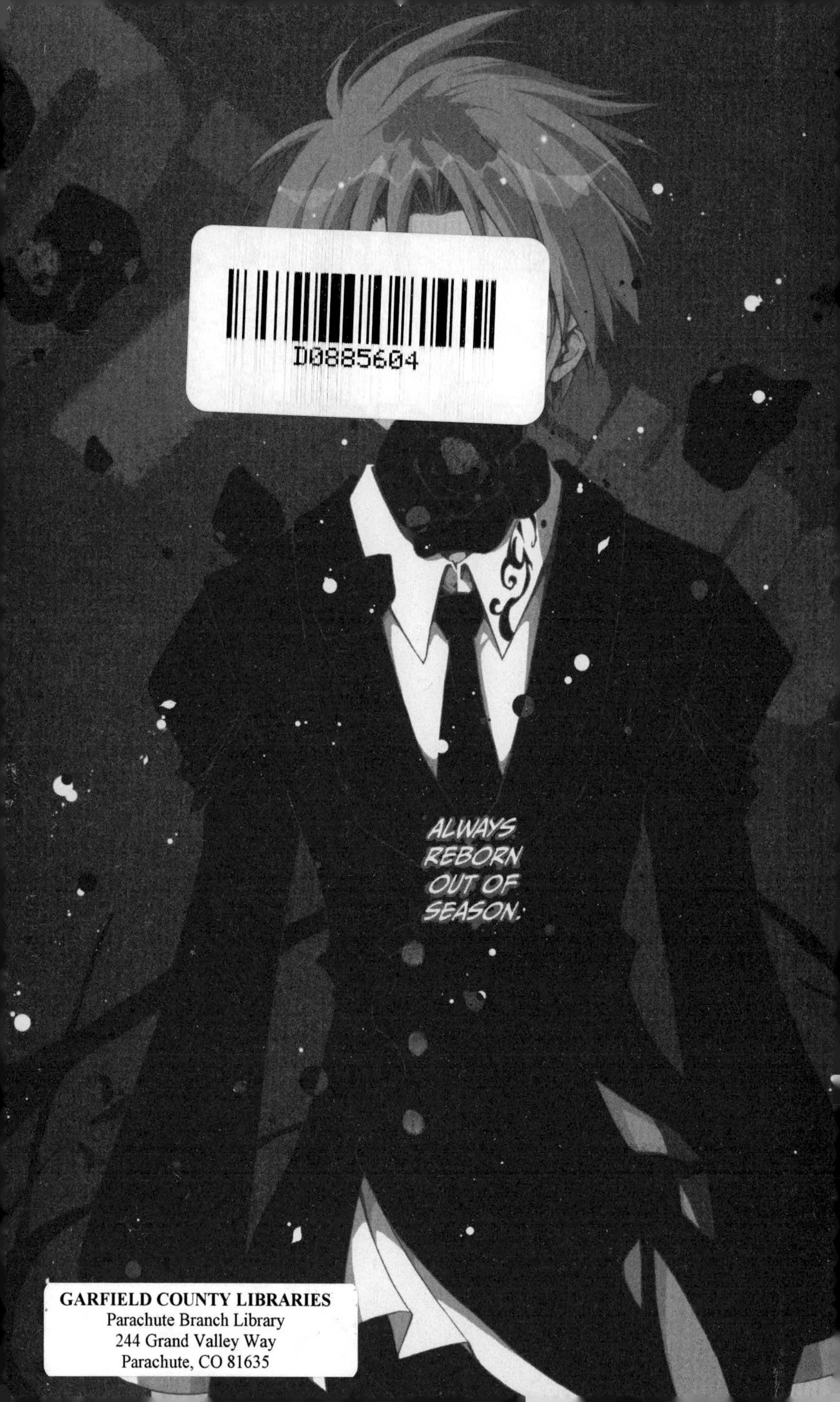
ALWAYS
REBORN
OUT OF
SEASON.

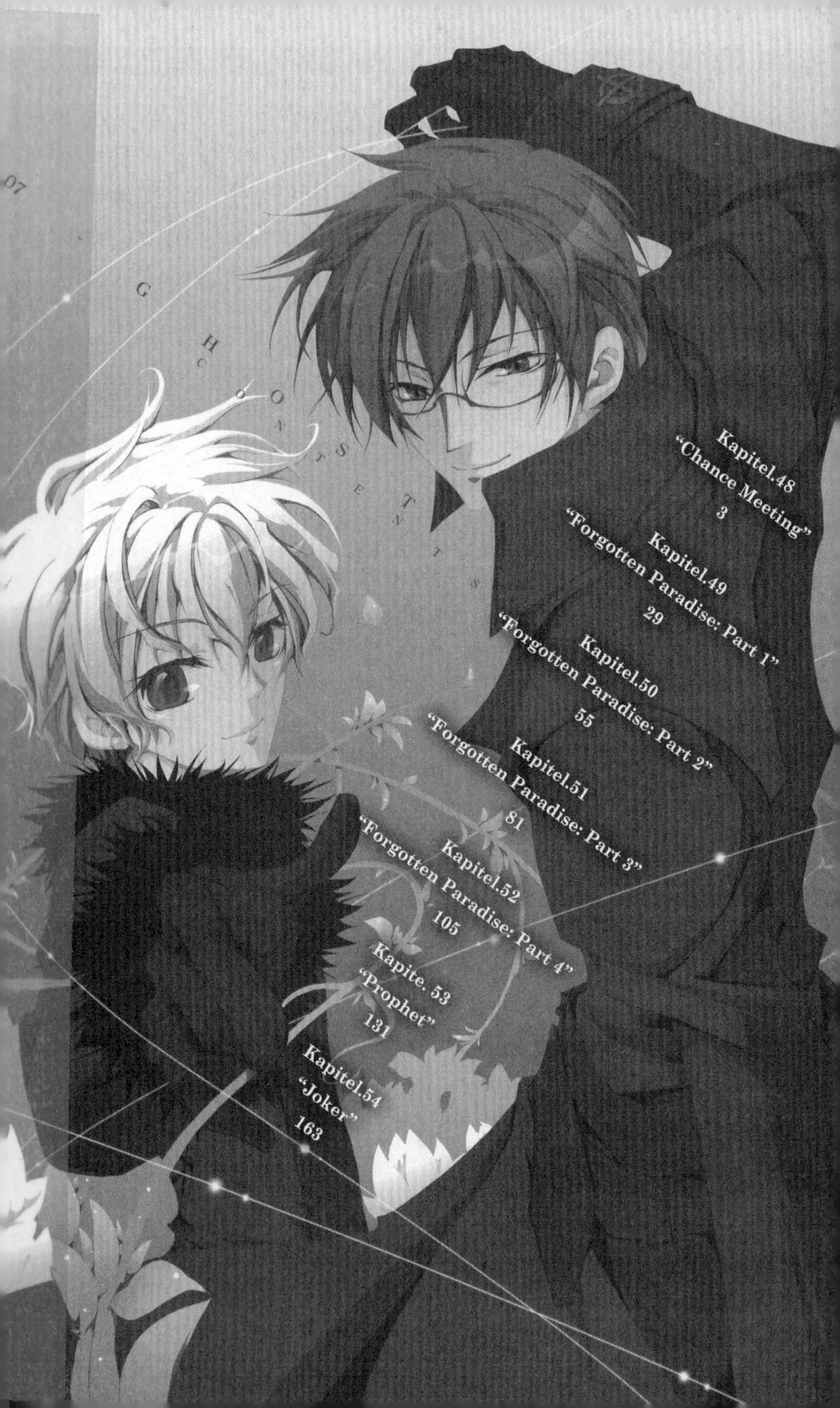

07
CONTENTS
Kapitel.48
"Chance Meeting"
3
Kapitel.49
"Forgotten Paradise: Part 1"
29
Kapitel.50
"Forgotten Paradise: Part 2"
55
Kapitel.51
"Forgotten Paradise: Part 3"
81
Kapitel.52
"Forgotten Paradise: Part 4"
105
Kapite. 53
"Prophet"
131
Kapitel.54
"Joker"
163

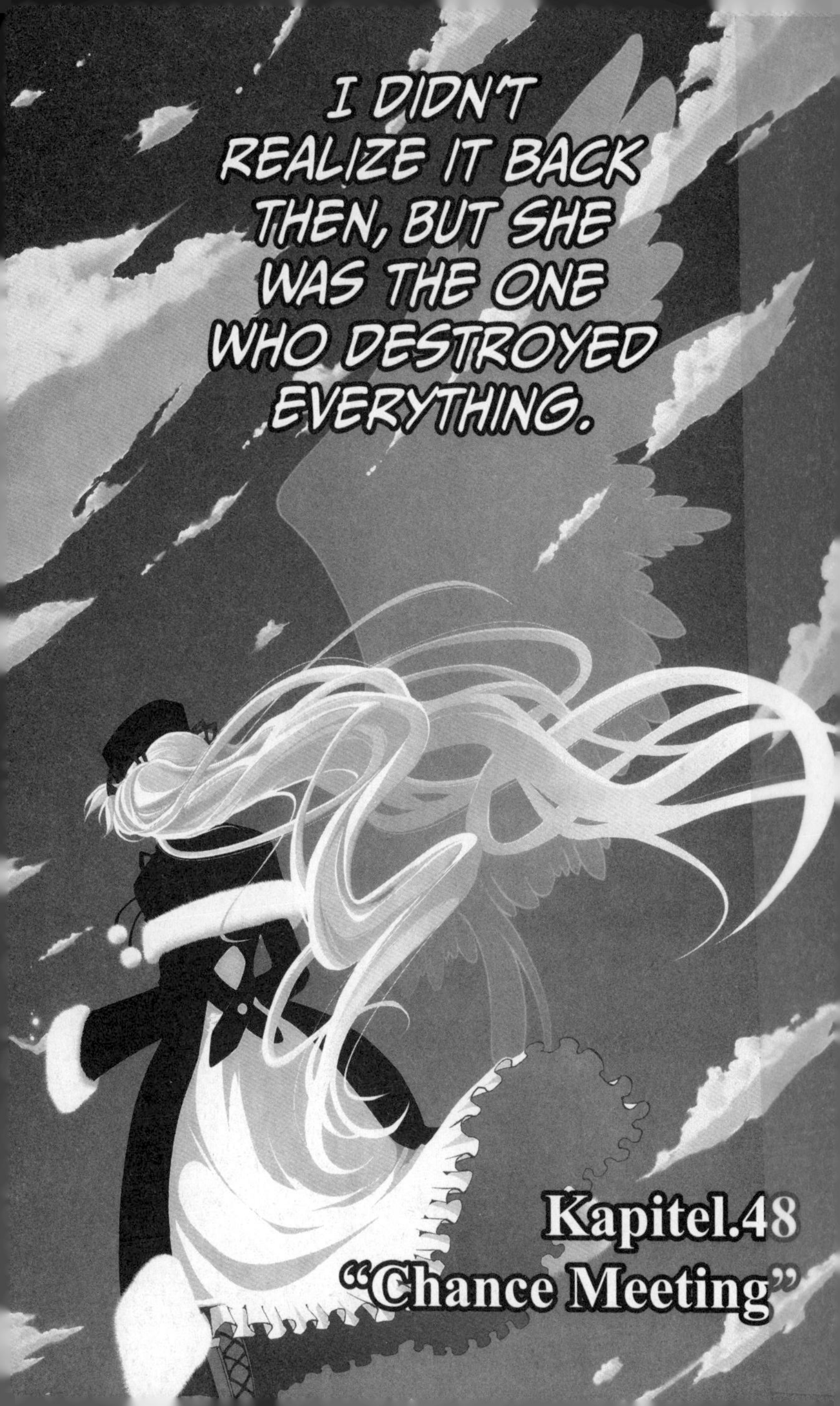
I DIDN'T REALIZE IT BACK THEN, BUT SHE WAS THE ONE WHO DESTROYED EVERYTHING.
Kapitel.48
"Chance Meeting"

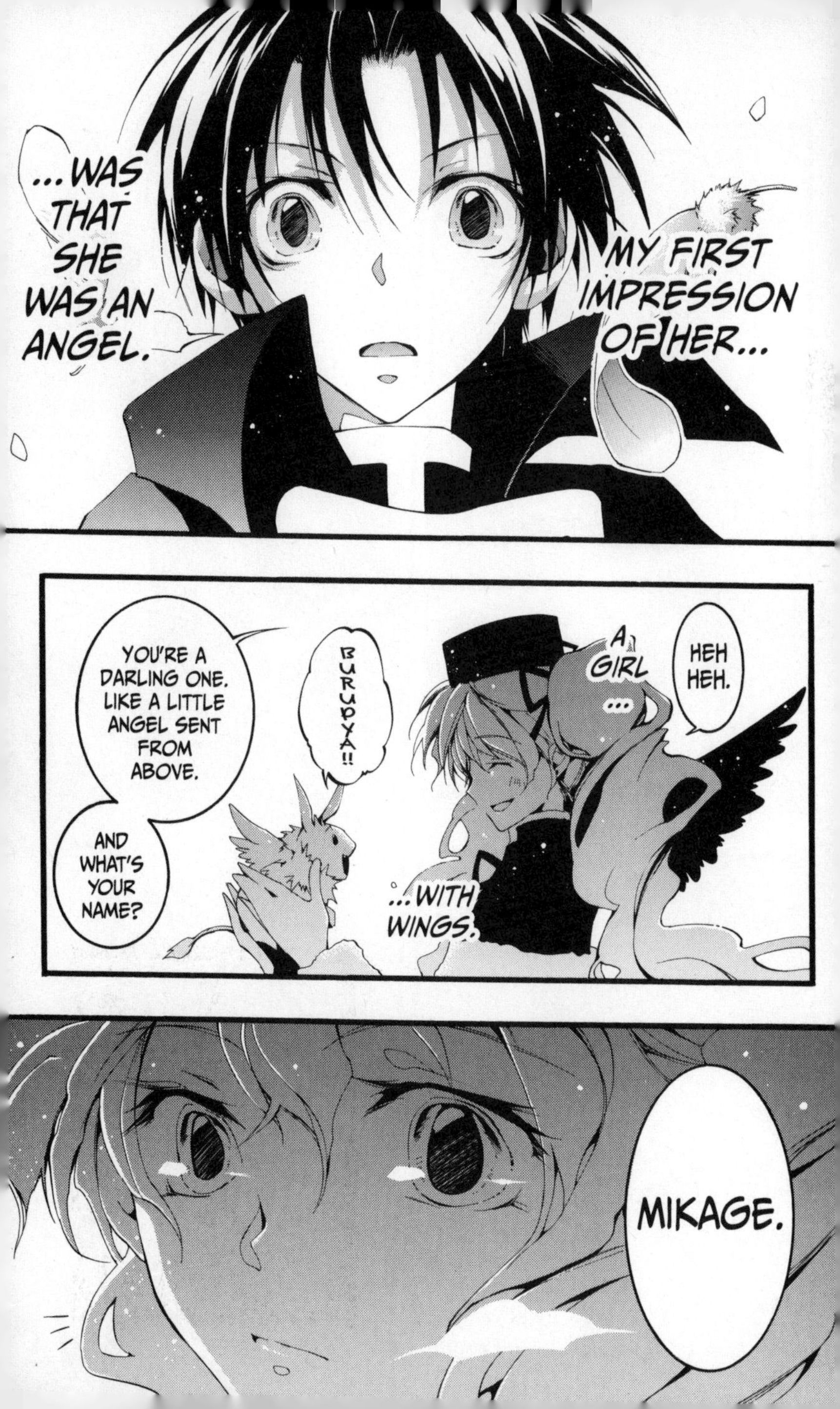
MY FIRST IMPRESSION OF HER...
...WAS THAT SHE WAS AN ANGEL.
HEH HEH.
A GIRL ...
...WITH WINGS.
BURUPYA!!
YOU'RE A DARLING ONE. LIKE A LITTLE ANGEL SENT FROM ABOVE.
AND WHAT'S YOUR NAME?
MIKAGE.

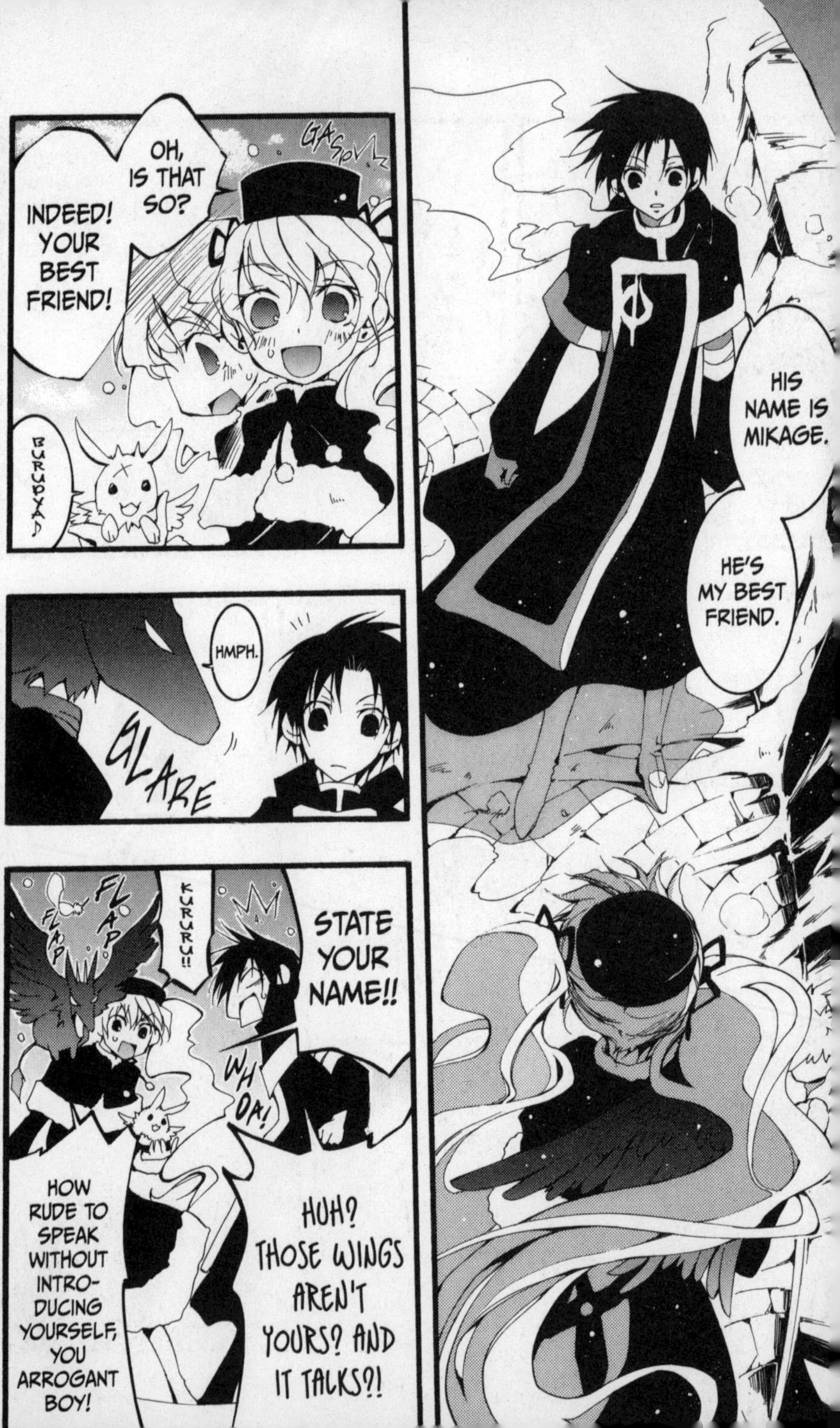
HIS NAME IS MIKAGE.
HE'S MY BEST FRIEND.
OH, IS THAT SO?
INDEED! YOUR BEST FRIEND!
BURUPYA♪
HMPH.
GLARE
STATE YOUR NAME!!
KURURU!!
FLAP
FLAP
WHOA!
HUH? THOSE WINGS AREN'T YOURS? AND IT TALKS?!
HOW RUDE TO SPEAK WITHOUT INTRO-DUCING YOURSELF, YOU ARROGANT BOY!

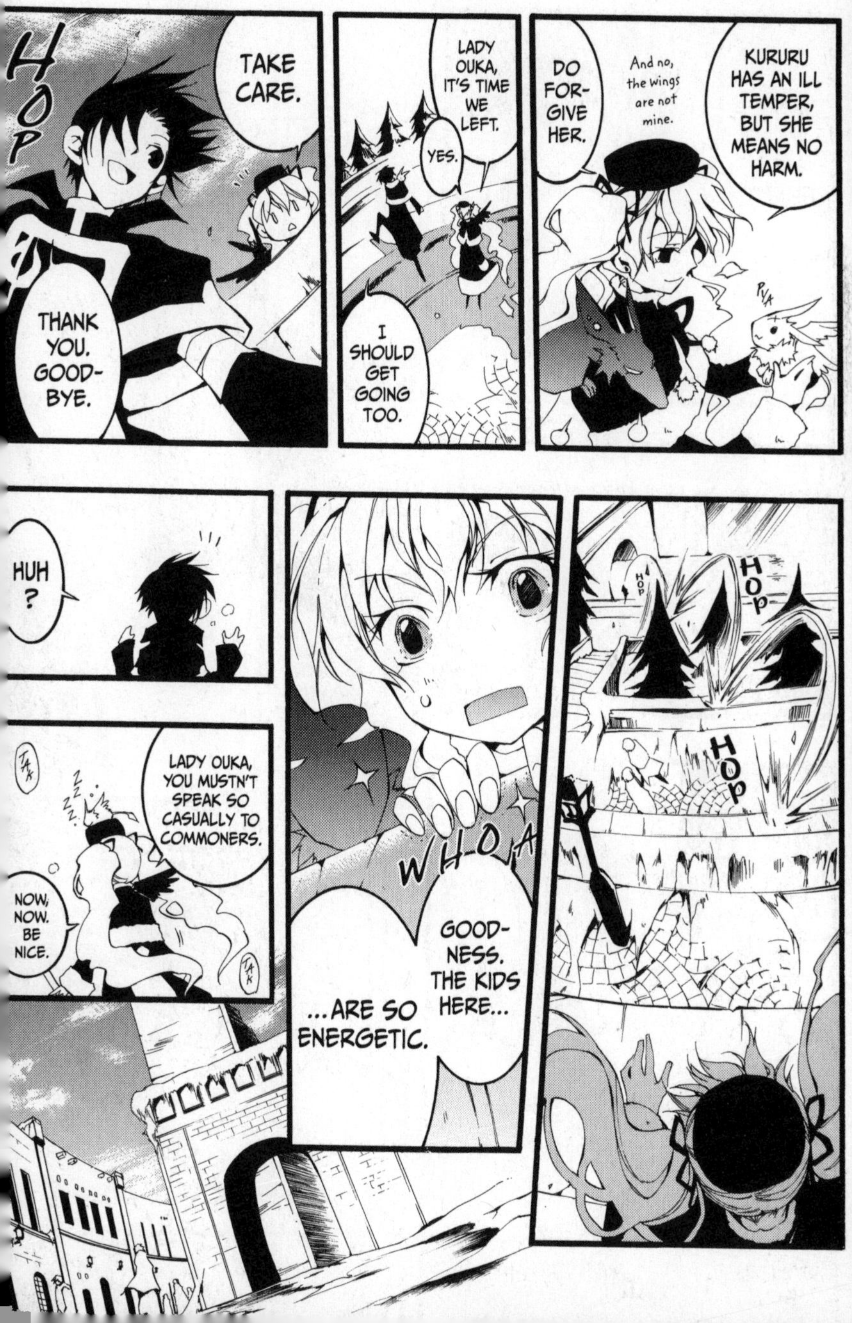
KURURU HAS AN ILL TEMPER, BUT SHE MEANS NO HARM.
And no, the wings are not mine.
DO FOR-GIVE HER.
PYA
LADY OUKA, IT'S TIME WE LEFT.
YES.
I SHOULD GET GOING TOO.
TAKE CARE.
HOP
THANK YOU. GOOD-BYE.
HOP
HOP
HOP
WHOA
GOOD-NESS. THE KIDS HERE...
...ARE SO ENERGETIC.
HUH?
TAK
LADY OUKA, YOU MUSTN'T SPEAK SO CASUALLY TO COMMONERS.
NOW, NOW. BE NICE.
TAK

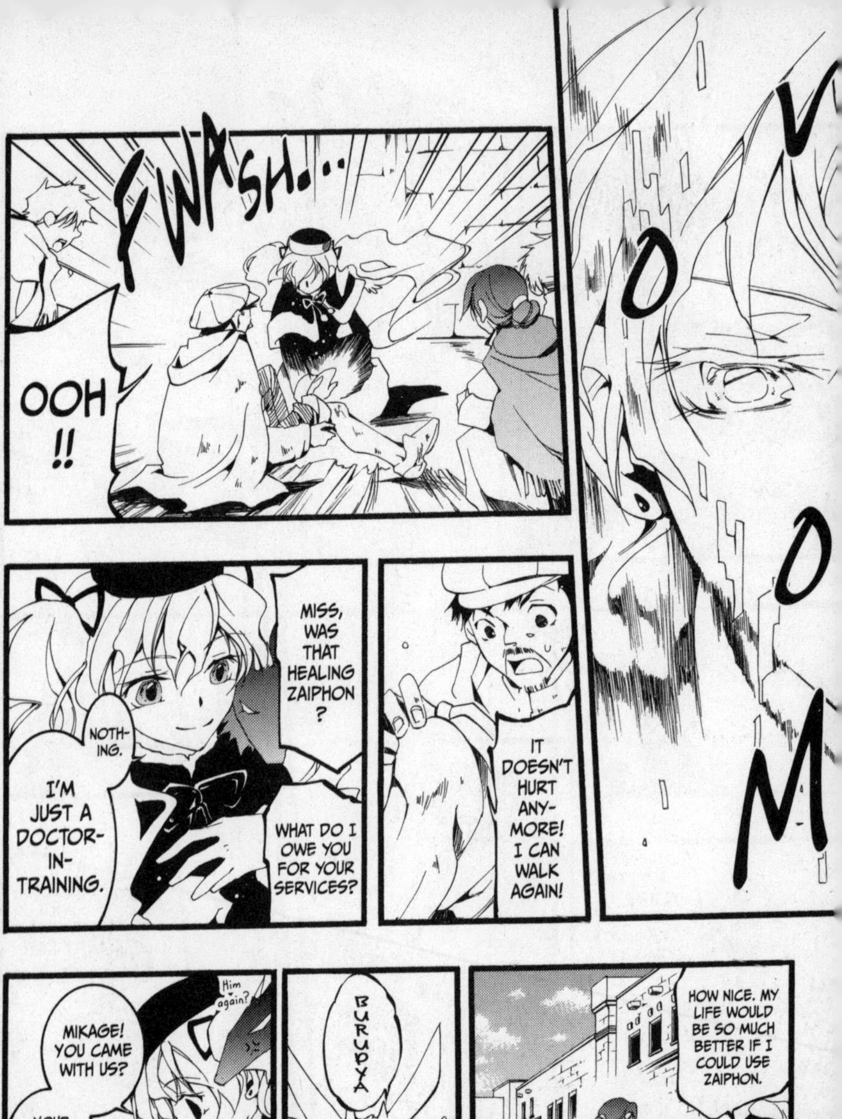
DOOM
FWASH...
OOH!!
IT DOESN'T HURT ANYMORE! I CAN WALK AGAIN!
MISS, WAS THAT HEALING ZAIPHON?
WHAT DO I OWE YOU FOR YOUR SERVICES?
NOTHING.
I'M JUST A DOCTOR-IN-TRAINING.
HOW NICE. MY LIFE WOULD BE SO MUCH BETTER IF I COULD USE ZAIPHON.
Next?
PLEASE HELP MY SON.
BURUPYA
Him again?
MIKAGE! YOU CAME WITH US?
YOUR FRIEND MUST BE WORRIED.

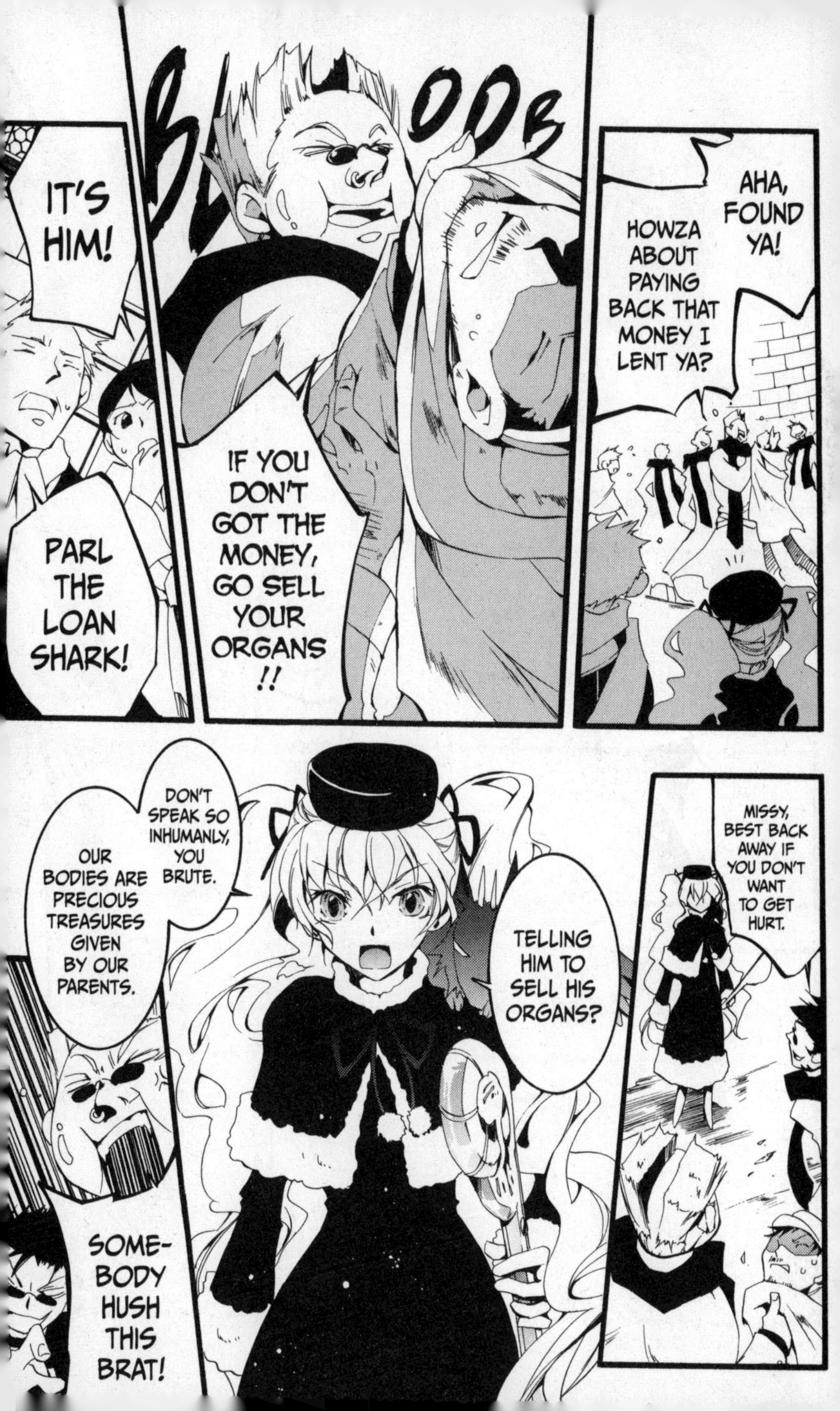
AHA, FOUND YA!
HOWZA ABOUT PAYING BACK THAT MONEY I LENT YA?
IF YOU DON'T GOT THE MONEY, GO SELL YOUR ORGANS!!
IT'S HIM!
PARL THE LOAN SHARK!
MISSY, BEST BACK AWAY IF YOU DON'T WANT TO GET HURT.
TELLING HIM TO SELL HIS ORGANS?
DON'T SPEAK SO INHUMANLY, YOU BRUTE.
OUR BODIES ARE PRECIOUS TREASURES GIVEN BY OUR PARENTS.
SOME-BODY HUSH THIS BRAT!

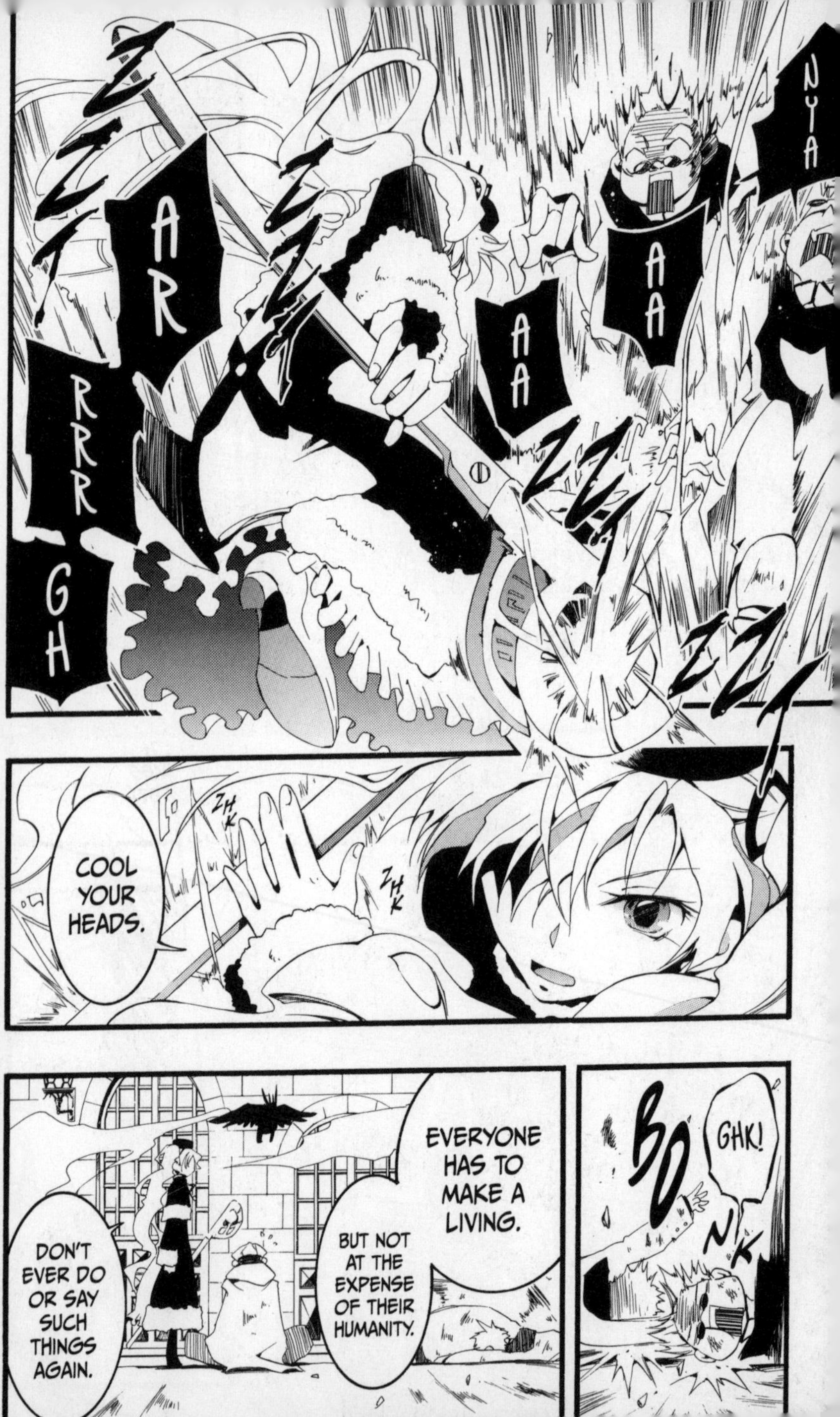
NYA
AA
AA
AR
RRRR
GH
ZHK
ZHK
COOL YOUR HEADS.
BONK
GHK!
EVERYONE HAS TO MAKE A LIVING.
BUT NOT AT THE EXPENSE OF THEIR HUMANITY.
DON'T EVER DO OR SAY SUCH THINGS AGAIN.

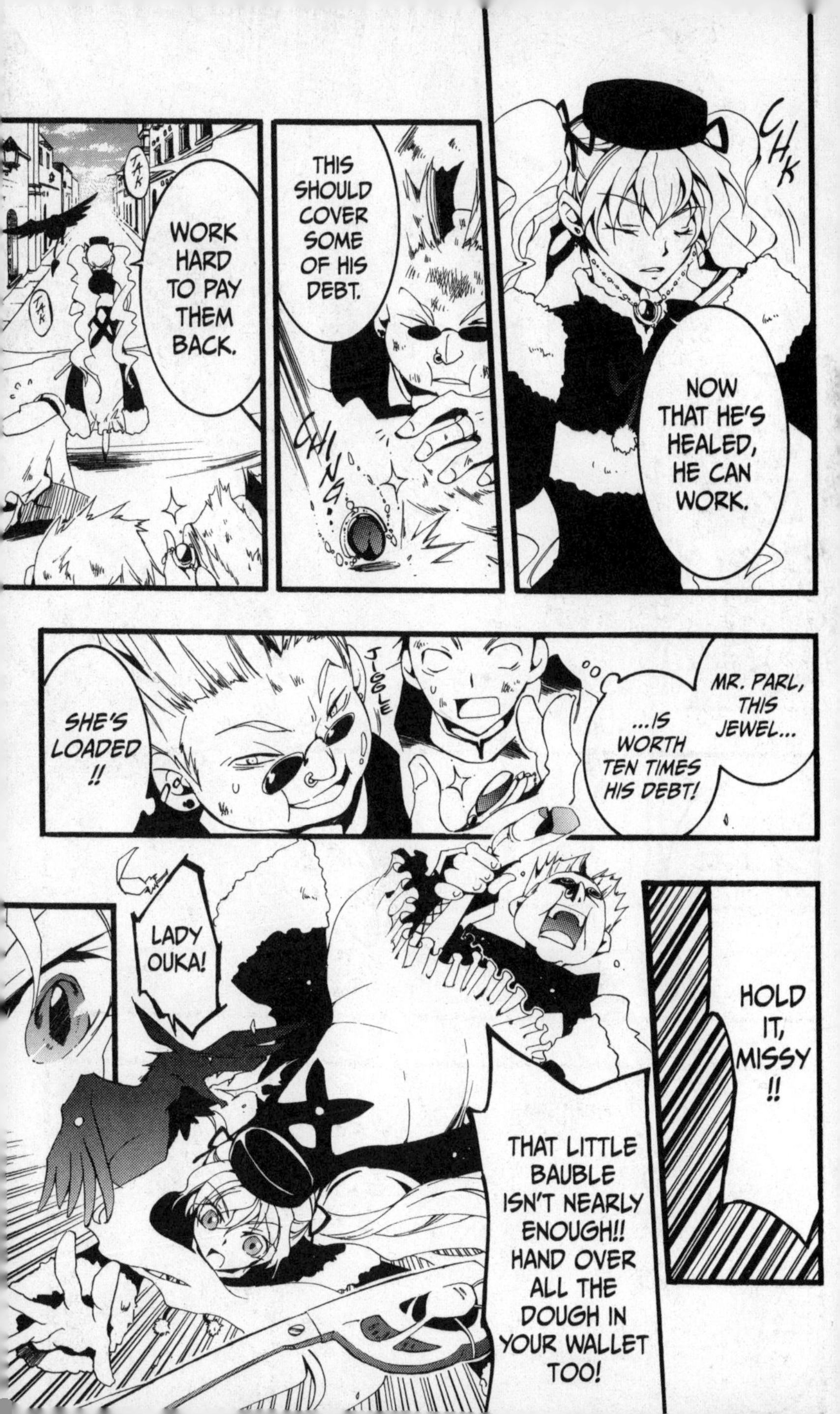
CHK
NOW THAT HE'S HEALED, HE CAN WORK.
THIS SHOULD COVER SOME OF HIS DEBT.
CHING
WORK HARD TO PAY THEM BACK.
MR. PARL, THIS JEWEL...
...IS WORTH TEN TIMES HIS DEBT!
JIGGLE
SHE'S LOADED !!
HOLD IT, MISSY !!
THAT LITTLE BAUBLE ISN'T NEARLY ENOUGH!! HAND OVER ALL THE DOUGH IN YOUR WALLET TOO!
LADY OUKA!

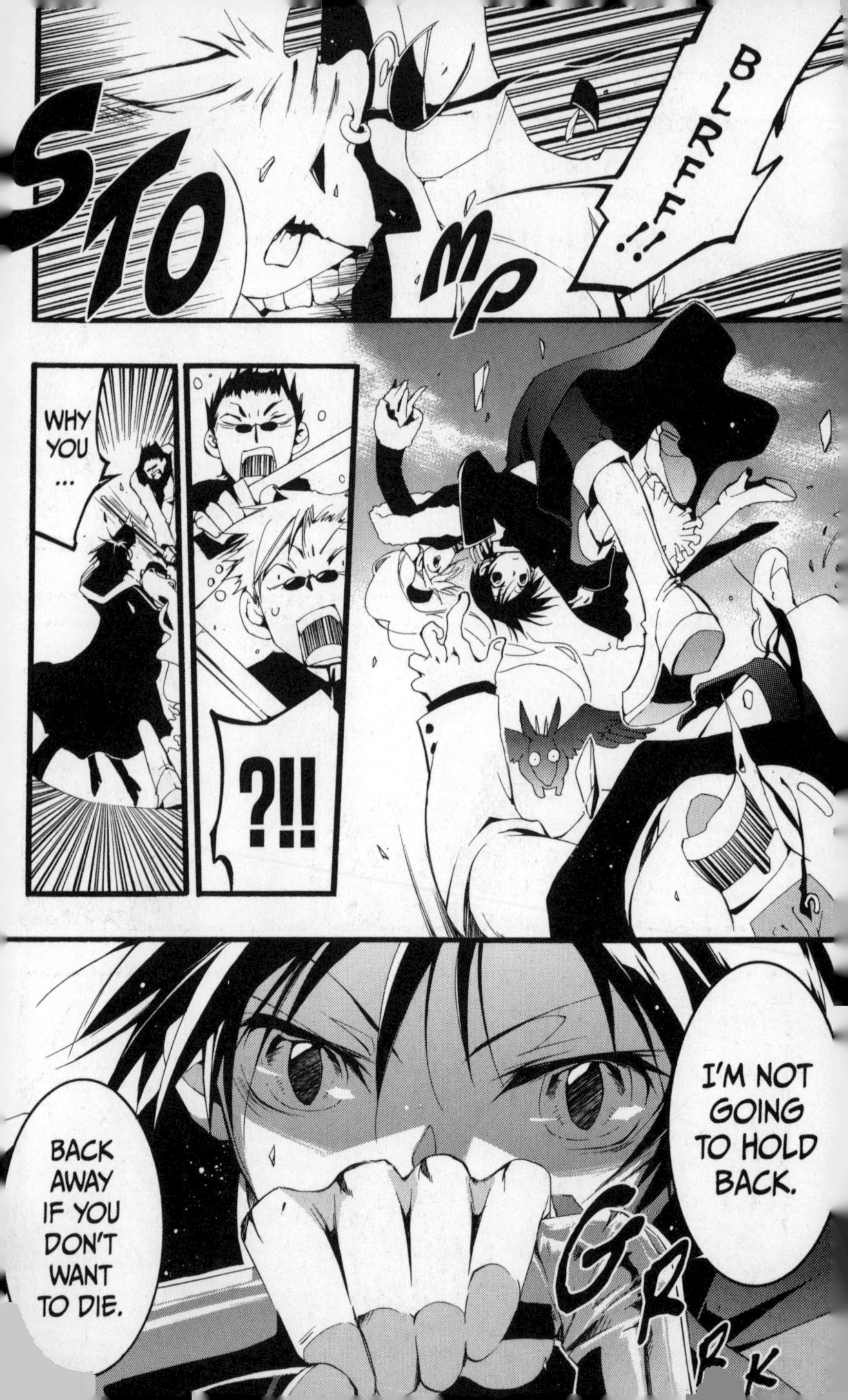
BLRFF!!
STOMP
?!!
WHY YOU ...
I'M NOT GOING TO HOLD BACK.
BACK AWAY IF YOU DON'T WANT TO DIE.
GRRK

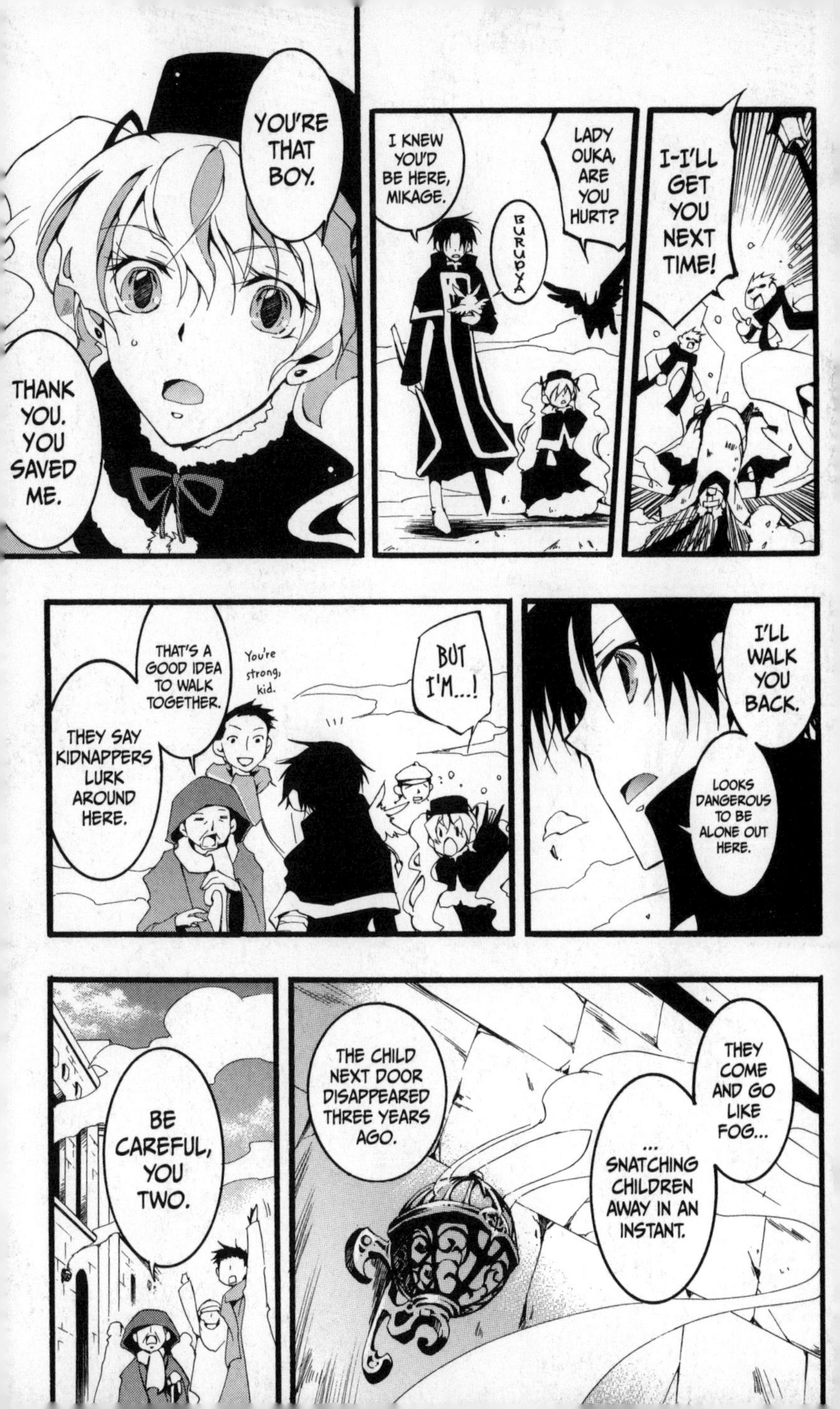
I-I'LL GET YOU NEXT TIME!
LADY OUKA, ARE YOU HURT?
I KNEW YOU'D BE HERE, MIKAGE.
BURUPYA
YOU'RE THAT BOY.
THANK YOU. YOU SAVED ME.
I'LL WALK YOU BACK.
LOOKS DANGEROUS TO BE ALONE OUT HERE.
BUT I'M...!
You're strong, kid.
THAT'S A GOOD IDEA TO WALK TOGETHER.
THEY SAY KIDNAPPERS LURK AROUND HERE.
THEY COME AND GO LIKE FOG...
...SNATCHING CHILDREN AWAY IN AN INSTANT.
THE CHILD NEXT DOOR DISAPPEARED THREE YEARS AGO.
BE CAREFUL, YOU TWO.

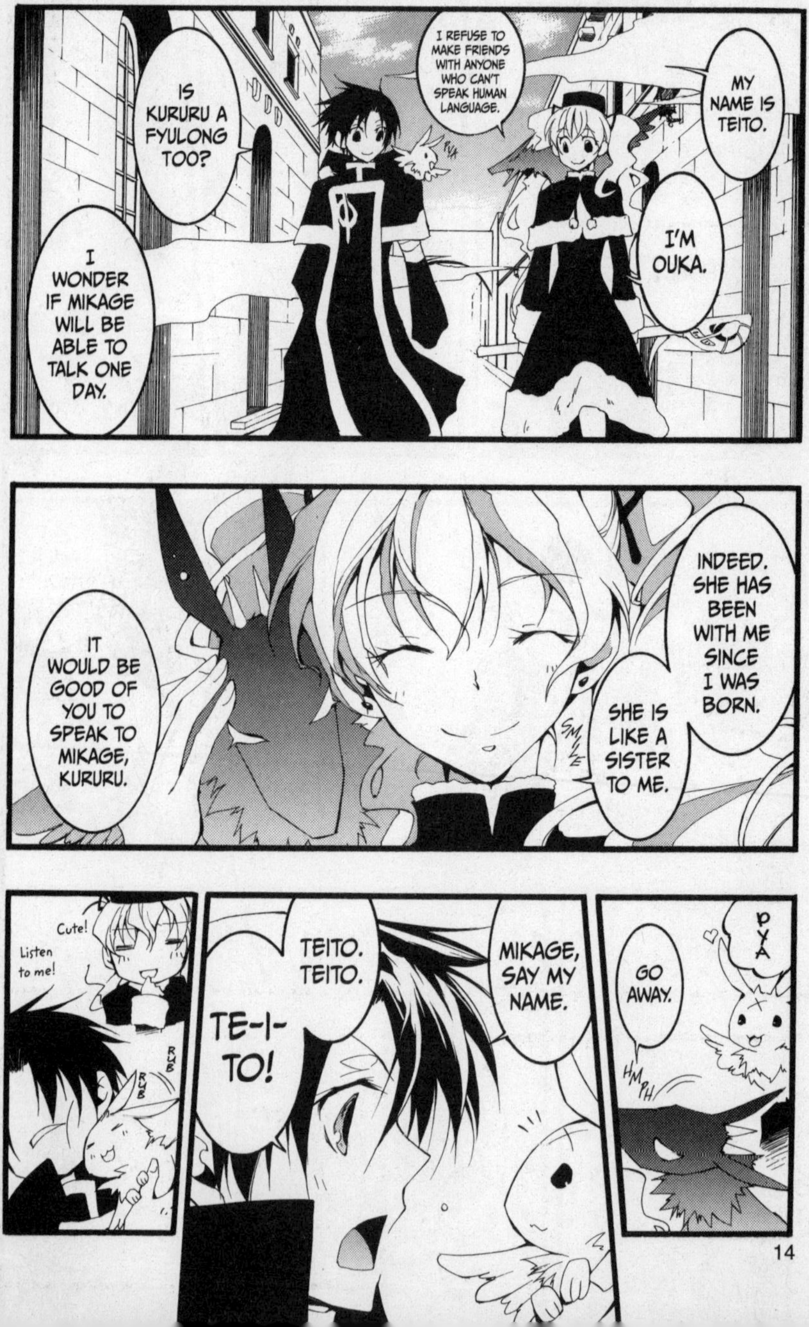

MY NAME IS TEITO.
I'M OUKA.
I REFUSE TO MAKE FRIENDS WITH ANYONE WHO CAN'T SPEAK HUMAN LANGUAGE.
PYA
IS KURURU A FYULONG TOO?
I WONDER IF MIKAGE WILL BE ABLE TO TALK ONE DAY.
INDEED. SHE HAS BEEN WITH ME SINCE I WAS BORN.
SHE IS LIKE A SISTER TO ME.
SMILE
IT WOULD BE GOOD OF YOU TO SPEAK TO MIKAGE, KURURU.
PYA
GO AWAY.
HMPH
MIKAGE, SAY MY NAME.
TEITO. TEITO.
TE-I-TO!
Cute!
Listen to me!
RUB
RUB

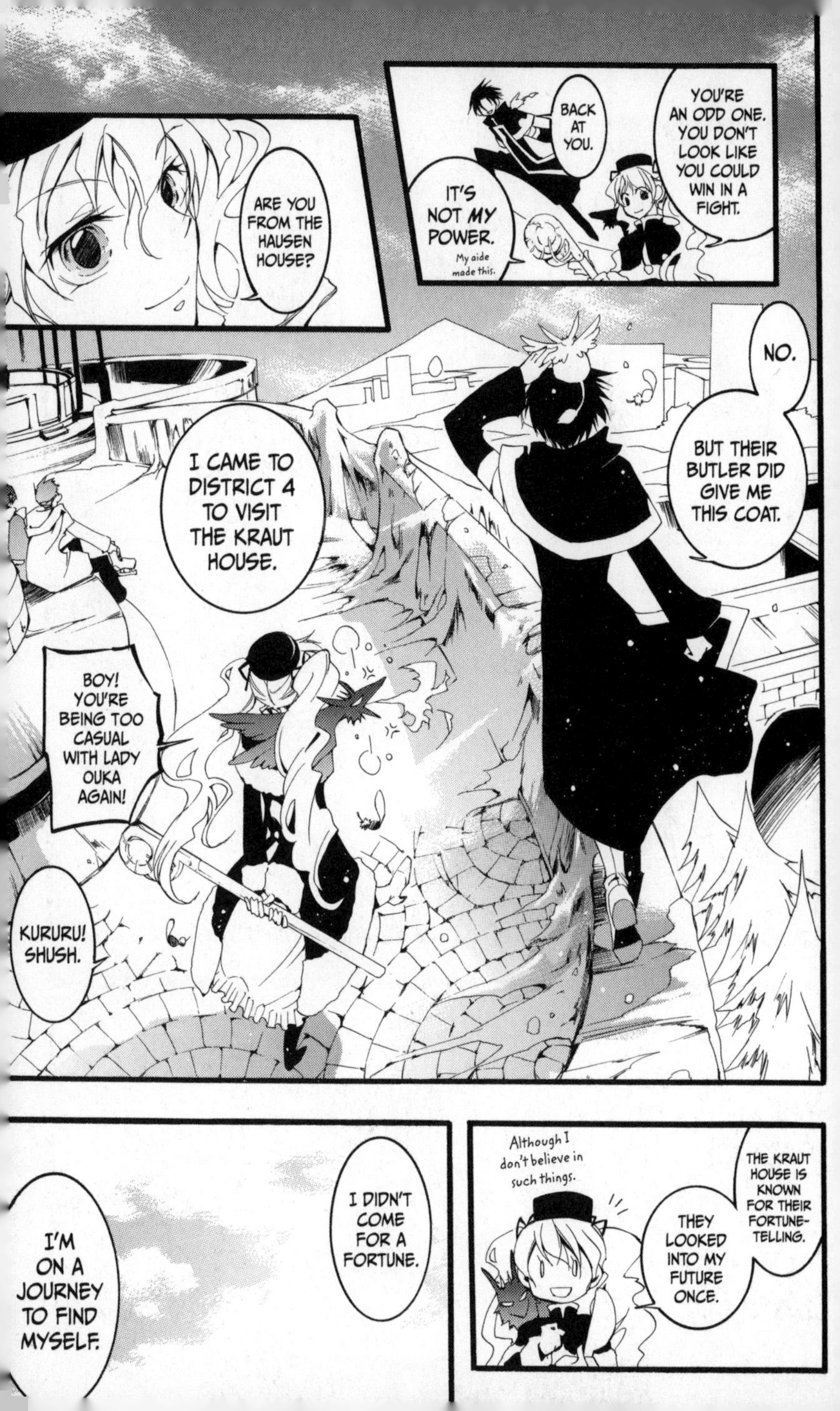
YOU'RE AN ODD ONE. YOU DON'T LOOK LIKE YOU COULD WIN IN A FIGHT.
BACK AT YOU.
IT'S NOT *MY* POWER.
My aide made this.
ARE YOU FROM THE HAUSEN HOUSE?
NO.
BUT THEIR BUTLER DID GIVE ME THIS COAT.
I CAME TO DISTRICT 4 TO VISIT THE KRAUT HOUSE.
BOY! YOU'RE BEING TOO CASUAL WITH LADY OUKA AGAIN!
KURURU! SHUSH.
THE KRAUT HOUSE IS KNOWN FOR THEIR FORTUNE-TELLING.
Although I don't believe in such things.
THEY LOOKED INTO MY FUTURE ONCE.
I DIDN'T COME FOR A FORTUNE.
I'M ON A JOURNEY TO FIND MYSELF.

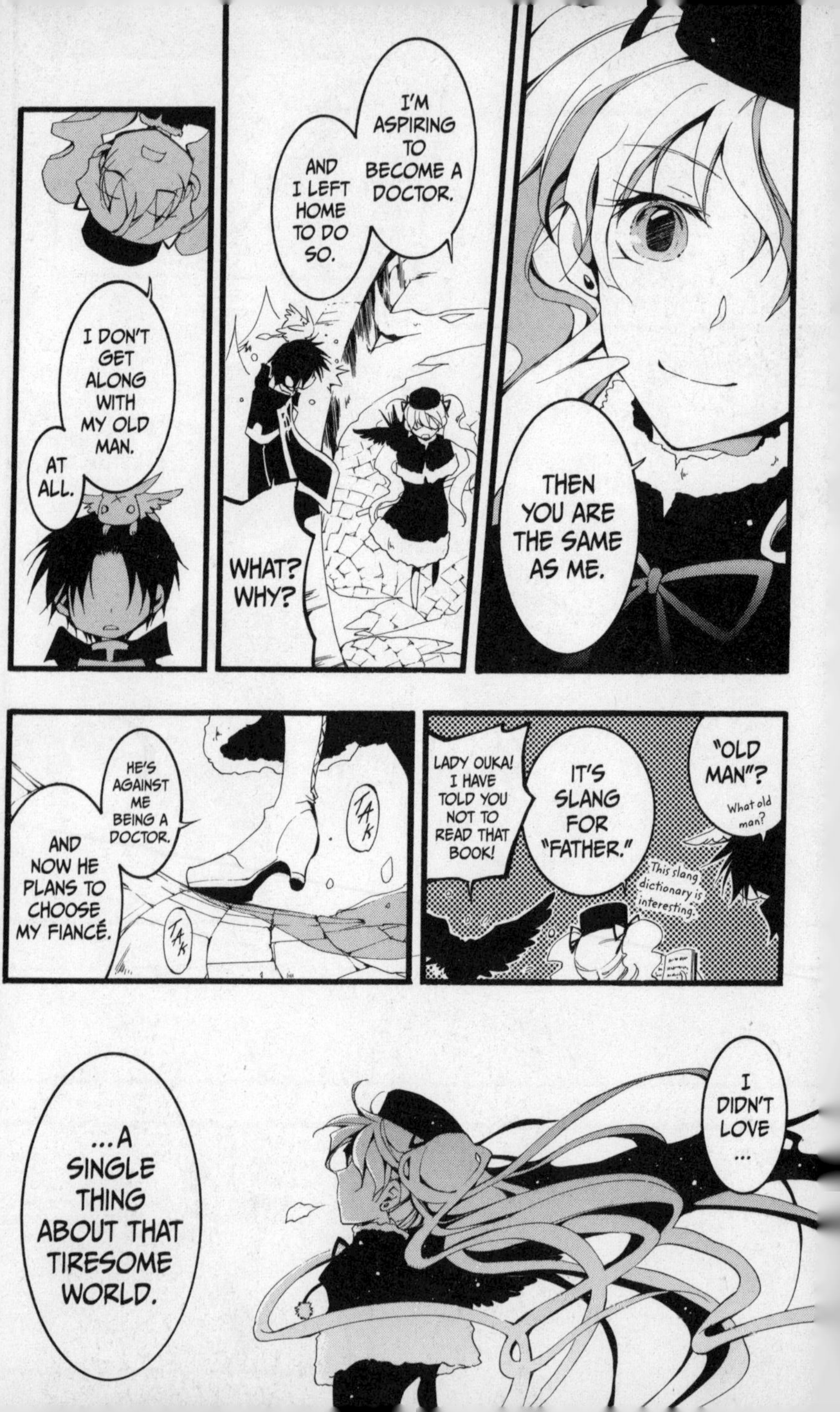
THEN YOU ARE THE SAME AS ME.
I'M ASPIRING TO BECOME A DOCTOR.
AND I LEFT HOME TO DO SO.
WHAT? WHY?
I DON'T GET ALONG WITH MY OLD MAN.
AT ALL.
"OLD MAN"?
What old man?
IT'S SLANG FOR "FATHER."
LADY OUKA! I HAVE TOLD YOU NOT TO READ THAT BOOK!
This slang dictionary is interesting.
TAK
HE'S AGAINST ME BEING A DOCTOR.
AND NOW HE PLANS TO CHOOSE MY FIANCÉ.
TAK
I DIDN'T LOVE...
...A SINGLE THING ABOUT THAT TIRESOME WORLD.

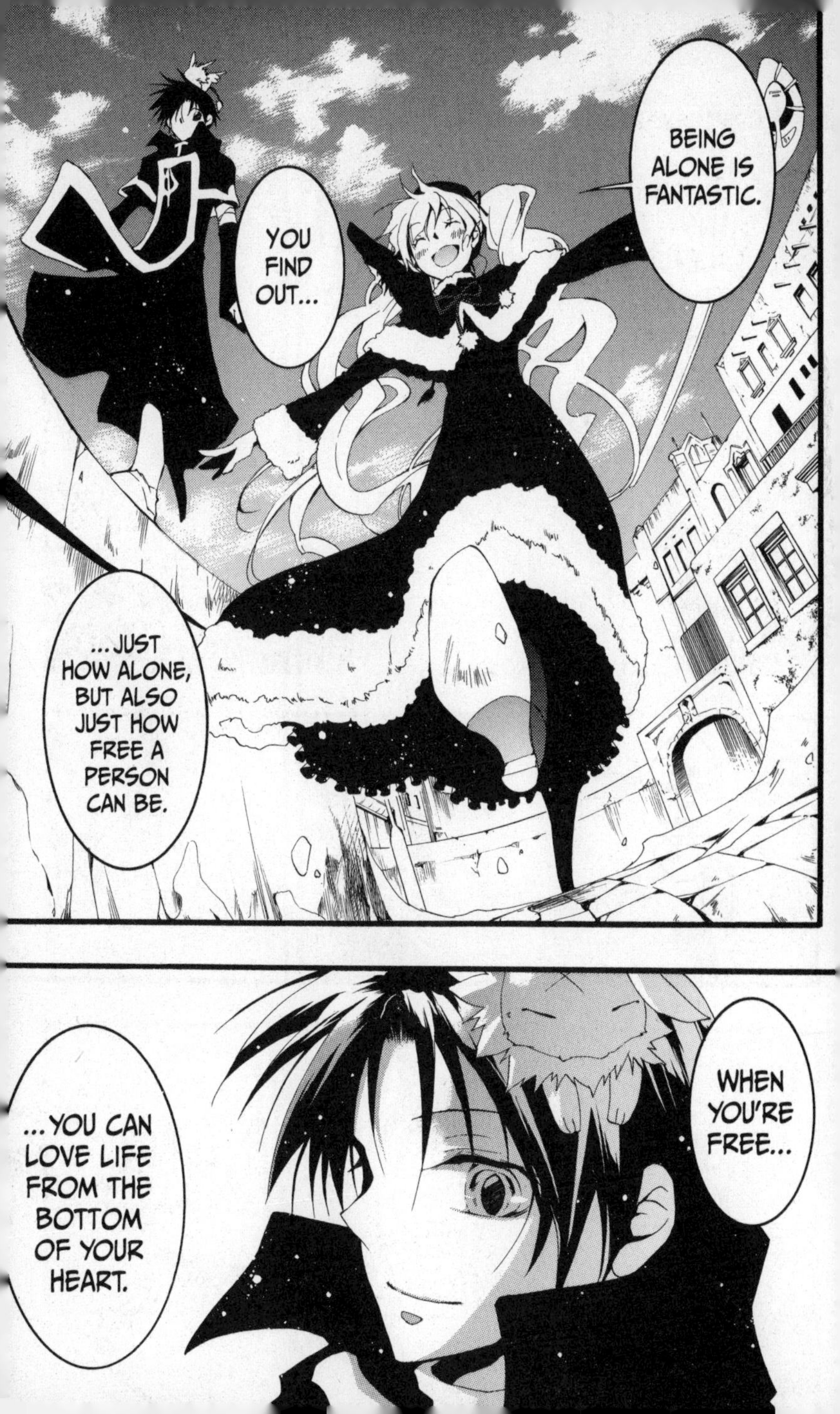
BEING ALONE IS FANTASTIC.
YOU FIND OUT...
...JUST HOW ALONE, BUT ALSO JUST HOW FREE A PERSON CAN BE.
WHEN YOU'RE FREE...
...YOU CAN LOVE LIFE FROM THE BOTTOM OF YOUR HEART.

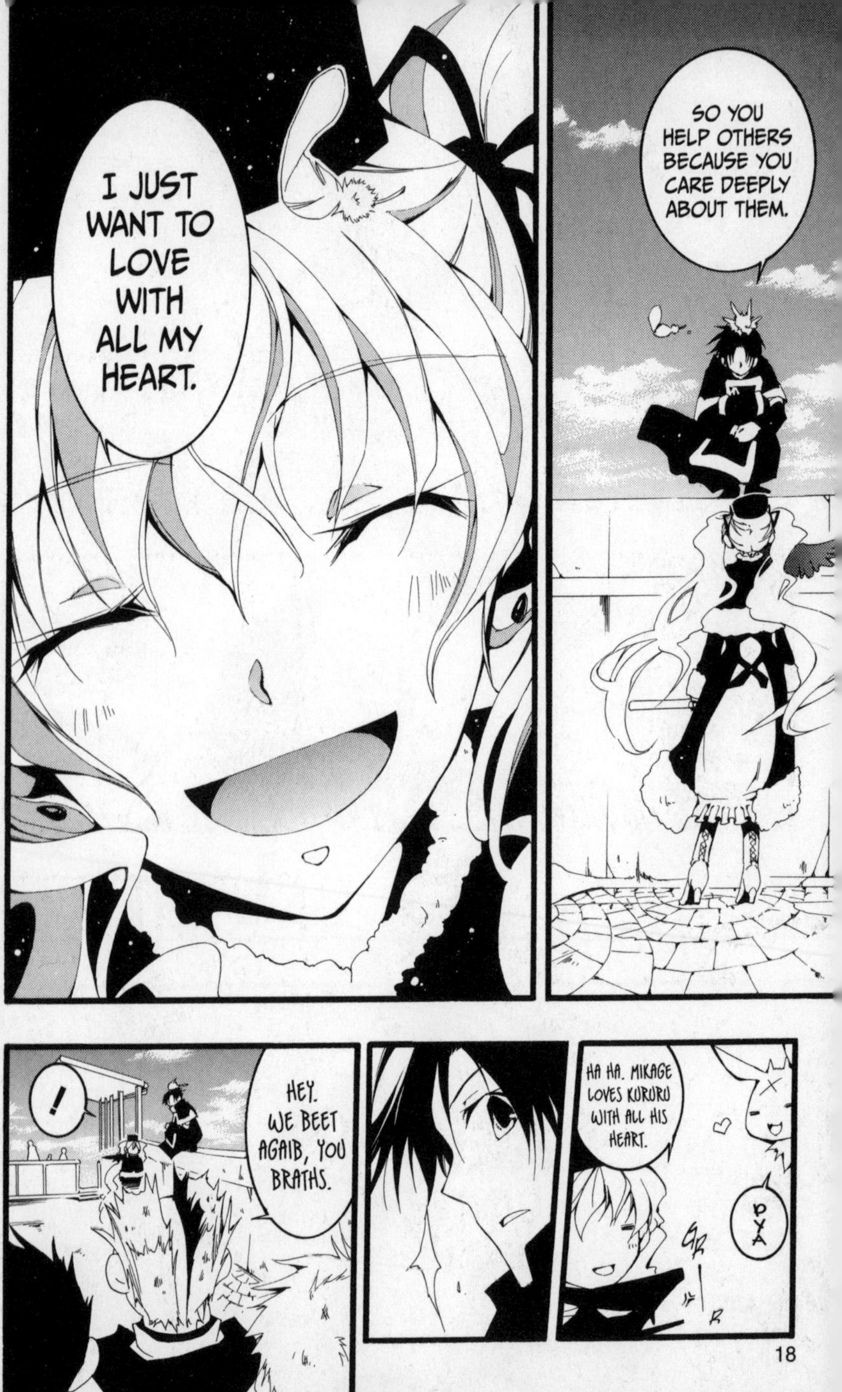
SO YOU HELP OTHERS BECAUSE YOU CARE DEEPLY ABOUT THEM.
I JUST WANT TO LOVE WITH ALL MY HEART.
HA HA. MIKAGE LOVES KURURU WITH ALL HIS HEART.
HEY. WE BEET AGAIB, YOU BRATHS.
!

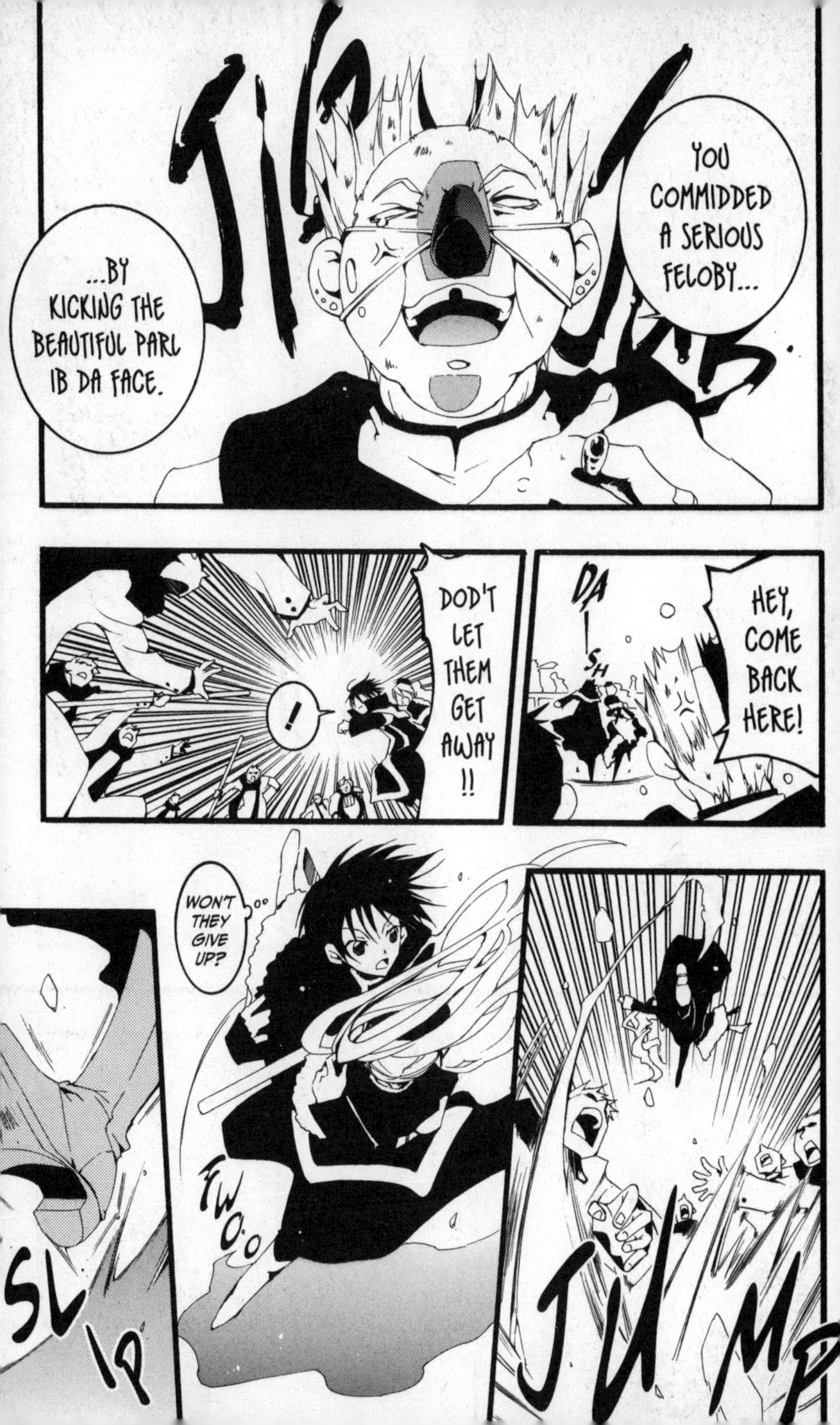
YOU COMMIDDED A SERIOUS FELOBY...
...BY KICKING THE BEAUTIFUL PARL IB DA FACE.
DASH
HEY, COME BACK HERE!
DOD'T LET THEM GET AWAY!!
!
JUMP
WON'T THEY GIVE UP?
FWOOO
SLIP

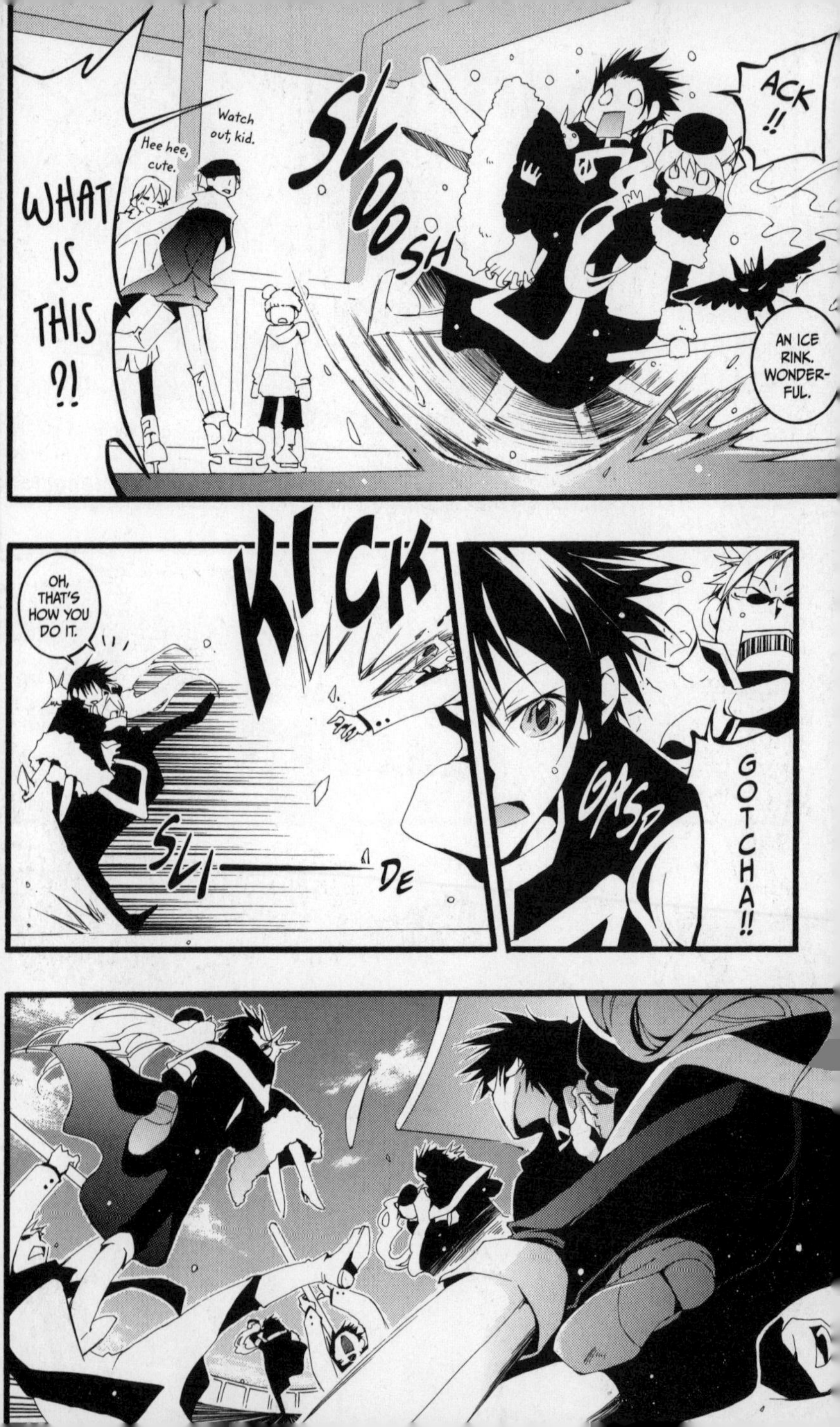
ACK!!
SLOOSH
Watch out, kid.
Hee hee, cute.
WHAT IS THIS ?!
AN ICE RINK. WONDERFUL.
GOTCHA!!
GASP
KICK
OH, THAT'S HOW YOU DO IT.
SLI————DE

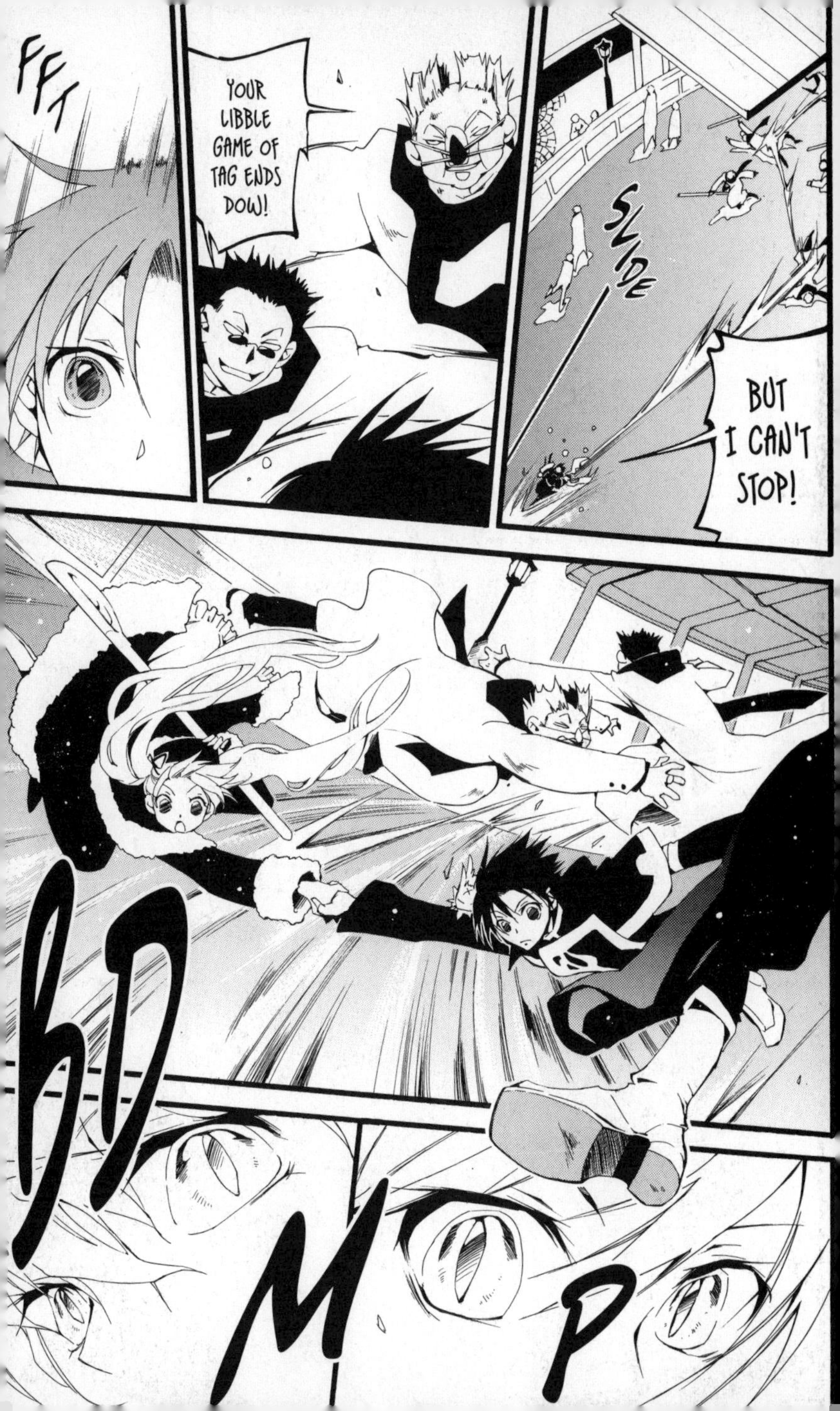
SLIDE
BUT I CAN'T STOP!
YOUR LIBBLE GAME OF TAG ENDS DOW!
FFT
BUMP

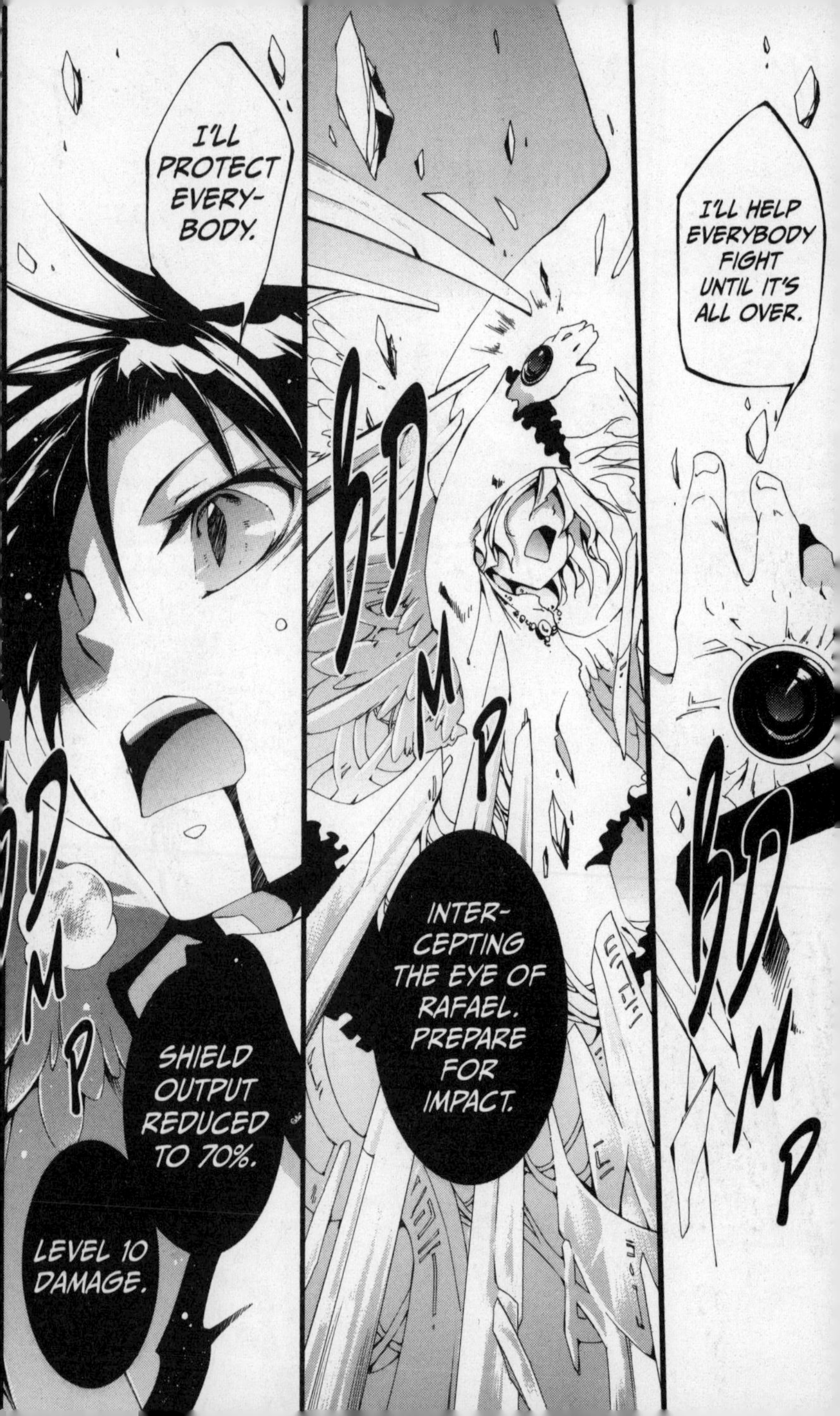
I'LL HELP EVERYBODY FIGHT UNTIL IT'S ALL OVER.
BDMP
BDMP
INTER-CEPTING THE EYE OF RAFAEL. PREPARE FOR IMPACT.
I'LL PROTECT EVERY-BODY.
BDMP
SHIELD OUTPUT REDUCED TO 70%.
LEVEL 10 DAMAGE.

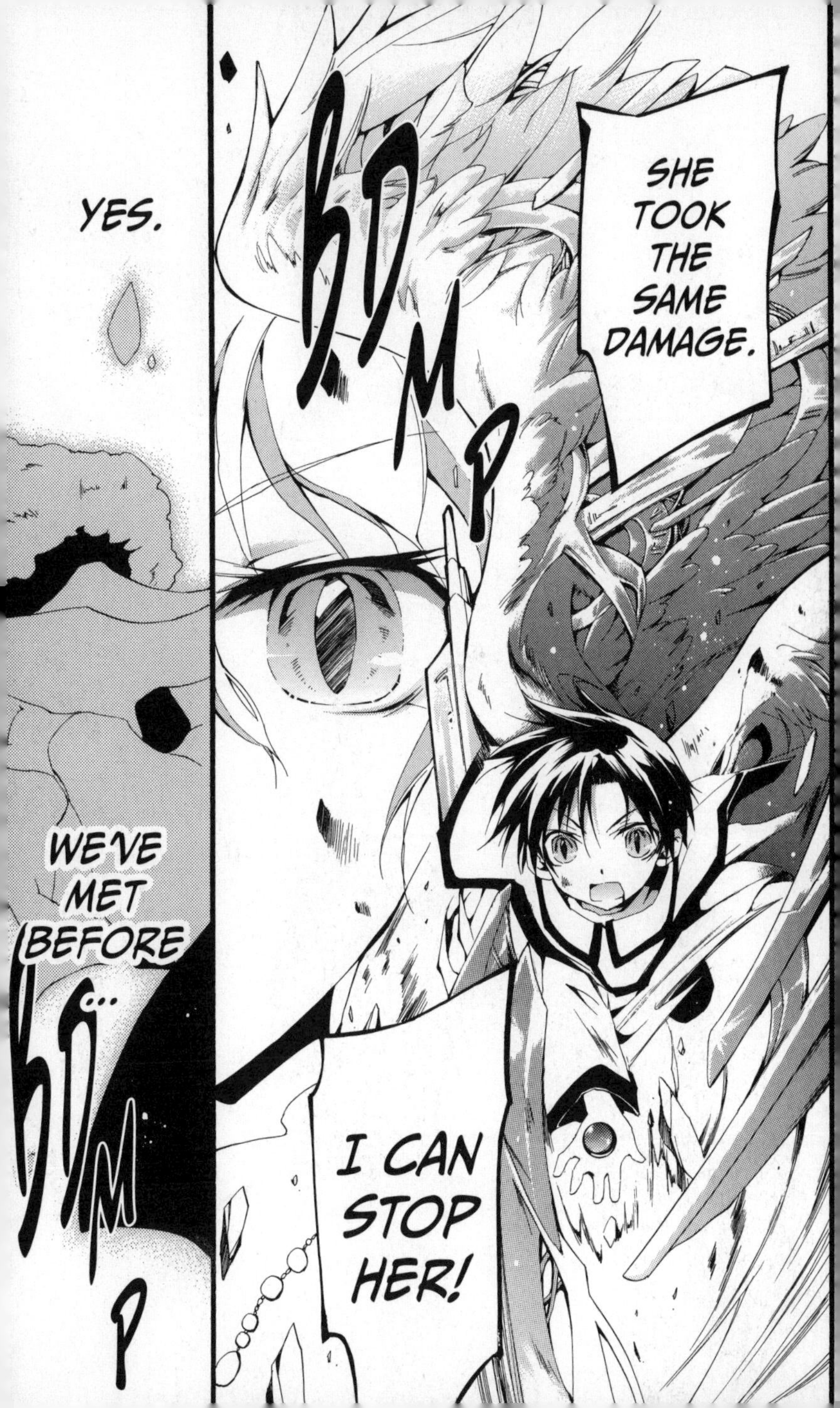
SHE TOOK THE SAME DAMAGE.
BDMP
I CAN STOP HER!
YES.
WE'VE MET BEFORE...
BDMP

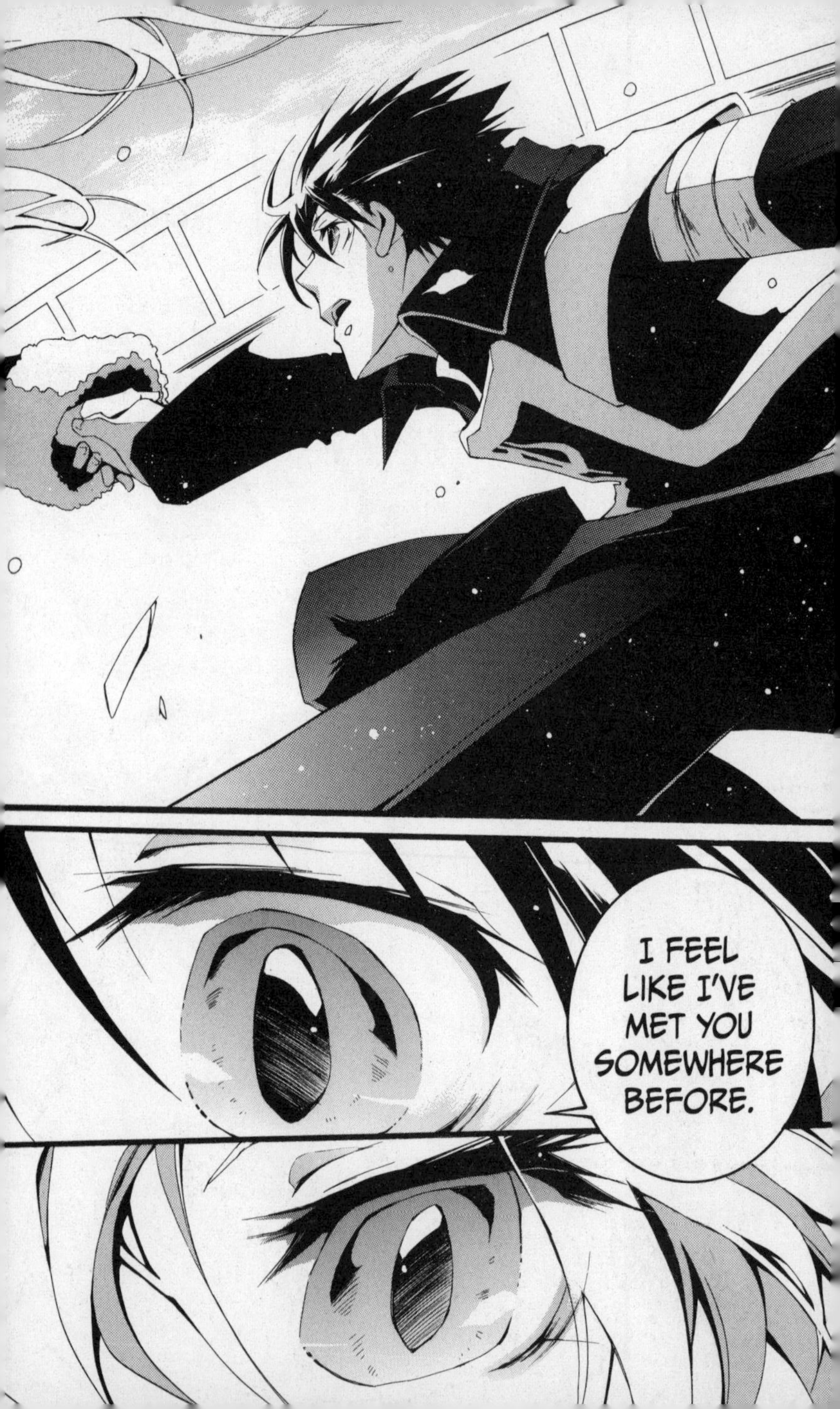
I FEEL LIKE I'VE MET YOU SOMEWHERE BEFORE.

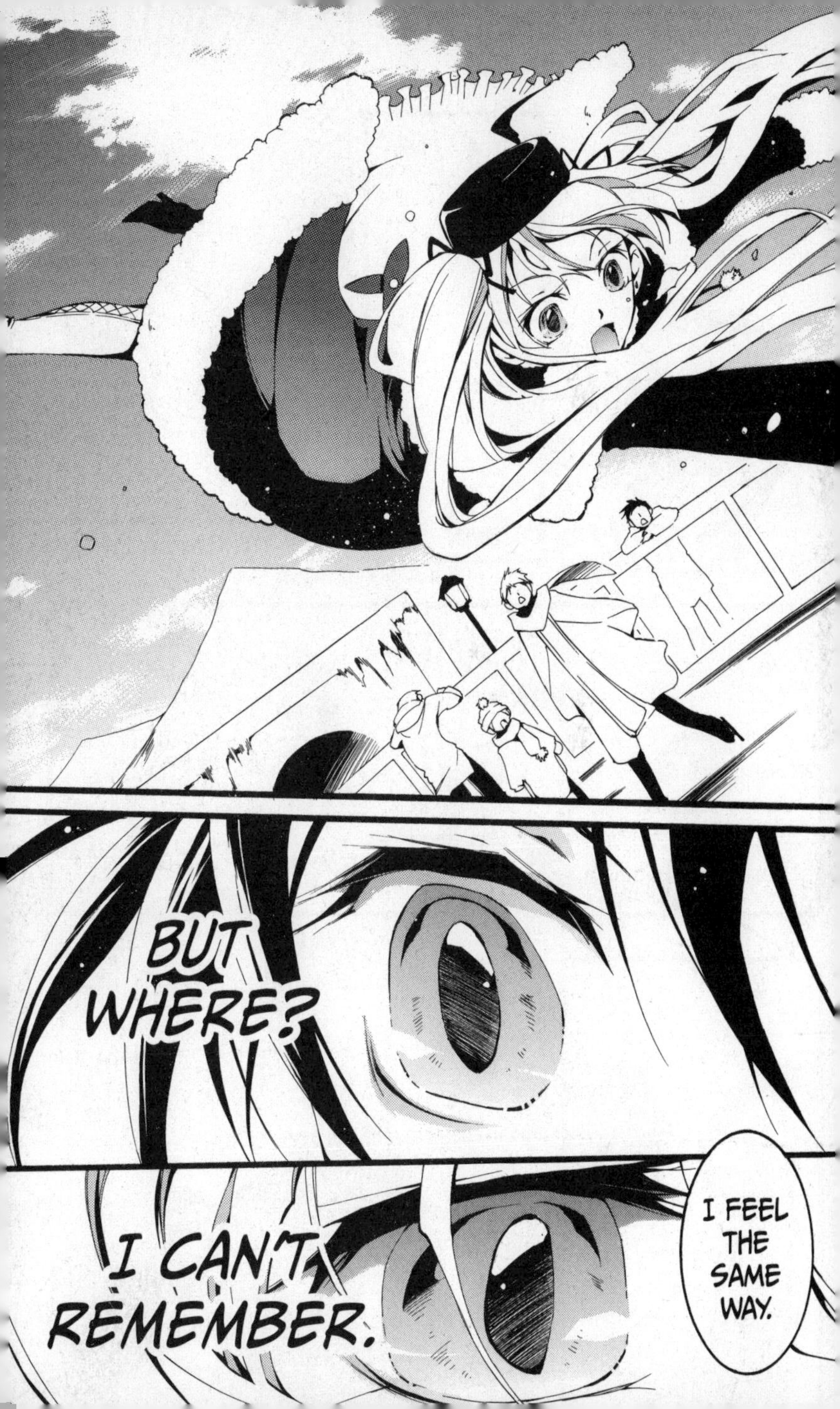
BUT WHERE?
I FEEL THE SAME WAY.
I CAN'T REMEMBER.

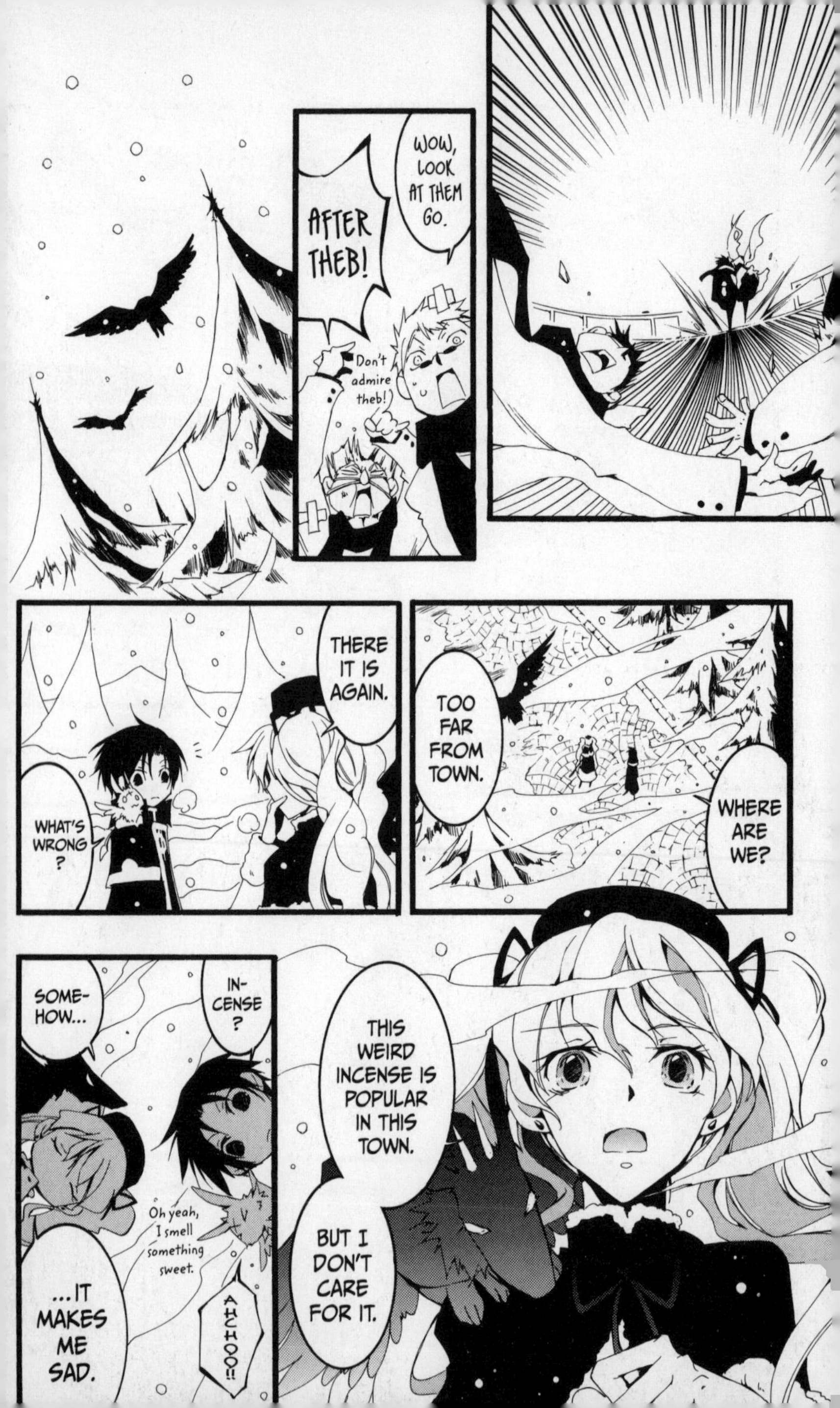

WOW, LOOK AT THEM GO.
AFTER THEB!
Don't admire theb!
WHERE ARE WE?
TOO FAR FROM TOWN.
THERE IT IS AGAIN.
WHAT'S WRONG?
THIS WEIRD INCENSE IS POPULAR IN THIS TOWN.
BUT I DON'T CARE FOR IT.
IN-CENSE?
SOME-HOW...
Oh yeah, I smell something sweet.
ACHOO!!
...IT MAKES ME SAD.

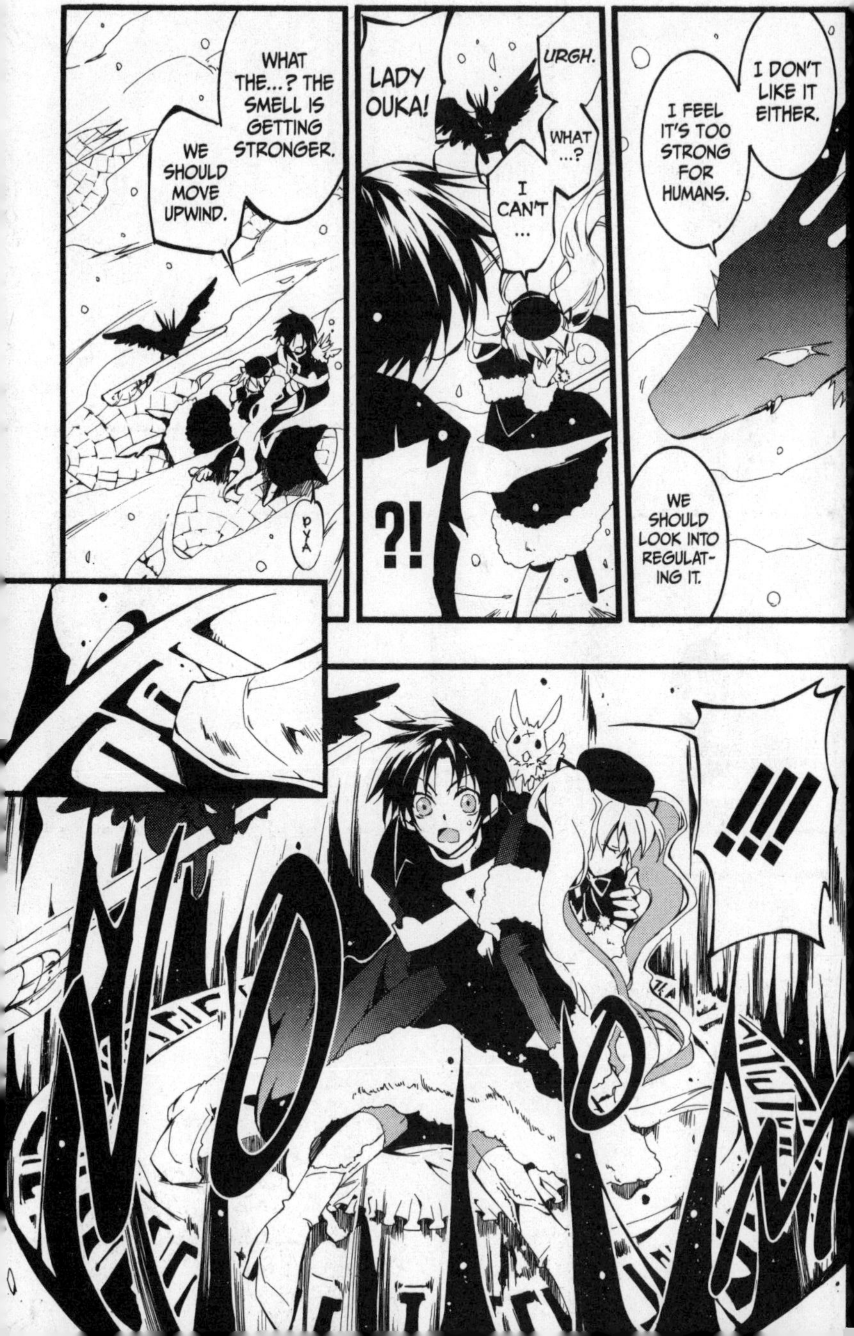
I DON'T LIKE IT EITHER.
I FEEL IT'S TOO STRONG FOR HUMANS.
WE SHOULD LOOK INTO REGULATING IT.
URGH.
WHAT ...?
I CAN'T ...
LADY OUKA!
?!
WHAT THE...? THE SMELL IS GETTING STRONGER.
WE SHOULD MOVE UPWIND.
PYA
!!!!

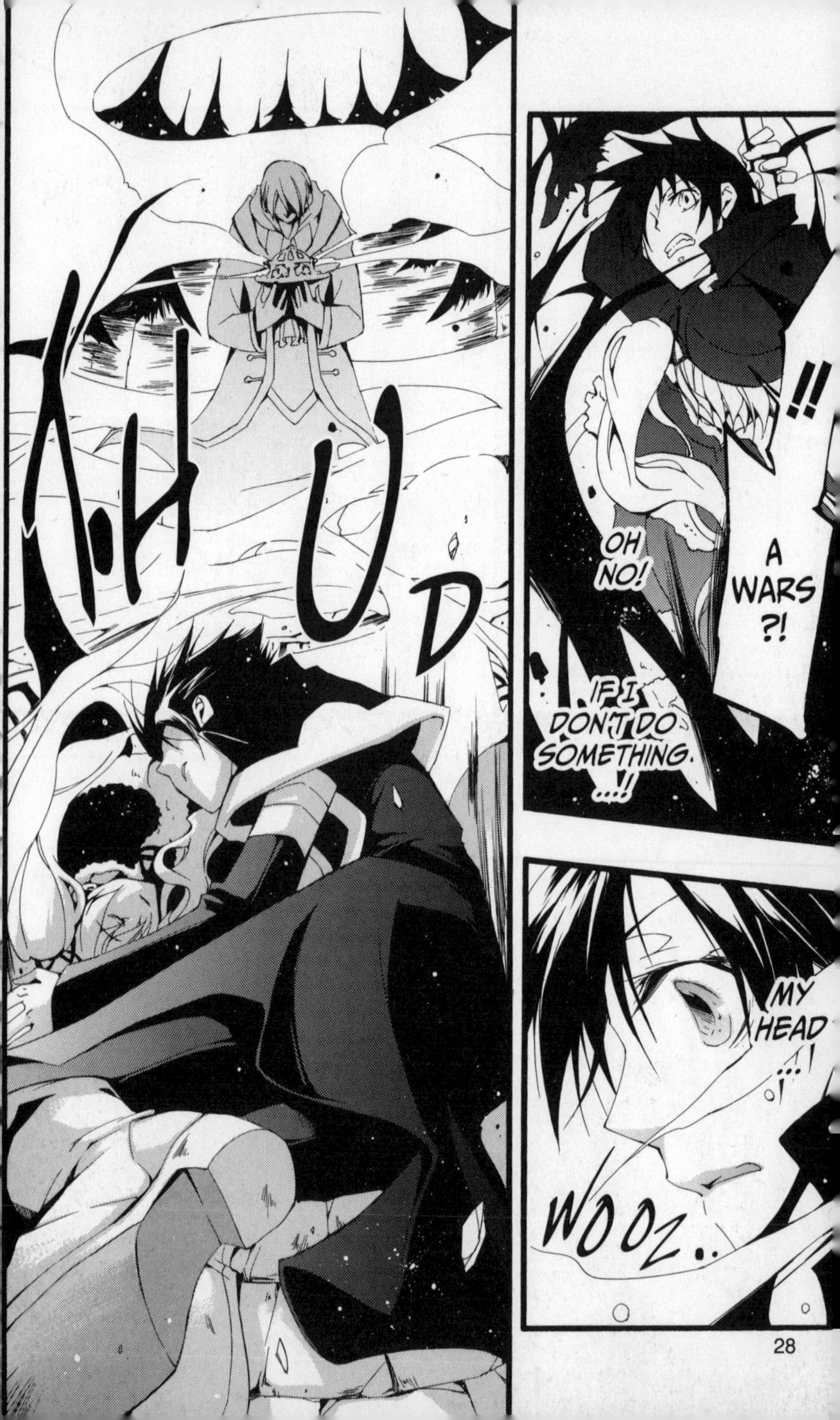
!!
A WARS ?!
OH NO!
IF I DON'T DO SOMETHING. ...!!
MY HEAD ...!
WOOZ..
THUD

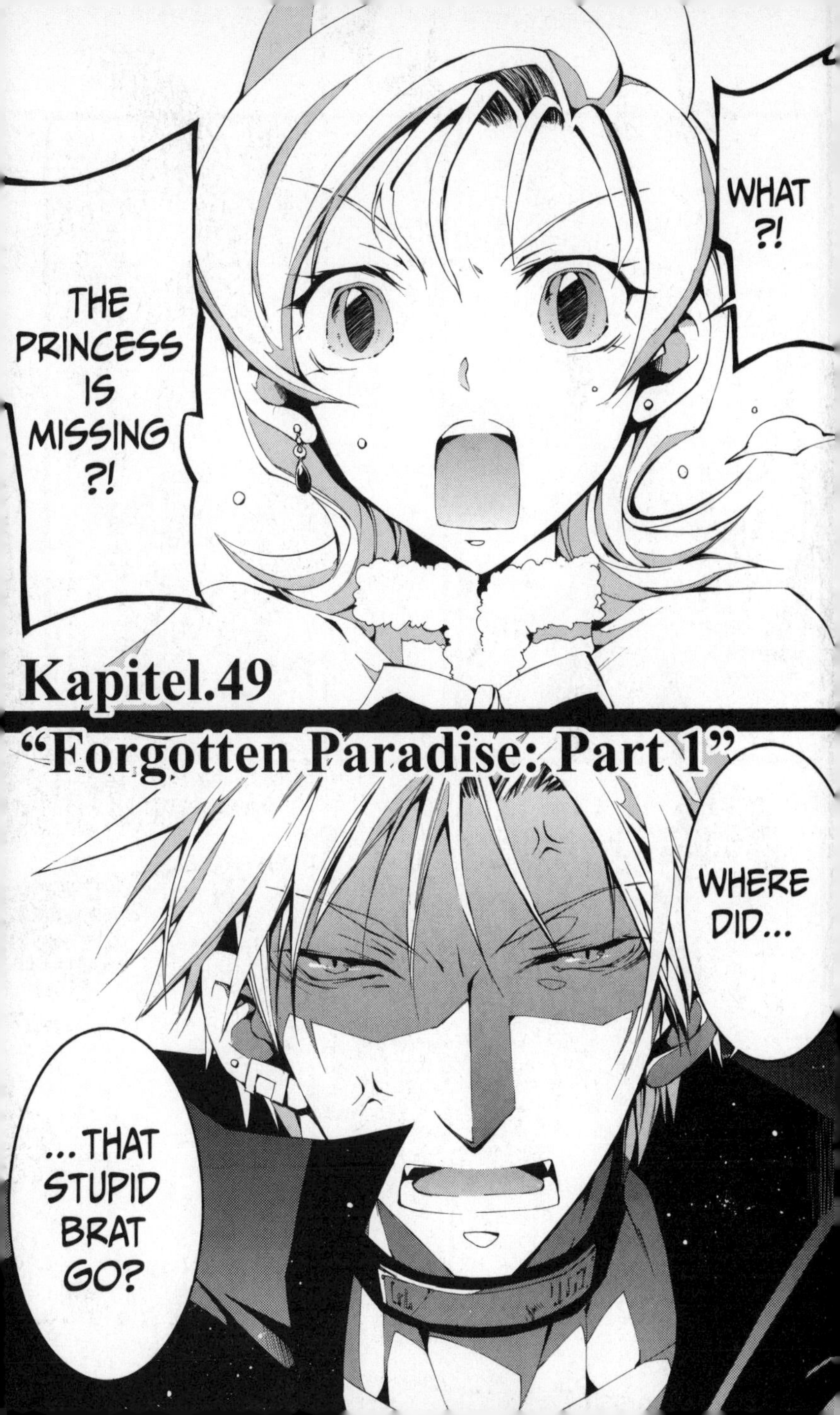
WHAT ?!
THE PRINCESS IS MISSING ?!
Kapitel.49
"Forgotten Paradise: Part 1"
WHERE DID...
...THAT STUPID BRAT GO?

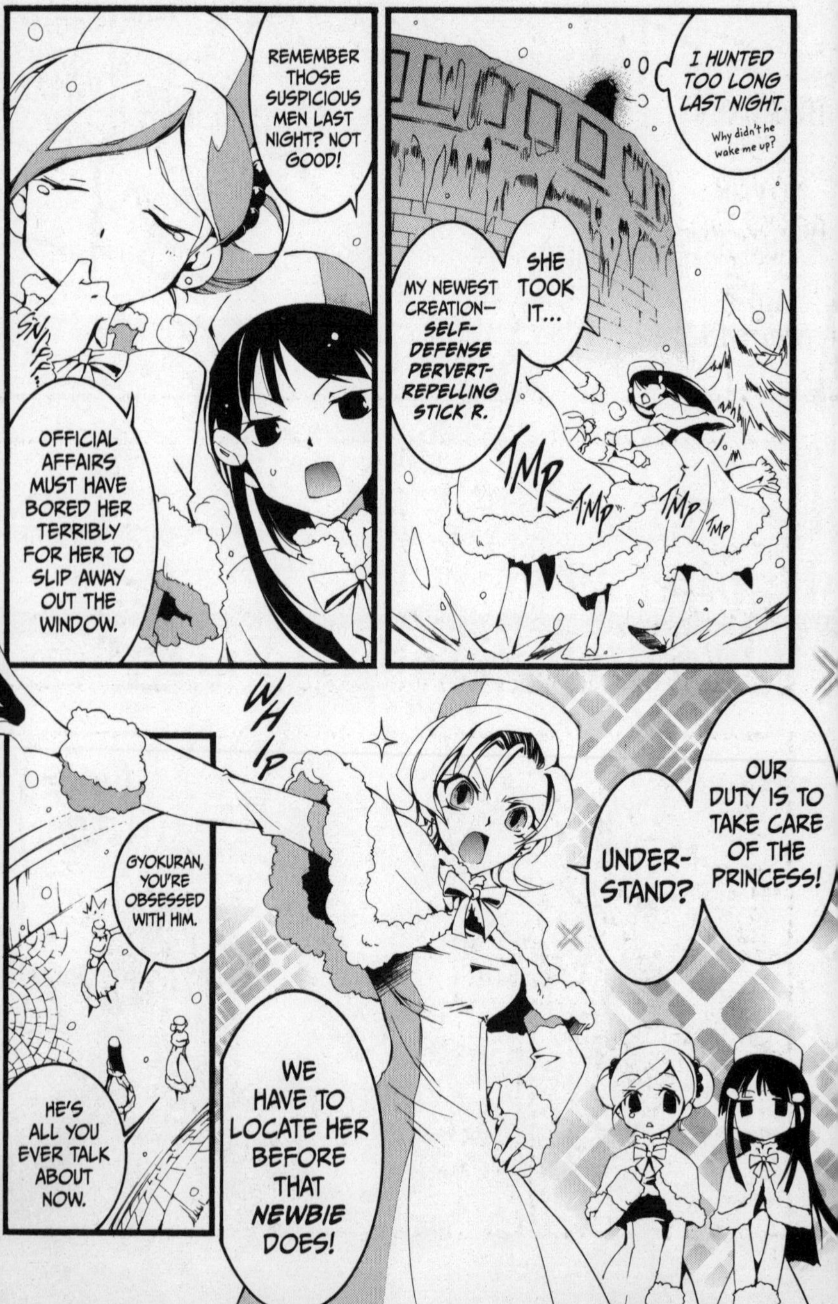
I HUNTED TOO LONG LAST NIGHT.
Why didn't he wake me up?
SHE TOOK IT...
MY NEWEST CREATION—SELF-DEFENSE PERVERT-REPELLING STICK R.
TMP TMP TMP TMP
REMEMBER THOSE SUSPICIOUS MEN LAST NIGHT? NOT GOOD!
SNIFF...
OFFICIAL AFFAIRS MUST HAVE BORED HER TERRIBLY FOR HER TO SLIP AWAY OUT THE WINDOW.
WHIP
OUR DUTY IS TO TAKE CARE OF THE PRINCESS!
UNDER-STAND?
WE HAVE TO LOCATE HER BEFORE THAT NEWBIE DOES!
GYOKURAN, YOU'RE OBSESSED WITH HIM.
HE'S ALL YOU EVER TALK ABOUT NOW.

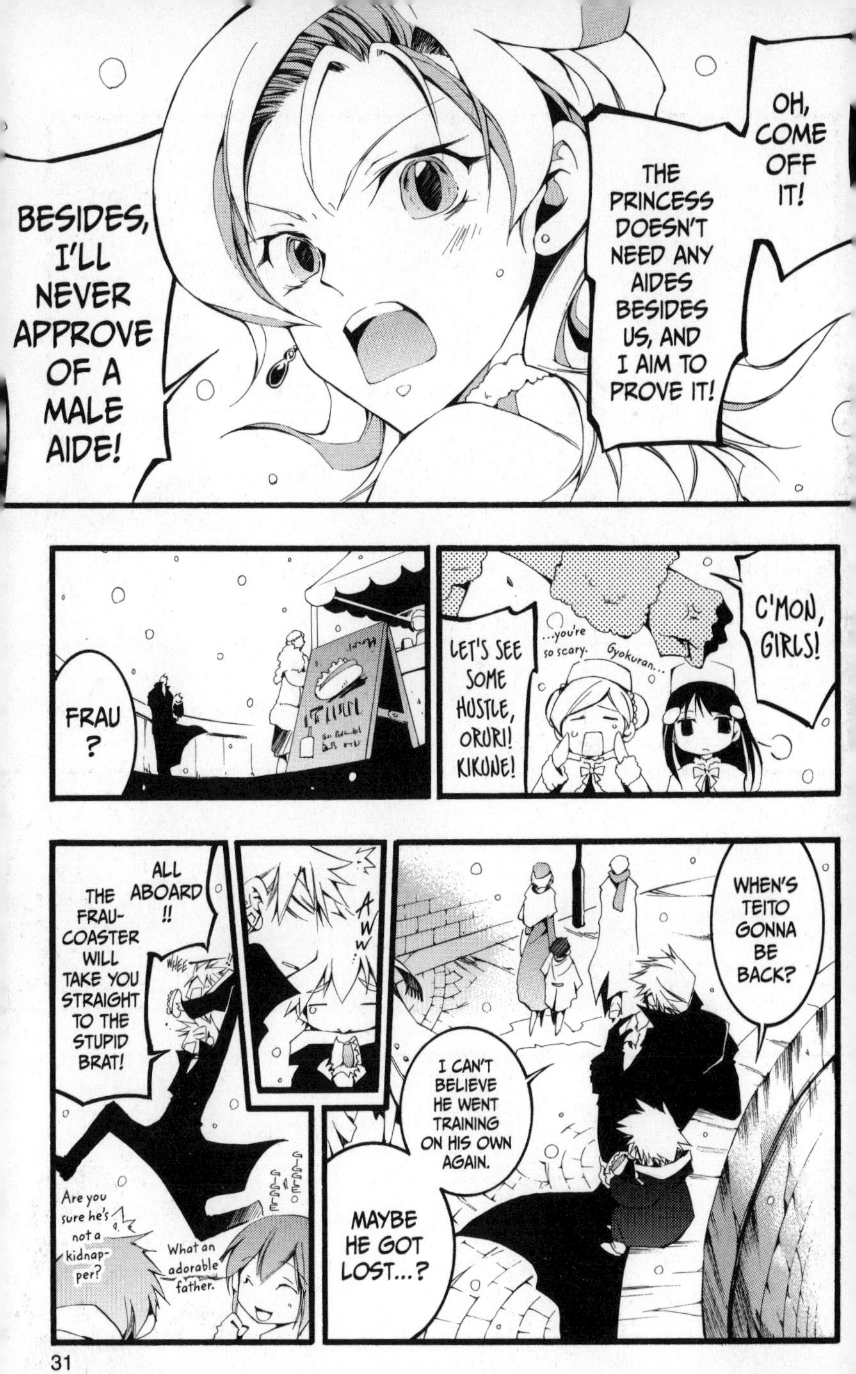
OH, COME OFF IT!
THE PRINCESS DOESN'T NEED ANY AIDES BESIDES US, AND I AIM TO PROVE IT!
BESIDES, I'LL NEVER APPROVE OF A MALE AIDE!
C'MON, GIRLS!
Gyokuran...
...you're so scary.
LET'S SEE SOME HUSTLE, ORURI! KIKUNE!
FRAU?
WHEN'S TEITO GONNA BE BACK?
I CAN'T BELIEVE HE WENT TRAINING ON HIS OWN AGAIN.
MAYBE HE GOT LOST...?
AWW...
ALL ABOARD!!
THE FRAU-COASTER WILL TAKE YOU STRAIGHT TO THE STUPID BRAT!
WHEE
GIGGLE GIGGLE
What an adorable father.
Are you sure he's not a kidnapper?

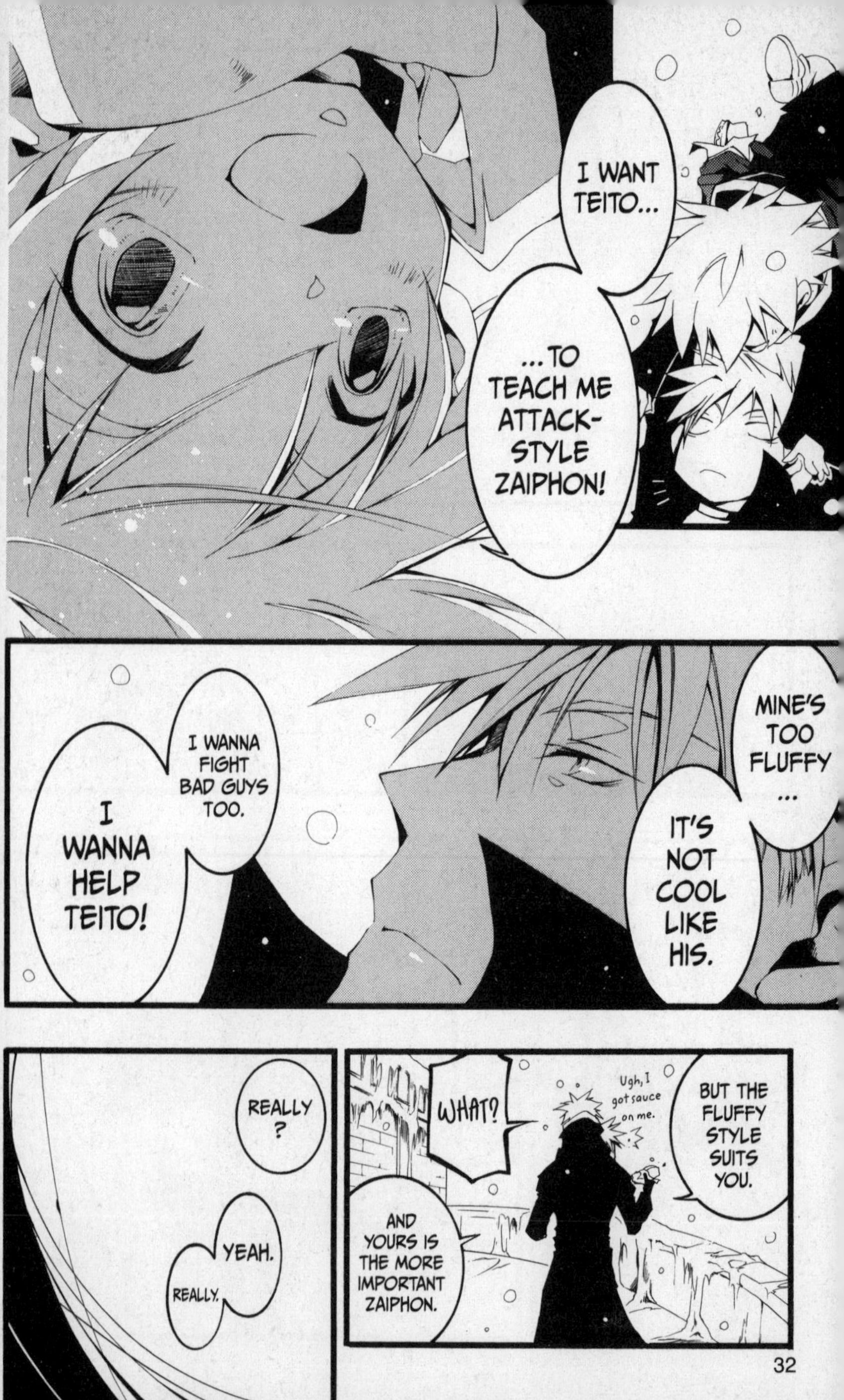
I WANT TEITO...
...TO TEACH ME ATTACK-STYLE ZAIPHON!
MINE'S TOO FLUFFY ...
IT'S NOT COOL LIKE HIS.
I WANNA FIGHT BAD GUYS TOO.
I WANNA HELP TEITO!
BUT THE FLUFFY STYLE SUITS YOU.
Ugh, I got sauce on me.
WHAT?
AND YOURS IS THE MORE IMPORTANT ZAIPHON.
REALLY ?
YEAH.
REALLY.

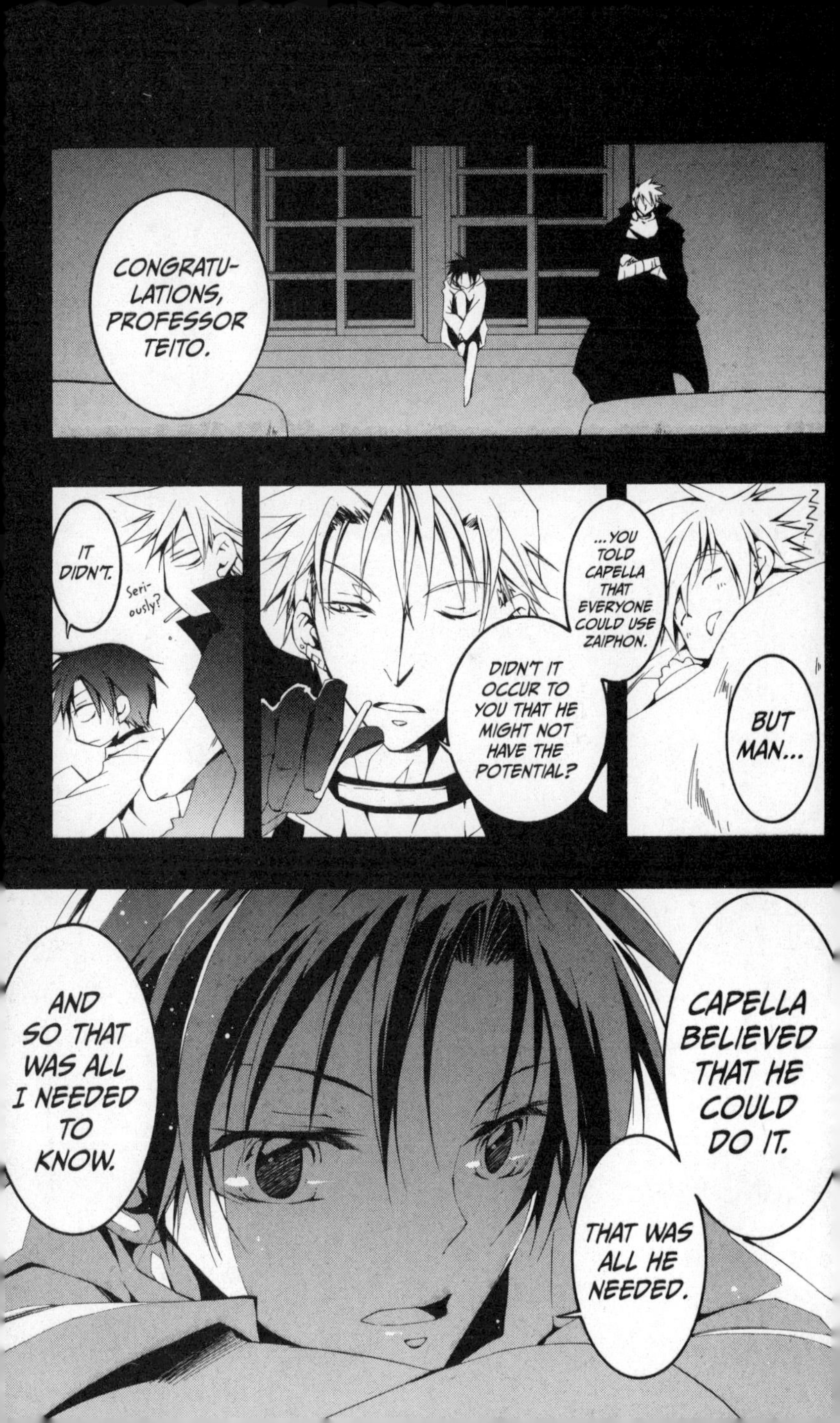
CONGRATU-LATIONS, PROFESSOR TEITO.
BUT MAN...
...YOU TOLD CAPELLA THAT EVERYONE COULD USE ZAIPHON.
DIDN'T IT OCCUR TO YOU THAT HE MIGHT NOT HAVE THE POTENTIAL?
IT DIDN'T.
Seri-ously?
CAPELLA BELIEVED THAT HE COULD DO IT.
THAT WAS ALL HE NEEDED.
AND SO THAT WAS ALL I NEEDED TO KNOW.

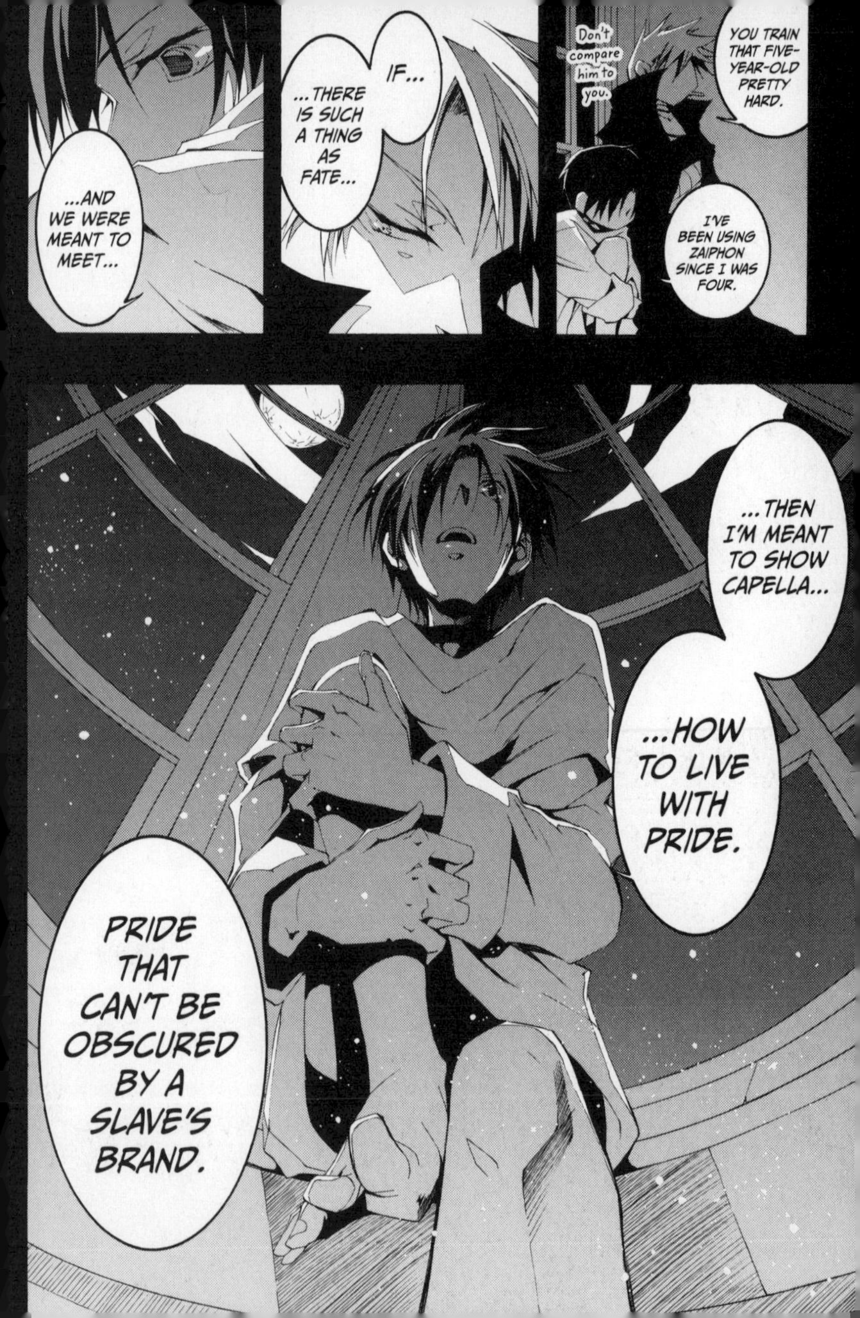
YOU TRAIN THAT FIVE-YEAR-OLD PRETTY HARD.
Don't compare him to you.
I'VE BEEN USING ZAIPHON SINCE I WAS FOUR.
IF...
...THERE IS SUCH A THING AS FATE...
...AND WE WERE MEANT TO MEET...
...THEN I'M MEANT TO SHOW CAPELLA...
...HOW TO LIVE WITH PRIDE.
PRIDE THAT CAN'T BE OBSCURED BY A SLAVE'S BRAND.

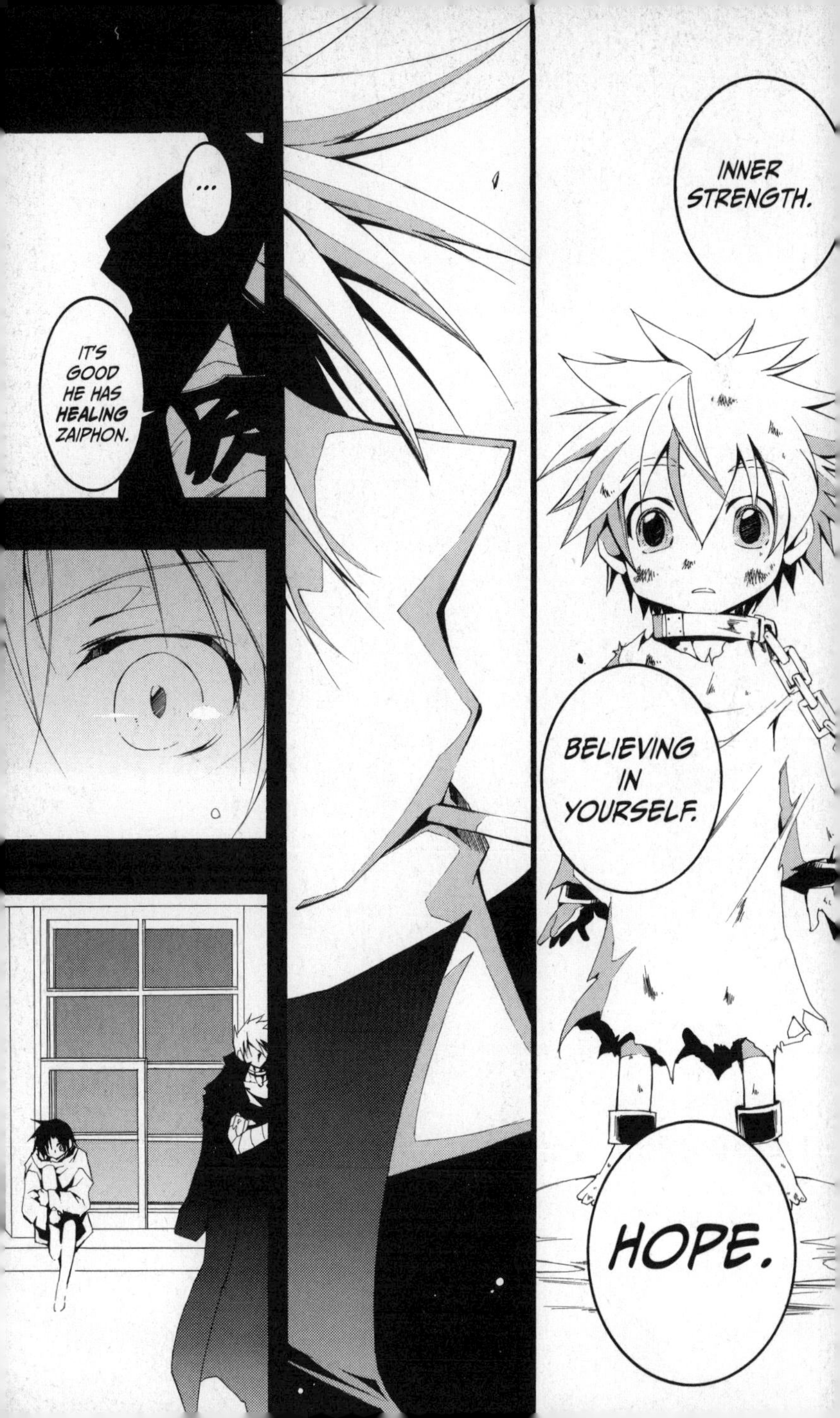
INNER STRENGTH.
BELIEVING IN YOURSELF.
HOPE.
...
IT'S GOOD HE HAS HEALING ZAIPHON.

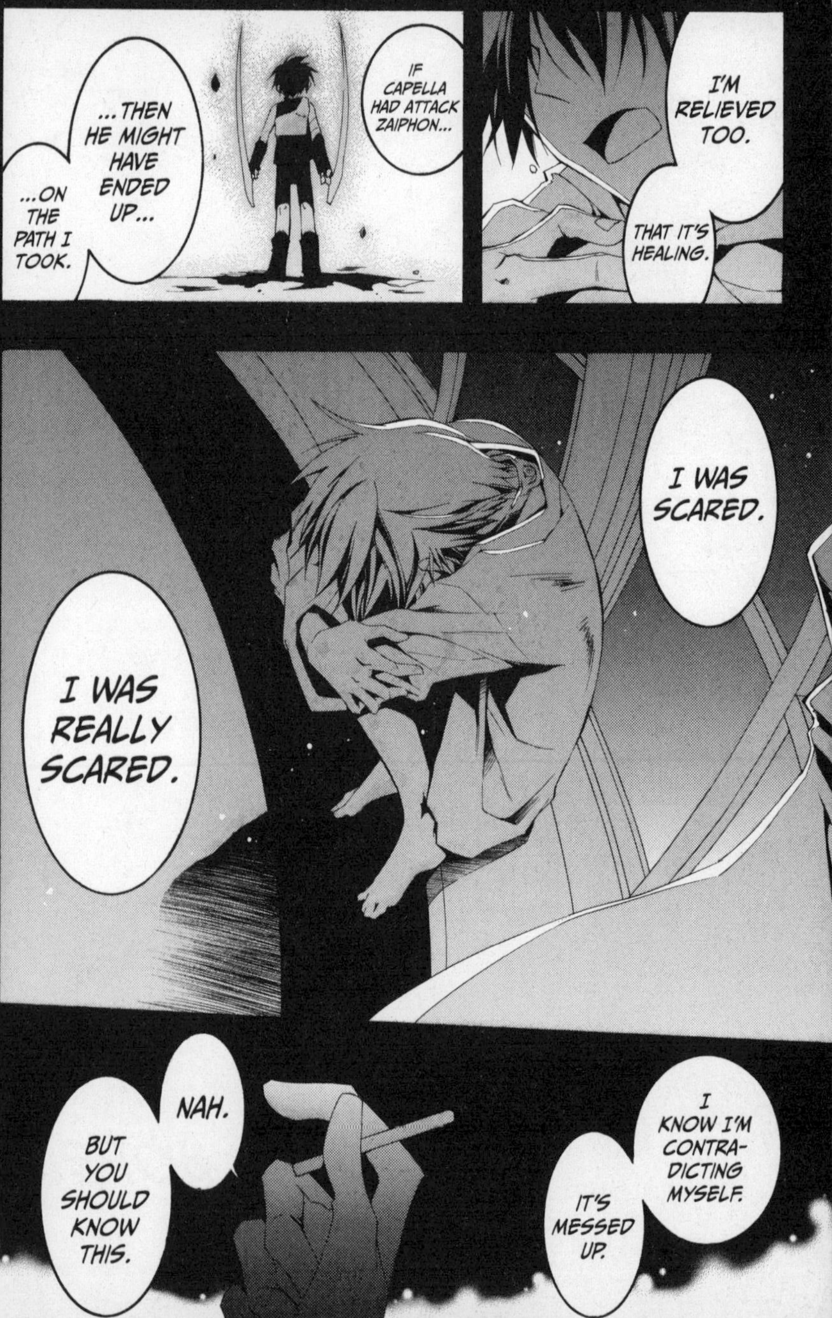
I'M RELIEVED TOO.
THAT IT'S HEALING.
IF CAPELLA HAD ATTACK ZAIPHON...
...THEN HE MIGHT HAVE ENDED UP...
...ON THE PATH I TOOK.
I WAS SCARED.
I WAS REALLY SCARED.
I KNOW I'M CONTRA-DICTING MYSELF.
IT'S MESSED UP.
NAH.
BUT YOU SHOULD KNOW THIS.

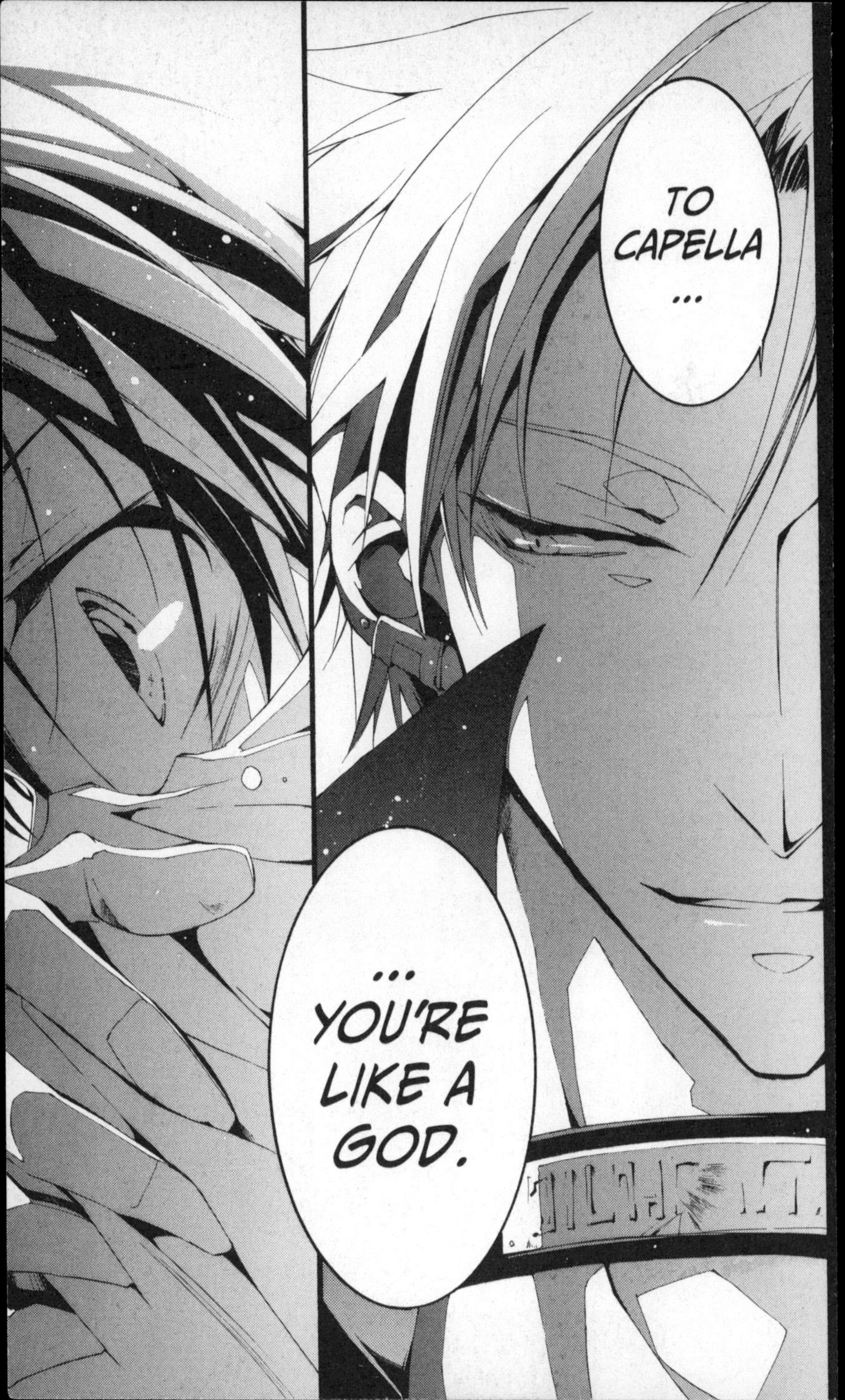
TO CAPELLA ...
... YOU'RE LIKE A GOD.

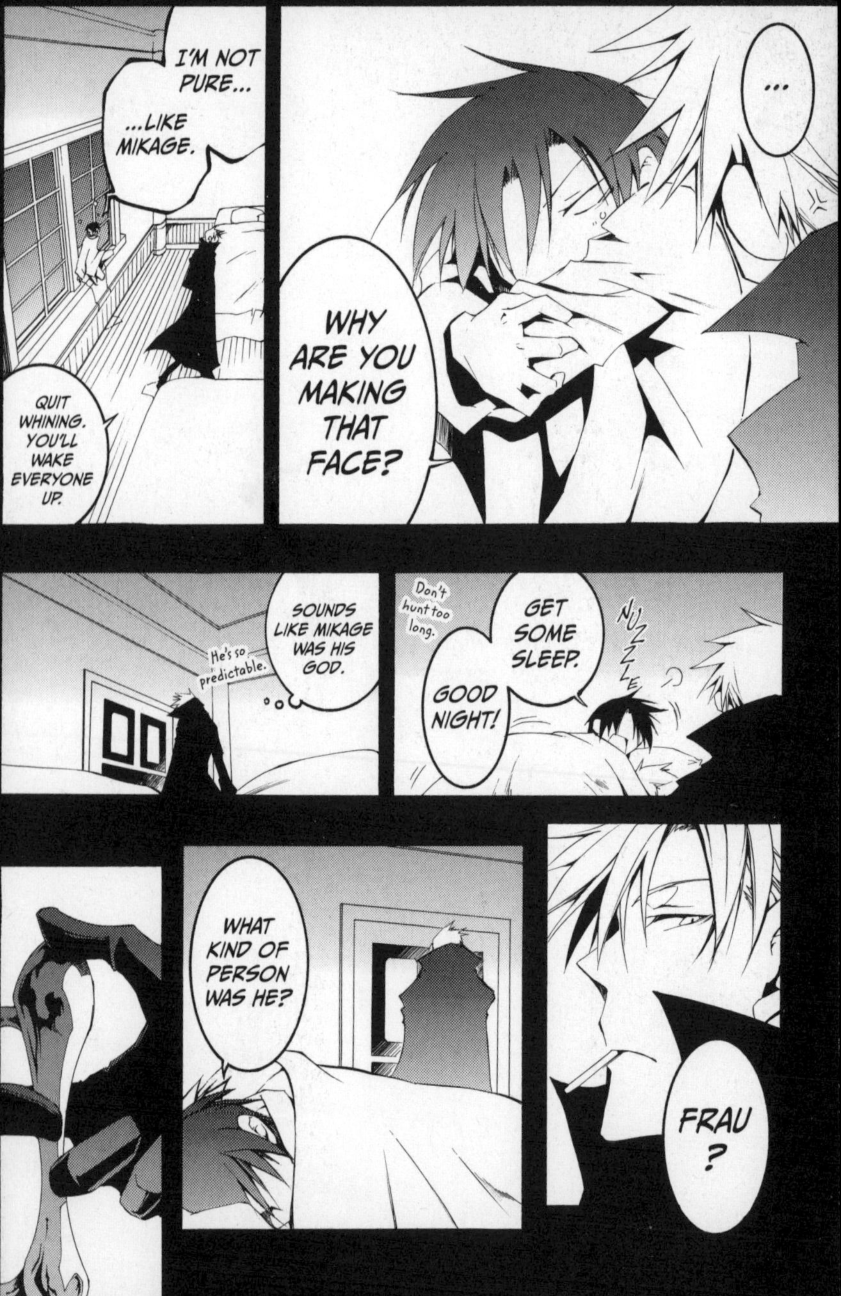
...
WHY ARE YOU MAKING THAT FACE?
I'M NOT PURE...
...LIKE MIKAGE.
QUIT WHINING. YOU'LL WAKE EVERYONE UP.
GET SOME SLEEP.
NUZZLE
Don't hunt too long.
GOOD NIGHT!
SOUNDS LIKE MIKAGE WAS HIS GOD.
He's so predictable.
FRAU?
WHAT KIND OF PERSON WAS HE?

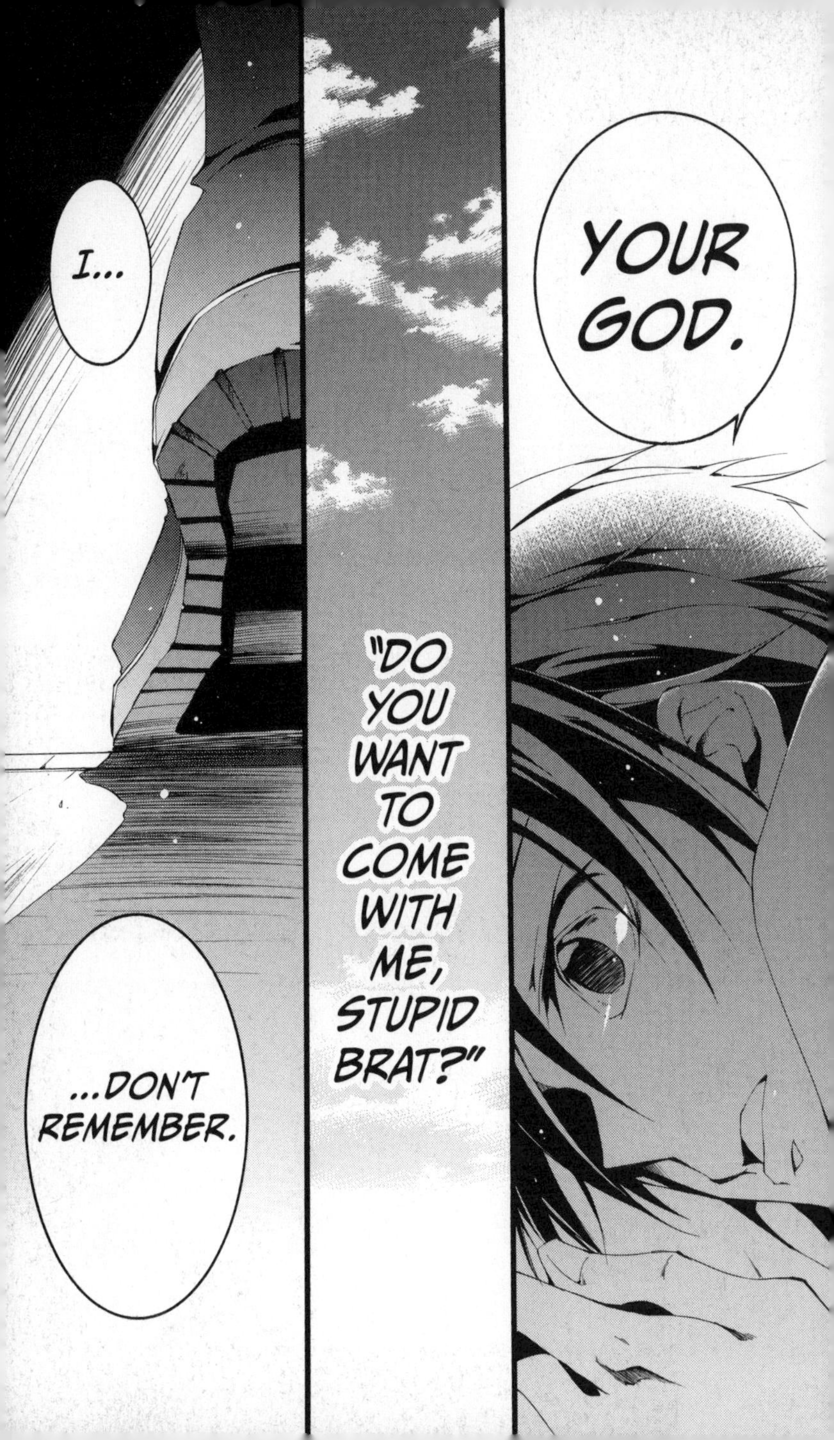
YOUR GOD.
"DO YOU WANT TO COME WITH ME, STUPID BRAT?"
I...
...DON'T REMEMBER.

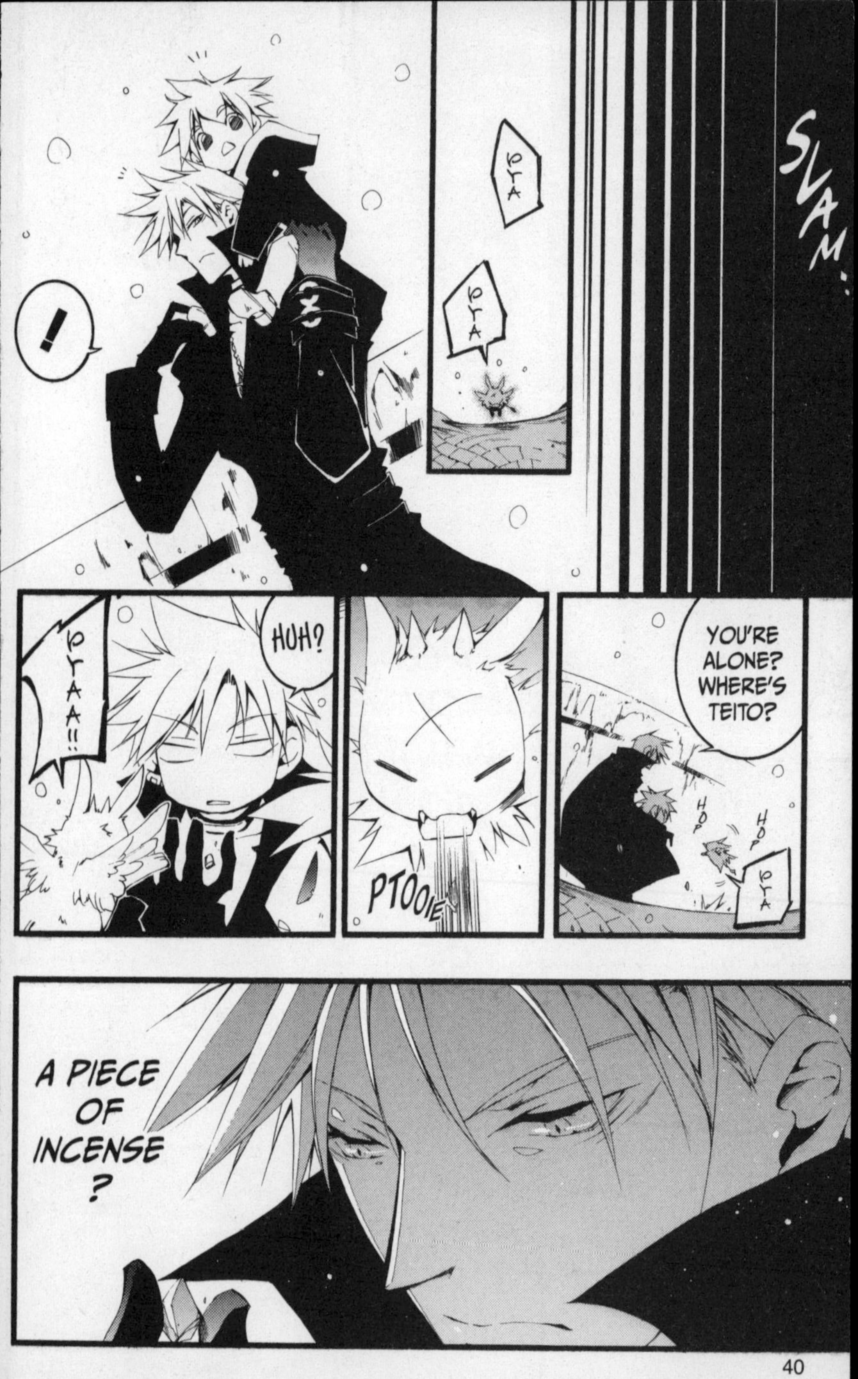

SLAM...
PYA
PYA
!
YOU'RE ALONE? WHERE'S TEITO?
HOP
HOP
PYA
PTOOIE
HUH?
PYAA!!
A PIECE OF INCENSE?

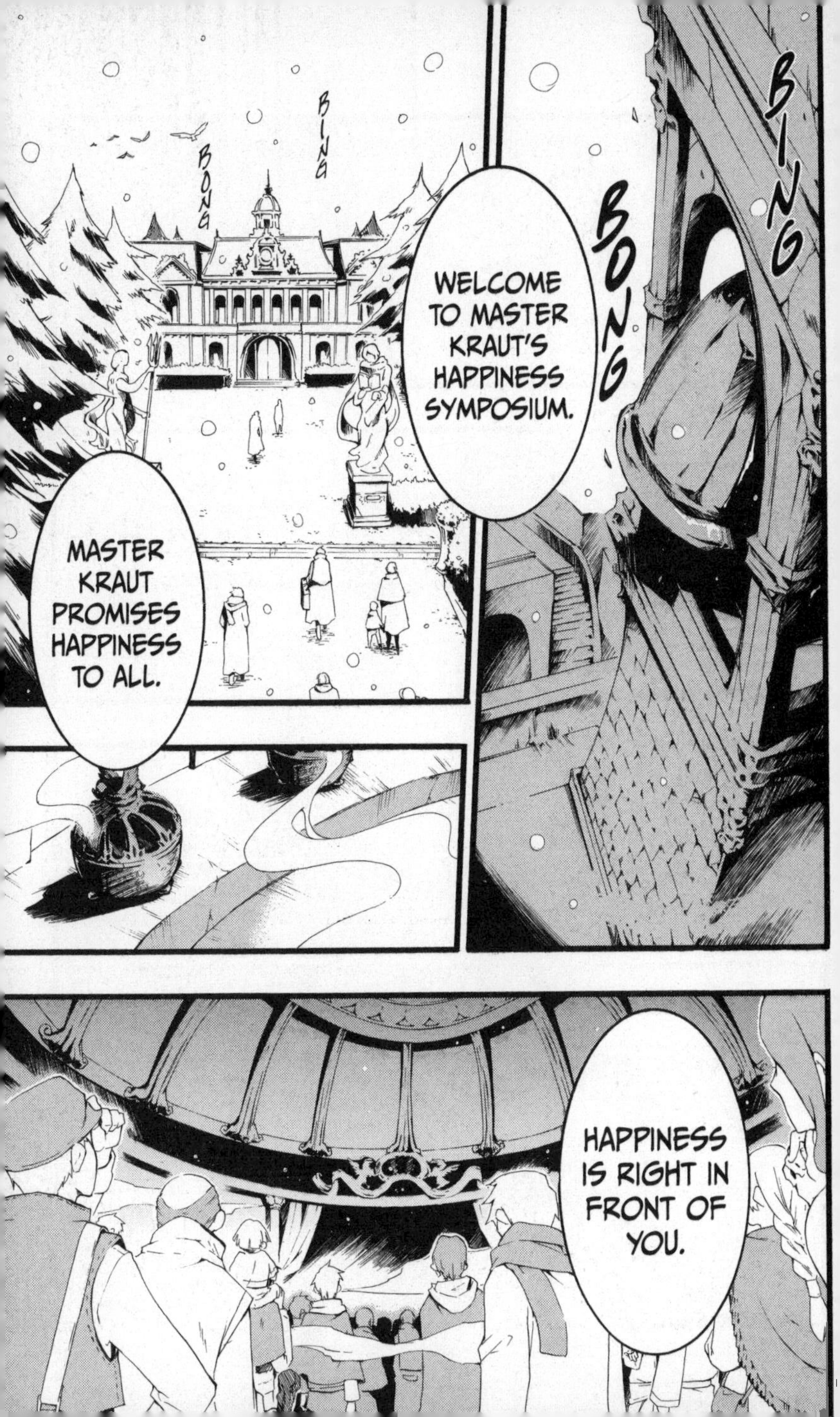
BING
BONG
WELCOME TO MASTER KRAUT'S HAPPINESS SYMPOSIUM.
BING
BONG
MASTER KRAUT PROMISES HAPPINESS TO ALL.
HAPPINESS IS RIGHT IN FRONT OF YOU.

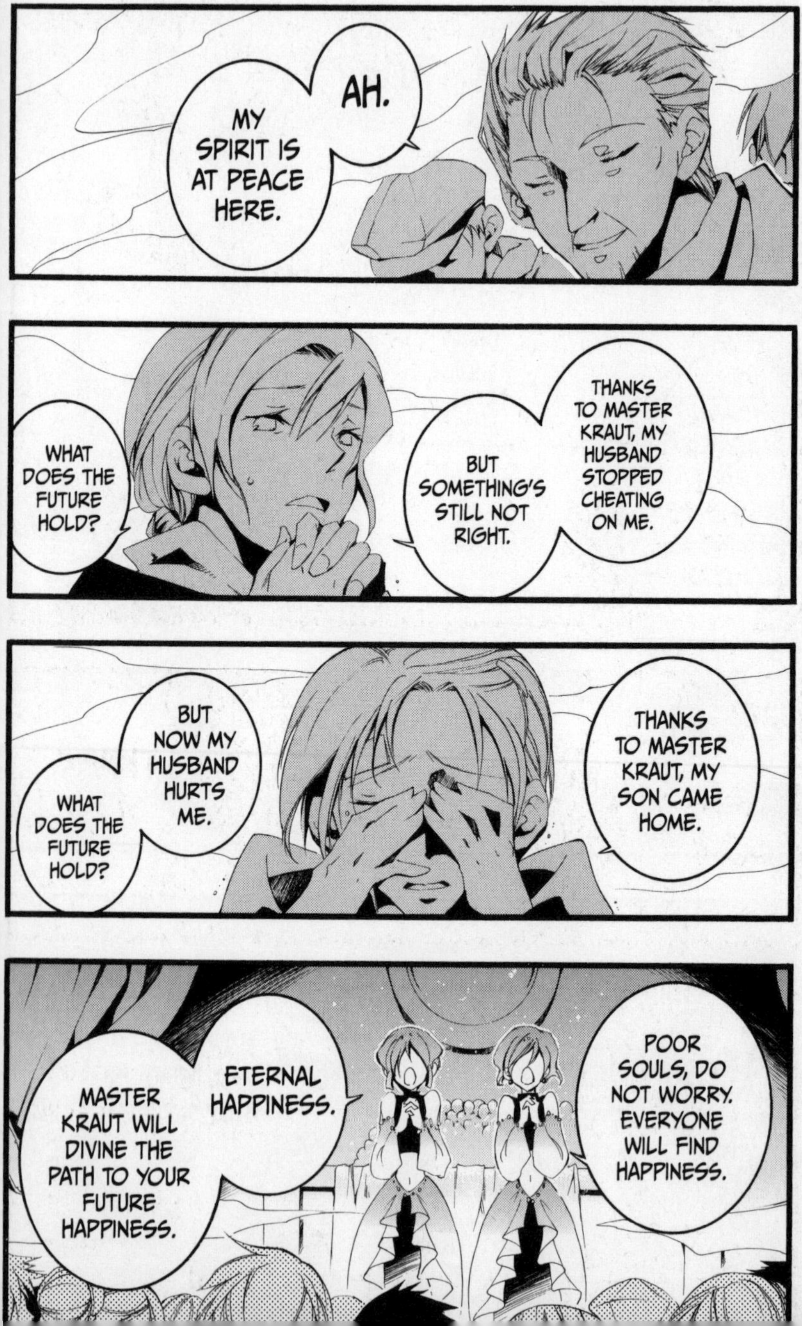
AH.
MY SPIRIT IS AT PEACE HERE.
THANKS TO MASTER KRAUT, MY HUSBAND STOPPED CHEATING ON ME.
BUT SOMETHING'S STILL NOT RIGHT.
WHAT DOES THE FUTURE HOLD?
THANKS TO MASTER KRAUT, MY SON CAME HOME.
BUT NOW MY HUSBAND HURTS ME.
WHAT DOES THE FUTURE HOLD?
POOR SOULS, DO NOT WORRY. EVERYONE WILL FIND HAPPINESS.
ETERNAL HAPPINESS.
MASTER KRAUT WILL DIVINE THE PATH TO YOUR FUTURE HAPPINESS.

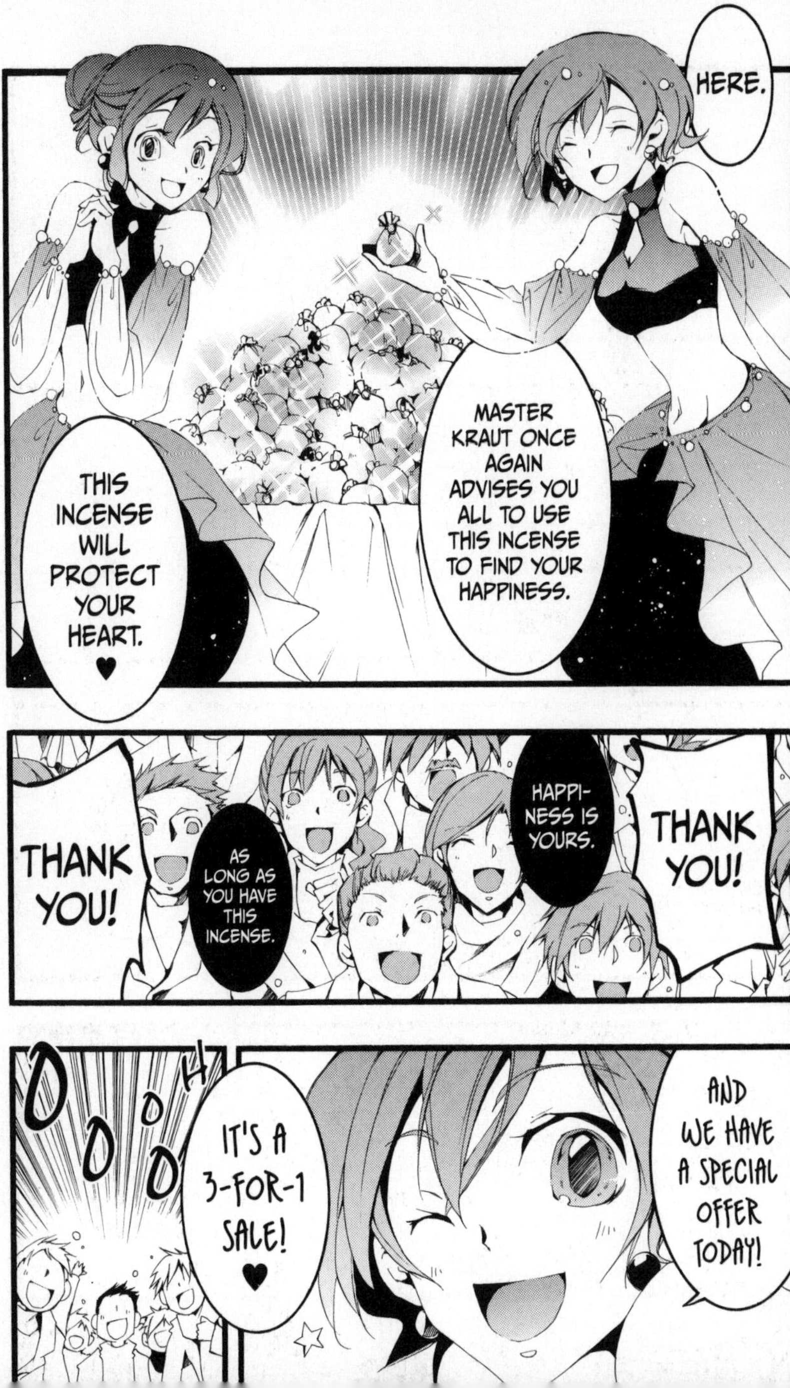
HERE.
MASTER KRAUT ONCE AGAIN ADVISES YOU ALL TO USE THIS INCENSE TO FIND YOUR HAPPINESS.
THIS INCENSE WILL PROTECT YOUR HEART. ♥
THANK YOU!
HAPPINESS IS YOURS.
AS LONG AS YOU HAVE THIS INCENSE.
THANK YOU!
AND WE HAVE A SPECIAL OFFER TODAY!
IT'S A 3-FOR-1 SALE! ♥
DOOOH

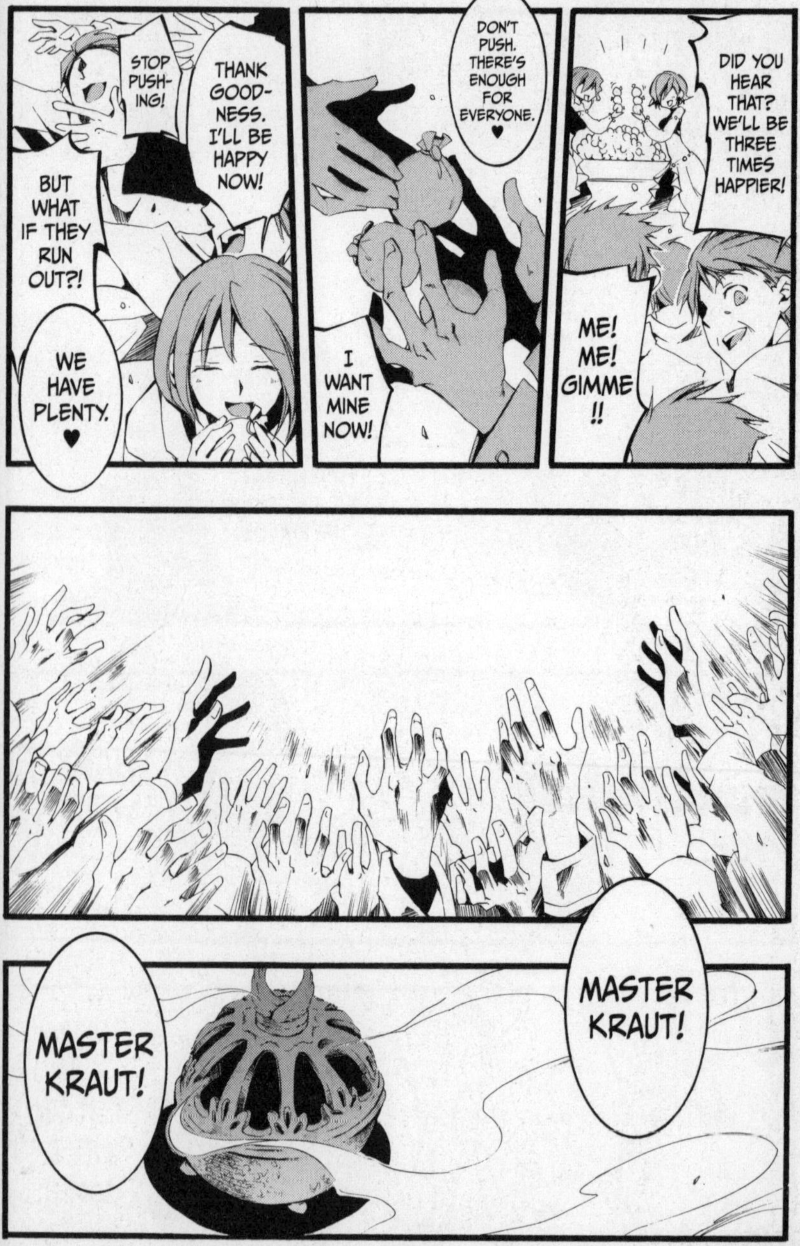
DID YOU HEAR THAT? WE'LL BE THREE TIMES HAPPIER!
ME! ME! GIMME!!
DON'T PUSH. THERE'S ENOUGH FOR EVERYONE. ♥
I WANT MINE NOW!
THANK GOODNESS. I'LL BE HAPPY NOW!
STOP PUSHING!
BUT WHAT IF THEY RUN OUT?!
WE HAVE PLENTY. ♥
MASTER KRAUT!
MASTER KRAUT!

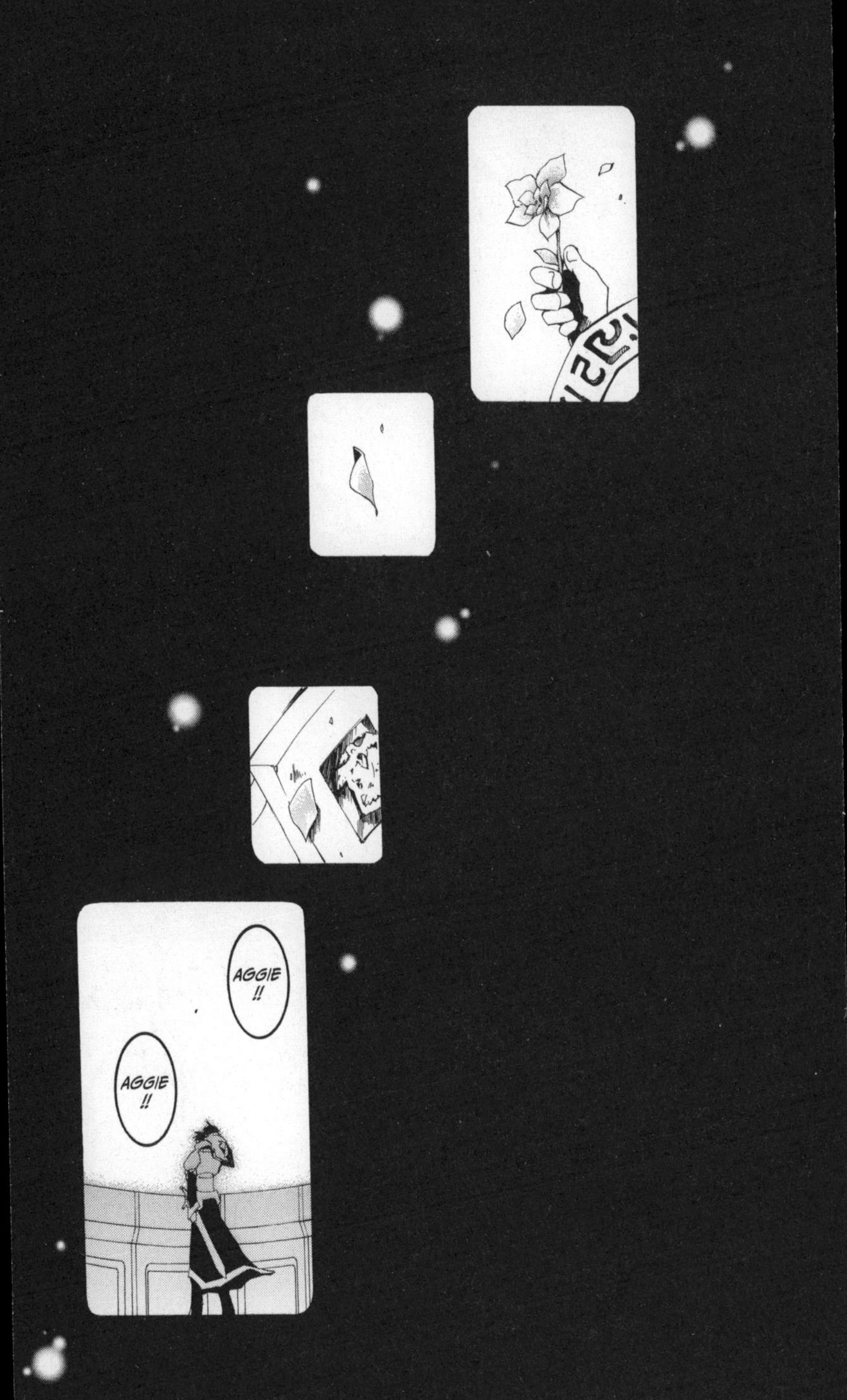
AGGIE!!
AGGIE!!

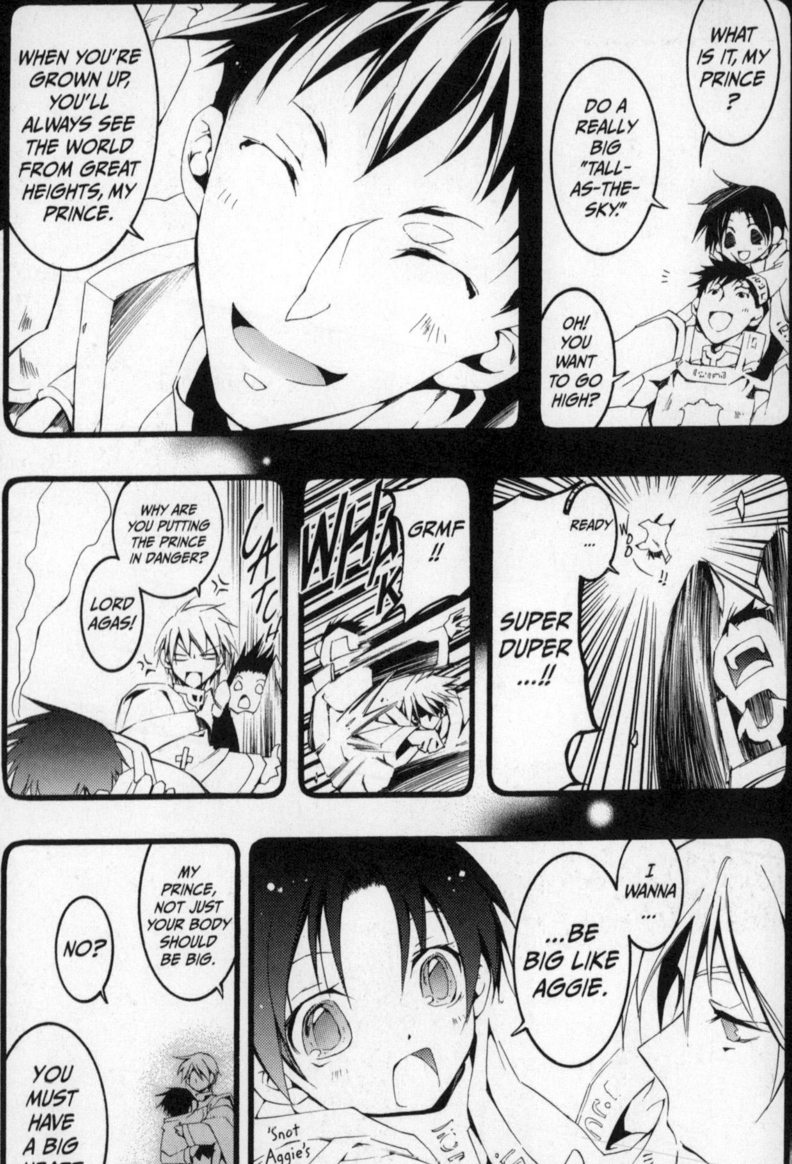
WHAT IS IT, MY PRINCE?
DO A REALLY BIG "TALL-AS-THE-SKY."
OH! YOU WANT TO GO HIGH?
WHEN YOU'RE GROWN UP, YOU'LL ALWAYS SEE THE WORLD FROM GREAT HEIGHTS, MY PRINCE.
READY...
SUPER DUPER...!!
WHACK
GRMF!!
CATCH
WHY ARE YOU PUTTING THE PRINCE IN DANGER?
LORD AGAS!
I WANNA...
...BE BIG LIKE AGGIE.
'Snot Aggie's fault.
MY PRINCE, NOT JUST YOUR BODY SHOULD BE BIG.
NO?
YOU MUST HAVE A BIG HEART TOO.

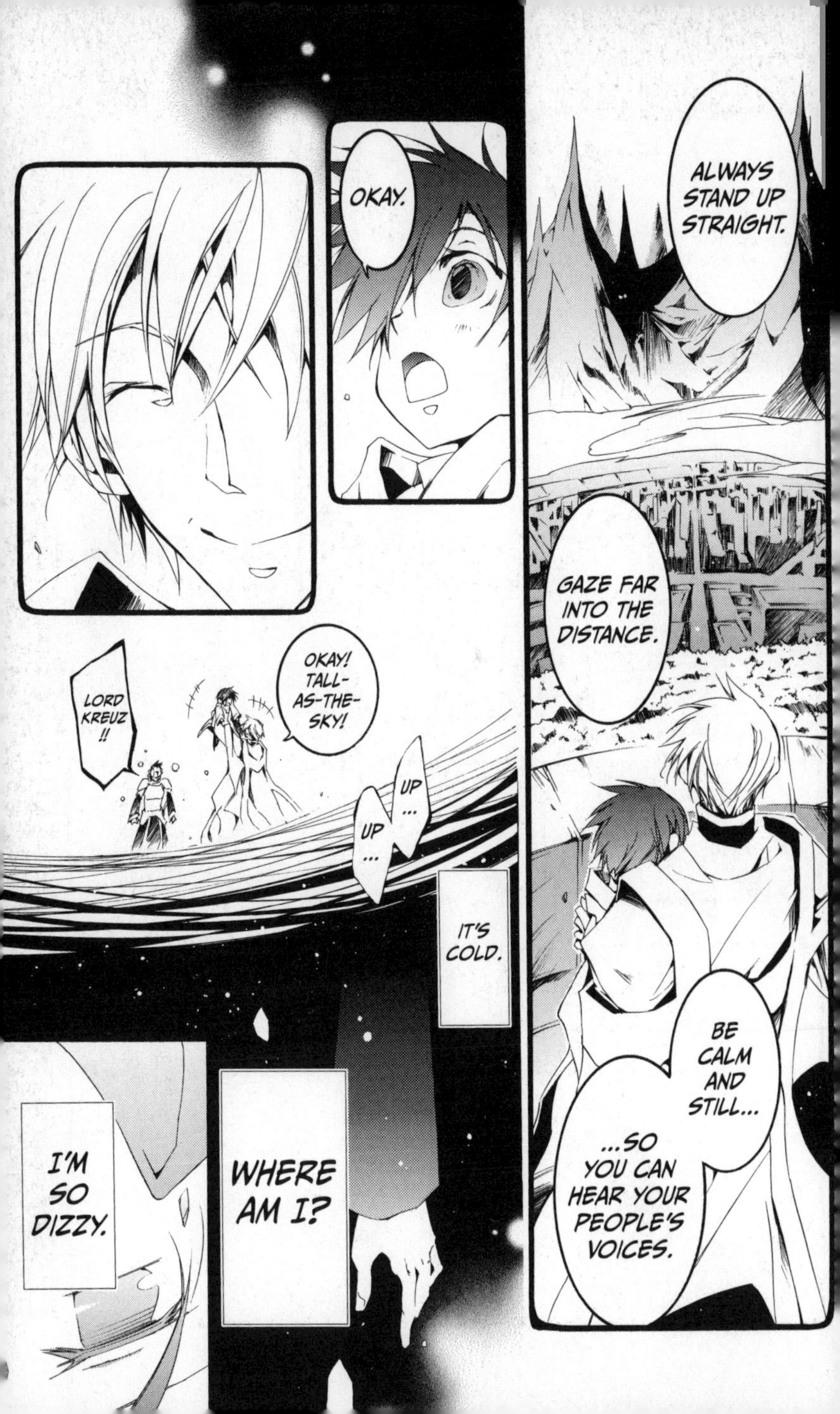
ALWAYS STAND UP STRAIGHT.
GAZE FAR INTO THE DISTANCE.
BE CALM AND STILL...
...SO YOU CAN HEAR YOUR PEOPLE'S VOICES.
OKAY.
OKAY! TALL-AS-THE-SKY!
LORD KREUZ !!
UP ...
UP ...
IT'S COLD.
WHERE AM I?
I'M SO DIZZY.

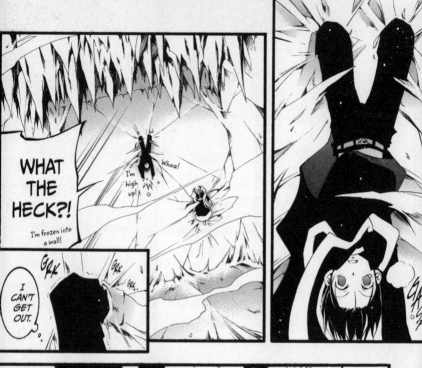

WHAT THE HECK?!

Whoa!

I'm high up!

I'm frozen into a wall!

GRK

GRK GRK

I CAN'T GET OUT.

JOOM

WHERE ARE KURURU AND MIKAGE?

TMP

KRAK

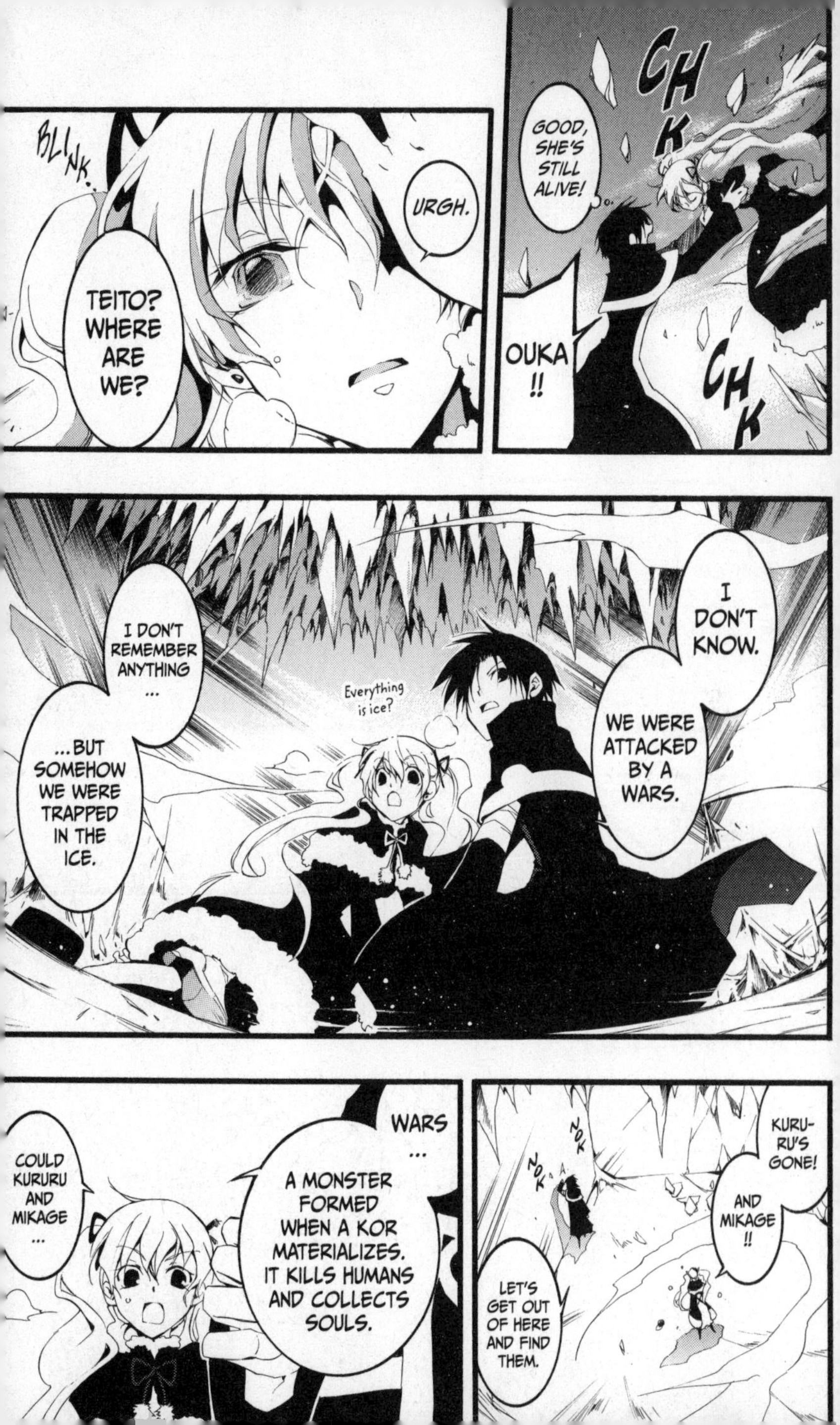
CHK
GOOD, SHE'S STILL ALIVE!
CHK
OUKA!!
URGH.
BLINK...
TEITO? WHERE ARE WE?
I DON'T KNOW.
WE WERE ATTACKED BY A WARS.
Everything is ice?
I DON'T REMEMBER ANYTHING...
...BUT SOMEHOW WE WERE TRAPPED IN THE ICE.
KURURU'S GONE!
AND MIKAGE!!
NOK
NOK
A...
LET'S GET OUT OF HERE AND FIND THEM.
WARS...
A MONSTER FORMED WHEN A KOR MATERIALIZES. IT KILLS HUMANS AND COLLECTS SOULS.
COULD KURURU AND MIKAGE...

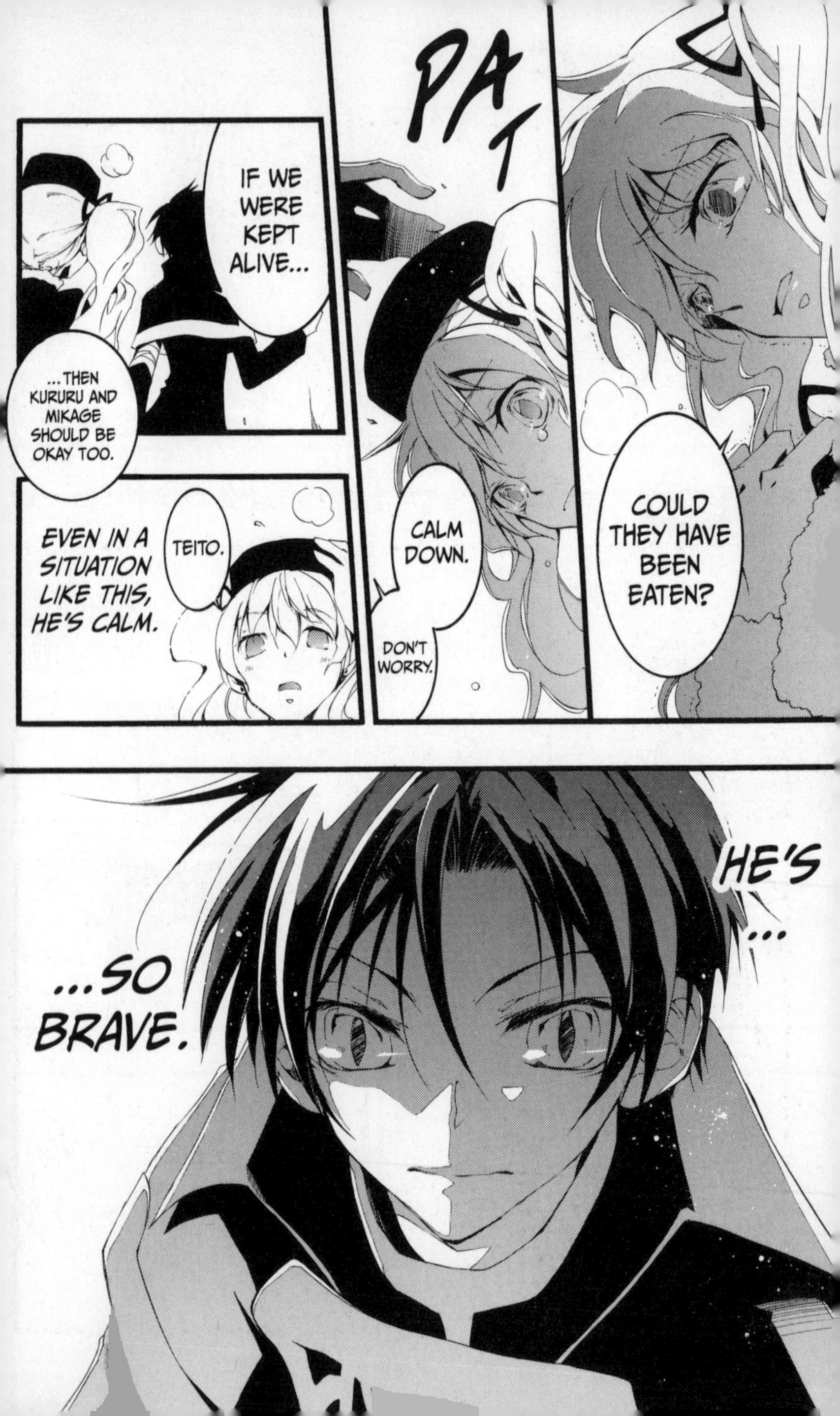
COULD THEY HAVE BEEN EATEN?
PAT
CALM DOWN.
DON'T WORRY.
IF WE WERE KEPT ALIVE...
...THEN KURURU AND MIKAGE SHOULD BE OKAY TOO.
TEITO.
EVEN IN A SITUATION LIKE THIS, HE'S CALM.
HE'S...
...SO BRAVE.

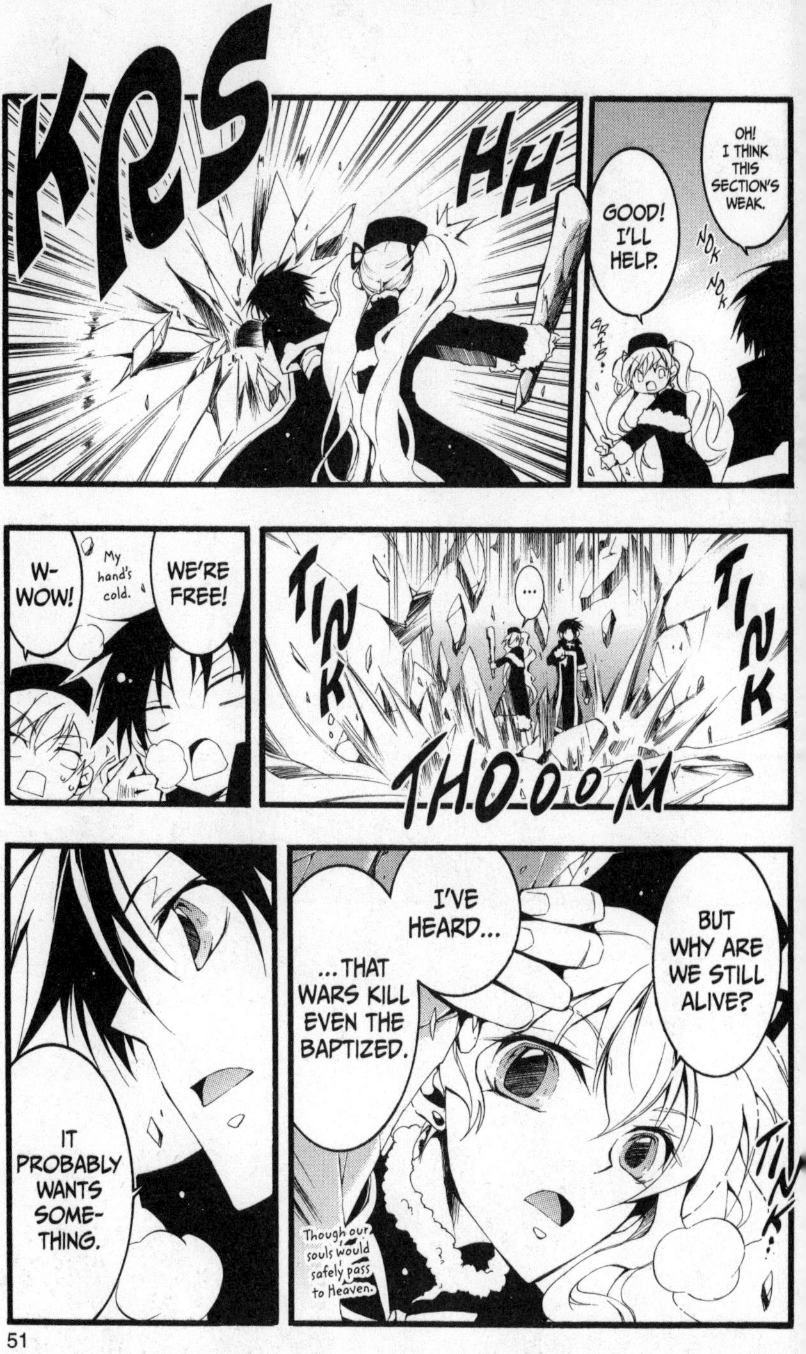
OH! I THINK THIS SECTION'S WEAK.
NOK NOK
GOOD! I'LL HELP.
GRAB
KRSHH
TINK
...
TINK
THOOOM
WE'RE FREE!
My hand's cold.
W-WOW!
BUT WHY ARE WE STILL ALIVE?
I'VE HEARD...
...THAT WARS KILL EVEN THE BAPTIZED.
Though our souls would safely pass to Heaven.
TINK...
IT PROBABLY WANTS SOME-THING.

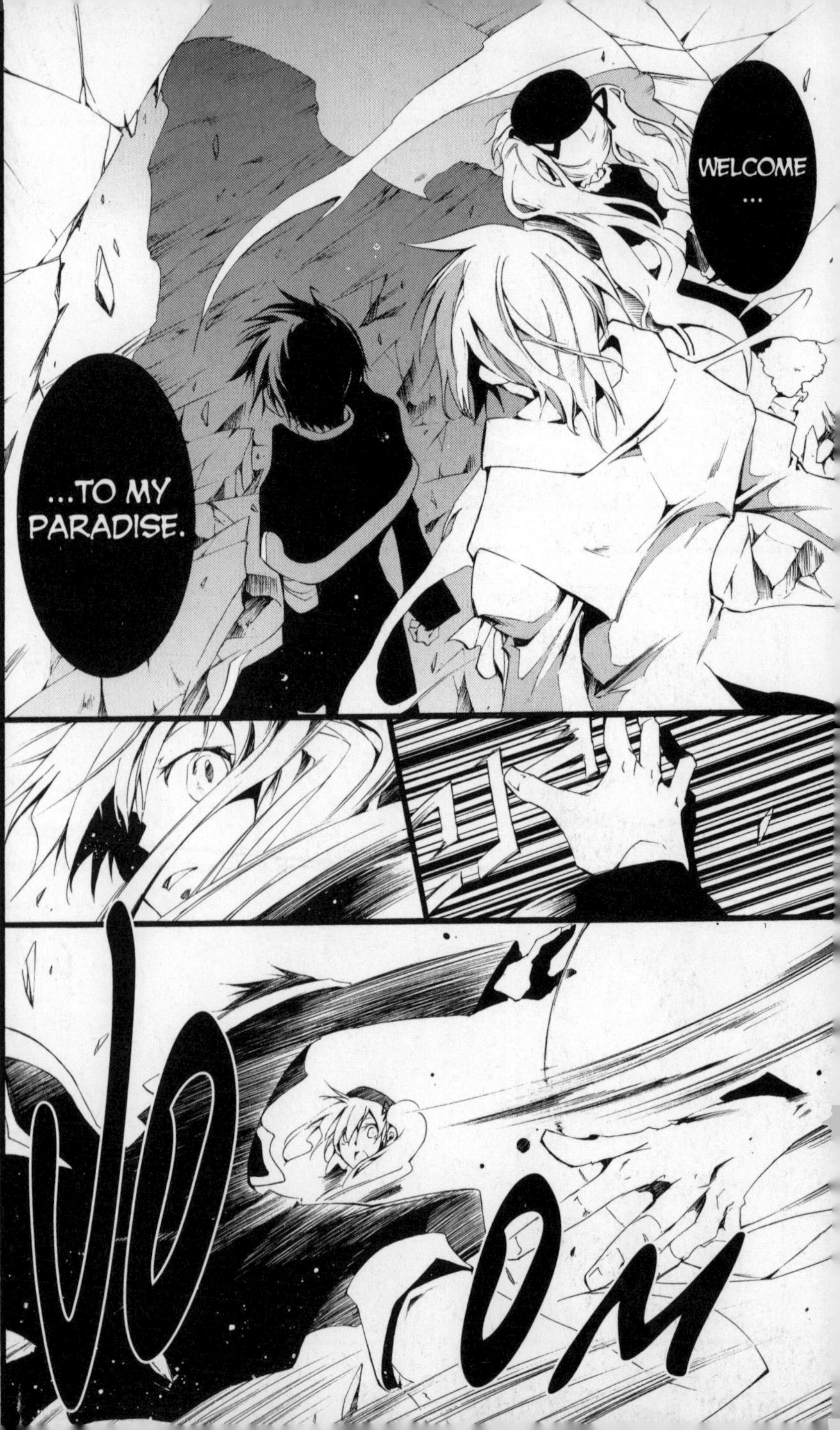
WELCOME ...
...TO MY PARADISE.

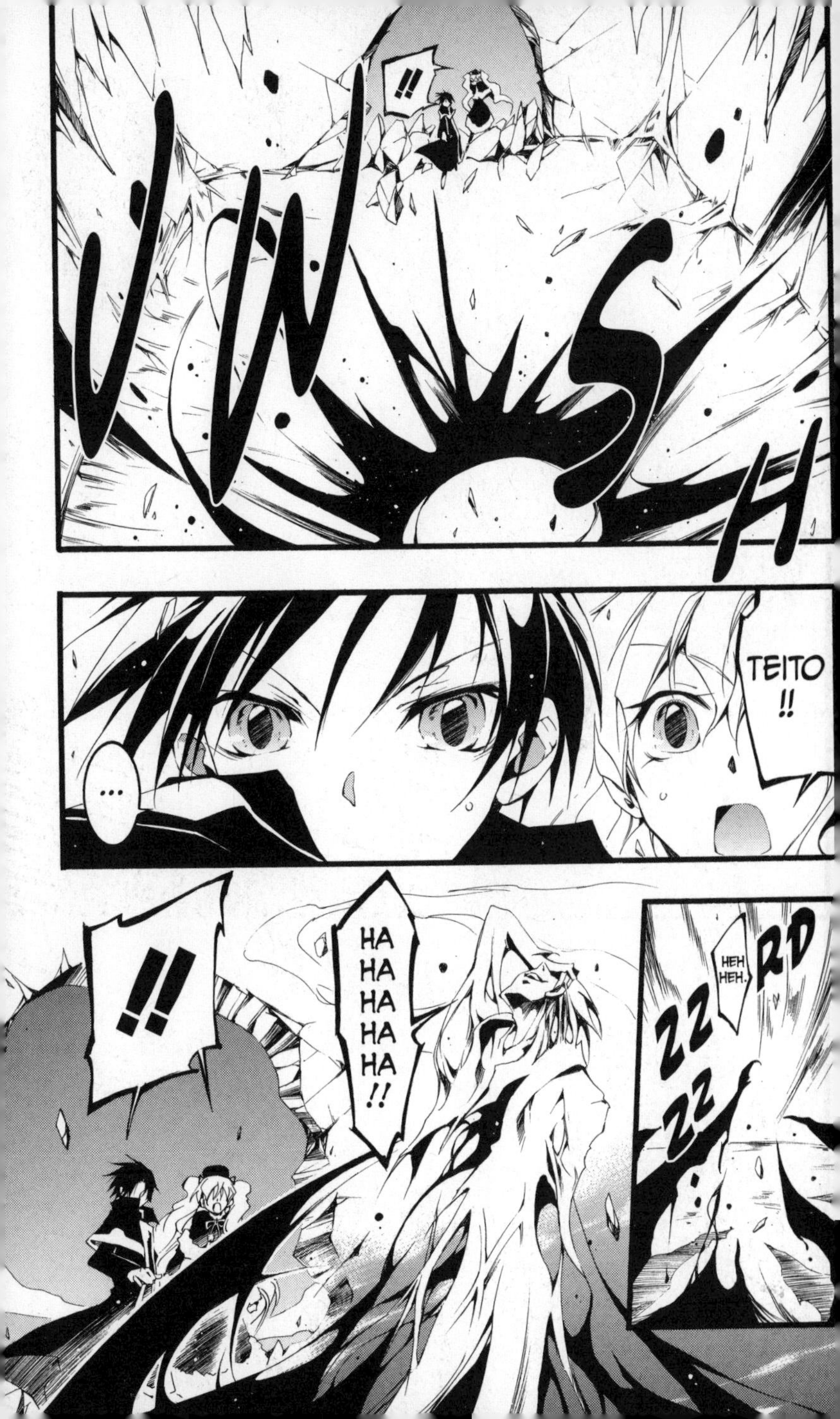
!!
VWSSH
TEITO !!
...
HEH HEH.
ZZZZRD
HA HA HA HA HA !!
!!

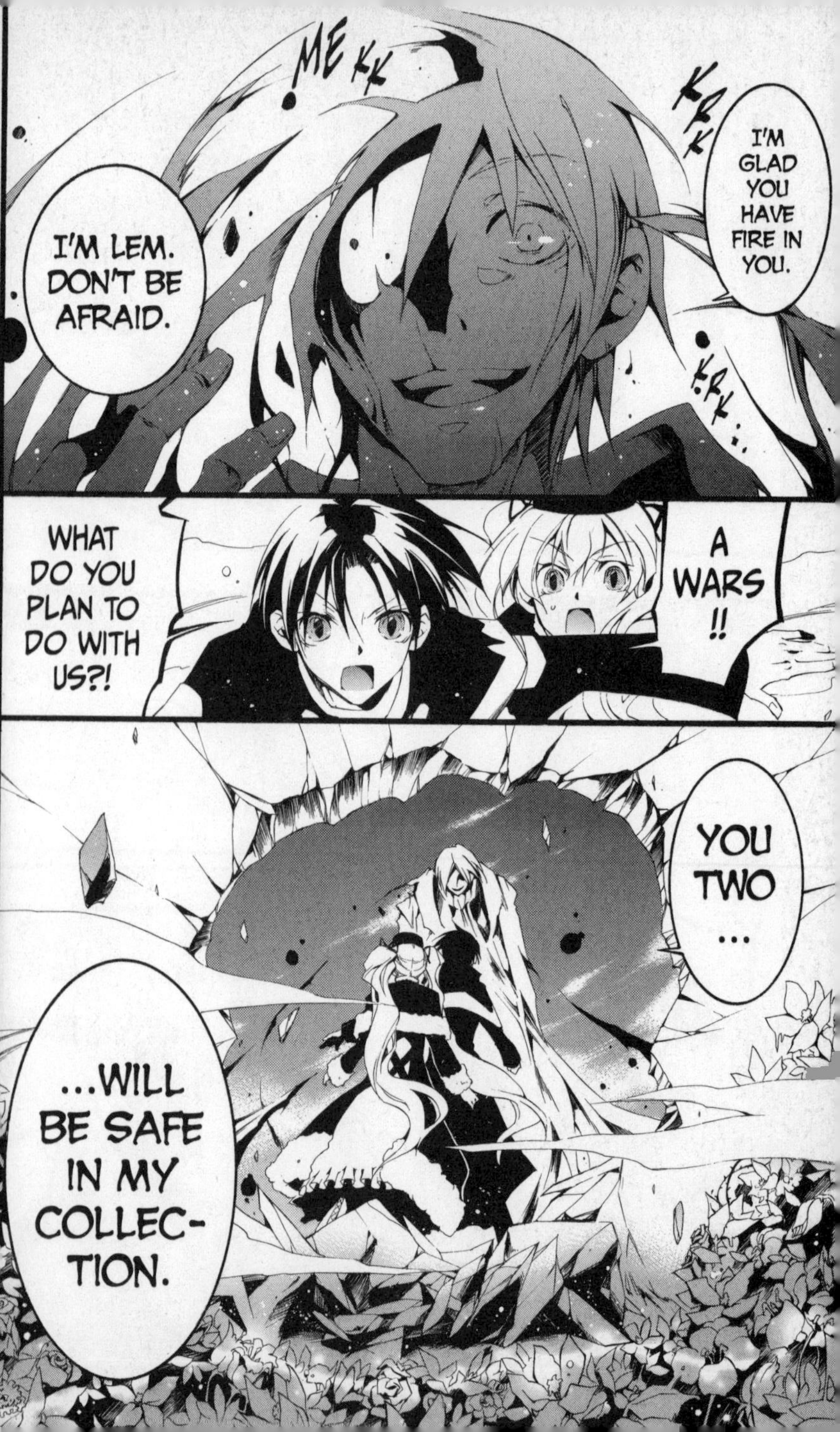
MEKK
KRKK
I'M GLAD YOU HAVE FIRE IN YOU.
I'M LEM. DON'T BE AFRAID.
KRK...
A WARS!!
WHAT DO YOU PLAN TO DO WITH US?!
YOU TWO...
...WILL BE SAFE IN MY COLLECTION.

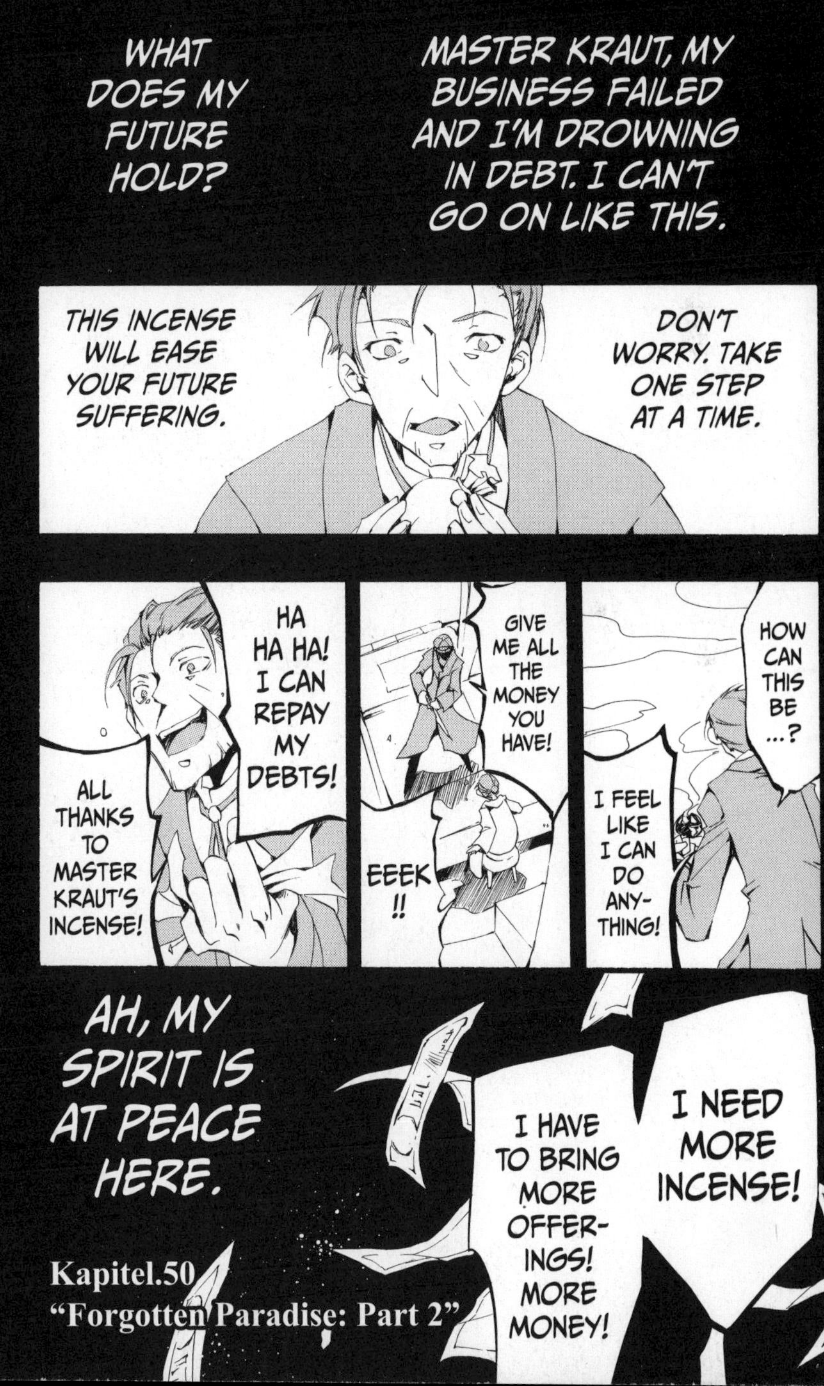

Kapitel.50 "Forgotten Paradise: Part 2"

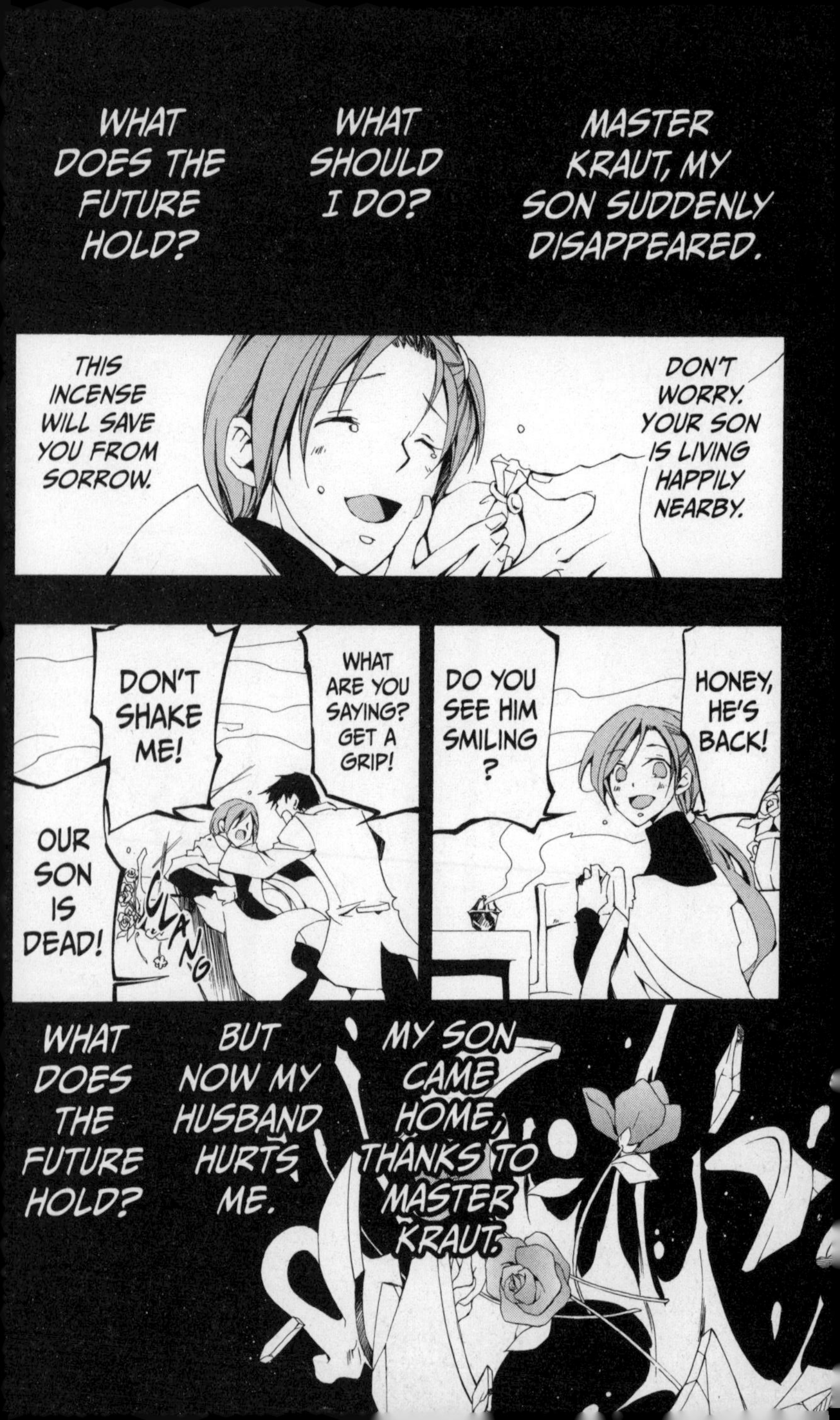
MASTER KRAUT, MY SON SUDDENLY DISAPPEARED.
WHAT SHOULD I DO?
WHAT DOES THE FUTURE HOLD?
DON'T WORRY. YOUR SON IS LIVING HAPPILY NEARBY.
THIS INCENSE WILL SAVE YOU FROM SORROW.
HONEY, HE'S BACK!
DO YOU SEE HIM SMILING?
WHAT ARE YOU SAYING? GET A GRIP!
DON'T SHAKE ME!
OUR SON IS DEAD!
CLANG
MY SON CAME HOME, THANKS TO MASTER KRAUT.
BUT NOW MY HUSBAND HURTS ME.
WHAT DOES THE FUTURE HOLD?

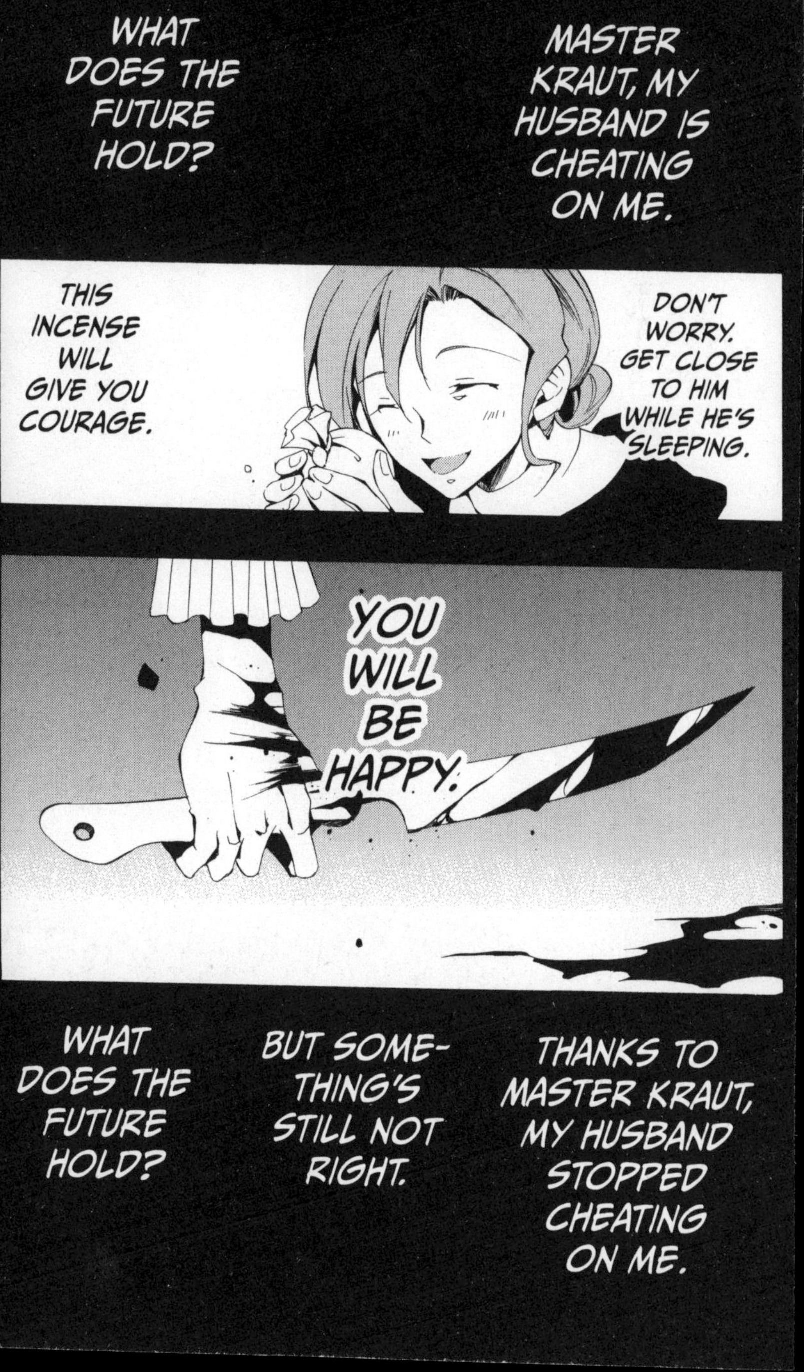
MASTER KRAUT, MY HUSBAND IS CHEATING ON ME.
WHAT DOES THE FUTURE HOLD?
DON'T WORRY. GET CLOSE TO HIM WHILE HE'S SLEEPING.
THIS INCENSE WILL GIVE YOU COURAGE.
YOU WILL BE HAPPY.
THANKS TO MASTER KRAUT, MY HUSBAND STOPPED CHEATING ON ME.
BUT SOME-THING'S STILL NOT RIGHT.
WHAT DOES THE FUTURE HOLD?

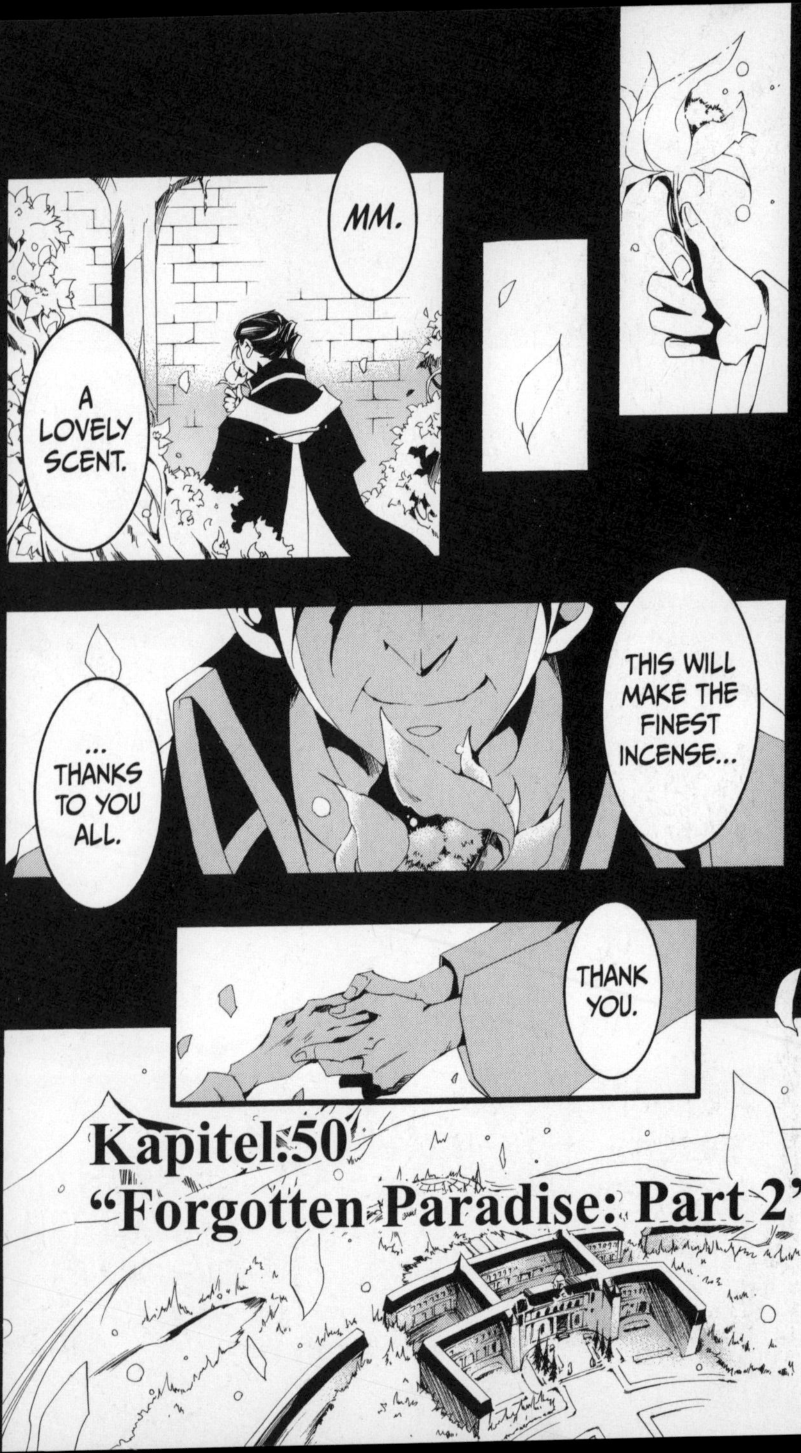
MM.
A LOVELY SCENT.
THIS WILL MAKE THE FINEST INCENSE...
... THANKS TO YOU ALL.
THANK YOU.
Kapitel.50
"Forgotten Paradise: Part 2"

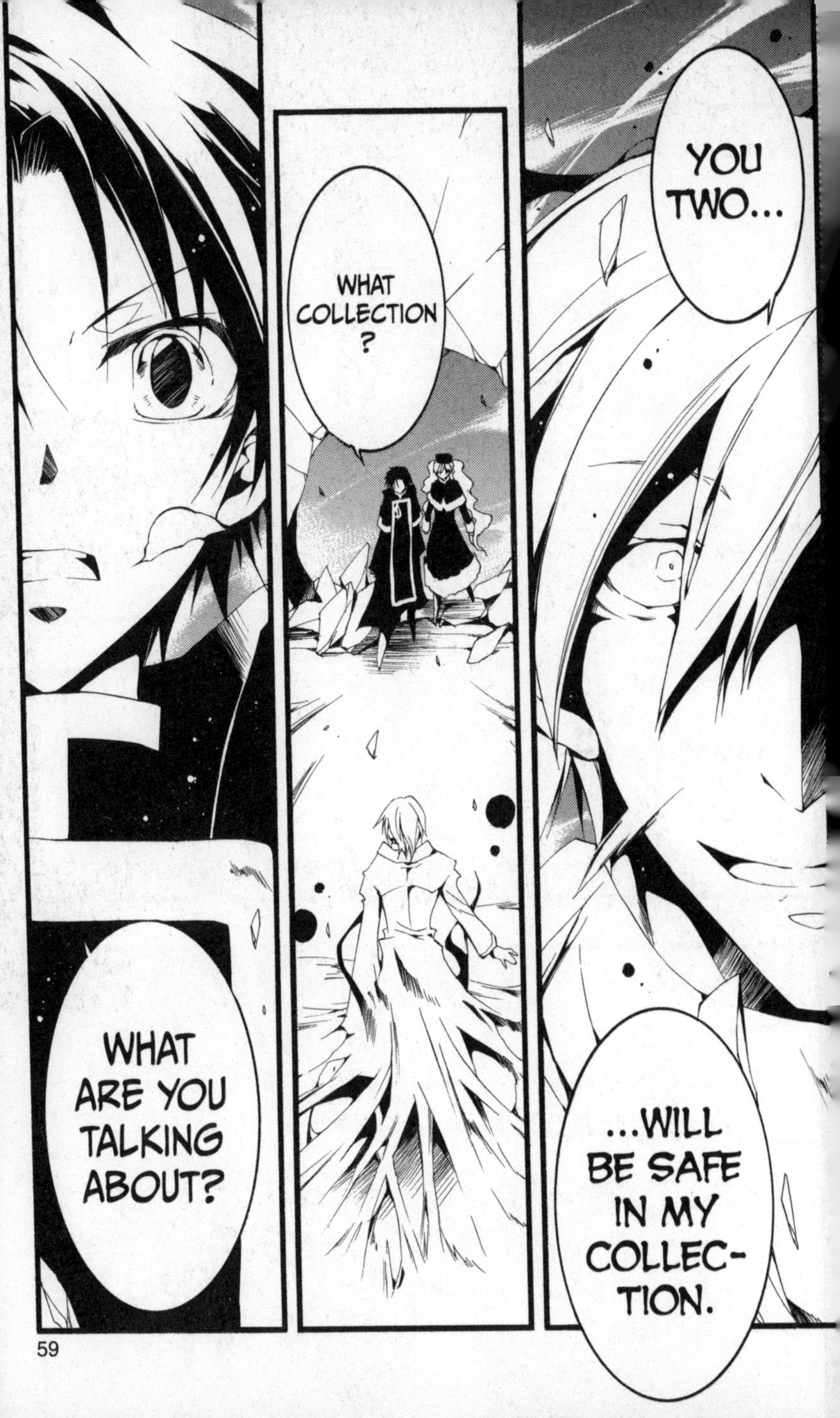
YOU TWO...
...WILL BE SAFE IN MY COLLECTION.
WHAT COLLECTION?
WHAT ARE YOU TALKING ABOUT?

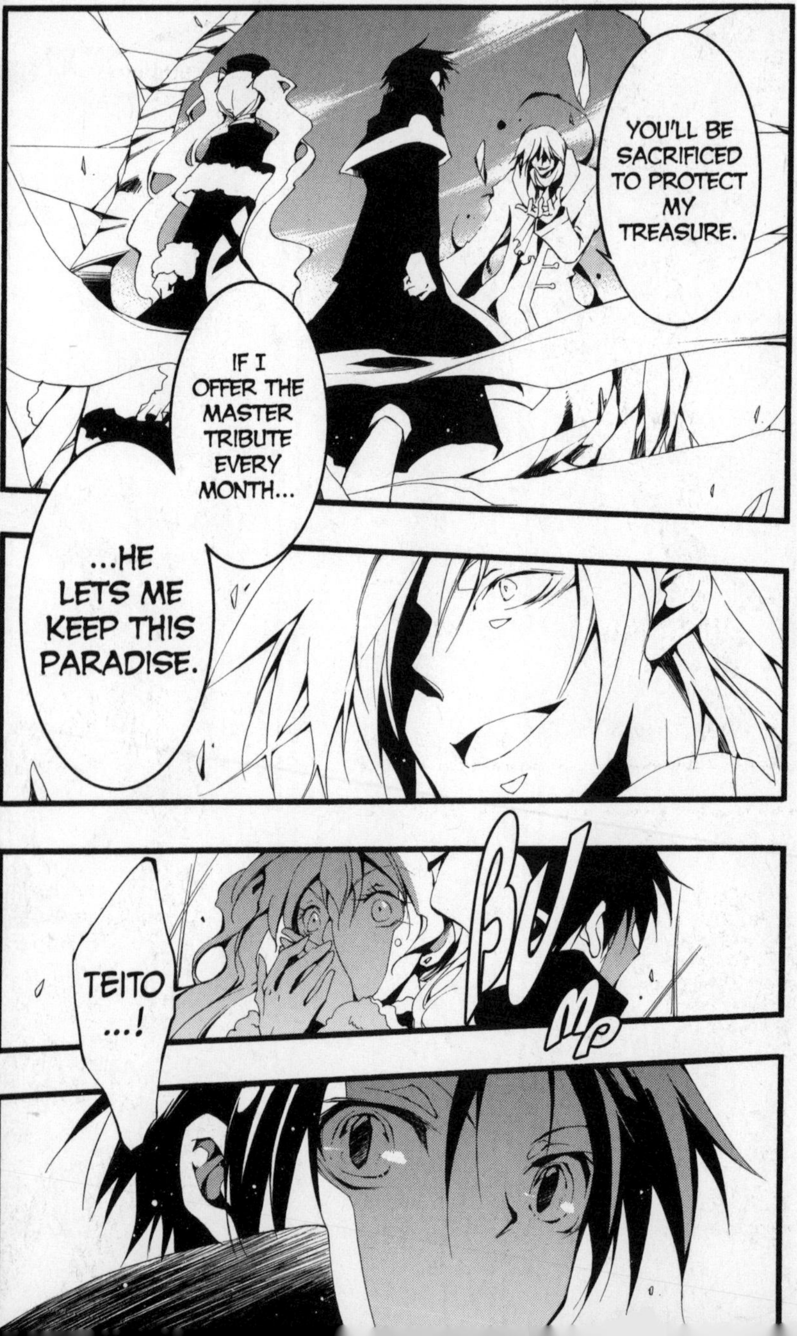
YOU'LL BE SACRIFICED TO PROTECT MY TREASURE.
IF I OFFER THE MASTER TRIBUTE EVERY MONTH...
...HE LETS ME KEEP THIS PARADISE.
BUMP
TEITO ...!

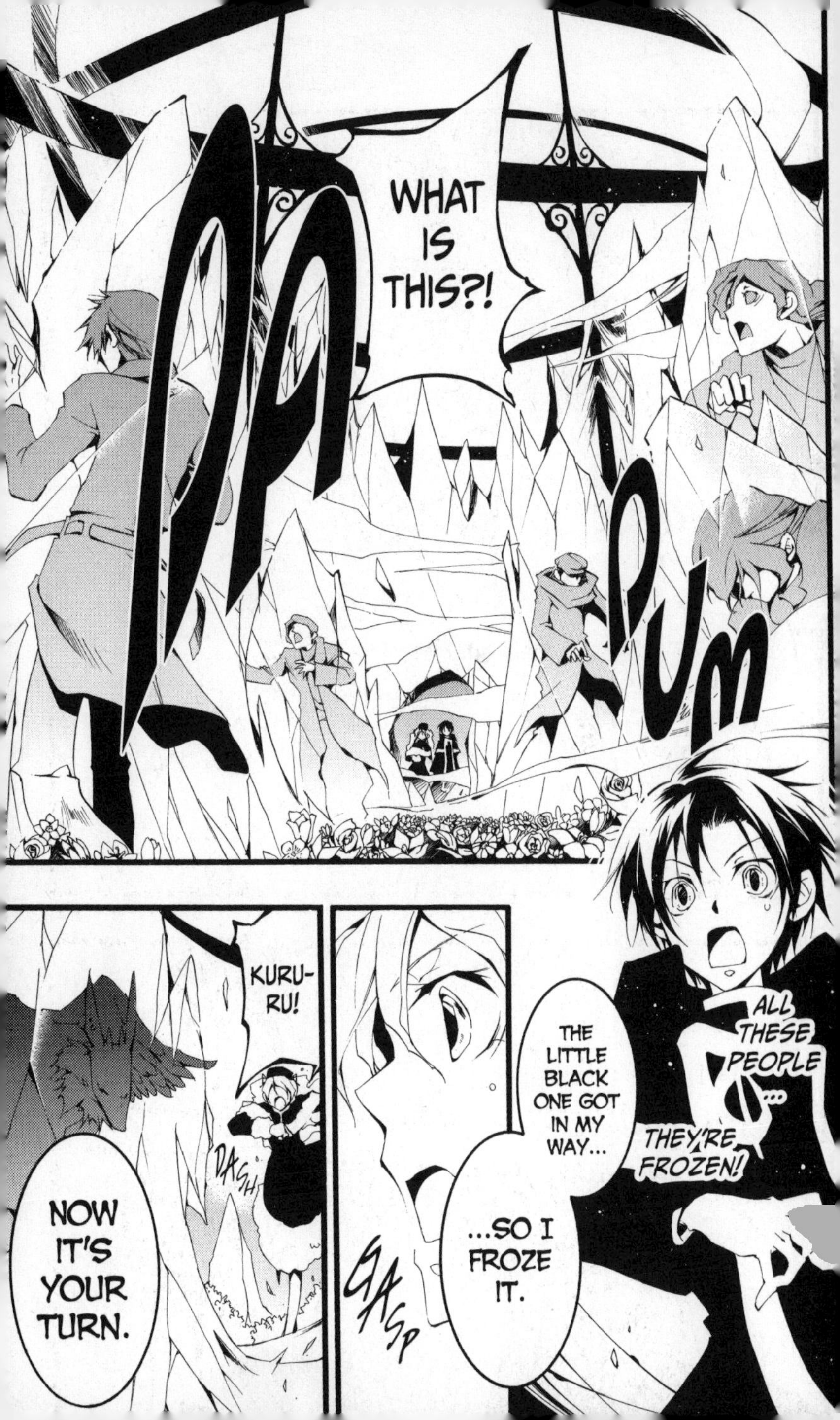
WHAT IS THIS?!
ALL THESE PEOPLE...
THEY'RE FROZEN!
THE LITTLE BLACK ONE GOT IN MY WAY...
...SO I FROZE IT.
GASP
KURU-RU!
DASH
NOW IT'S YOUR TURN.

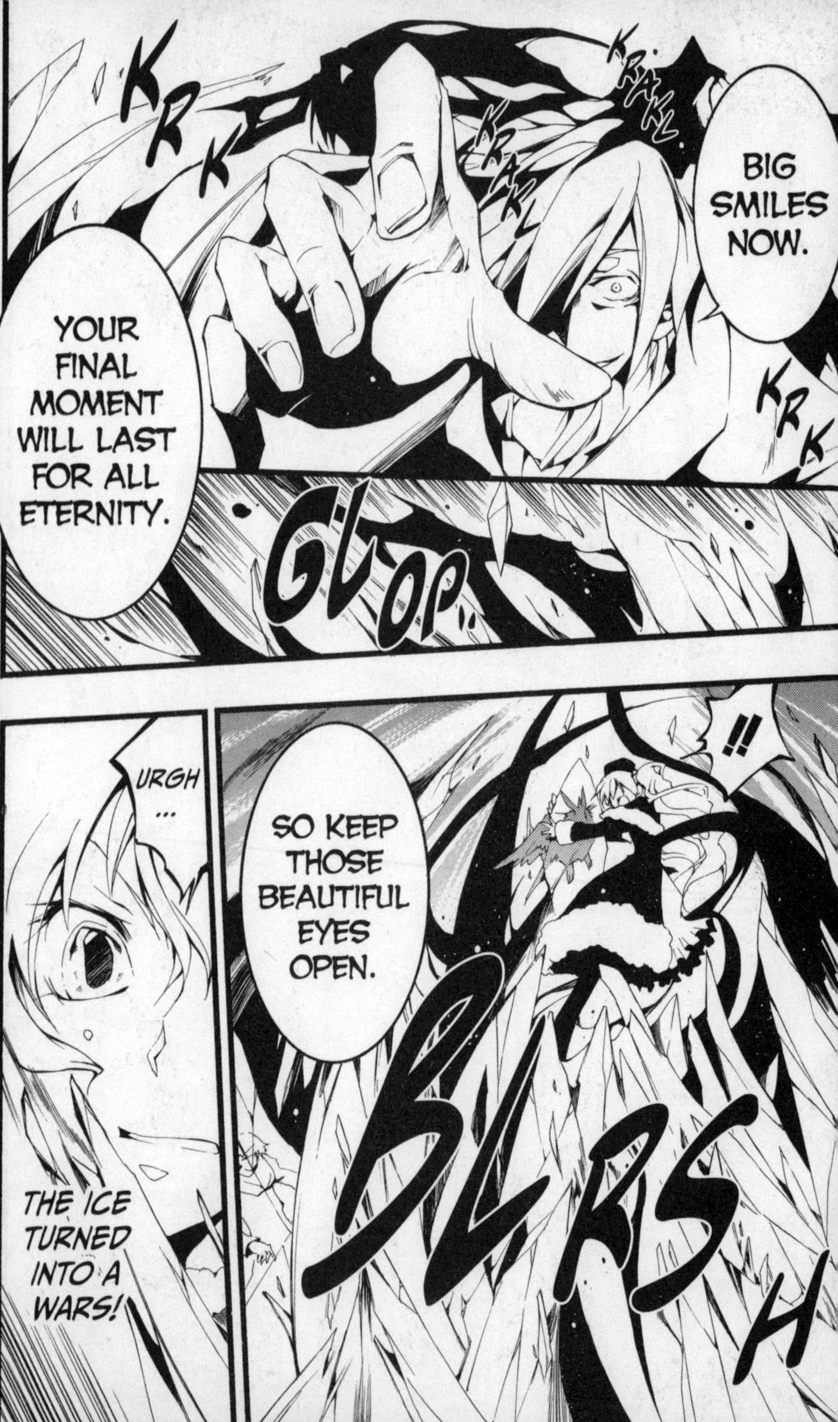
BIG SMILES NOW.
KRAKL
KRAKL
KRK
KRK
YOUR FINAL MOMENT WILL LAST FOR ALL ETERNITY.
GLOOP..
!!
SO KEEP THOSE BEAUTIFUL EYES OPEN.
URGH ...
THE ICE TURNED INTO A WARS!

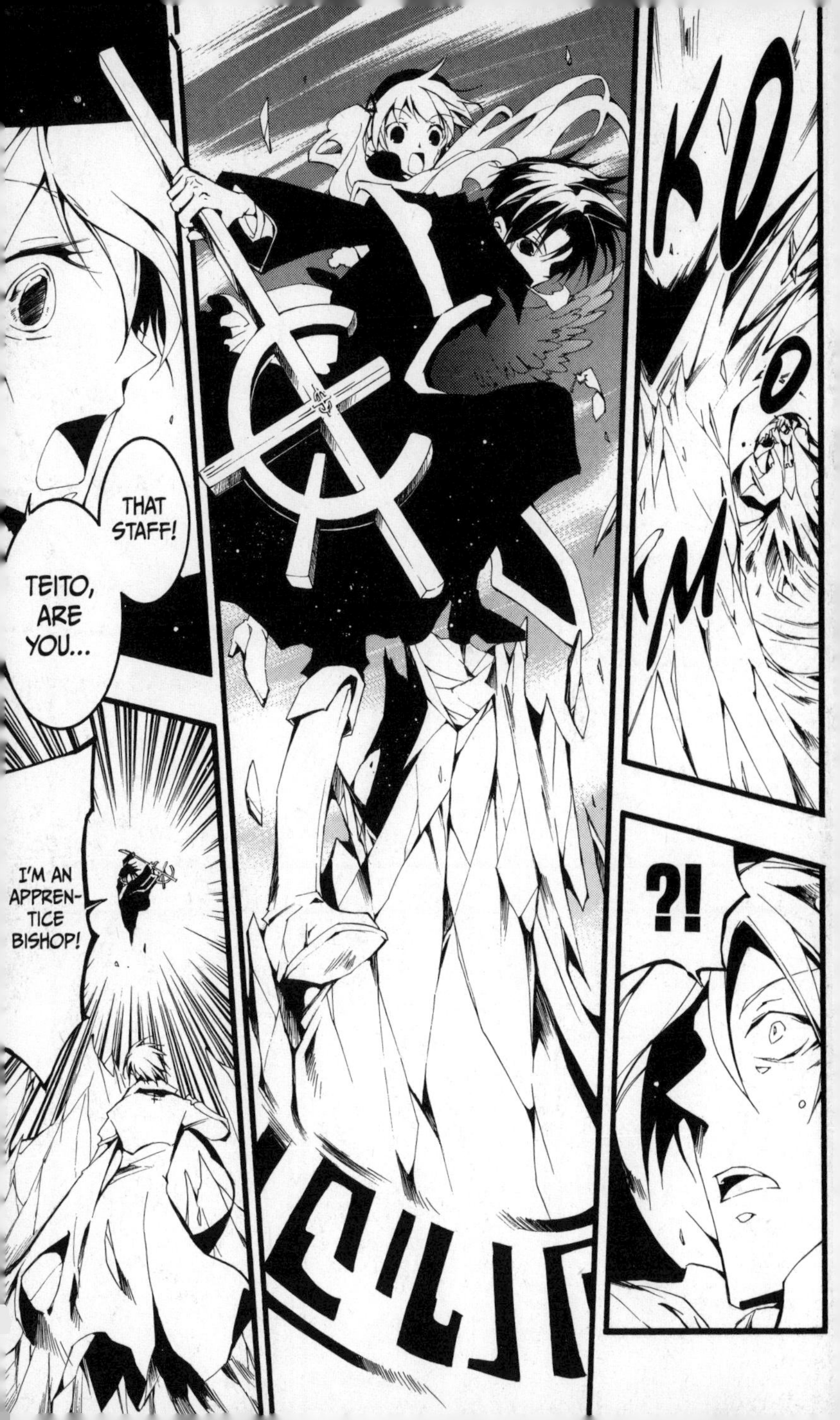
?!
THAT STAFF!
TEITO, ARE YOU...
I'M AN APPRENTICE BISHOP!

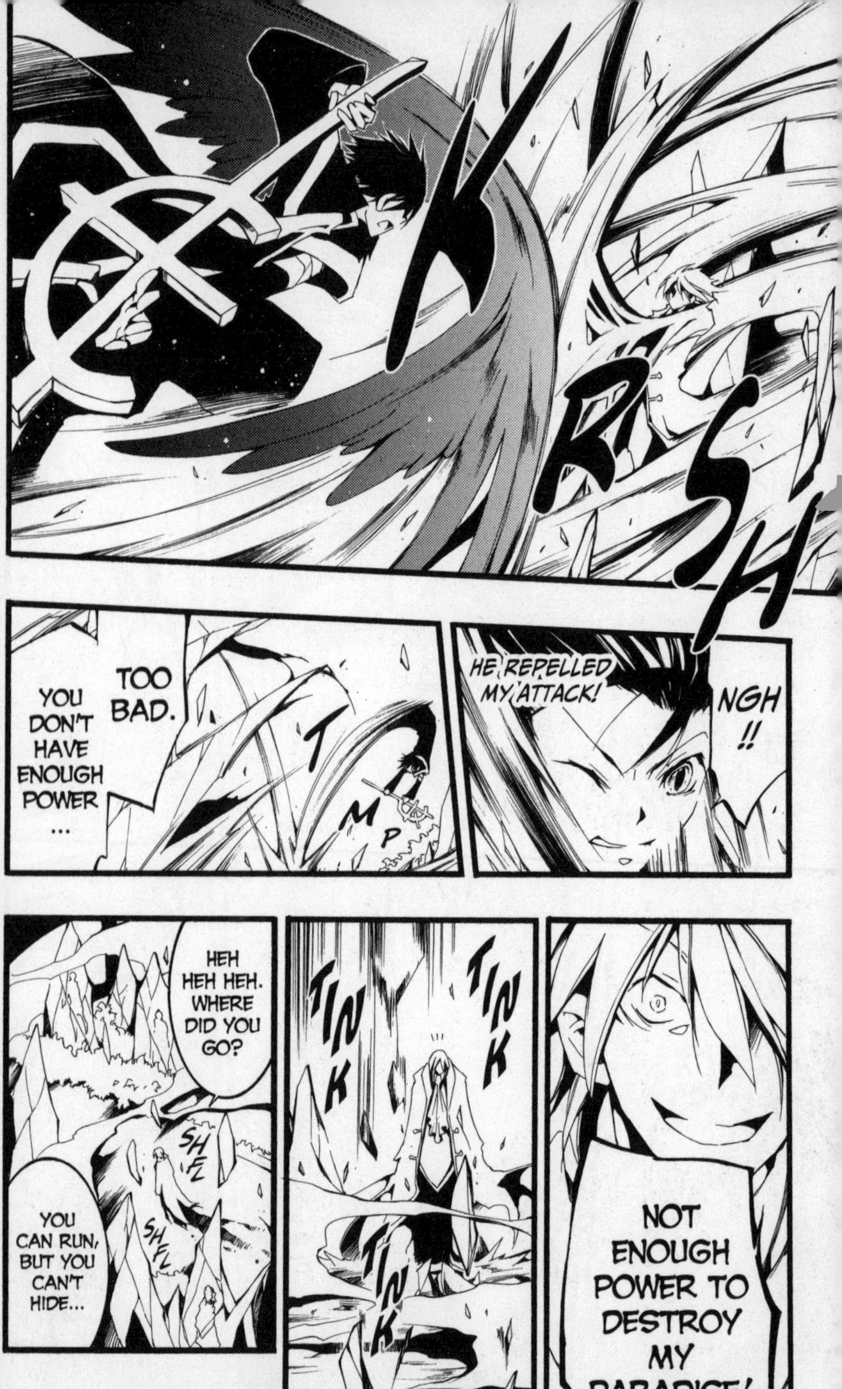
BASH
NGH!!
HE REPELLED MY ATTACK!
TOO BAD.
YOU DON'T HAVE ENOUGH POWER...
TMP
NOT ENOUGH POWER TO DESTROY MY PARADISE!
TINK
TINK
TINK
HEH HEH HEH. WHERE DID YOU GO?
SHFL
SHFL
YOU CAN RUN, BUT YOU CAN'T HIDE...

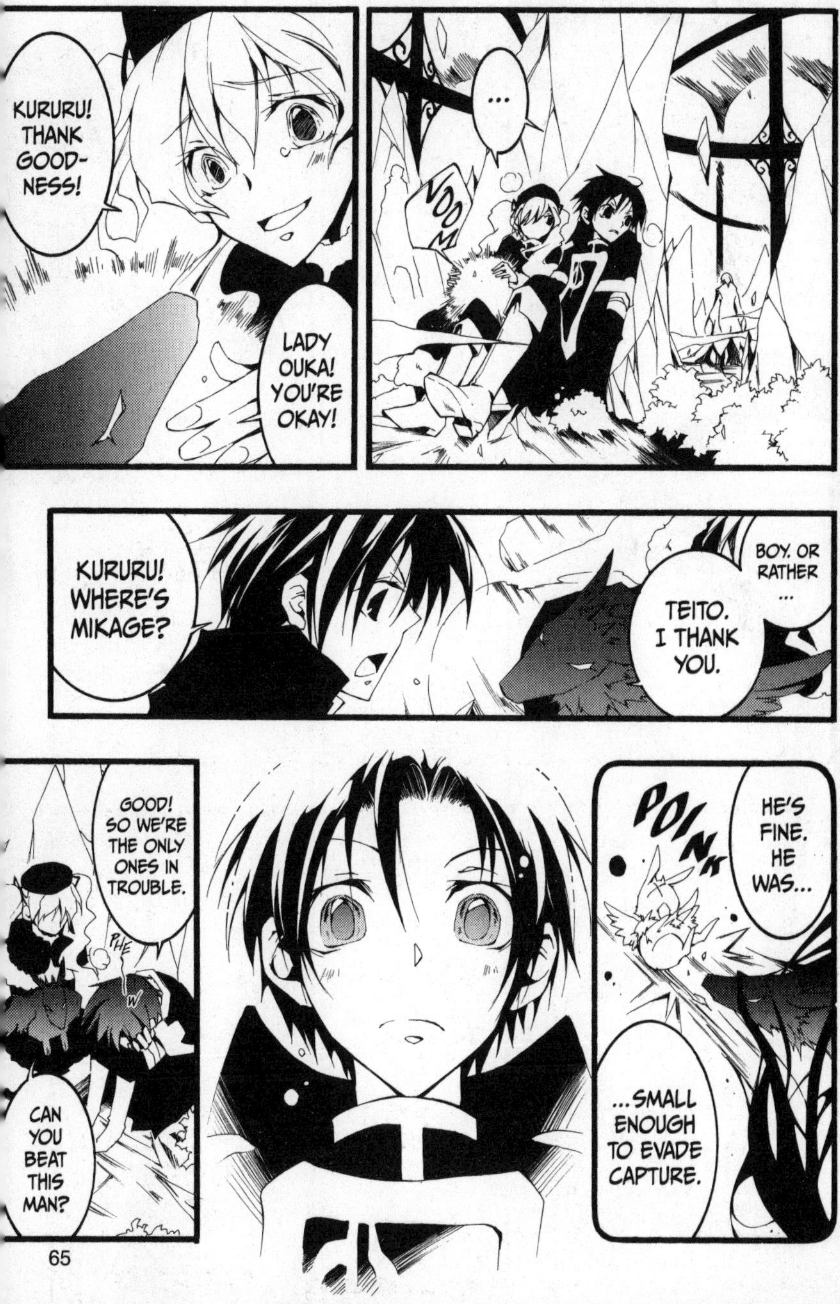
...
VOOM
LADY OUKA! YOU'RE OKAY!
KURURU! THANK GOODNESS!
BOY. OR RATHER ...
TEITO. I THANK YOU.
KURURU! WHERE'S MIKAGE?
POINK
HE'S FINE. HE WAS...
...SMALL ENOUGH TO EVADE CAPTURE.
GOOD! SO WE'RE THE ONLY ONES IN TROUBLE.
PHEW
CAN YOU BEAT THIS MAN?

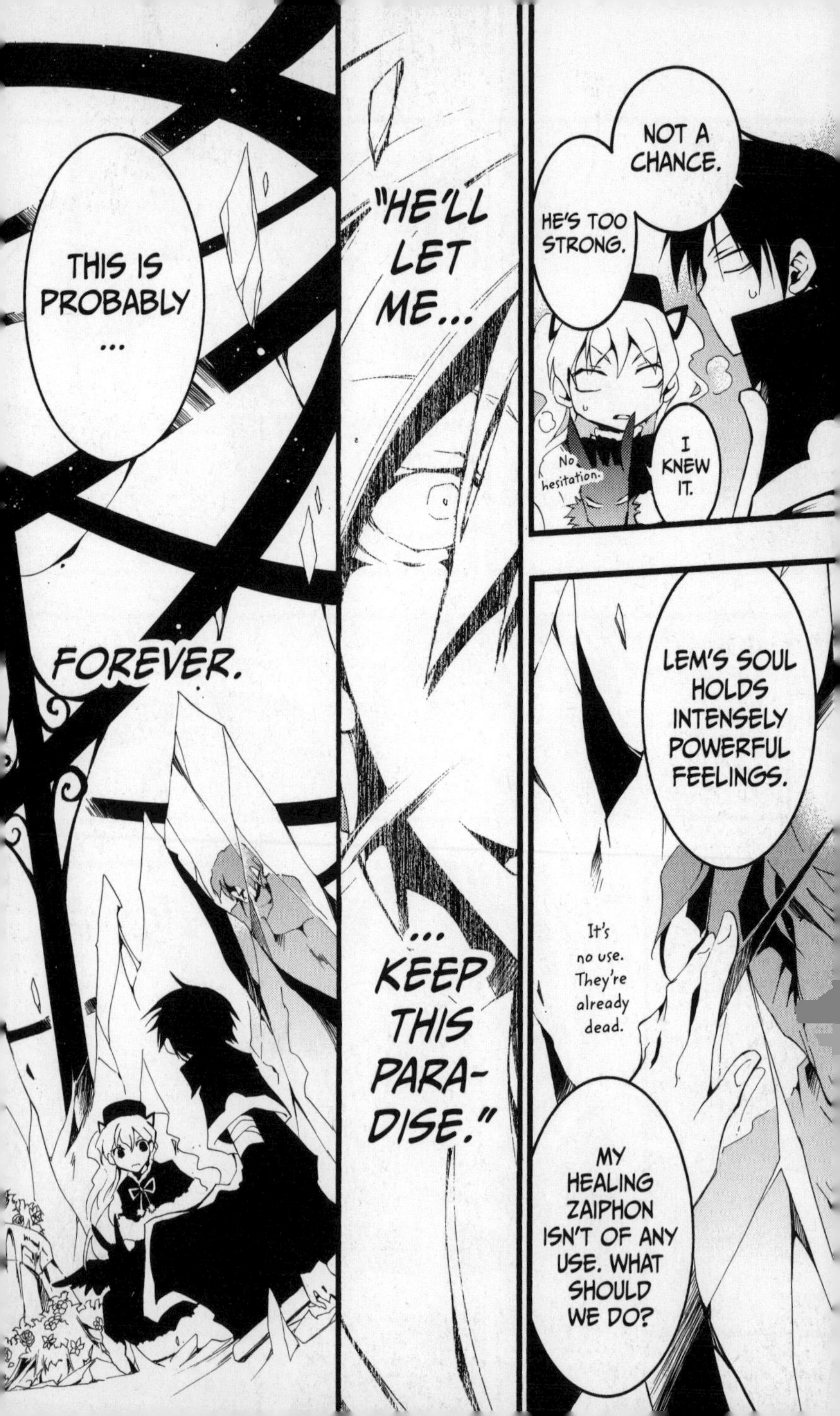

NOT A CHANCE.
HE'S TOO STRONG.
I KNEW IT.
No hesitation.
LEM'S SOUL HOLDS INTENSELY POWERFUL FEELINGS.
It's no use. They're already dead.
MY HEALING ZAIPHON ISN'T OF ANY USE. WHAT SHOULD WE DO?
"HE'LL LET ME...
... KEEP THIS PARA-DISE."
THIS IS PROBABLY ...
FOREVER.

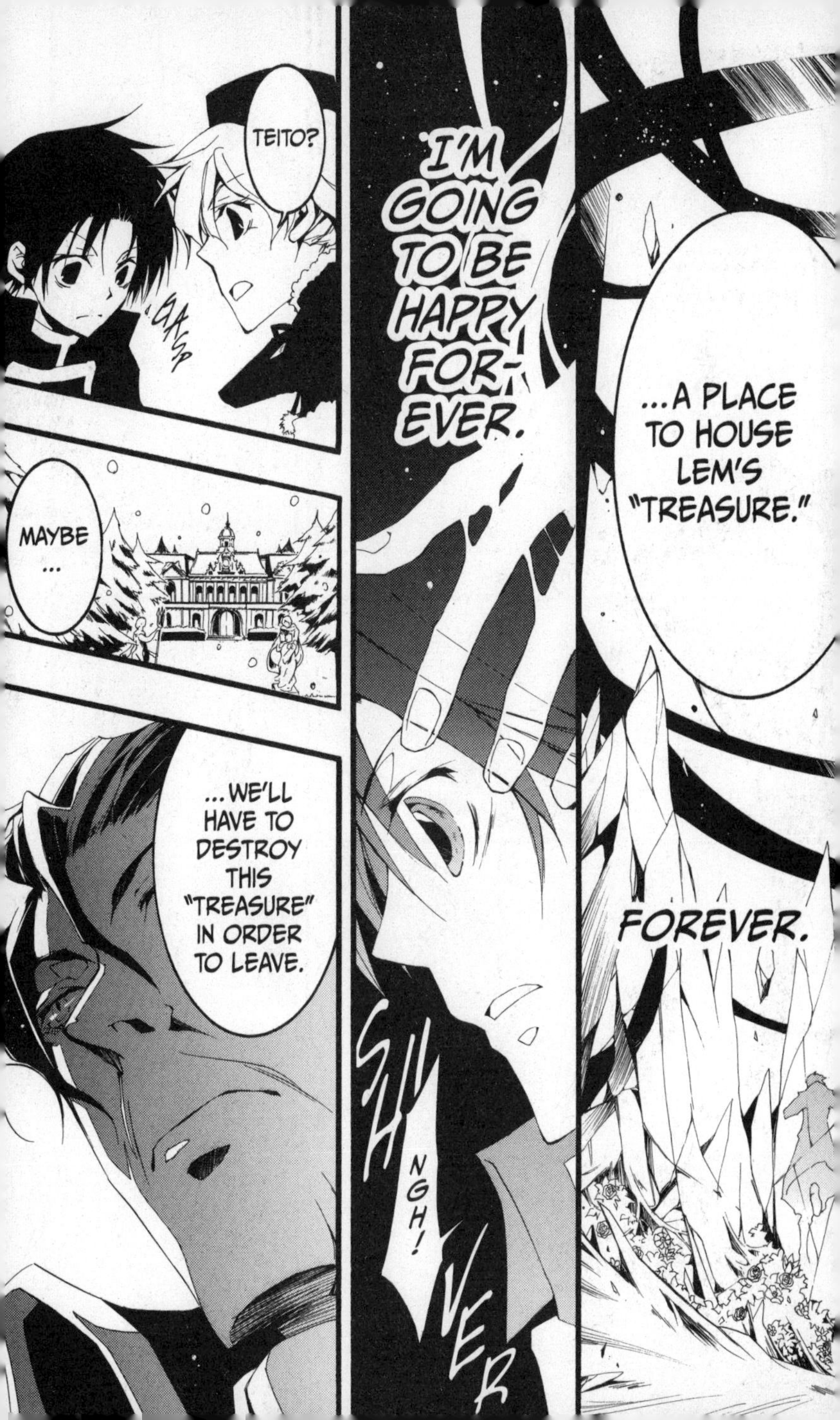
...A PLACE TO HOUSE LEM'S "TREASURE."
FOREVER.
I'M GOING TO BE HAPPY FOR-EVER.
SHIVER
NGH!
TEITO?
MAYBE...
...WE'LL HAVE TO DESTROY THIS "TREASURE" IN ORDER TO LEAVE.

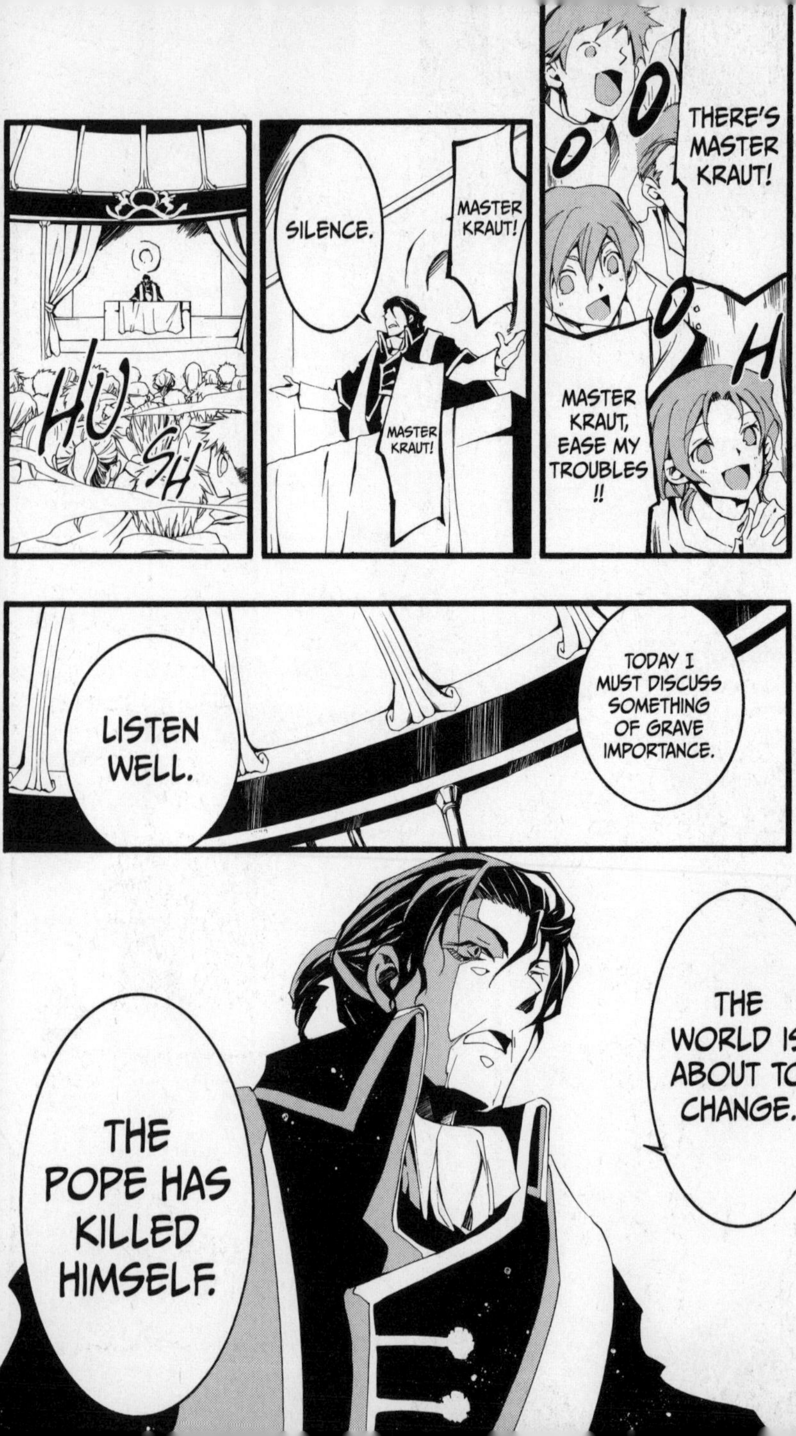
THERE'S MASTER KRAUT!
OOOOH
MASTER KRAUT, EASE MY TROUBLES!!
MASTER KRAUT!
SILENCE.
MASTER KRAUT!
HUSH
TODAY I MUST DISCUSS SOMETHING OF GRAVE IMPORTANCE.
LISTEN WELL.
THE WORLD IS ABOUT TO CHANGE.
THE POPE HAS KILLED HIMSELF.

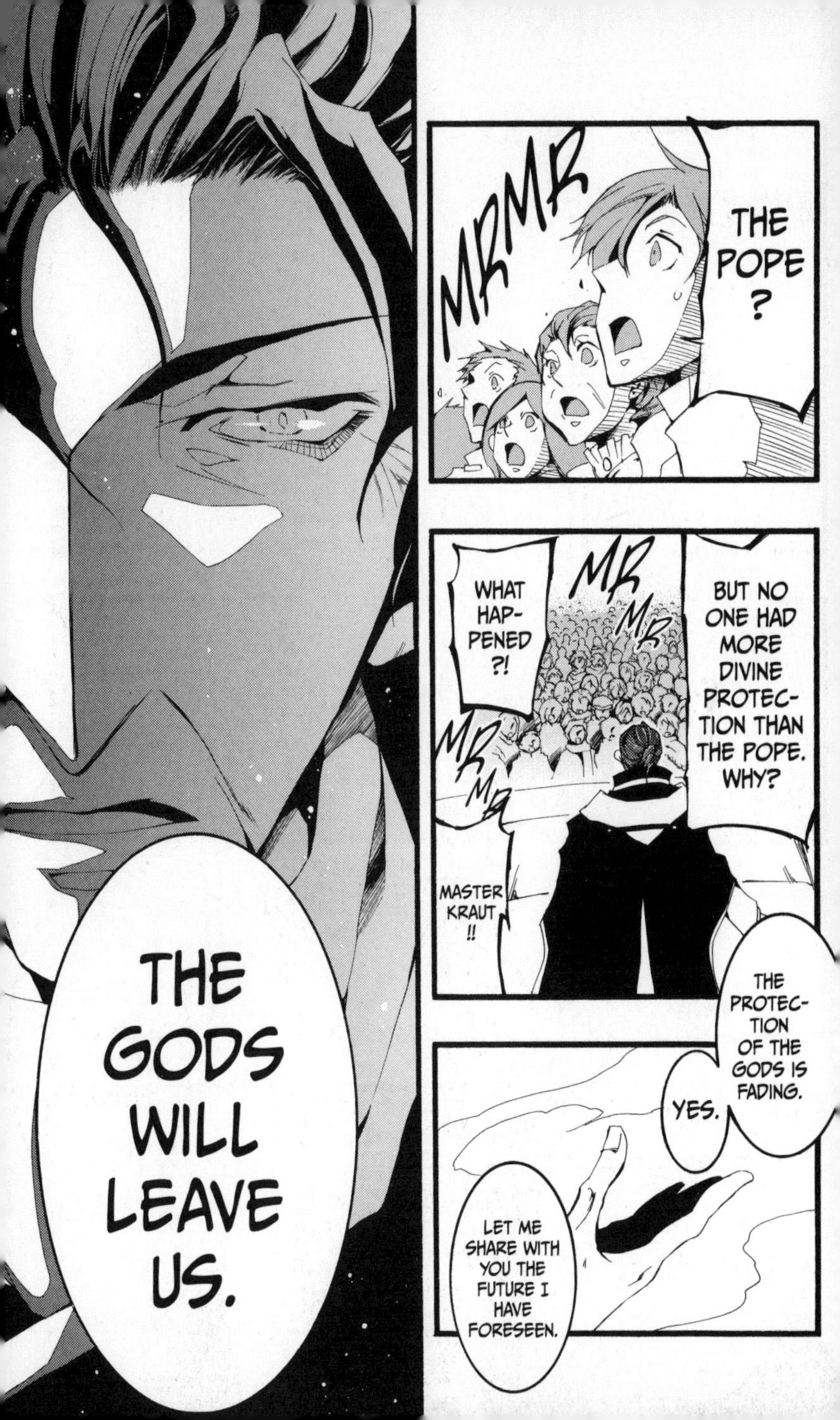
THE POPE?
MRMR
BUT NO ONE HAD MORE DIVINE PROTECTION THAN THE POPE. WHY?
MR MR
WHAT HAPPENED?!
MR MR
MASTER KRAUT!!
THE PROTECTION OF THE GODS IS FADING.
YES.
LET ME SHARE WITH YOU THE FUTURE I HAVE FORESEEN.
THE GODS WILL LEAVE US.

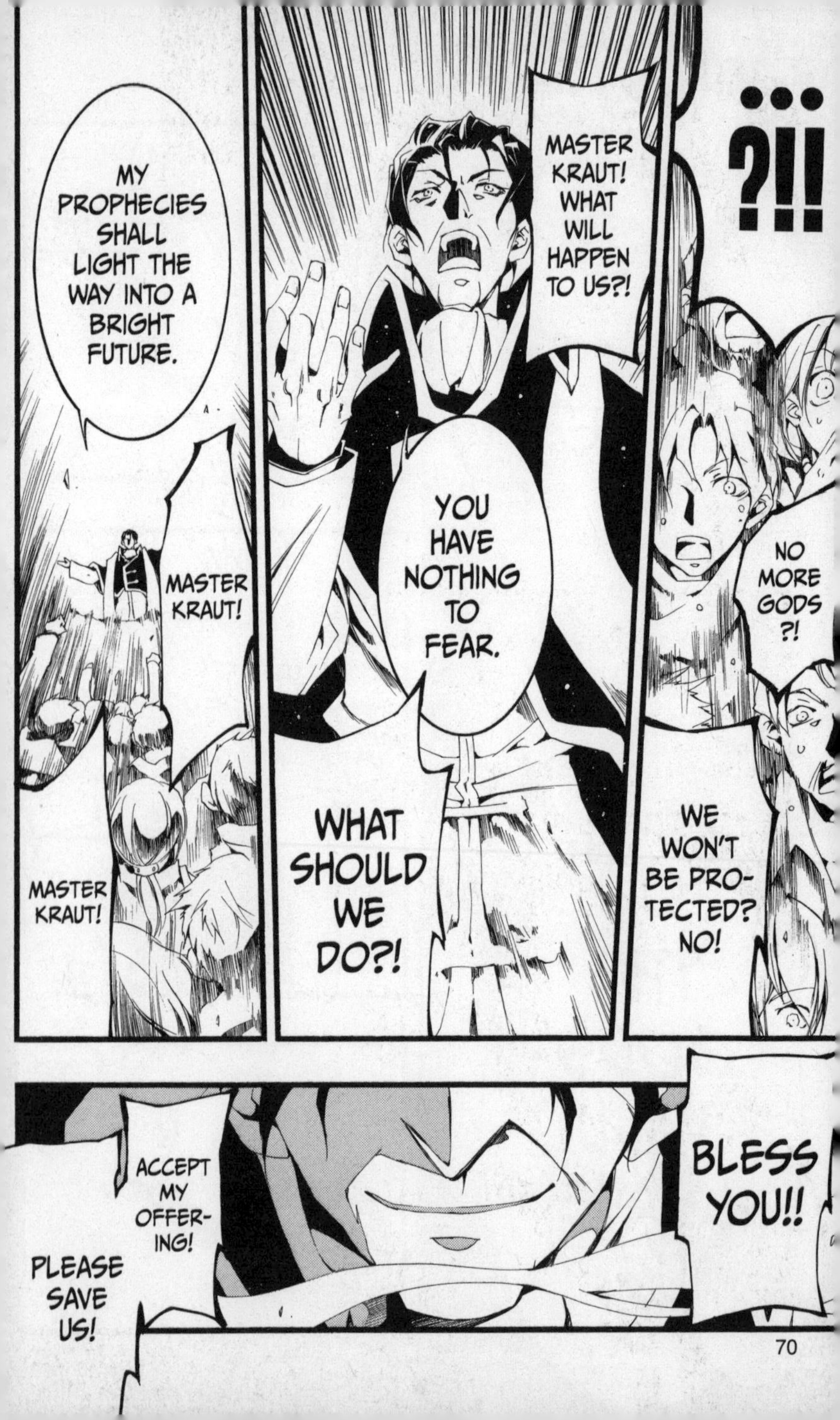
...?!!
NO MORE GODS ?!
WE WON'T BE PRO-TECTED? NO!
MASTER KRAUT! WHAT WILL HAPPEN TO US?!
YOU HAVE NOTHING TO FEAR.
WHAT SHOULD WE DO?!
MY PROPHECIES SHALL LIGHT THE WAY INTO A BRIGHT FUTURE.
MASTER KRAUT!
MASTER KRAUT!
BLESS YOU!!
ACCEPT MY OFFER-ING!
PLEASE SAVE US!

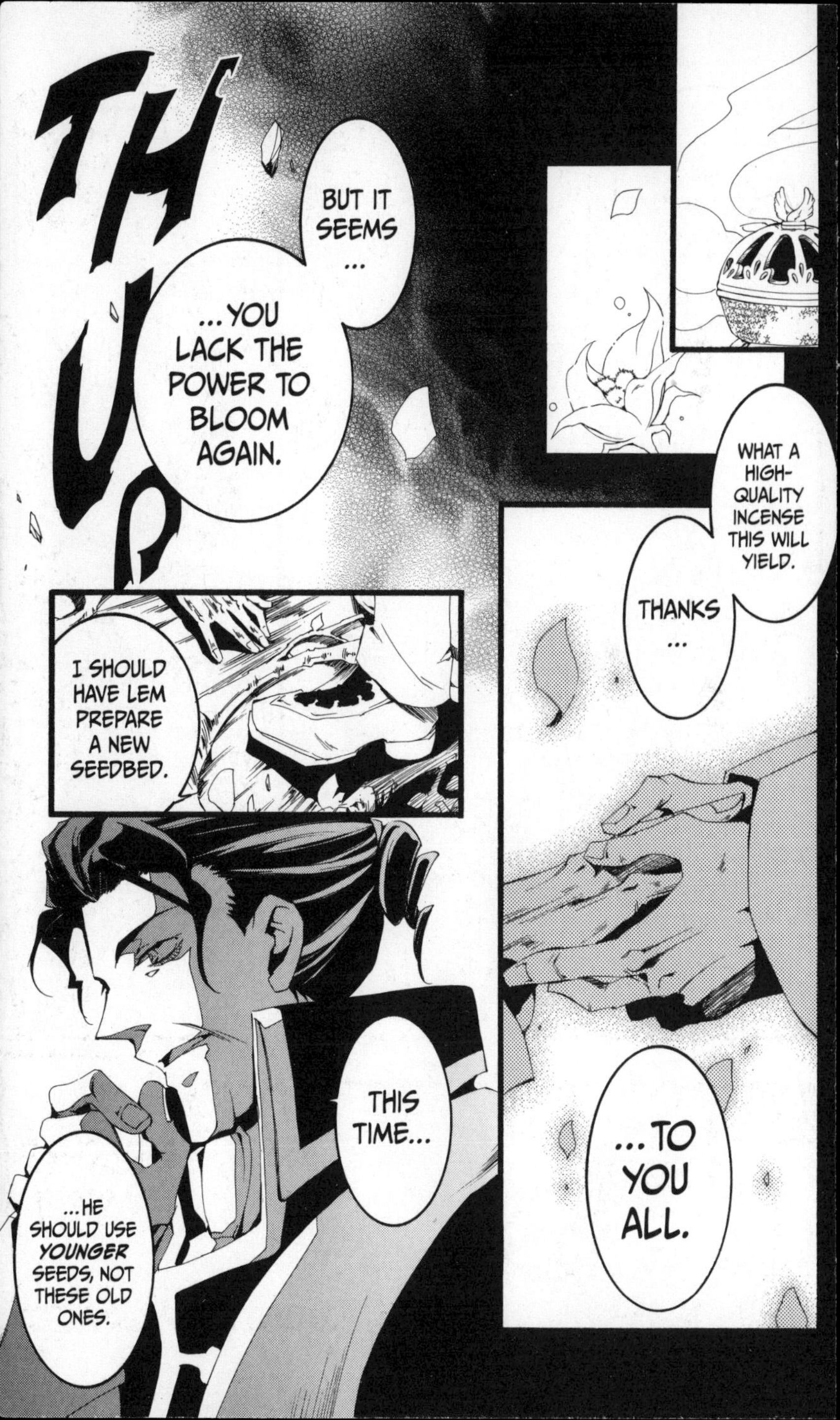
WHAT A HIGH-QUALITY INCENSE THIS WILL YIELD.
THANKS...
...TO YOU ALL.
BUT IT SEEMS...
...YOU LACK THE POWER TO BLOOM AGAIN.
THU
I SHOULD HAVE LEM PREPARE A NEW SEEDBED.
THIS TIME...
...HE SHOULD USE *YOUNGER* SEEDS, NOT THESE OLD ONES.

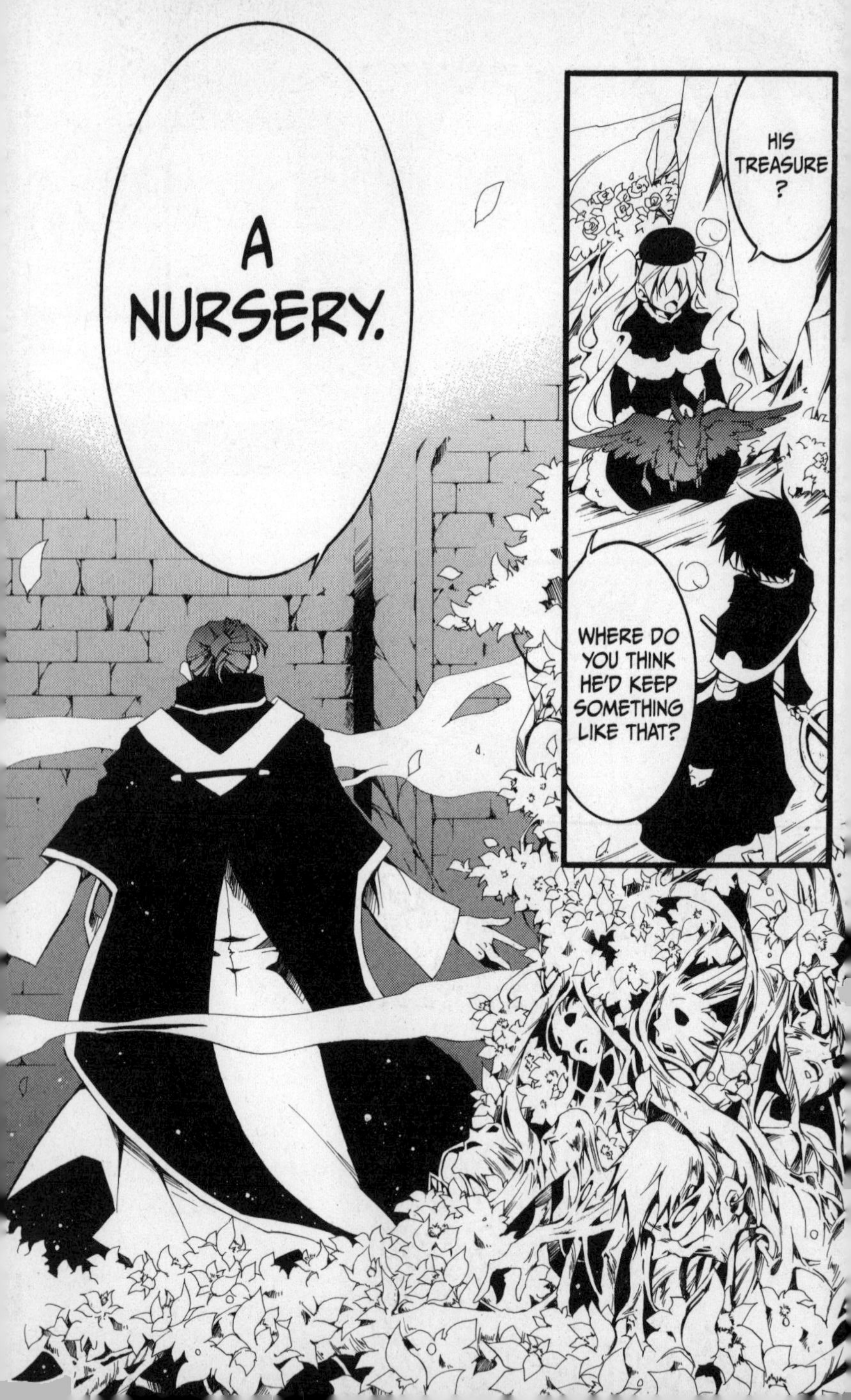
HIS TREASURE?
WHERE DO YOU THINK HE'D KEEP SOMETHING LIKE THAT?
A NURSERY.

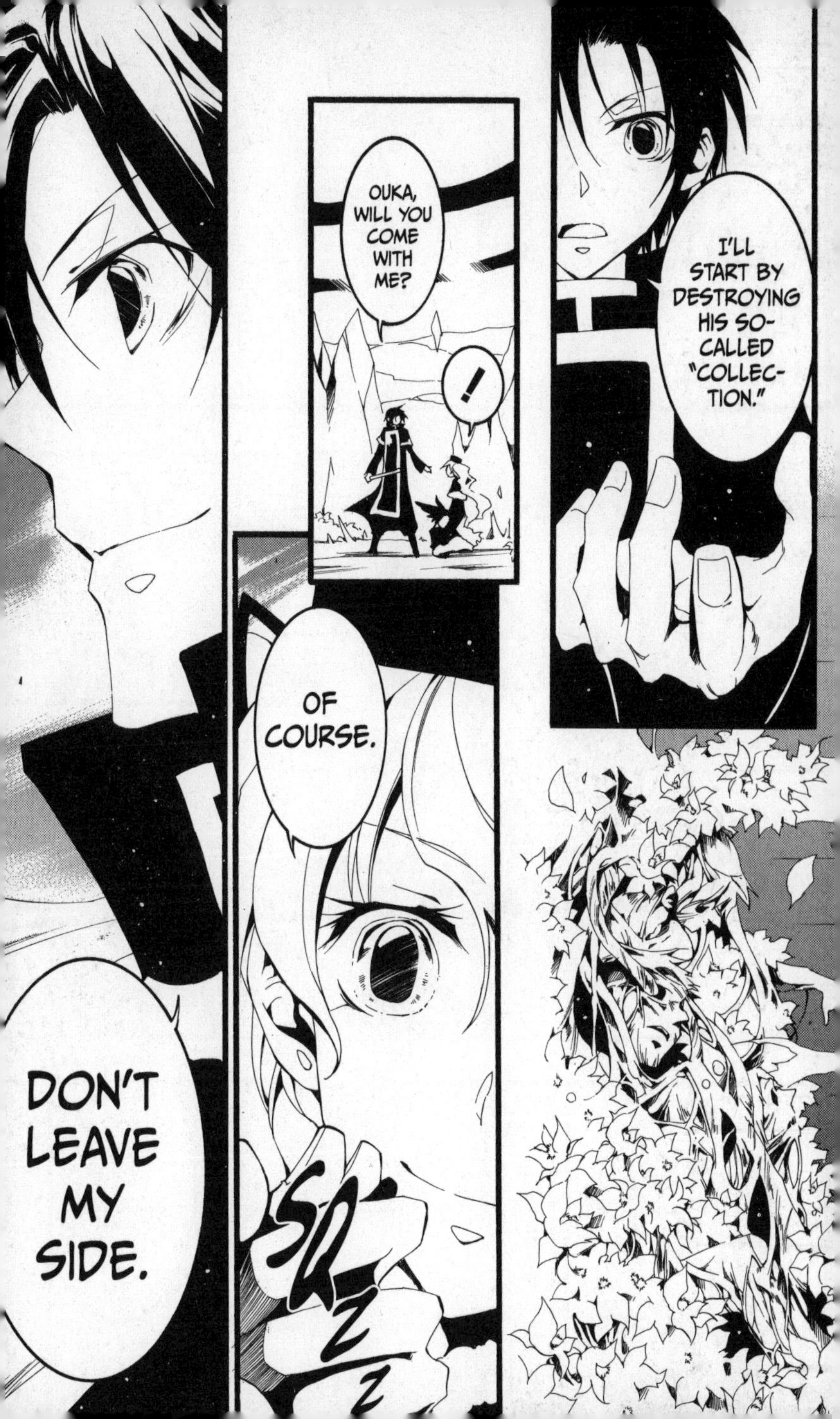
I'LL START BY DESTROYING HIS SO-CALLED "COLLECTION."
OUKA, WILL YOU COME WITH ME?
!
OF COURSE.
SZZZ
DON'T LEAVE MY SIDE.

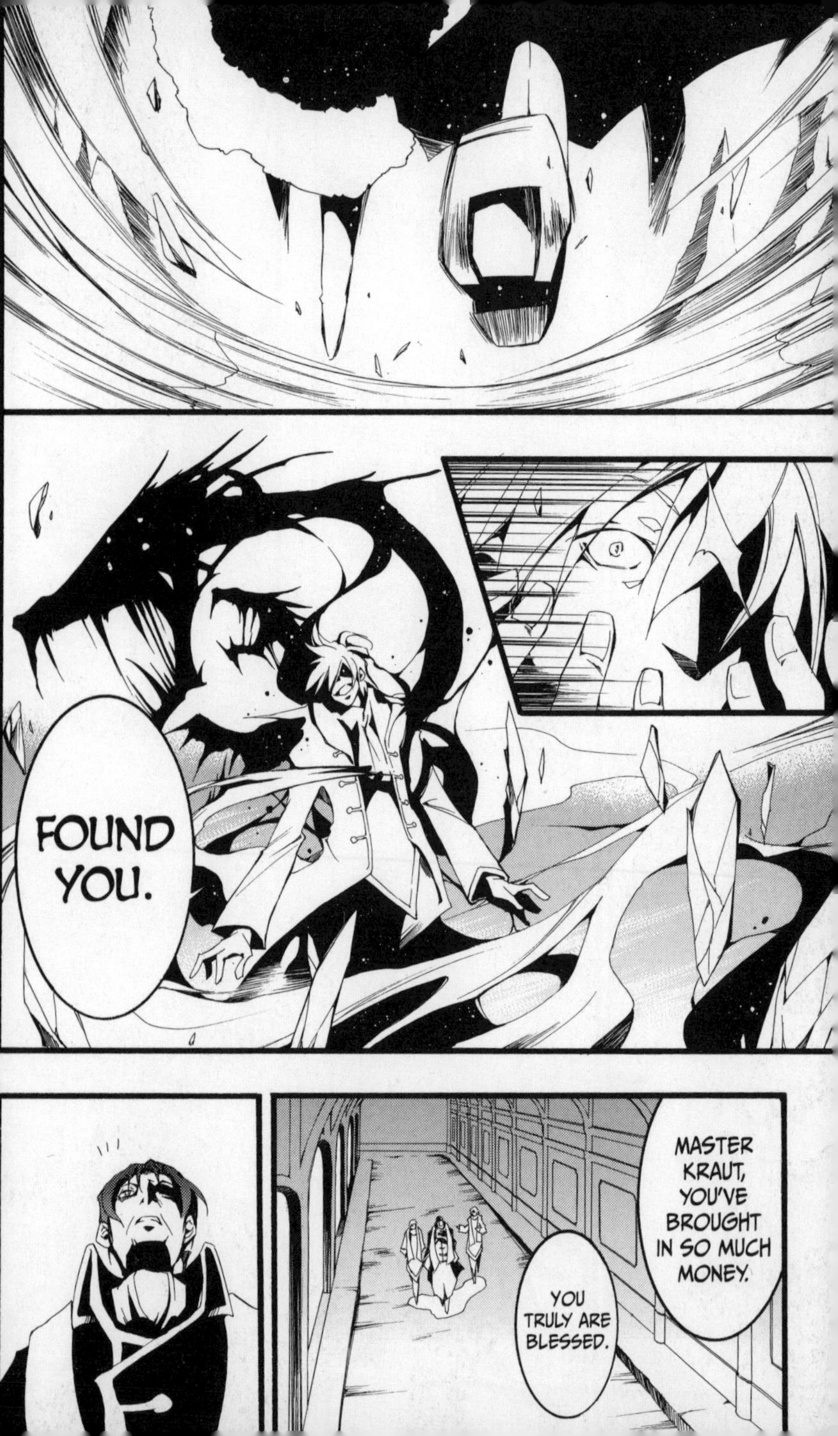
FOUND YOU.
MASTER KRAUT, YOU'VE BROUGHT IN SO MUCH MONEY.
YOU TRULY ARE BLESSED.

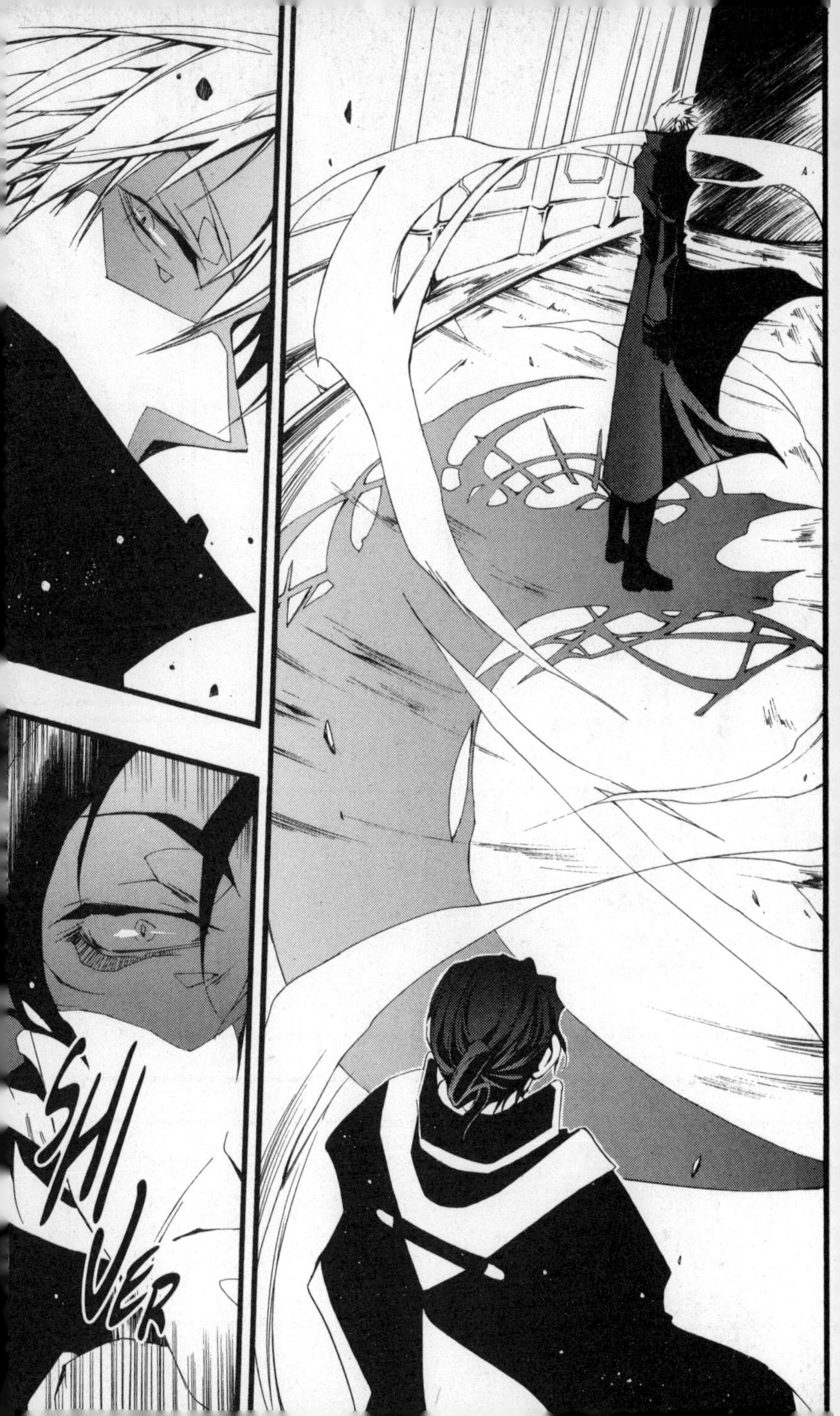
SHIVER

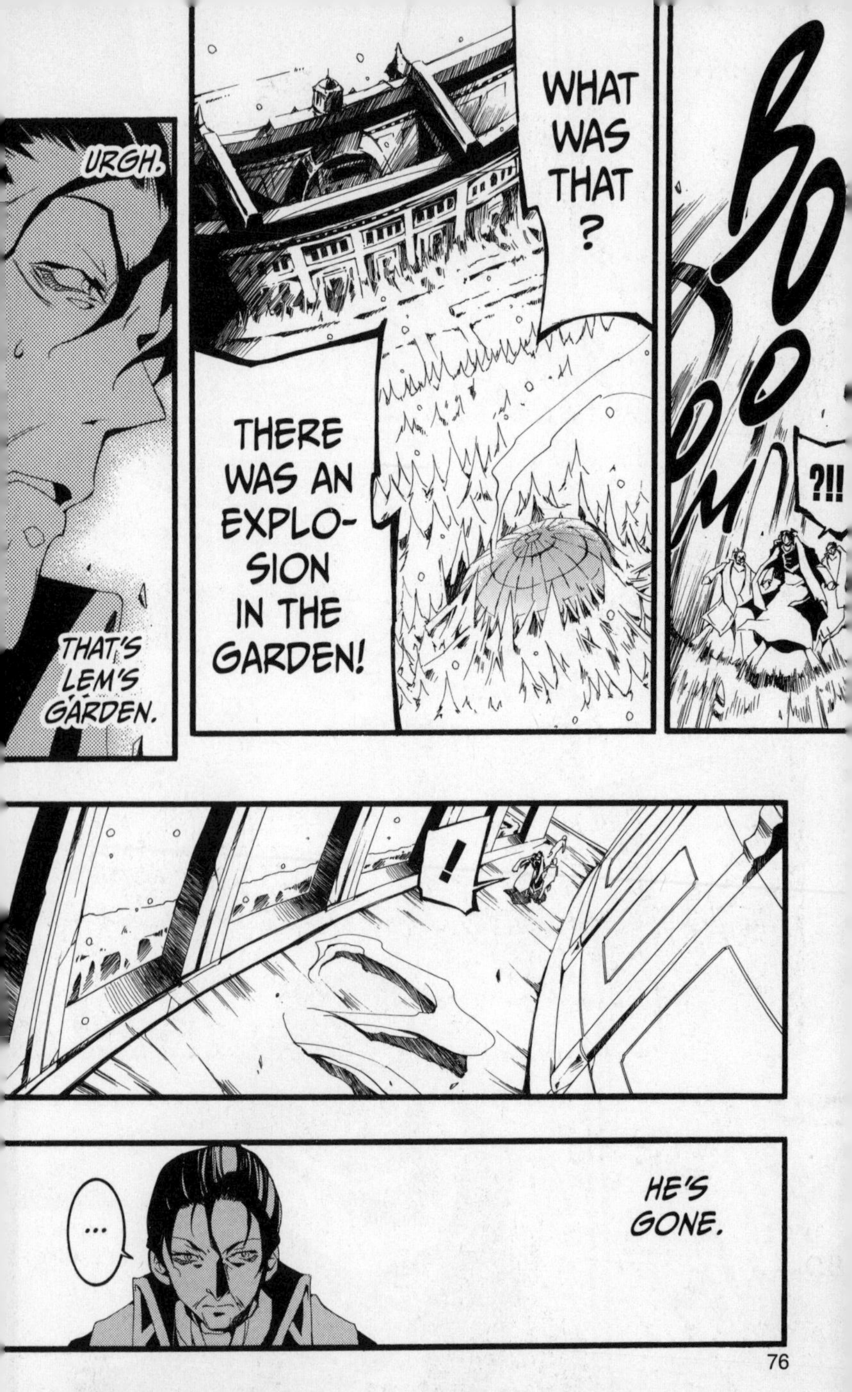
BOOOOM
?!!
WHAT WAS THAT?
THERE WAS AN EXPLOSION IN THE GARDEN!
URGH.
THAT'S LEM'S GARDEN.
!
HE'S GONE.
...

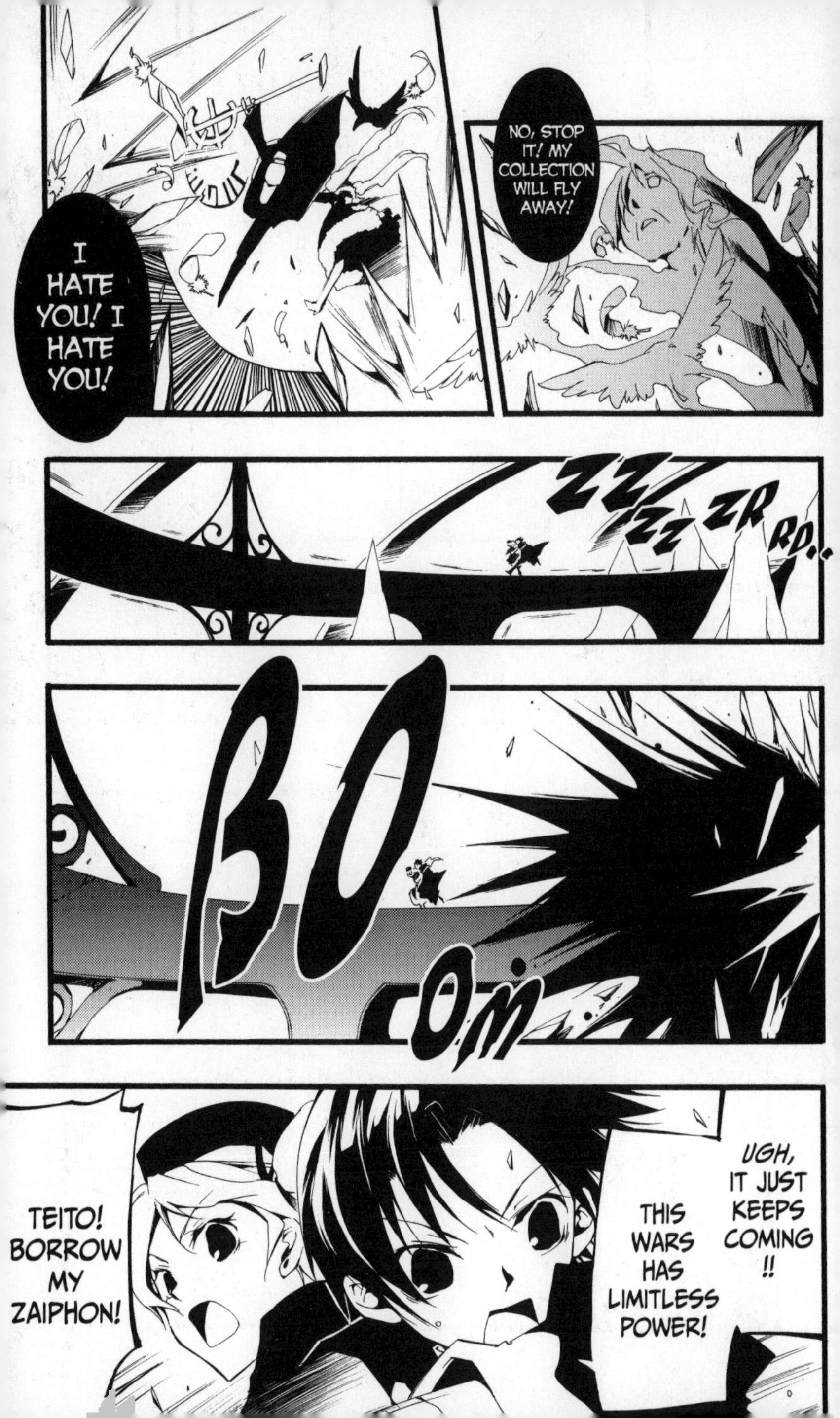
NO, STOP IT! MY COLLECTION WILL FLY AWAY!
I HATE YOU! I HATE YOU!
ZZZZZZRRD..
BOOM
UGH, IT JUST KEEPS COMING !!
THIS WARS HAS LIMITLESS POWER!
TEITO! BORROW MY ZAIPHON!

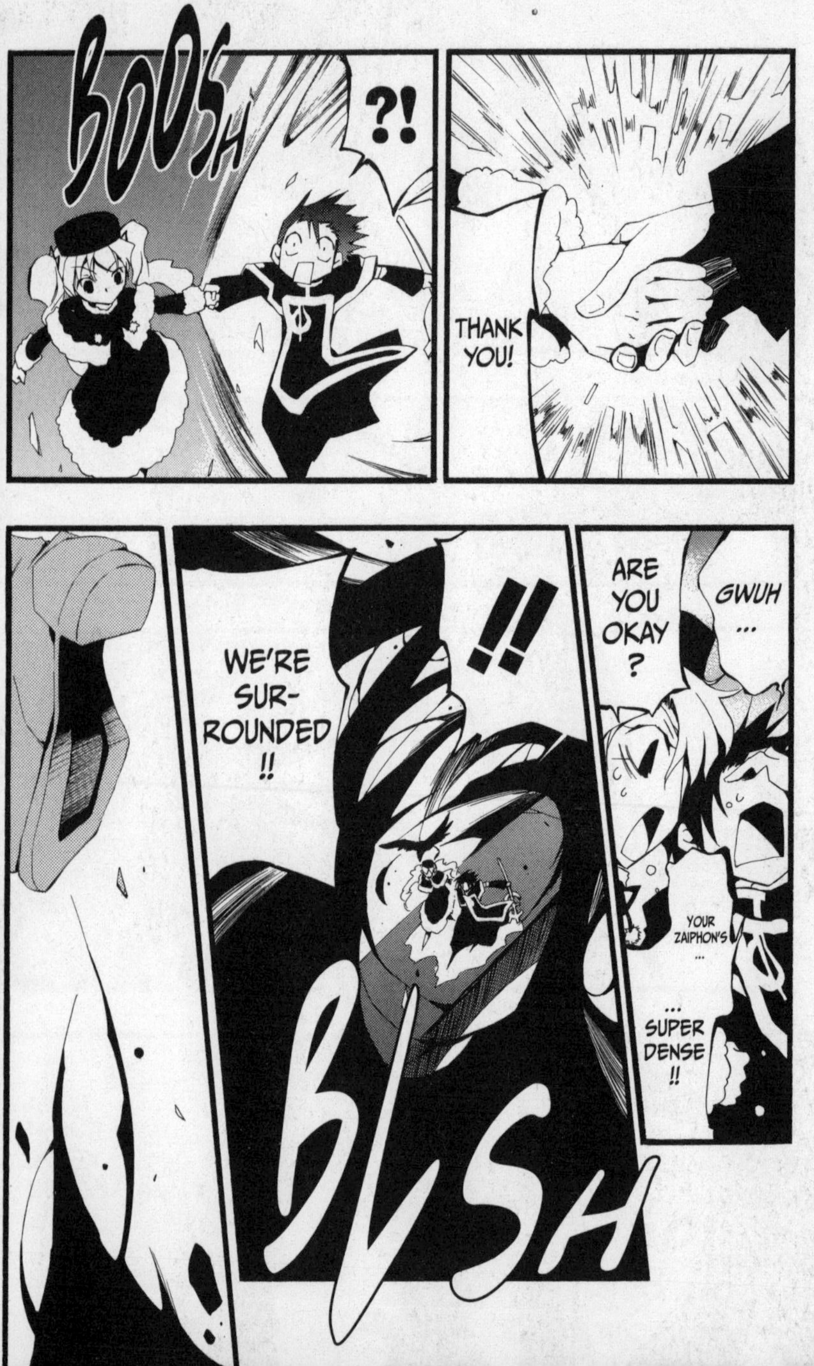
THANK YOU!
BOOSH
?!
ARE YOU OKAY?
GWUH ...
YOUR ZAIPHON'S ...
... SUPER DENSE !!
!!
WE'RE SUR-ROUNDED !!

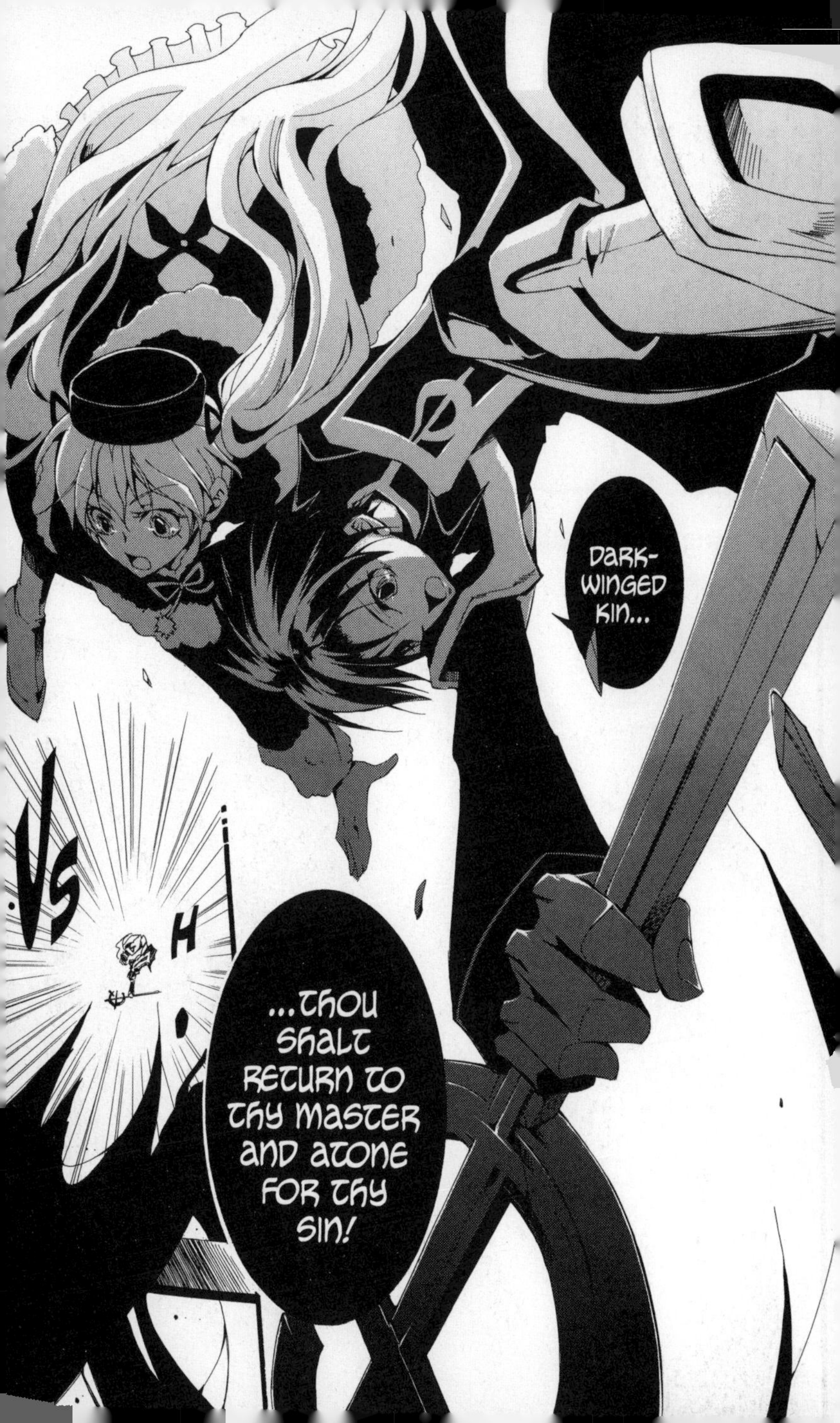
DARK-WINGED KIN...
...THOU SHALT RETURN TO THY MASTER AND ATONE FOR THY SIN!
VS
H

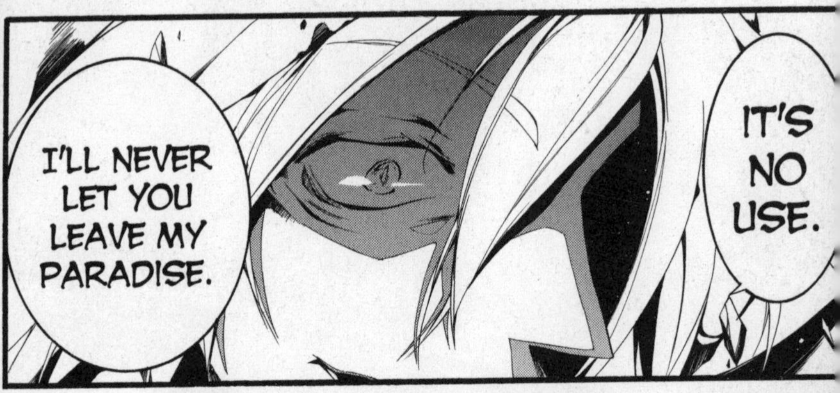
IT'S NO USE.
I'LL NEVER LET YOU LEAVE MY PARADISE.

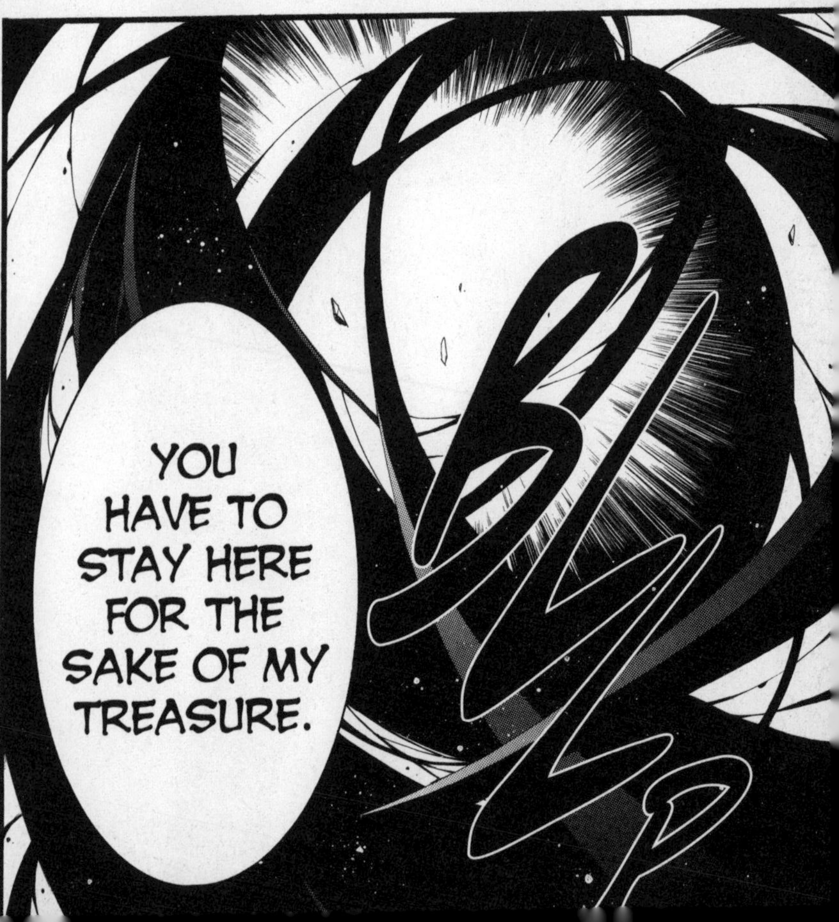
YOU HAVE TO STAY HERE FOR THE SAKE OF MY TREASURE.

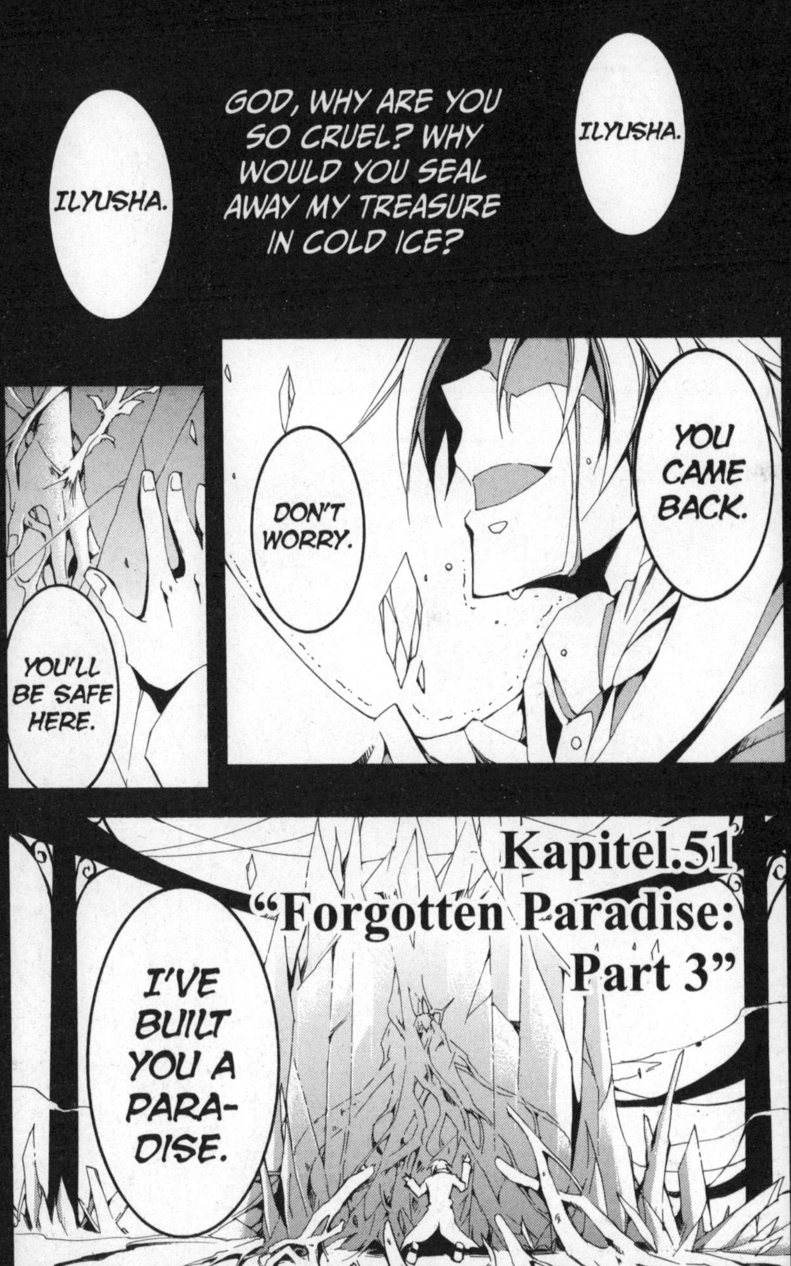
ILYUSHA.
GOD, WHY ARE YOU SO CRUEL? WHY WOULD YOU SEAL AWAY MY TREASURE IN COLD ICE?
ILYUSHA.
YOU CAME BACK.
DON'T WORRY.
YOU'LL BE SAFE HERE.
Kapitel.51 "Forgotten Paradise: Part 3"
I'VE BUILT YOU A PARA-DISE.

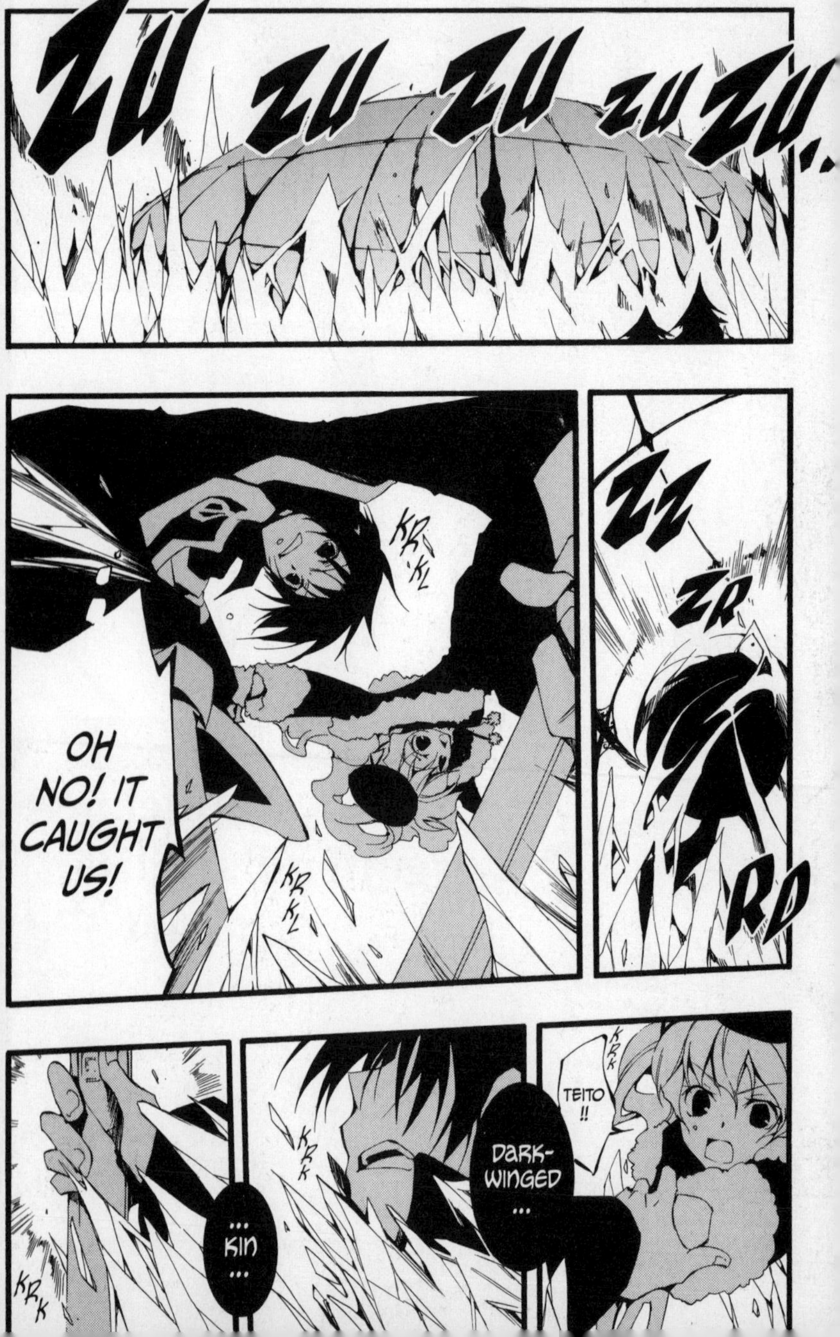
ZU ZU ZU ZU ZU ZU..
ZZ
ZR
RD
KRKL
OH NO! IT CAUGHT US!
KRKL
KRK
TEITO!!
DARK-WINGED...
KRK
...KIN...
KRK

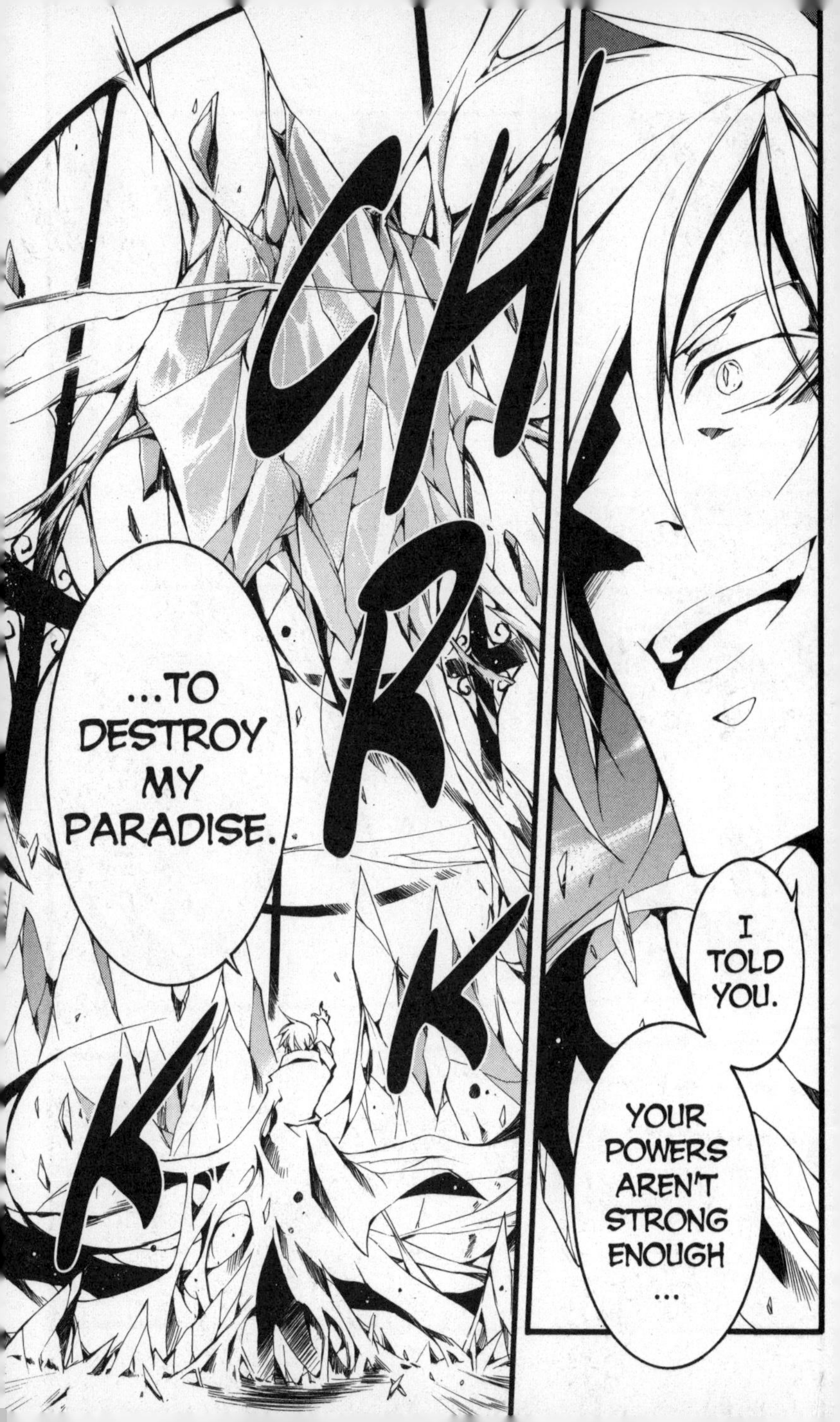
I TOLD YOU.
YOUR POWERS AREN'T STRONG ENOUGH ...
...TO DESTROY MY PARADISE.
CHKKK

SHFL

SHFL

I MUST COLLECT MORE.

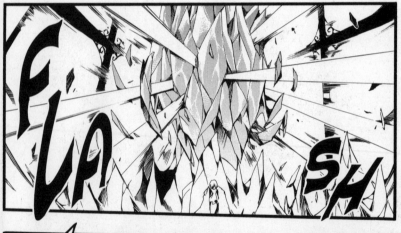

FLIP

SH

?!

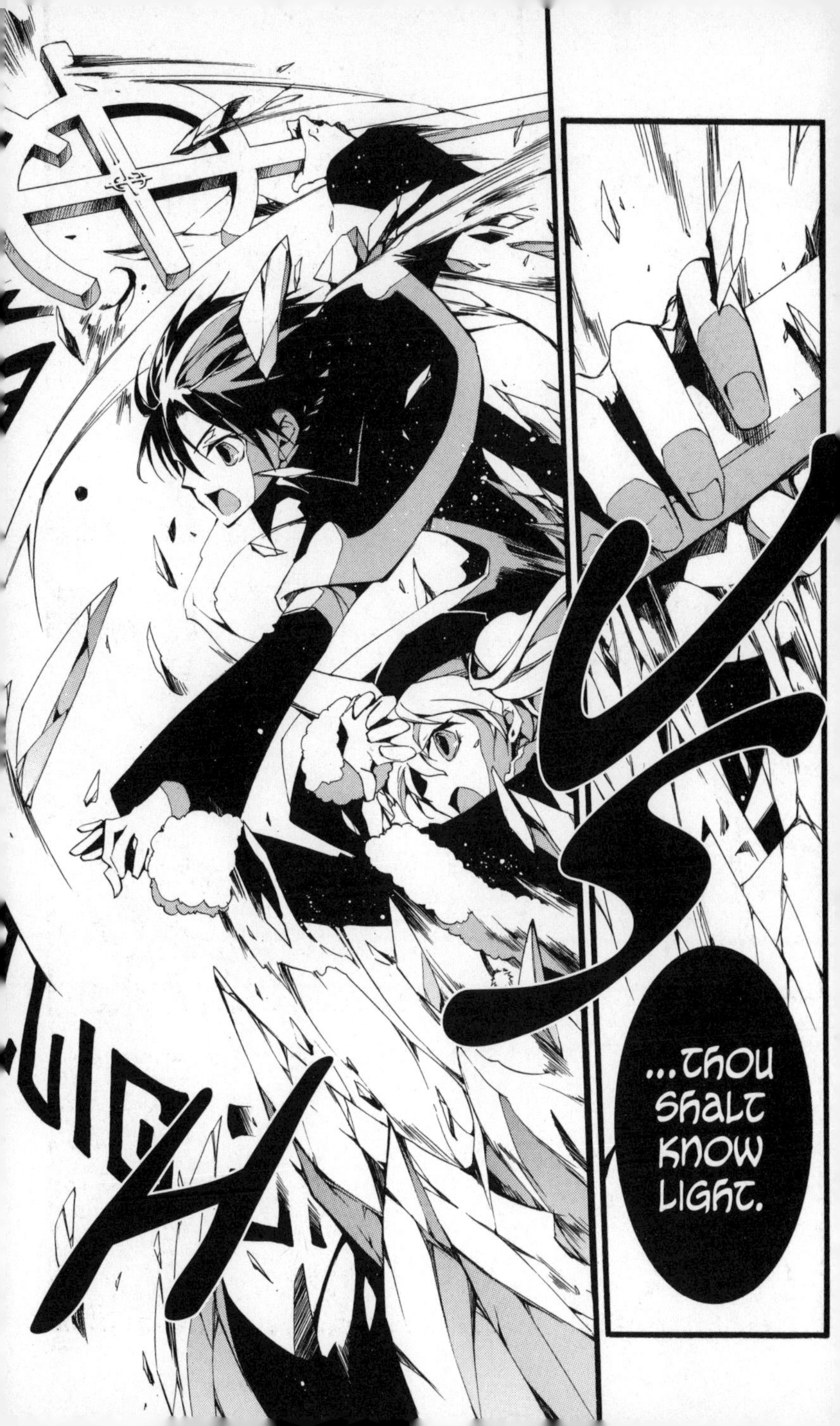
...THOU SHALT KNOW LIGHT.

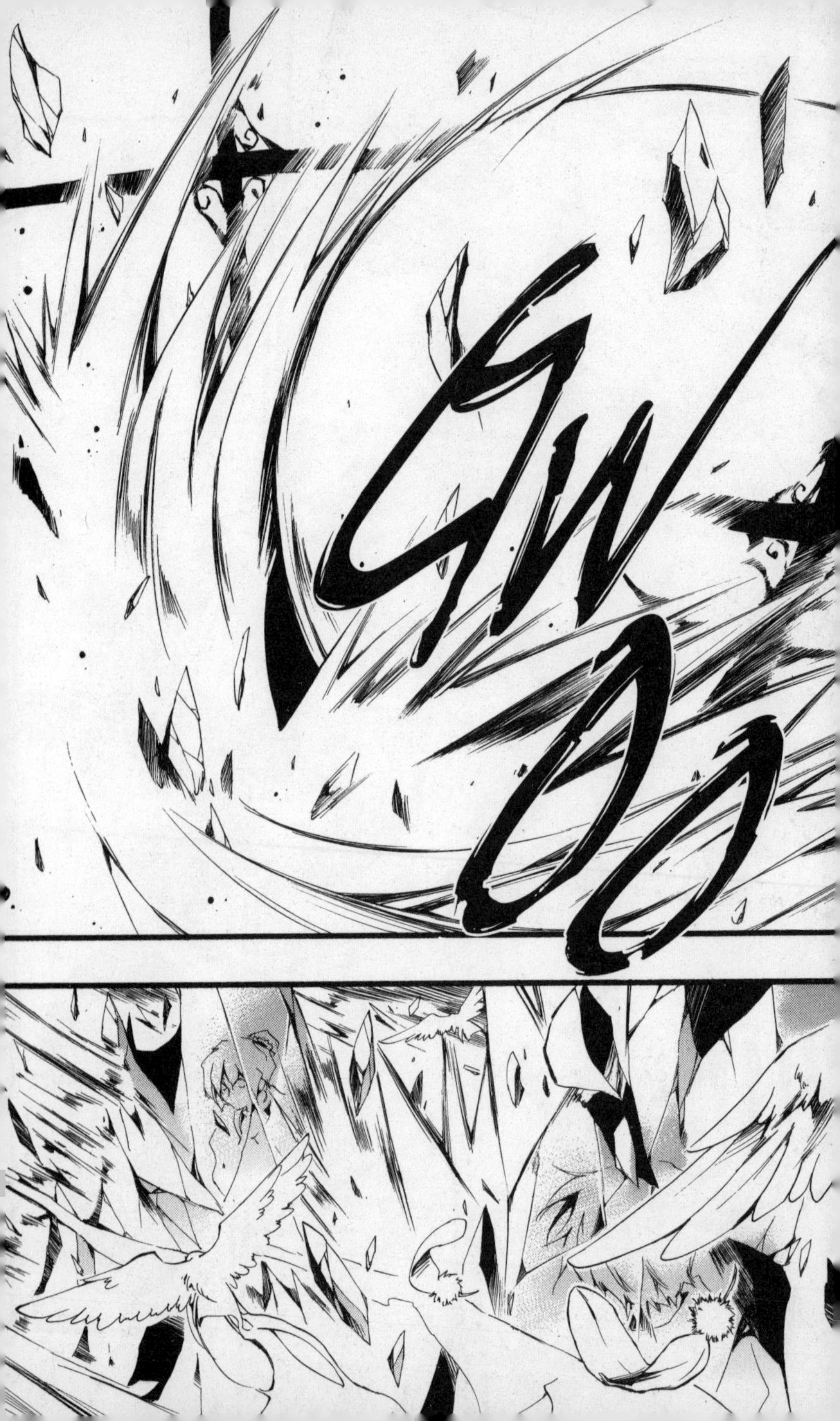
GWOO

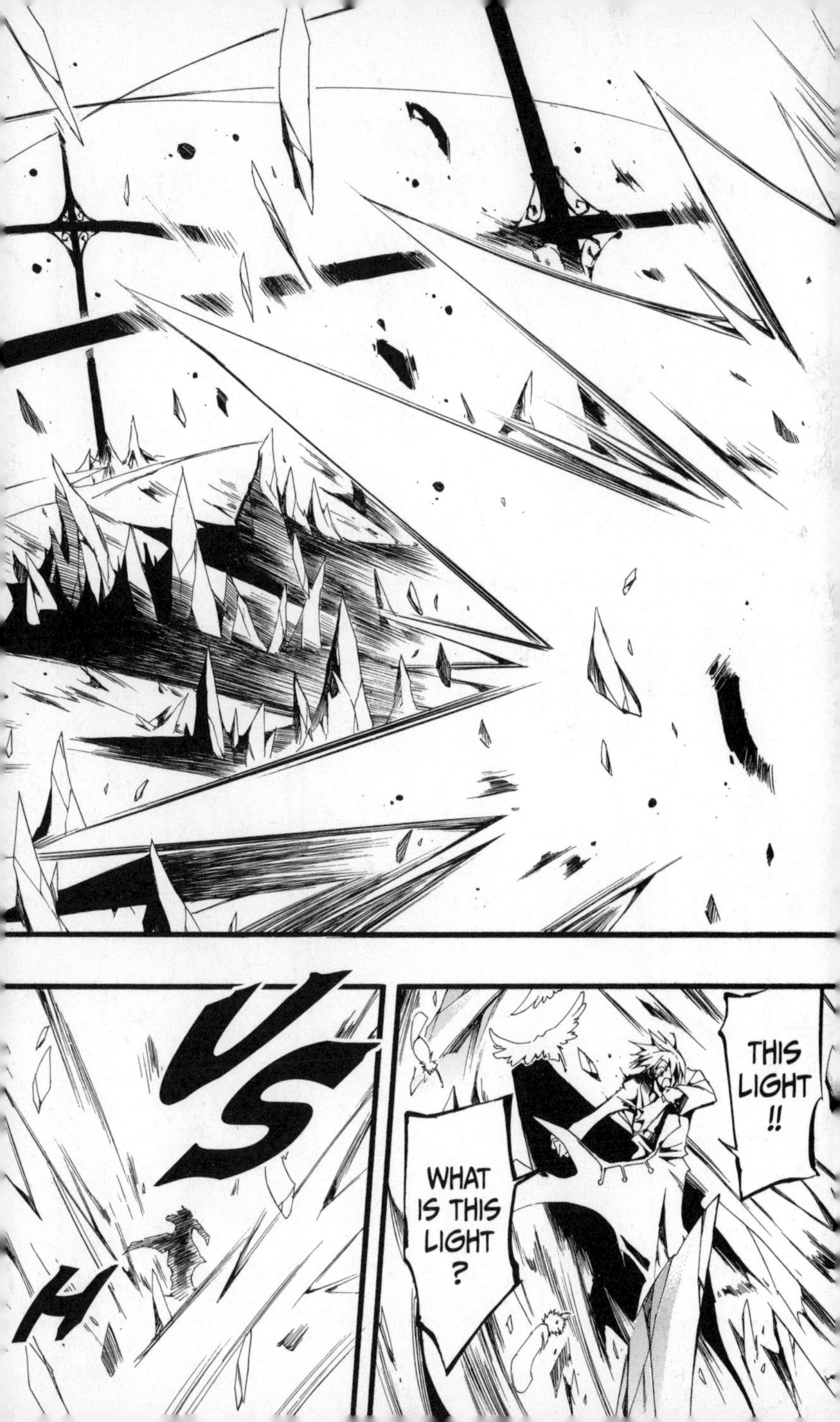
THIS LIGHT !!
WHAT IS THIS LIGHT ?
VS
H

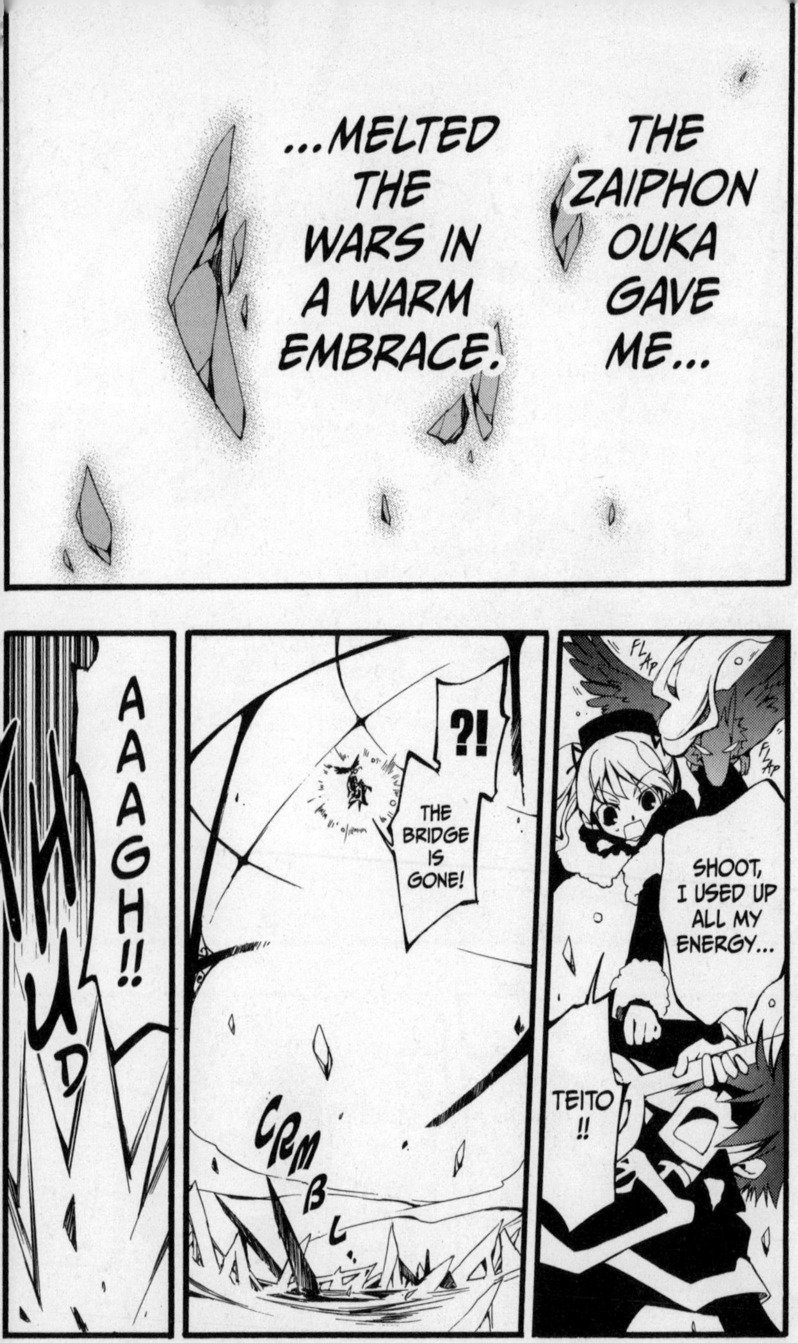
THE ZAIPHON OUKA GAVE ME...
...MELTED THE WARS IN A WARM EMBRACE.
FLAP
FLAP
SHOOT, I USED UP ALL MY ENERGY...
TEITO!!
?!
THE BRIDGE IS GONE!
CRMBL
AAAAGH!!

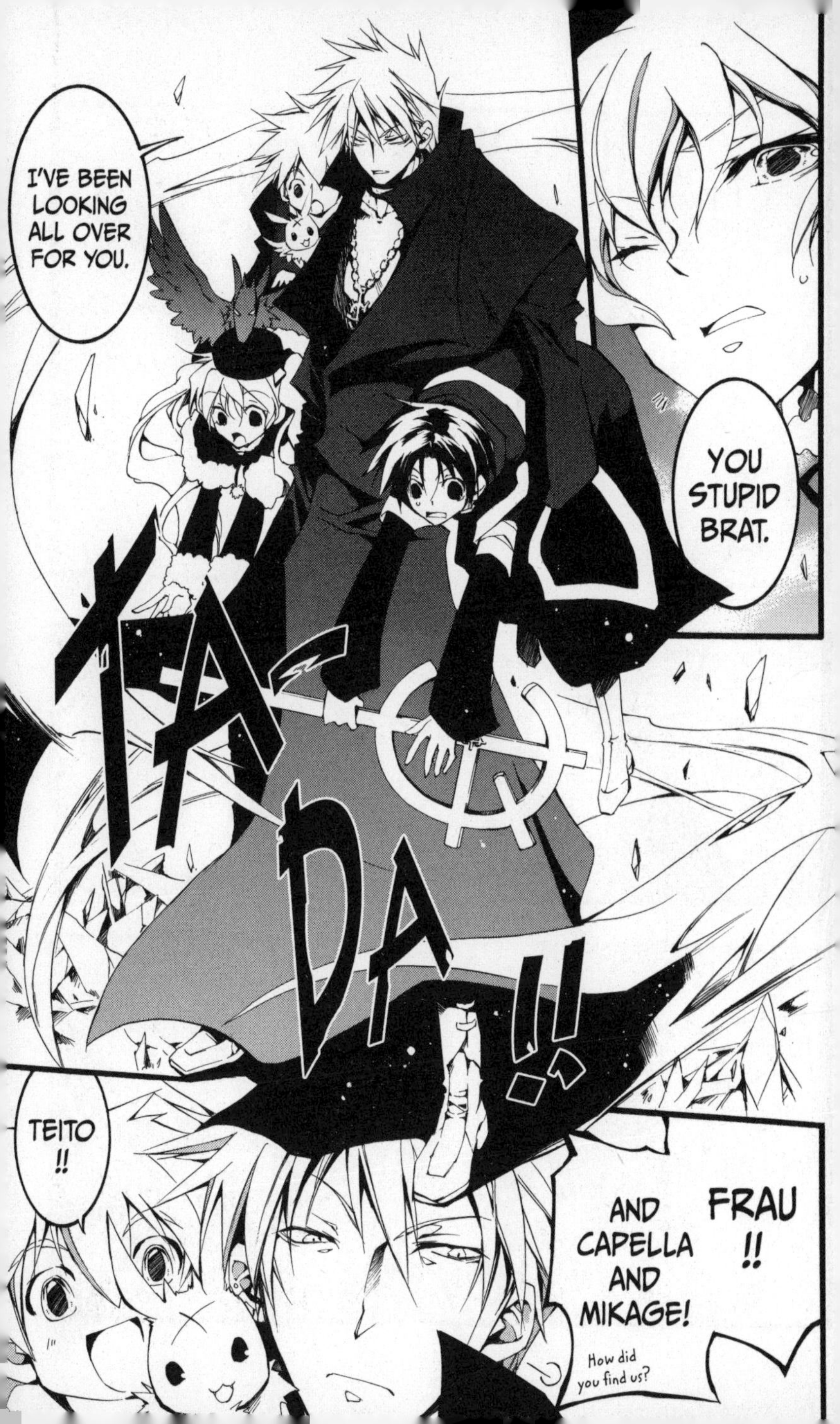
YOU STUPID BRAT.
I'VE BEEN LOOKING ALL OVER FOR YOU.
TA-DA!!
FRAU!!
AND CAPELLA AND MIKAGE!
How did you find us?
TEITO!!

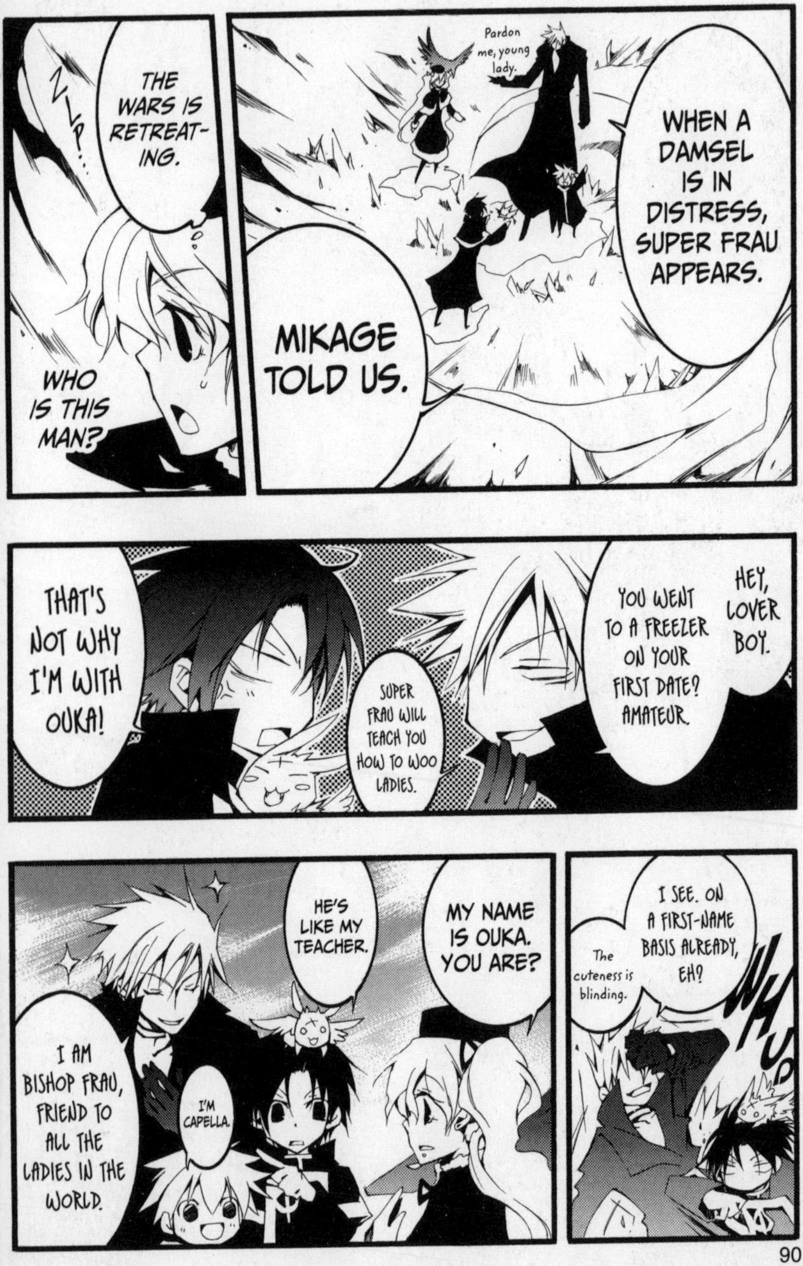

WHEN A DAMSEL IS IN DISTRESS, SUPER FRAU APPEARS.
Pardon me, young lady.
MIKAGE TOLD US.
THE WARS IS RETREATING.
WHO IS THIS MAN?
HEY, LOVER BOY.
YOU WENT TO A FREEZER ON YOUR FIRST DATE? AMATEUR.
SUPER FRAU WILL TEACH YOU HOW TO WOO LADIES.
THAT'S NOT WHY I'M WITH OUKA!
I SEE. ON A FIRST-NAME BASIS ALREADY, EH?
The cuteness is blinding.
MY NAME IS OUKA. YOU ARE?
HE'S LIKE MY TEACHER.
I AM BISHOP FRAU, FRIEND TO ALL THE LADIES IN THE WORLD.
I'M CAPELLA.

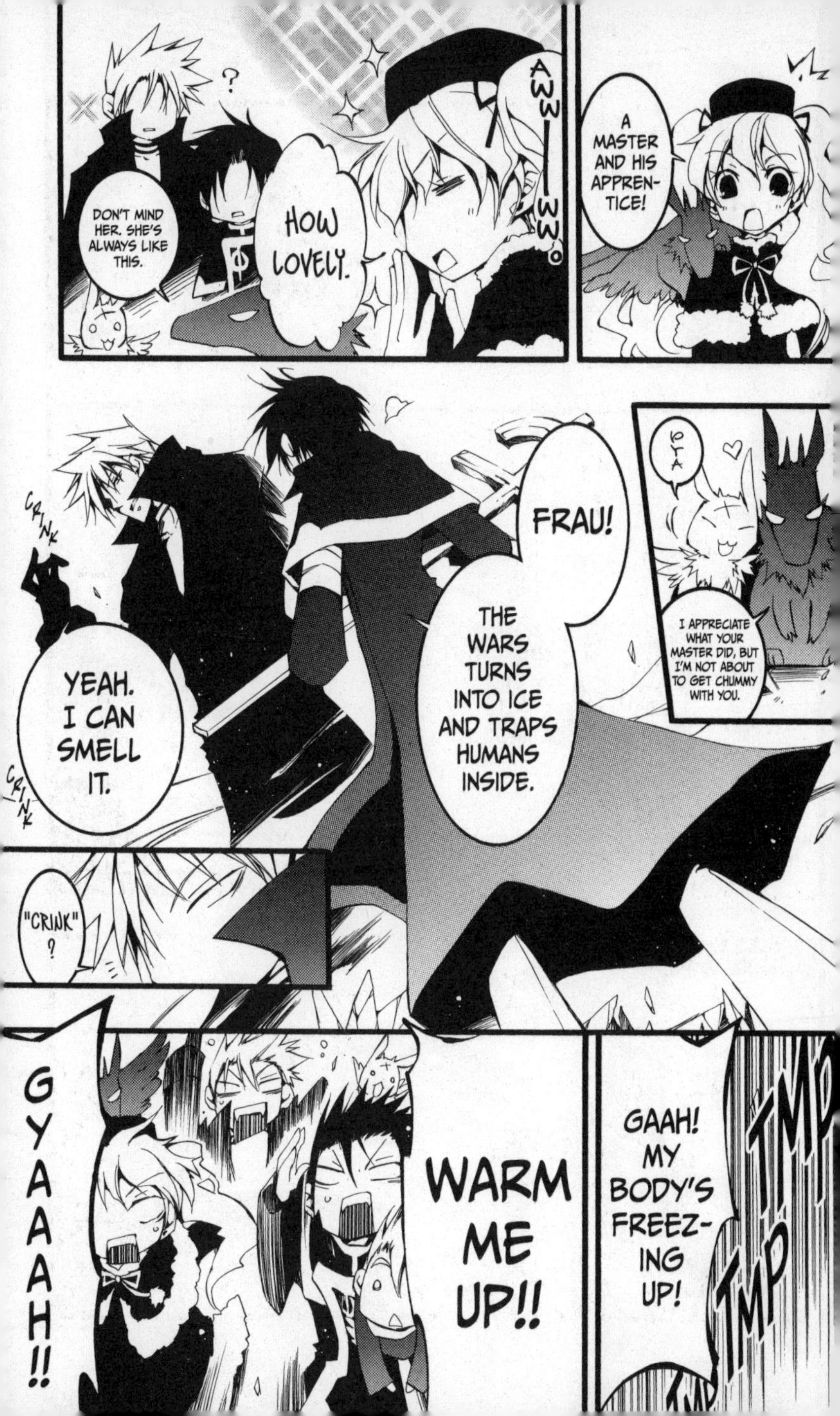
A MASTER AND HIS APPREN-TICE!
AWW—WW♡
HOW LOVELY.
?
DON'T MIND HER. SHE'S ALWAYS LIKE THIS.
I APPRECIATE WHAT YOUR MASTER DID, BUT I'M NOT ABOUT TO GET CHUMMY WITH YOU.
FRAU!
THE WARS TURNS INTO ICE AND TRAPS HUMANS INSIDE.
CRINK
YEAH. I CAN SMELL IT.
CRINK
"CRINK"?
TMP TMP
GAAH! MY BODY'S FREEZ-ING UP!
WARM ME UP!!
GYAAAAH!!

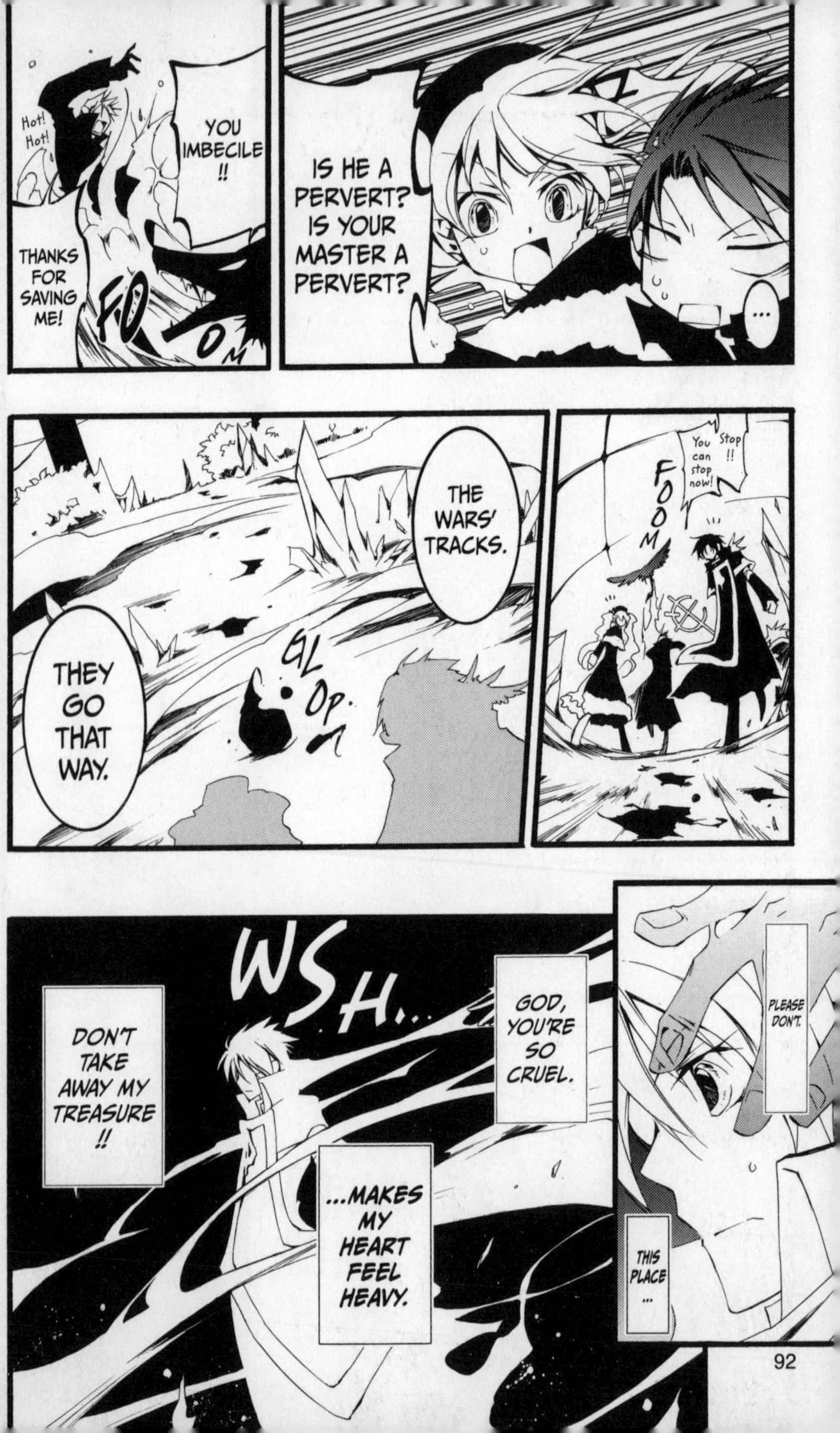
IS HE A PERVERT? IS YOUR MASTER A PERVERT?
...
Hot! Hot!
YOU IMBECILE !!
THANKS FOR SAVING ME!
FOOM
Stop !!
You can stop now!
FOOM
THE WARS' TRACKS.
THEY GO THAT WAY.
GLOP
PLEASE DON'T.
THIS PLACE ...
GOD, YOU'RE SO CRUEL.
WSH...
...MAKES MY HEART FEEL HEAVY.
DON'T TAKE AWAY MY TREASURE !!

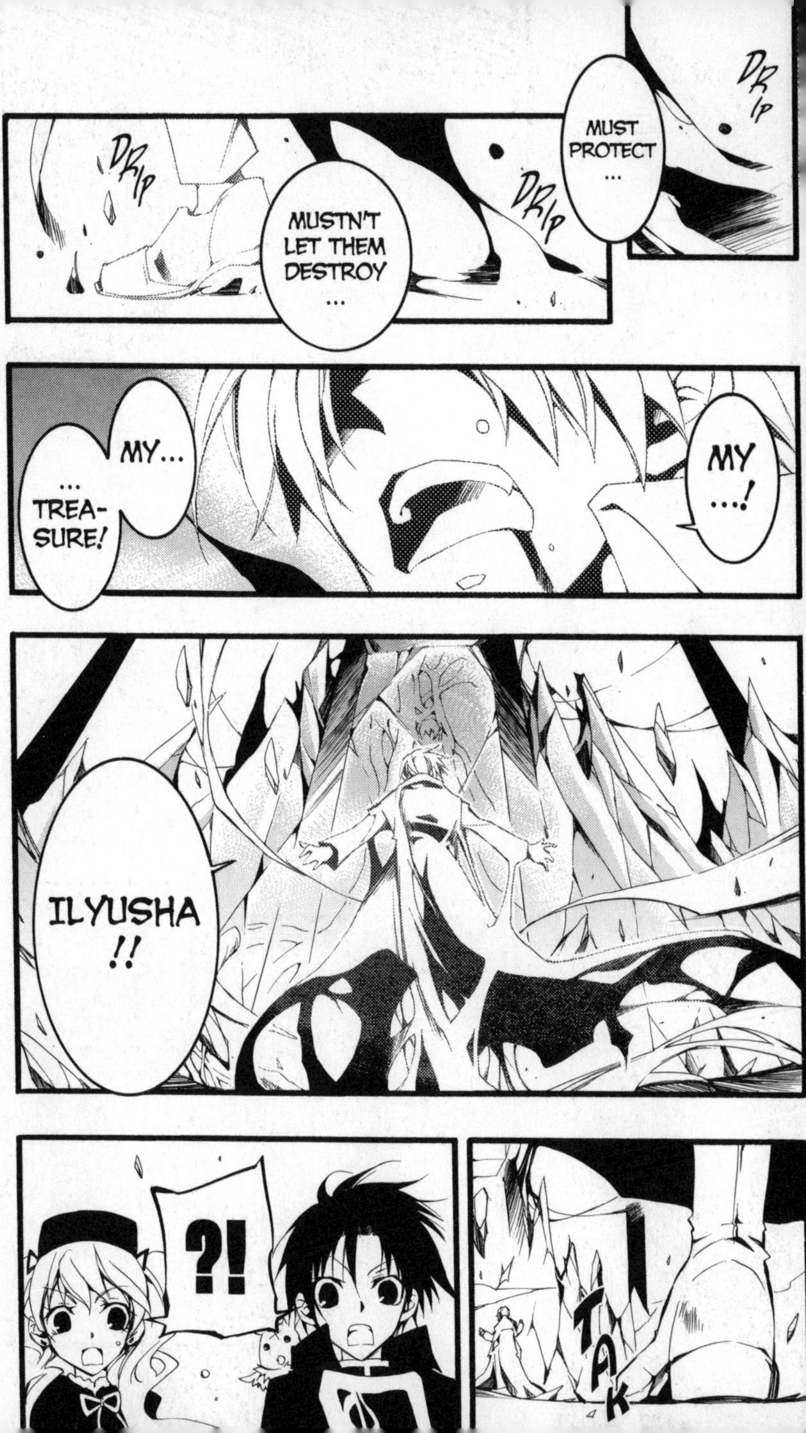
DRIP
MUST PROTECT ...
DRIP
MUSTN'T LET THEM DESTROY ...
DRIP
MY ...!
MY... ... TREA-SURE!
ILYUSHA !!
TAK
?!

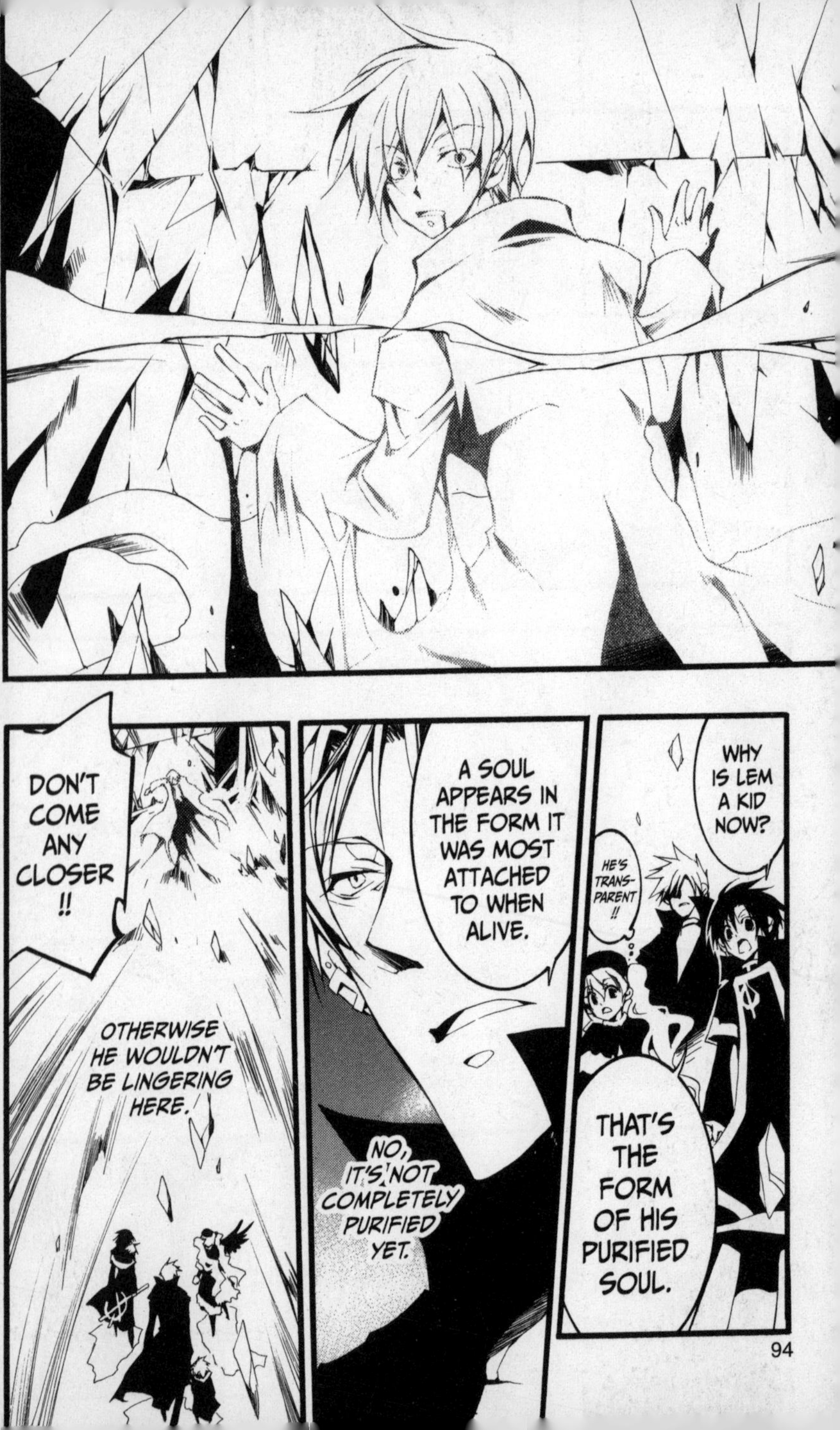
WHY IS LEM A KID NOW?
HE'S TRANS-PARENT !!
THAT'S THE FORM OF HIS PURIFIED SOUL.
A SOUL APPEARS IN THE FORM IT WAS MOST ATTACHED TO WHEN ALIVE.
NO, IT'S NOT COMPLETELY PURIFIED YET.
DON'T COME ANY CLOSER !!
OTHERWISE HE WOULDN'T BE LINGERING HERE.

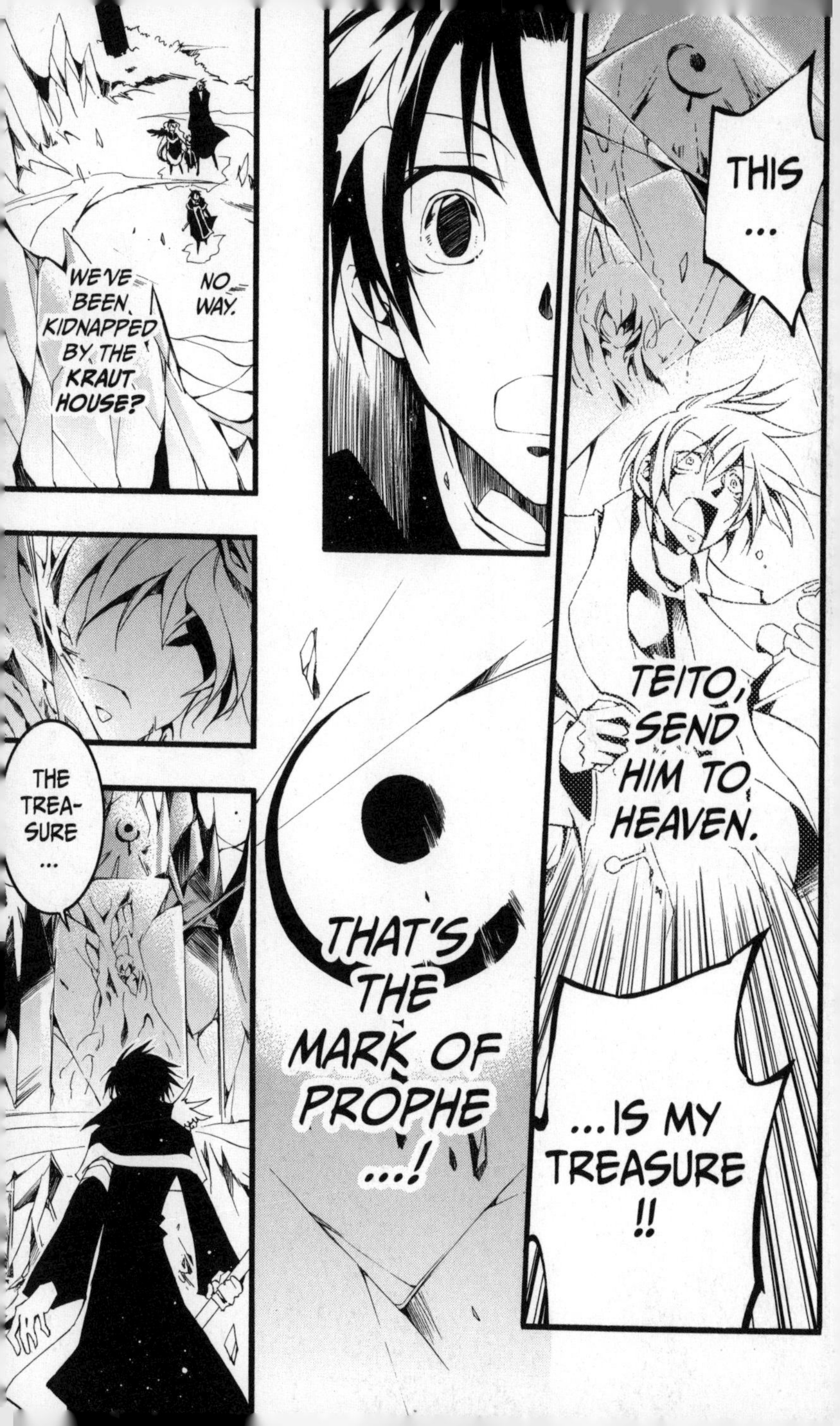
THIS ...
TEITO, SEND HIM TO HEAVEN.
...IS MY TREASURE !!
NO WAY.
WE'VE BEEN KIDNAPPED BY THE KRAUT HOUSE?
THE TREASURE ...
THAT'S THE MARK OF PROPHE ...!

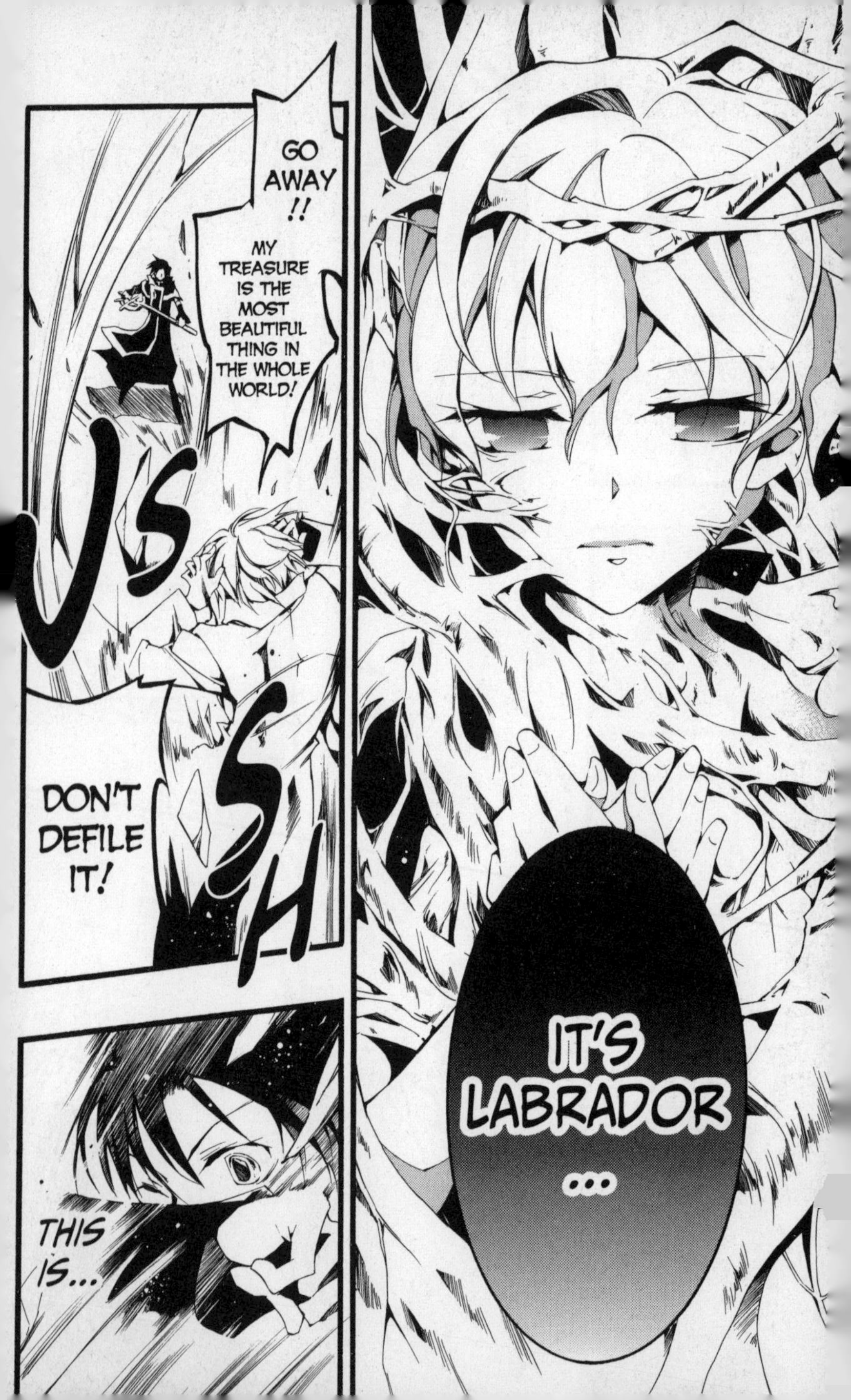
IT'S LABRADOR ...
GO AWAY!!
MY TREASURE IS THE MOST BEAUTIFUL THING IN THE WHOLE WORLD!
DON'T DEFILE IT!
THIS IS...

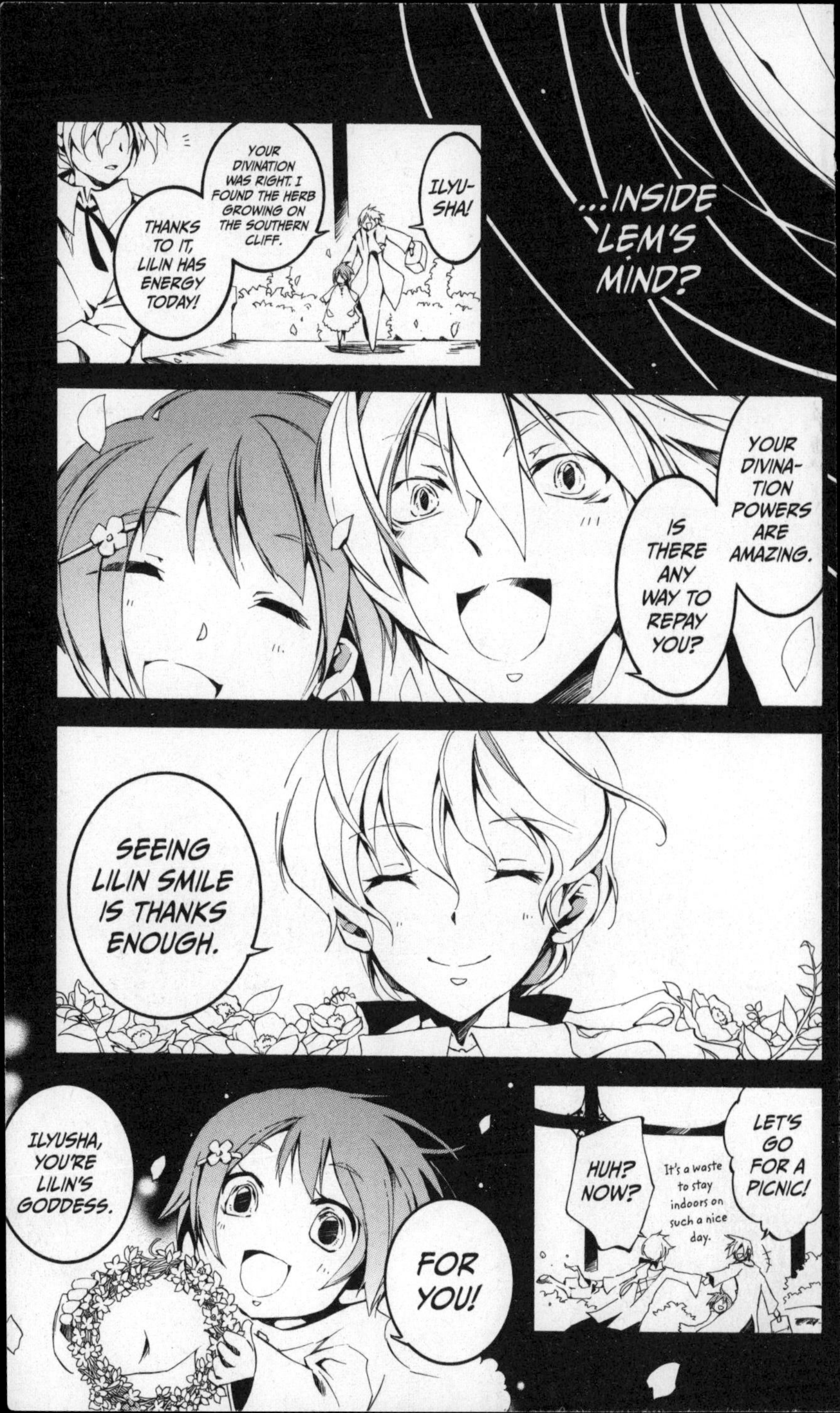
...INSIDE LEM'S MIND?
ILYUSHA!
YOUR DIVINATION WAS RIGHT. I FOUND THE HERB GROWING ON THE SOUTHERN CLIFF.
THANKS TO IT, LILIN HAS ENERGY TODAY!
YOUR DIVINATION POWERS ARE AMAZING.
IS THERE ANY WAY TO REPAY YOU?
SEEING LILIN SMILE IS THANKS ENOUGH.
LET'S GO FOR A PICNIC!
It's a waste to stay indoors on such a nice day.
HUH? NOW?
FOR YOU!
ILYUSHA, YOU'RE LILIN'S GODDESS.

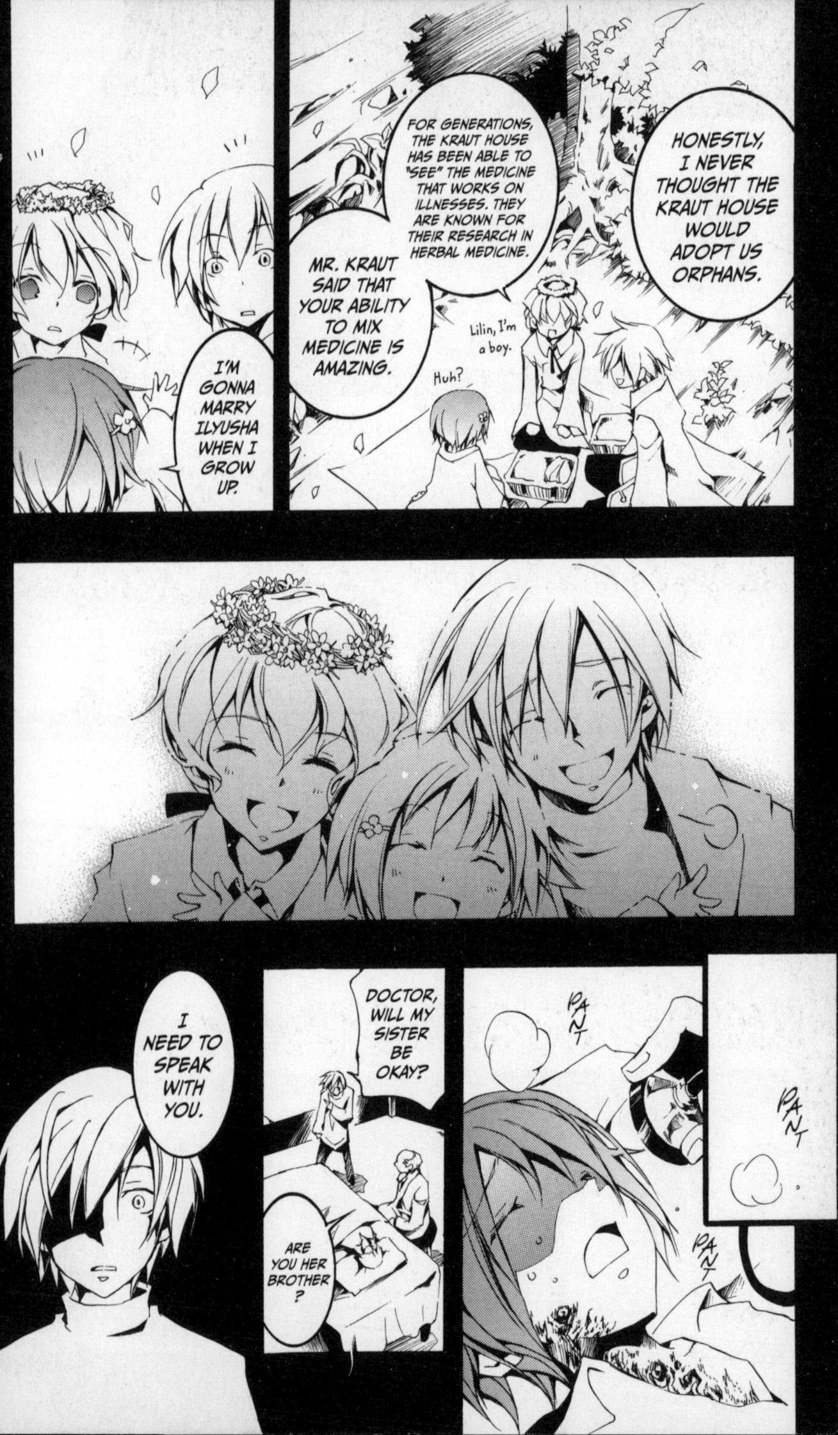
HONESTLY, I NEVER THOUGHT THE KRAUT HOUSE WOULD ADOPT US ORPHANS.
FOR GENERATIONS, THE KRAUT HOUSE HAS BEEN ABLE TO "SEE" THE MEDICINE THAT WORKS ON ILLNESSES. THEY ARE KNOWN FOR THEIR RESEARCH IN HERBAL MEDICINE.
MR. KRAUT SAID THAT YOUR ABILITY TO MIX MEDICINE IS AMAZING.
Lilin, I'm a boy.
Huh?
I'M GONNA MARRY ILYUSHA WHEN I GROW UP.
PANT
PANT
PANT
DOCTOR, WILL MY SISTER BE OKAY?
ARE YOU HER BROTHER?
I NEED TO SPEAK WITH YOU.

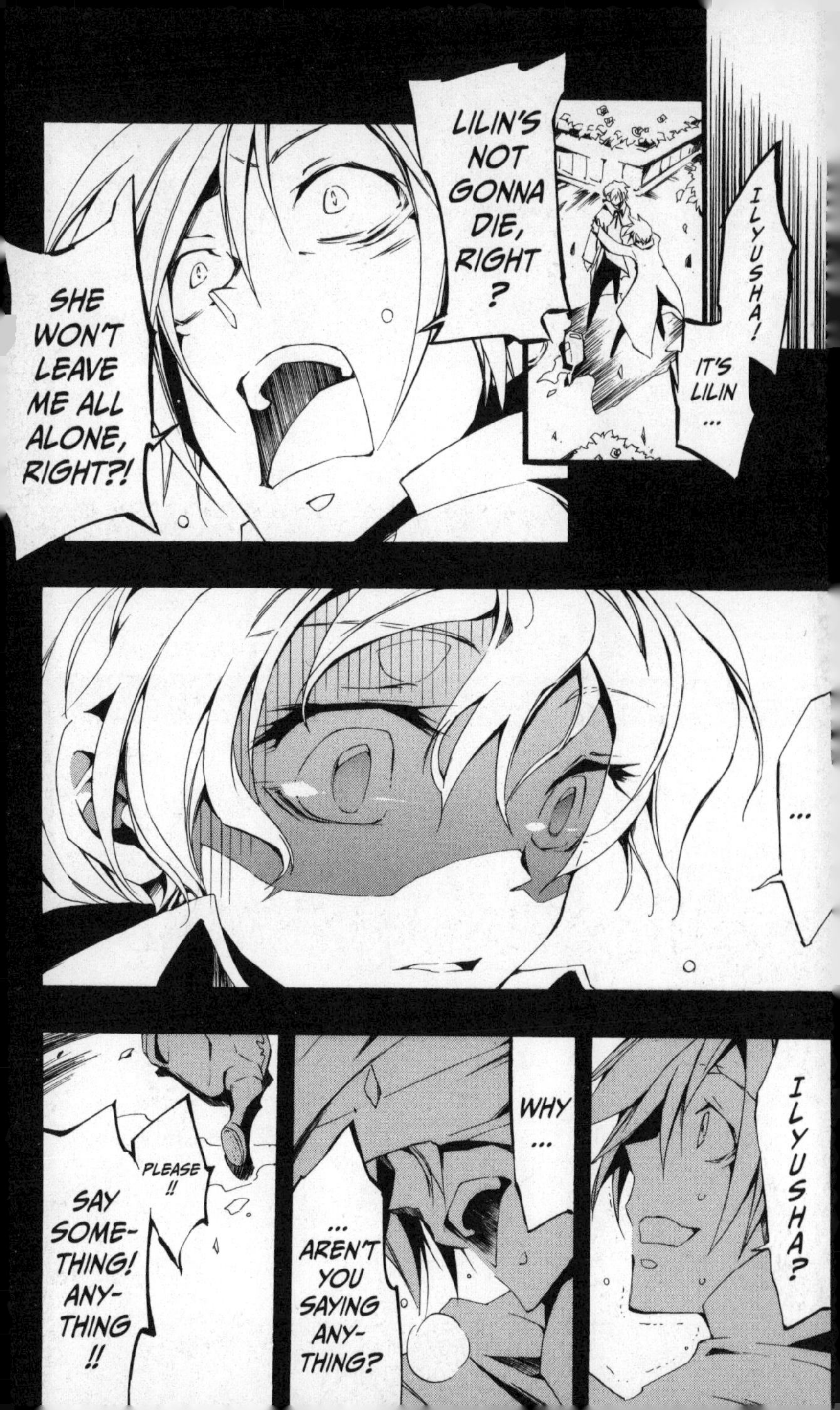
ILYUSHA!
IT'S LILIN...
LILIN'S NOT GONNA DIE, RIGHT?
SHE WON'T LEAVE ME ALL ALONE, RIGHT?!
...
ILYUSHA?
WHY...
...AREN'T YOU SAYING ANYTHING?
PLEASE!!
SAY SOMETHING! ANYTHING!!

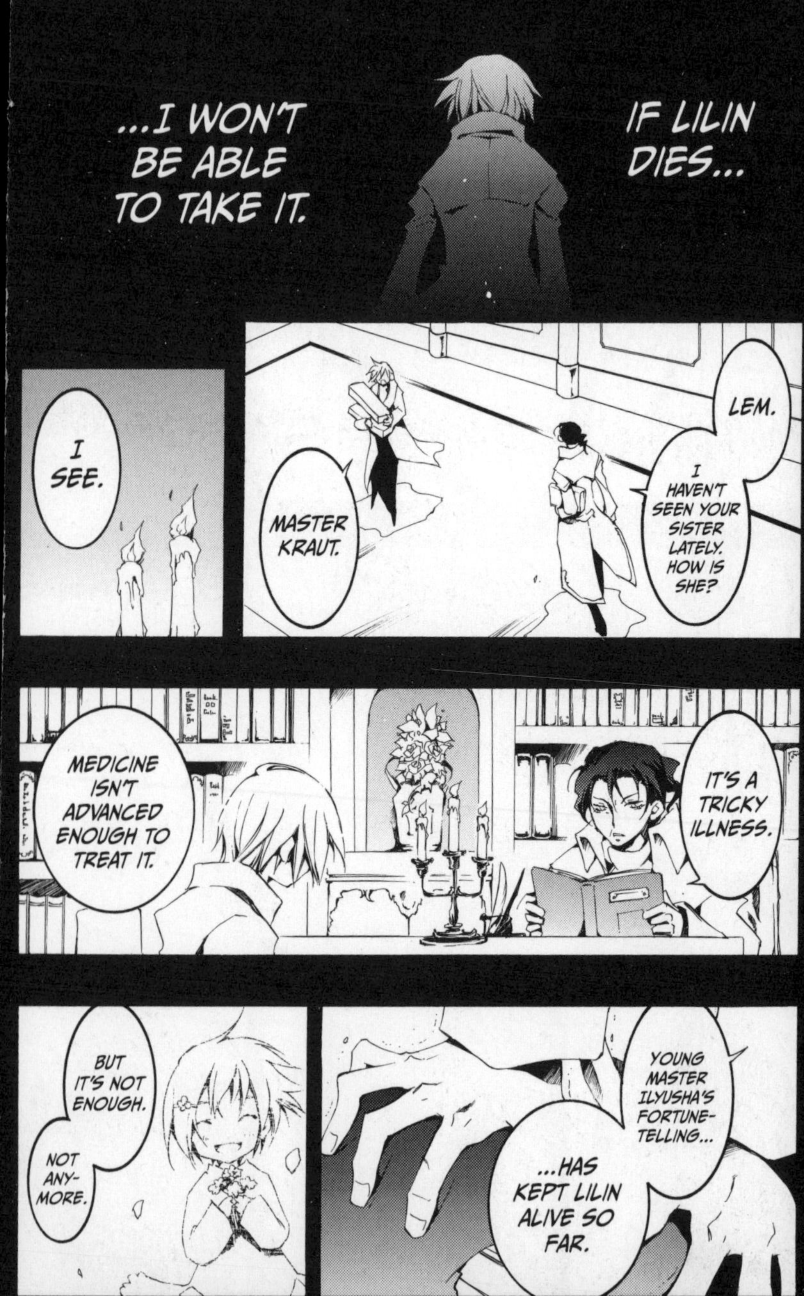
IF LILIN DIES...
...I WON'T BE ABLE TO TAKE IT.
LEM.
I HAVEN'T SEEN YOUR SISTER LATELY. HOW IS SHE?
MASTER KRAUT.
I SEE.
IT'S A TRICKY ILLNESS.
MEDICINE ISN'T ADVANCED ENOUGH TO TREAT IT.
YOUNG MASTER ILYUSHA'S FORTUNE-TELLING...
...HAS KEPT LILIN ALIVE SO FAR.
BUT IT'S NOT ENOUGH.
NOT ANYMORE.

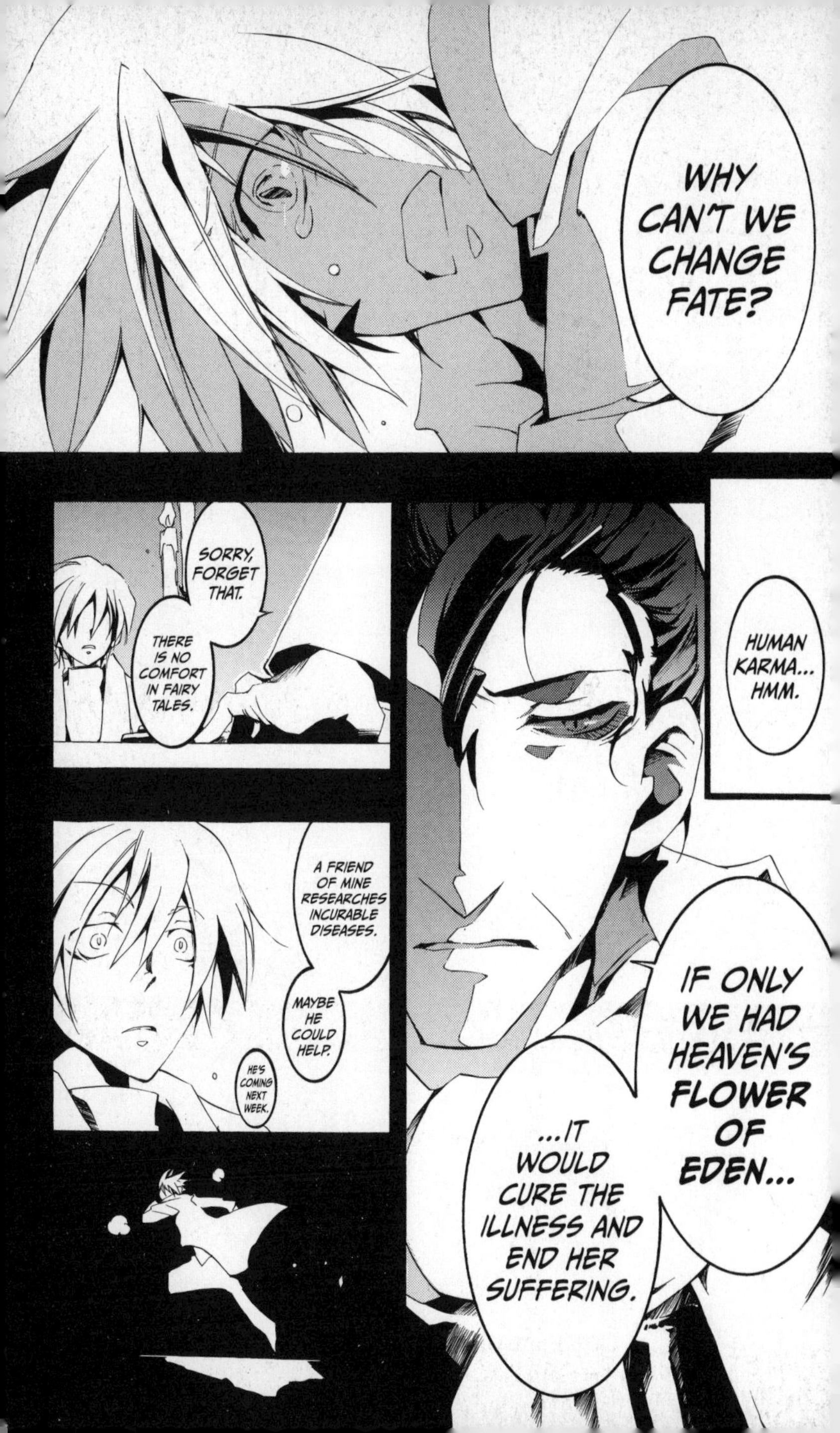
WHY CAN'T WE CHANGE FATE?
HUMAN KARMA... HMM.
IF ONLY WE HAD HEAVEN'S FLOWER OF EDEN...
...IT WOULD CURE THE ILLNESS AND END HER SUFFERING.
SORRY, FORGET THAT.
THERE IS NO COMFORT IN FAIRY TALES.
A FRIEND OF MINE RESEARCHES INCURABLE DISEASES.
MAYBE HE COULD HELP.
HE'S COMING NEXT WEEK.

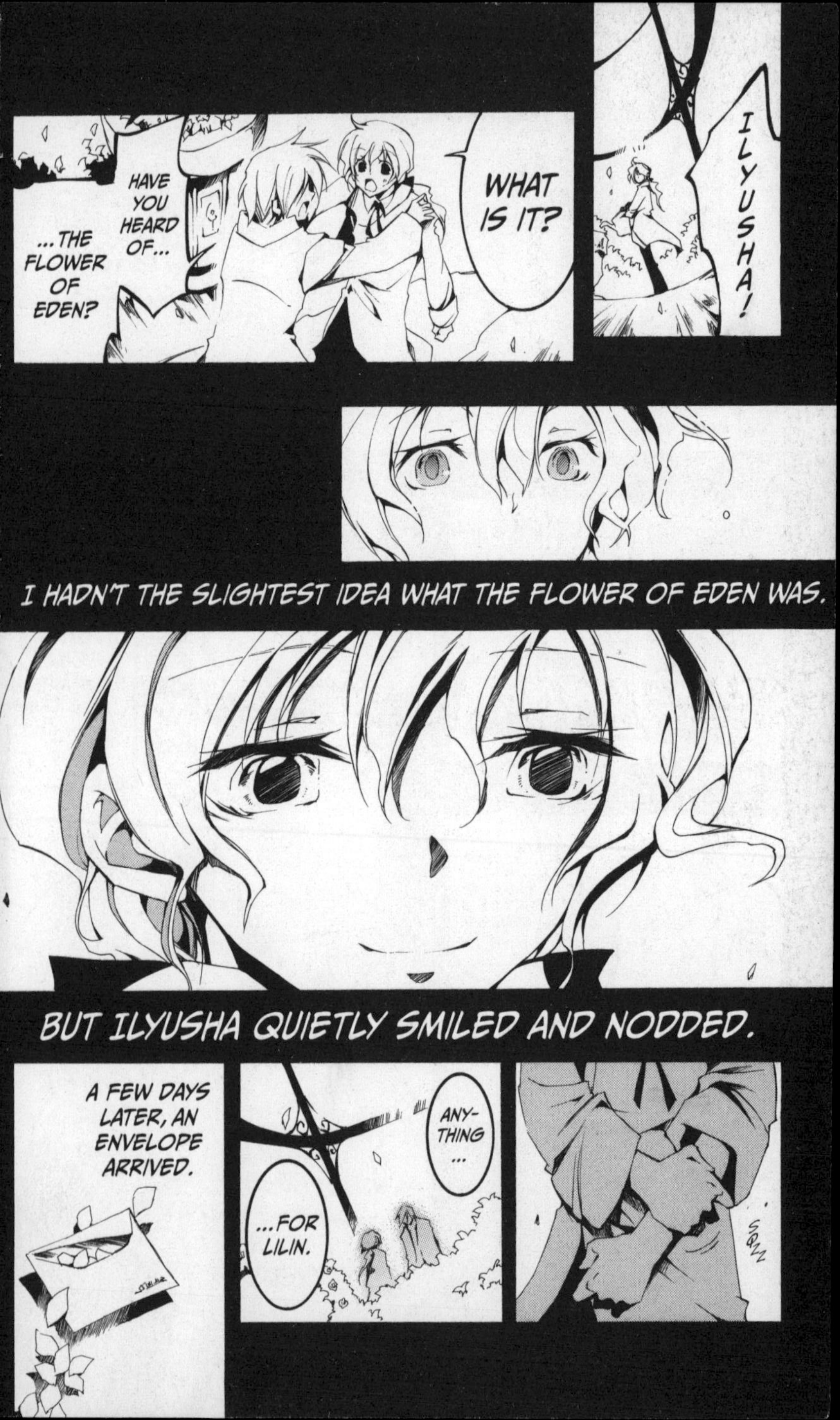
ILYUSHA!
WHAT IS IT?
HAVE YOU HEARD OF...
...THE FLOWER OF EDEN?
I HADN'T THE SLIGHTEST IDEA WHAT THE FLOWER OF EDEN WAS.
BUT ILYUSHA QUIETLY SMILED AND NODDED.
ANY-THING...
...FOR LILIN.
A FEW DAYS LATER, AN ENVELOPE ARRIVED.

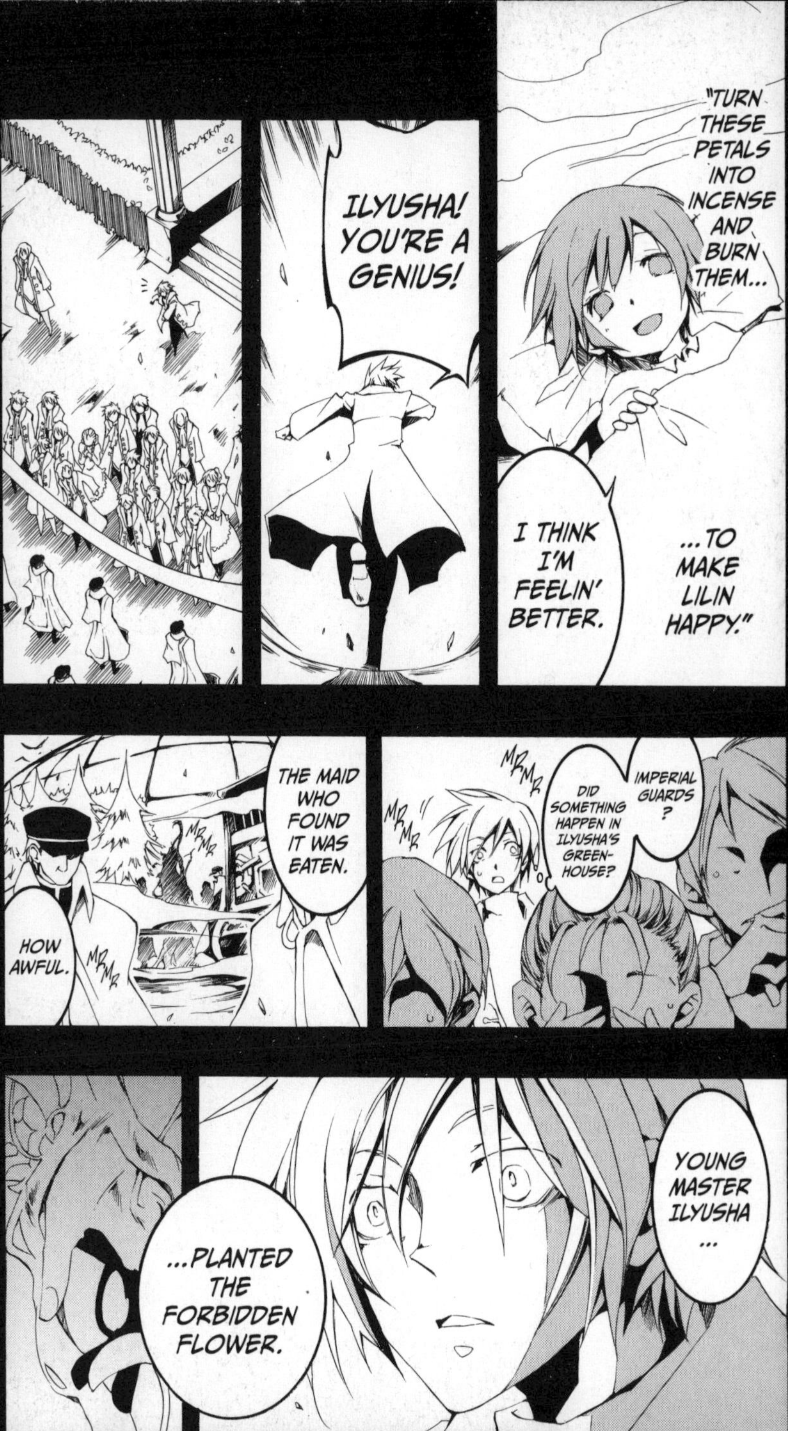
"TURN THESE PETALS INTO INCENSE AND BURN THEM...
...TO MAKE LILIN HAPPY."
I THINK I'M FEELIN' BETTER.
ILYUSHA! YOU'RE A GENIUS!
MRMR
IMPERIAL GUARDS?
DID SOMETHING HAPPEN IN ILYUSHA'S GREEN-HOUSE?
MRMR
THE MAID WHO FOUND IT WAS EATEN.
MRMR
HOW AWFUL.
MRMR
YOUNG MASTER ILYUSHA...
...PLANTED THE FORBIDDEN FLOWER.

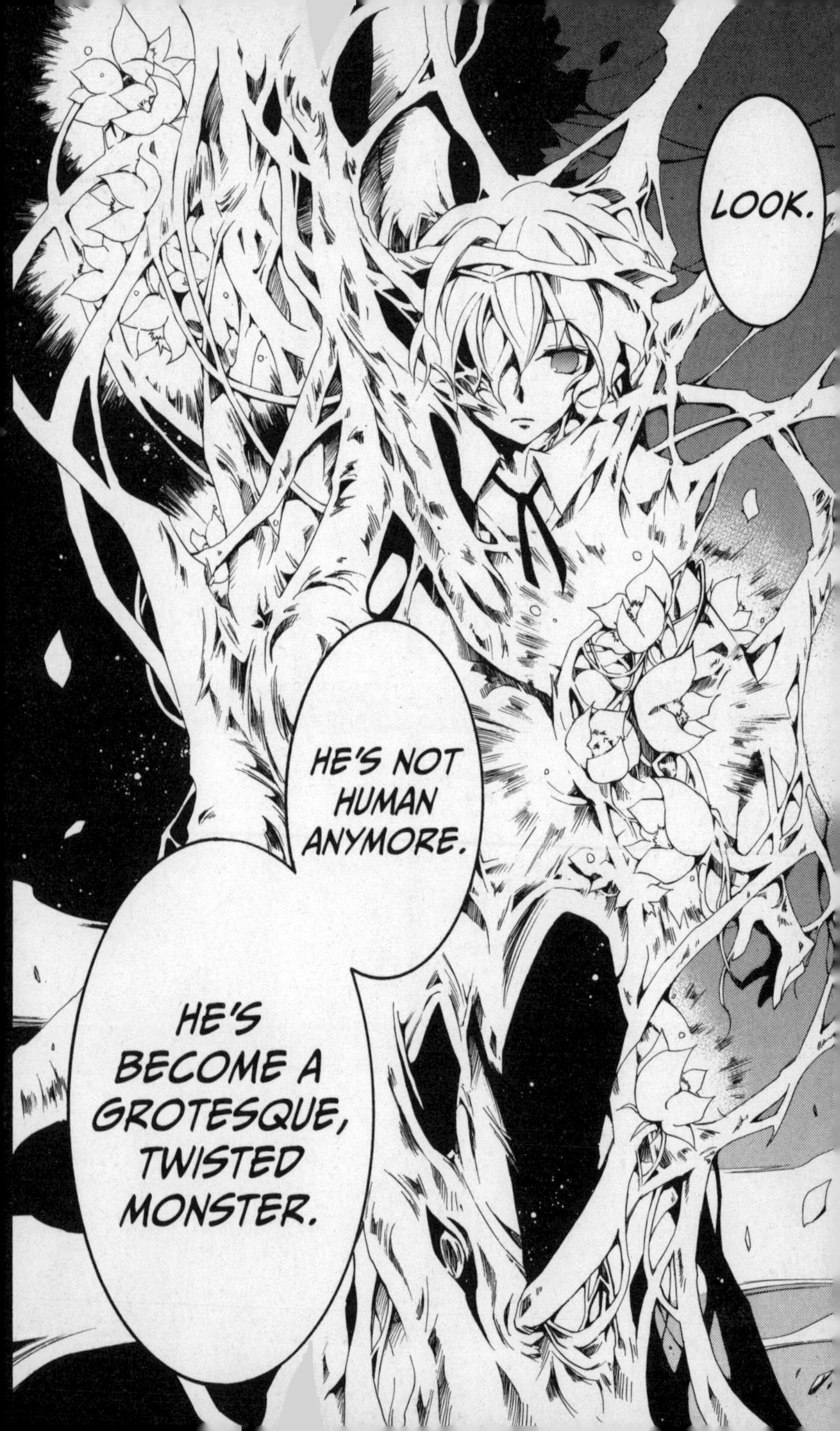
LOOK.
HE'S NOT HUMAN ANYMORE.
HE'S BECOME A GROTESQUE, TWISTED MONSTER.

Kapitel.52
"Forgotten Paradise: Part 4"

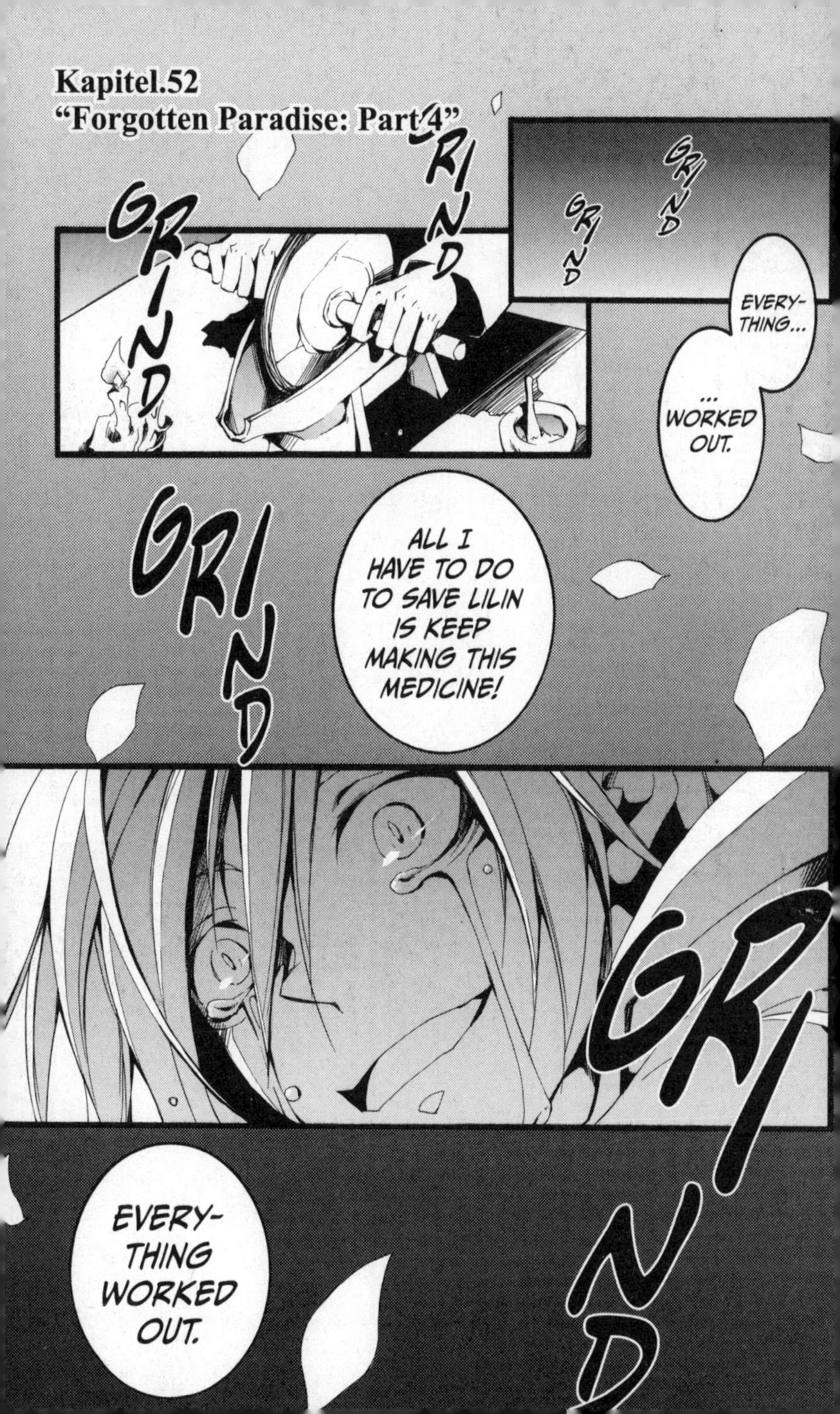
GRIND
GRIND
GRIND
GRIND
EVERY-THING...
...WORKED OUT.
GRIND
ALL I HAVE TO DO TO SAVE LILIN IS KEEP MAKING THIS MEDICINE!
GRIND
EVERY-THING WORKED OUT.

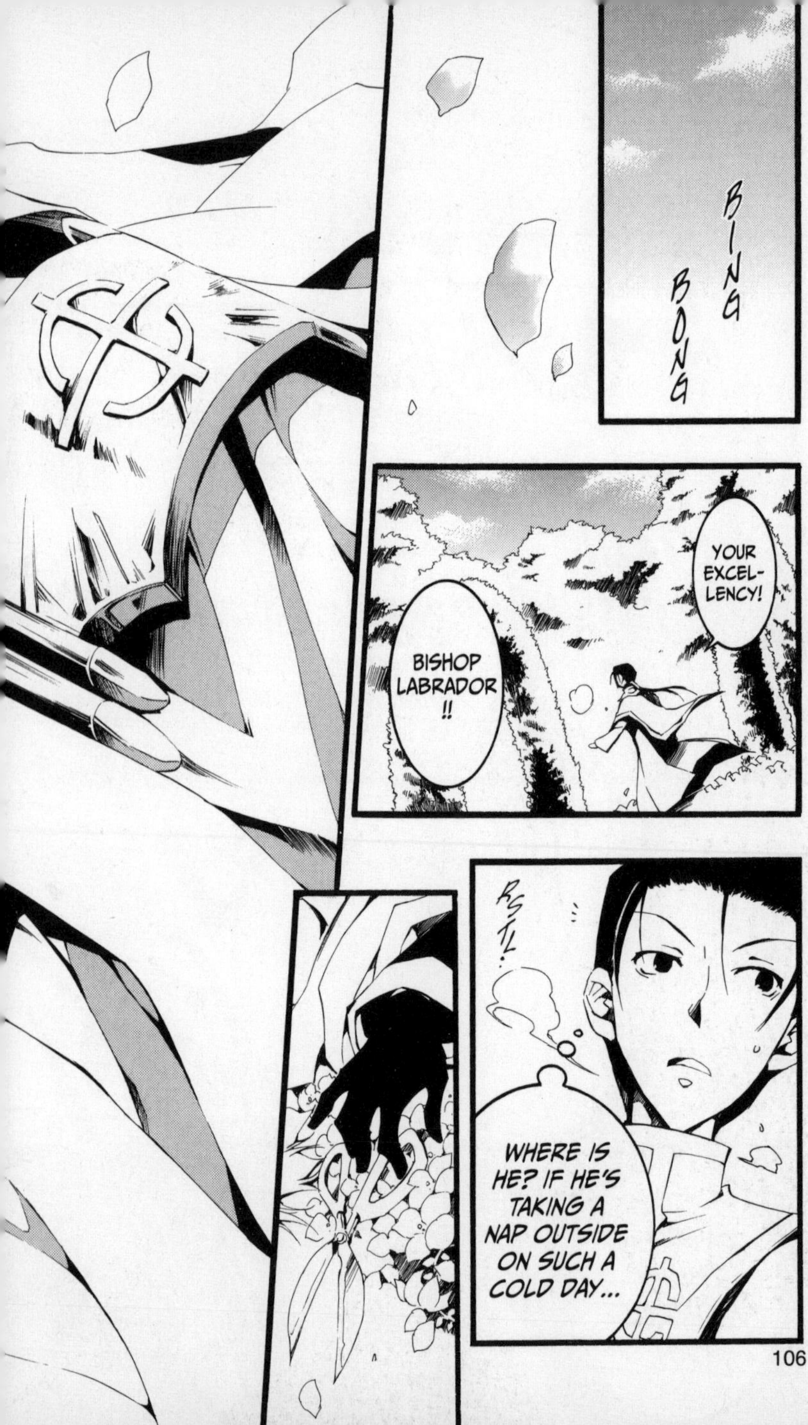
BING BONG
YOUR EXCEL-LENCY!
BISHOP LABRADOR !!
RSTL
WHERE IS HE? IF HE'S TAKING A NAP OUTSIDE ON SUCH A COLD DAY...

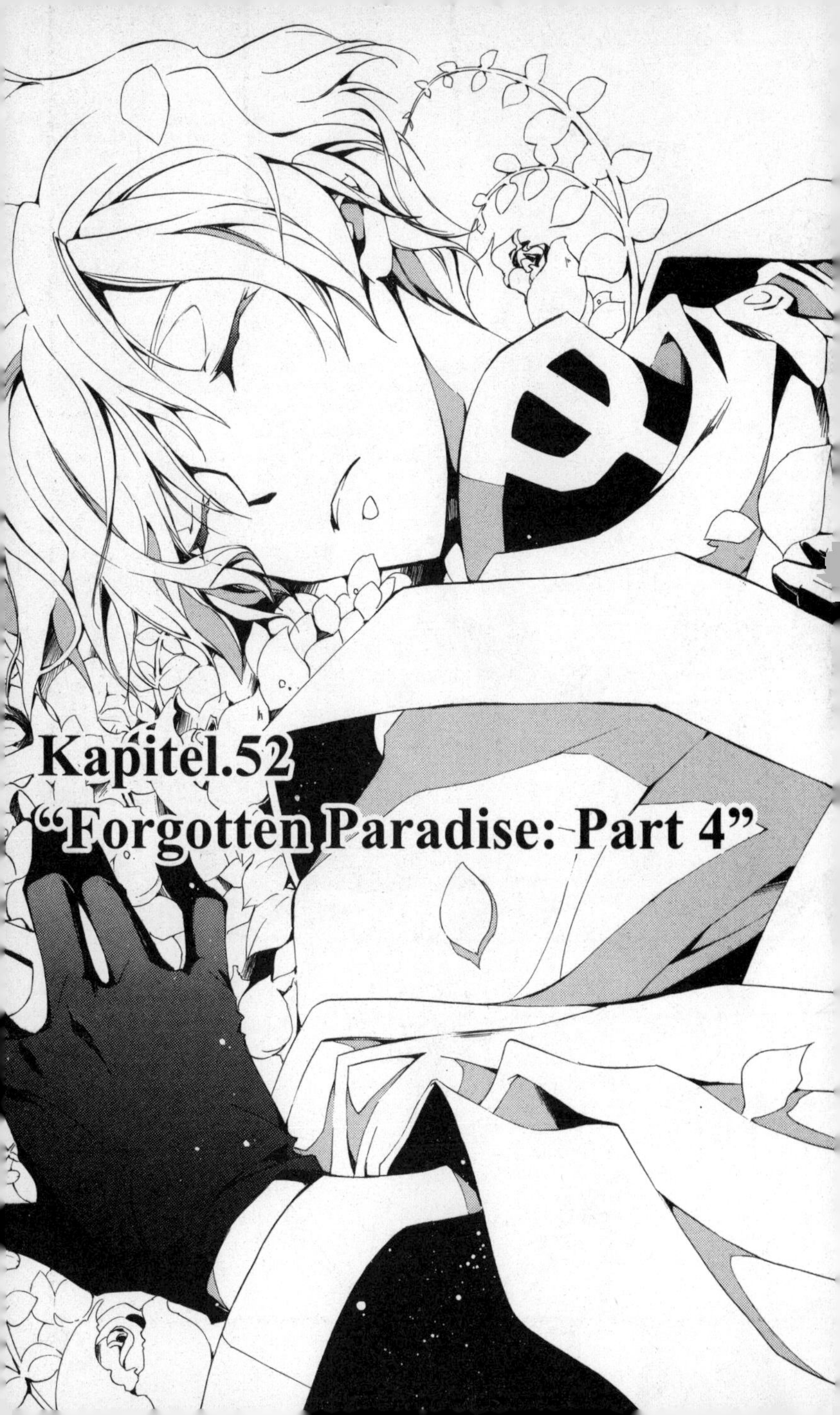
Kapitel.52
“Forgotten Paradise: Part 4”

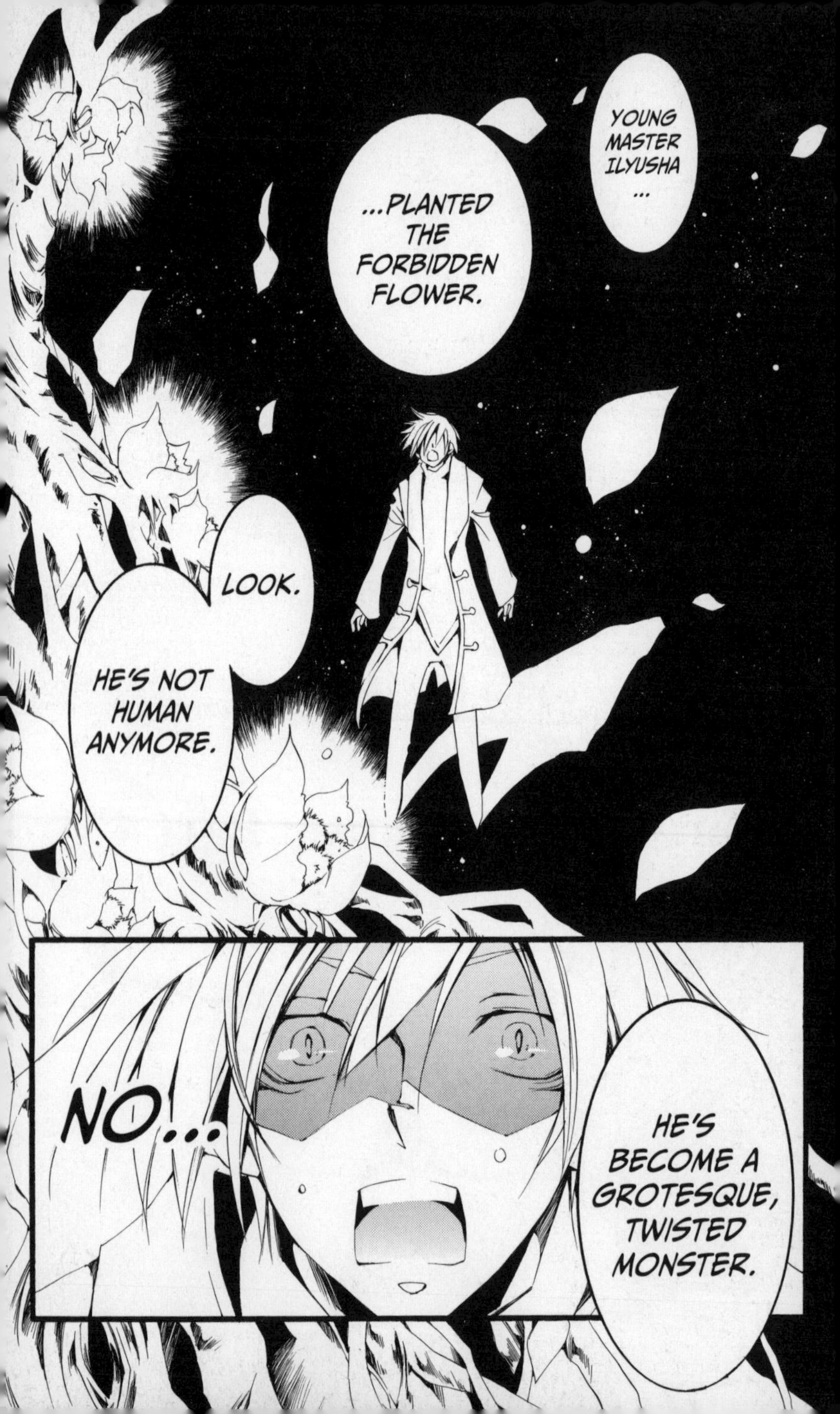
YOUNG MASTER ILYUSHA...
...PLANTED THE FORBIDDEN FLOWER.
LOOK.
HE'S NOT HUMAN ANYMORE.
HE'S BECOME A GROTESQUE, TWISTED MONSTER.
NO...

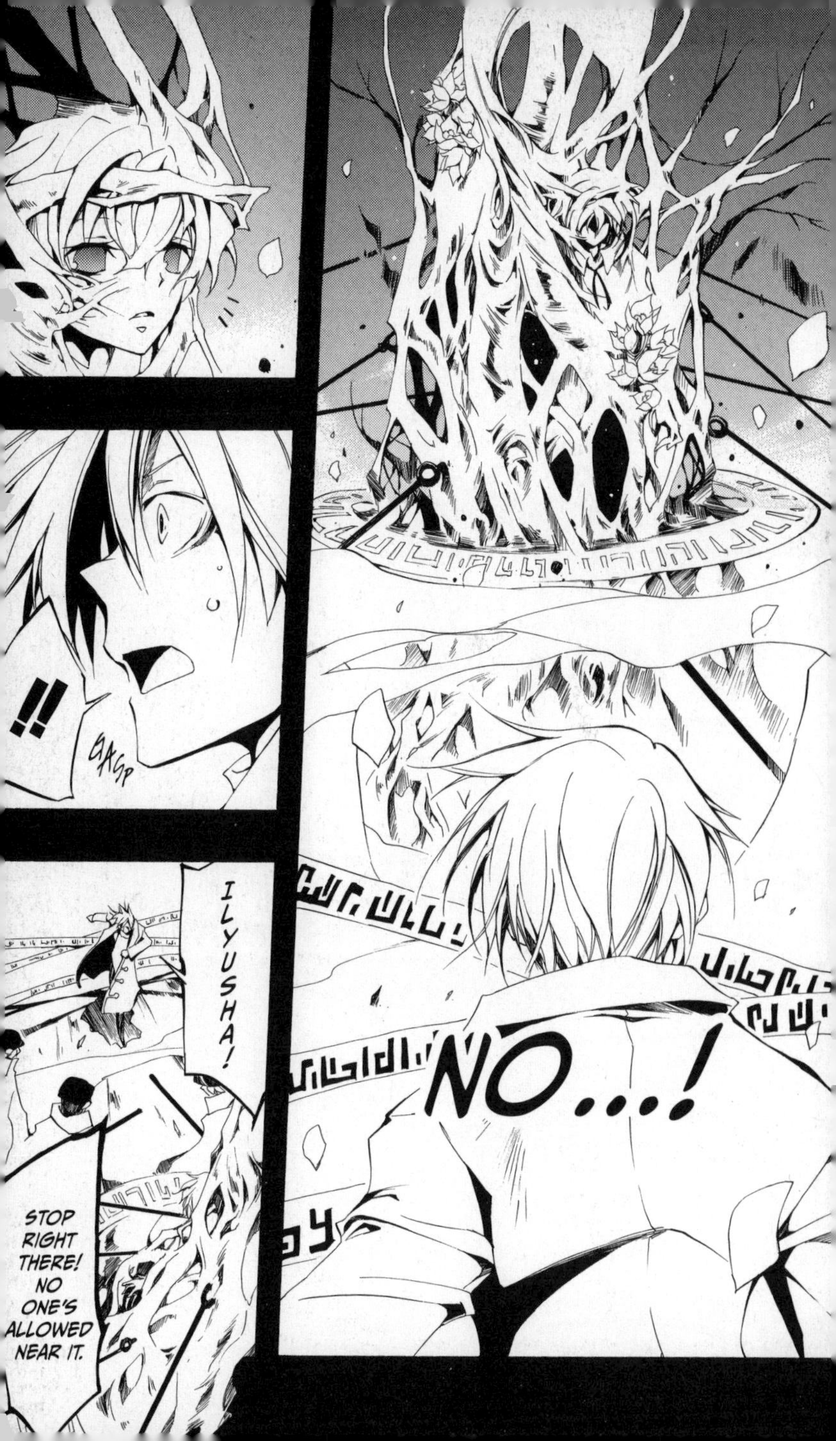
NO...!
!!
GASP
ILYUSHA!
STOP RIGHT THERE! NO ONE'S ALLOWED NEAR IT.

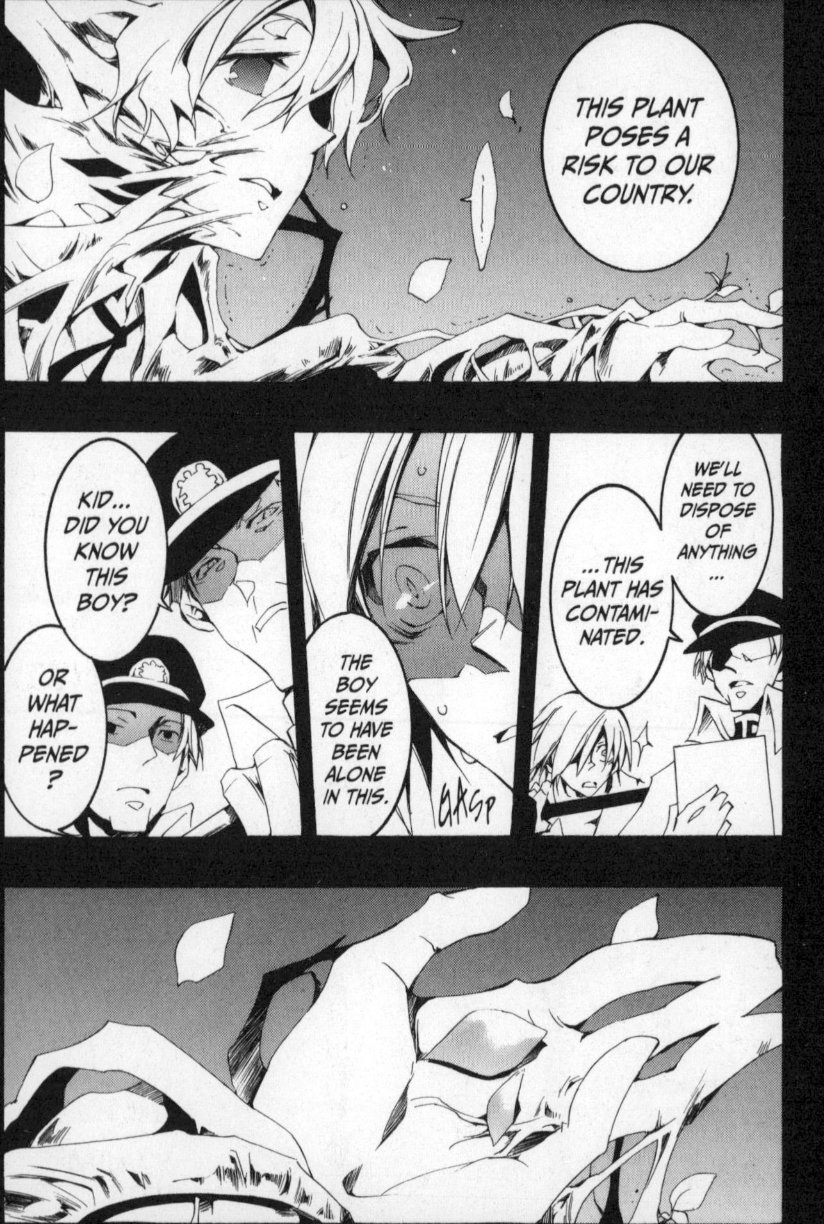
THIS PLANT POSES A RISK TO OUR COUNTRY.
WE'LL NEED TO DISPOSE OF ANYTHING...
...THIS PLANT HAS CONTAMINATED.
THE BOY SEEMS TO HAVE BEEN ALONE IN THIS.
GASP
KID... DID YOU KNOW THIS BOY?
OR WHAT HAPPENED?

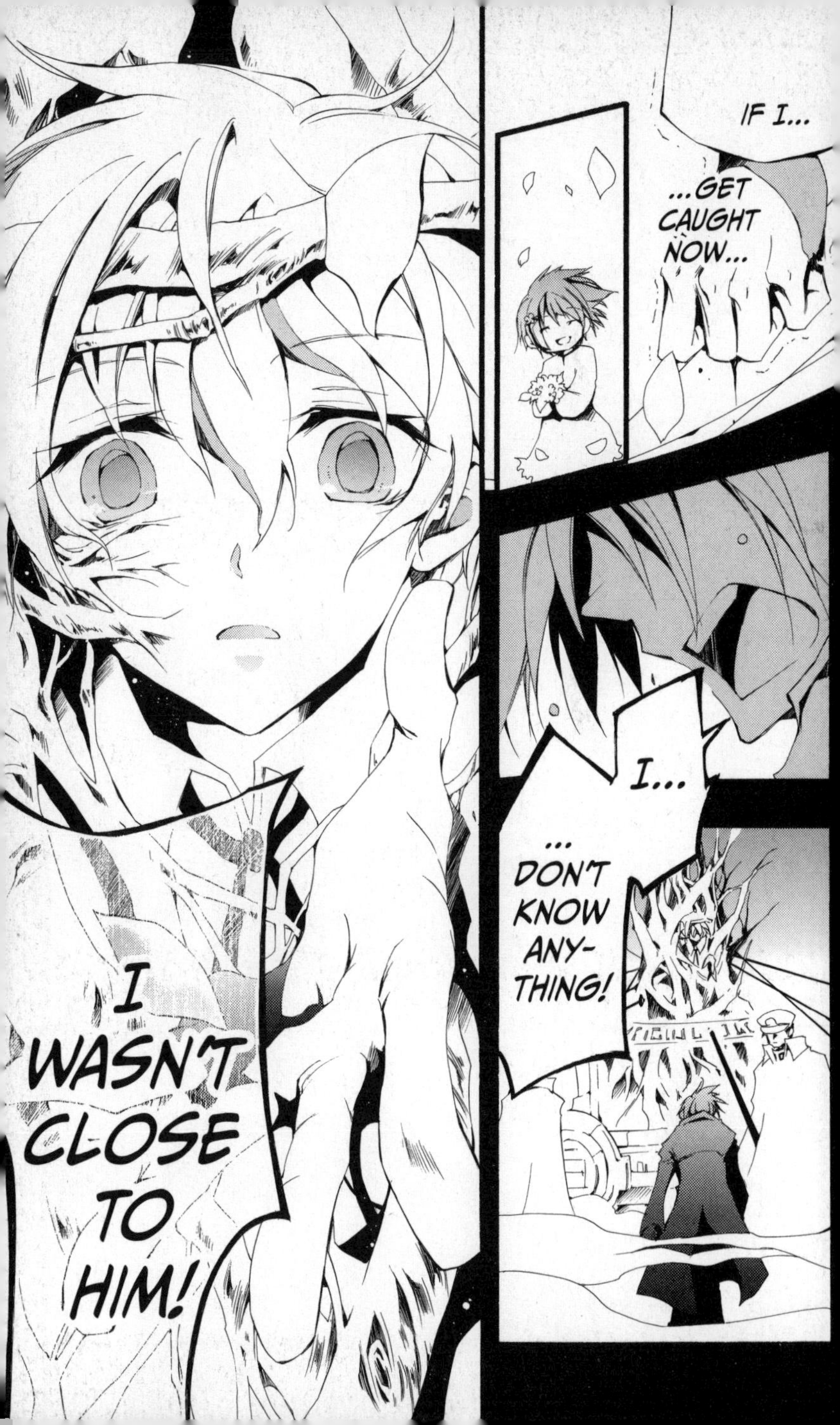
IF I...
...GET CAUGHT NOW...
I...
...DON'T KNOW ANY-THING!
I WASN'T CLOSE TO HIM!

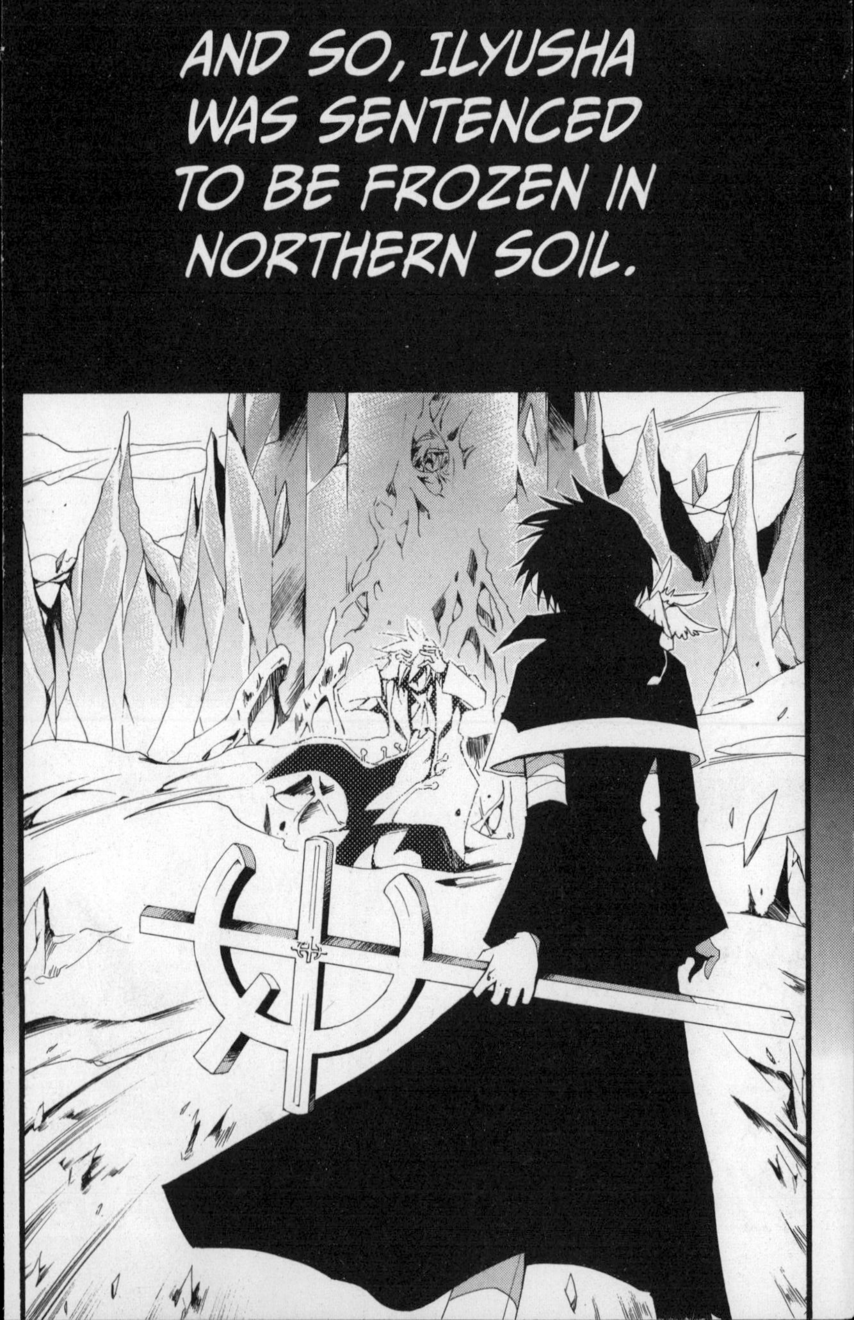
AND SO, ILYUSHA WAS SENTENCED TO BE FROZEN IN NORTHERN SOIL.

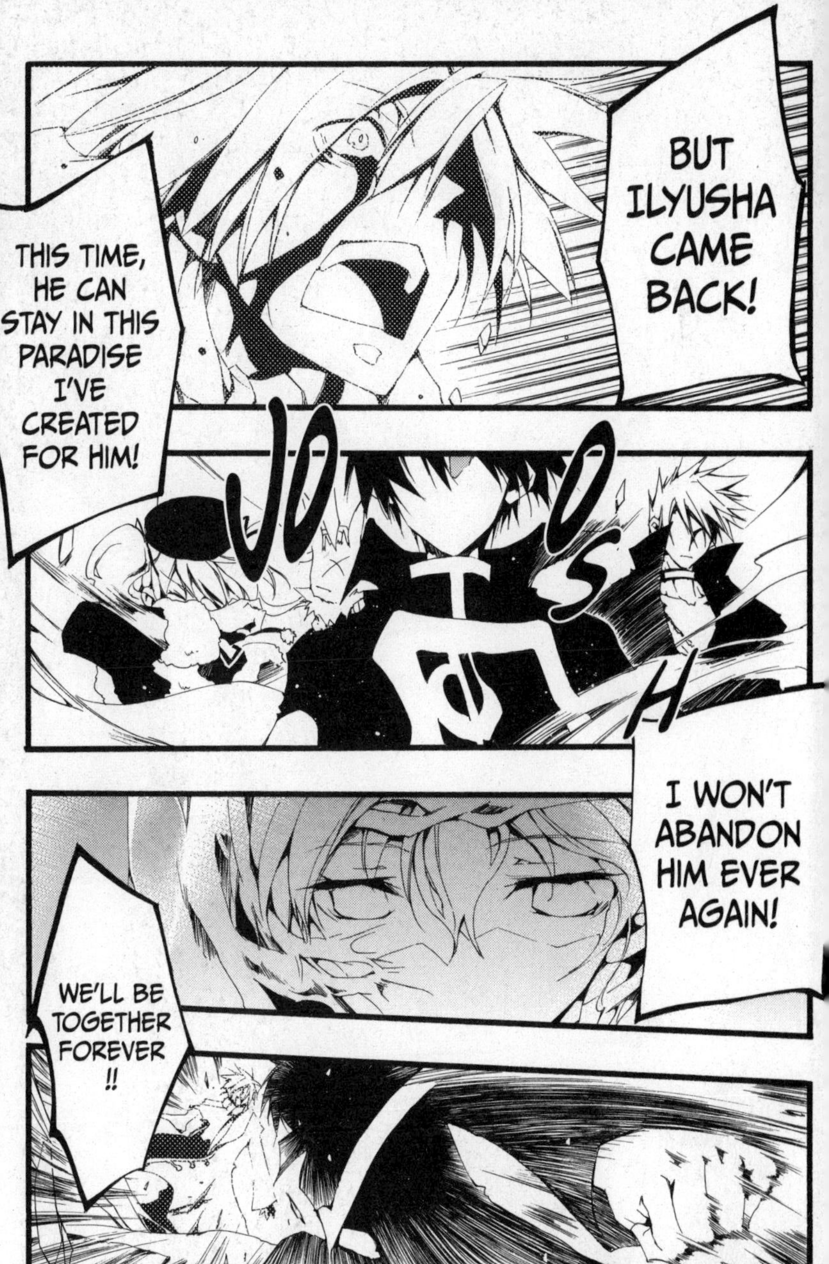
BUT ILYUSHA CAME BACK!
THIS TIME, HE CAN STAY IN THIS PARADISE I'VE CREATED FOR HIM!
JOOSH
I WON'T ABANDON HIM EVER AGAIN!
WE'LL BE TOGETHER FOREVER !!

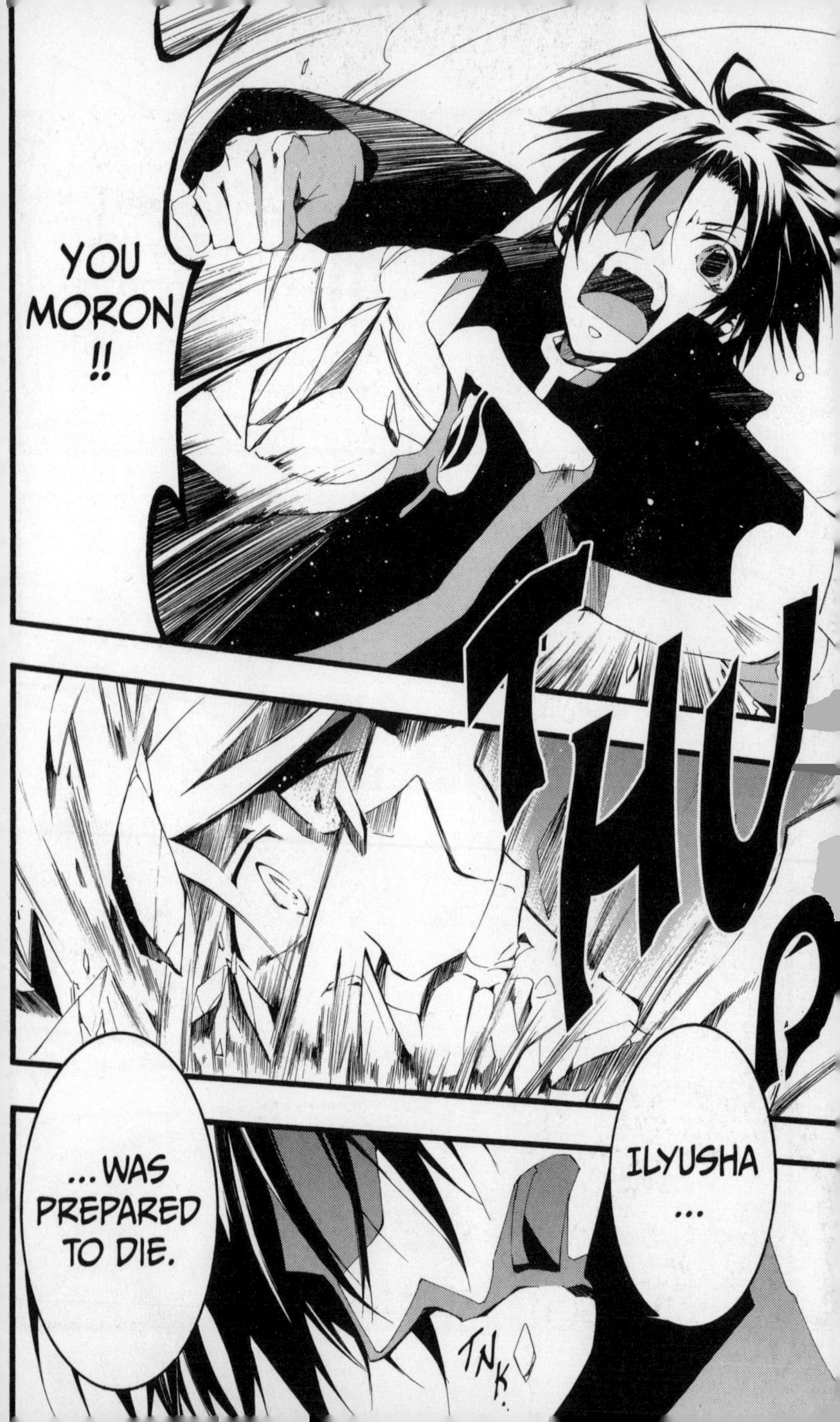
YOU MORON !!
THU
ILYUSHA ...
...WAS PREPARED TO DIE.
TNK

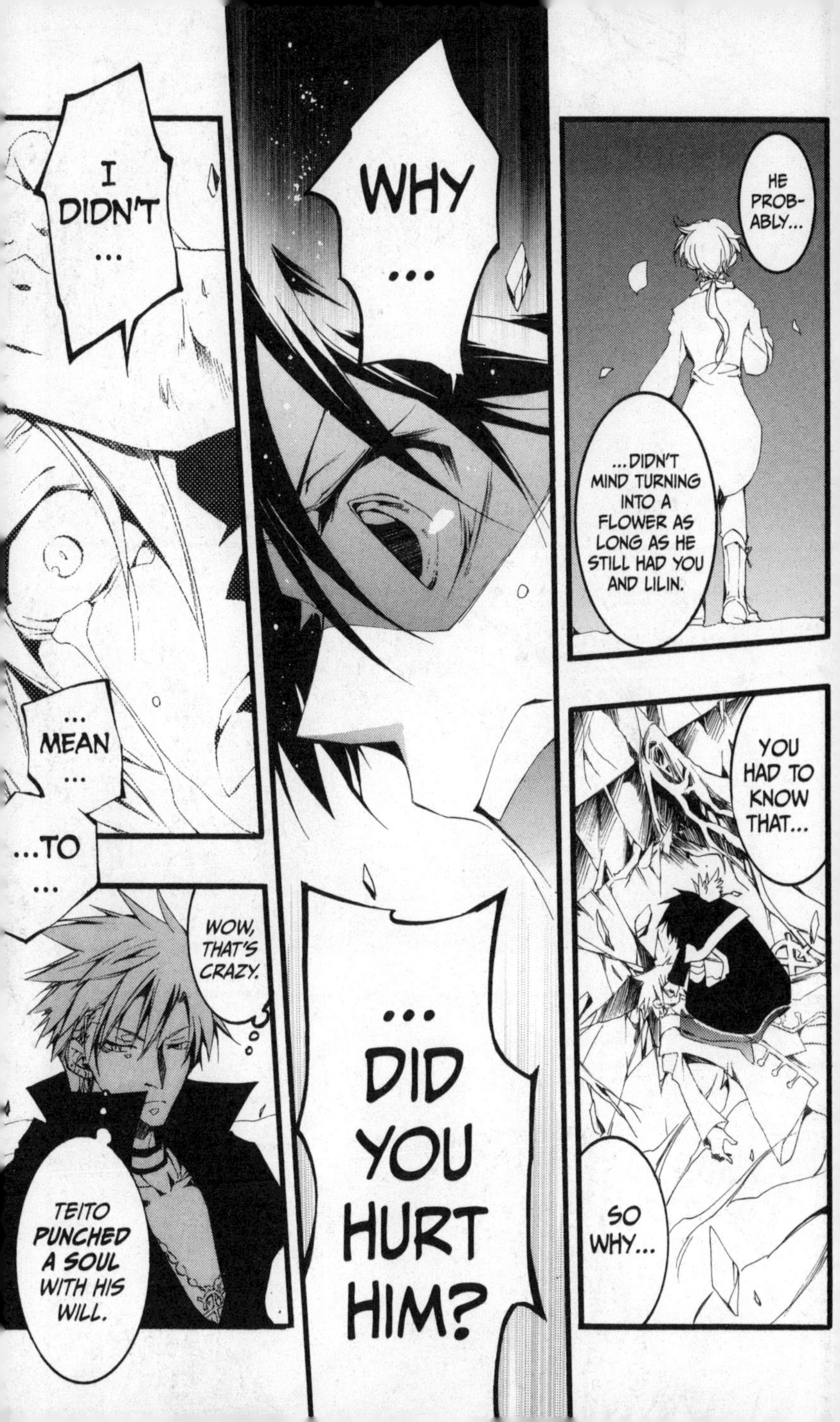
HE PROBABLY...
...DIDN'T MIND TURNING INTO A FLOWER AS LONG AS HE STILL HAD YOU AND LILIN.
YOU HAD TO KNOW THAT...
SO WHY...
WHY ...
... DID YOU HURT HIM?
I DIDN'T ...
... MEAN ...
...TO ...
WOW, THAT'S CRAZY.
TEITO PUNCHED A SOUL WITH HIS WILL.

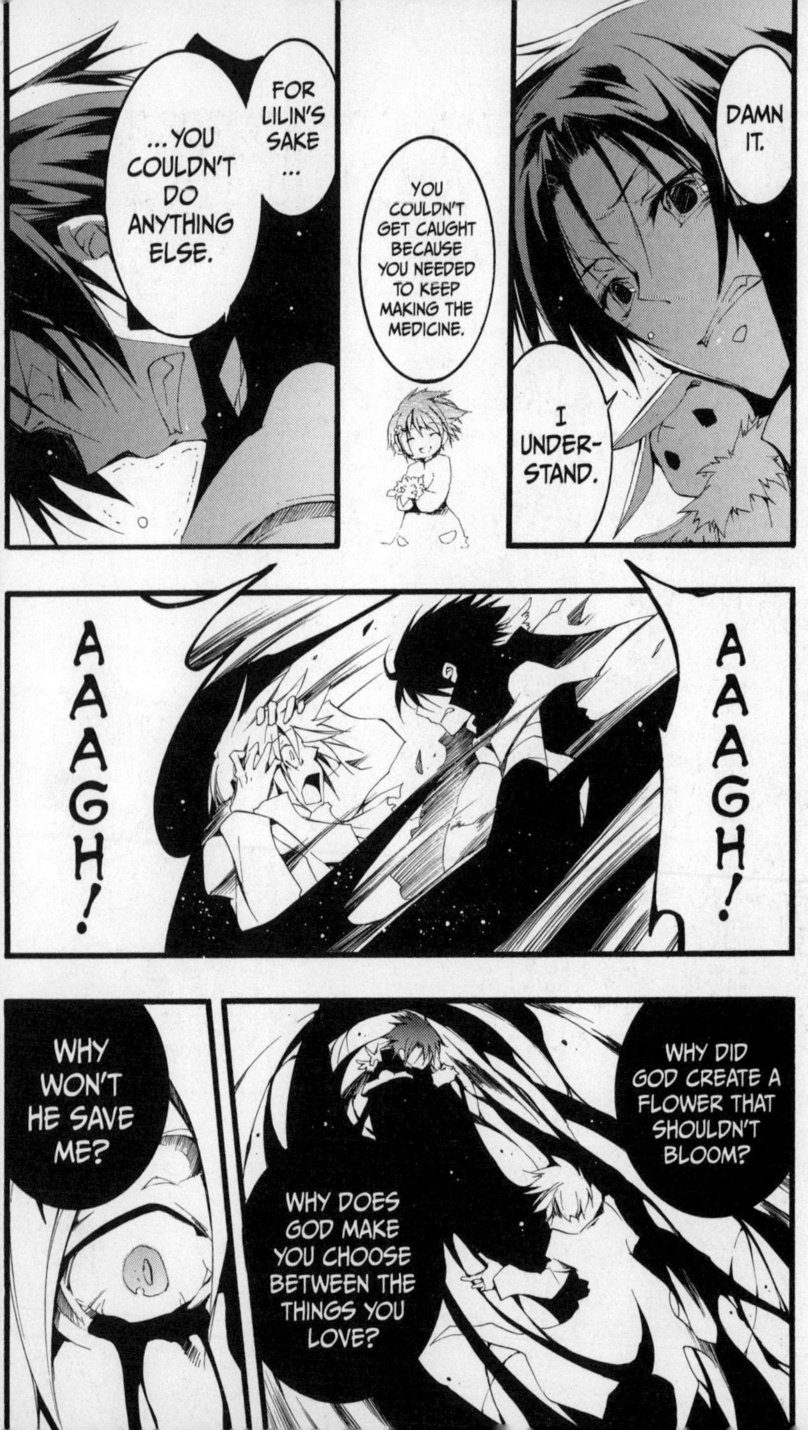
DAMN IT.
I UNDER-STAND.
YOU COULDN'T GET CAUGHT BECAUSE YOU NEEDED TO KEEP MAKING THE MEDICINE.
FOR LILIN'S SAKE ...
...YOU COULDN'T DO ANYTHING ELSE.
AAAGH!
AAAGH!
WHY DID GOD CREATE A FLOWER THAT SHOULDN'T BLOOM?
WHY DOES GOD MAKE YOU CHOOSE BETWEEN THE THINGS YOU LOVE?
WHY WON'T HE SAVE ME?

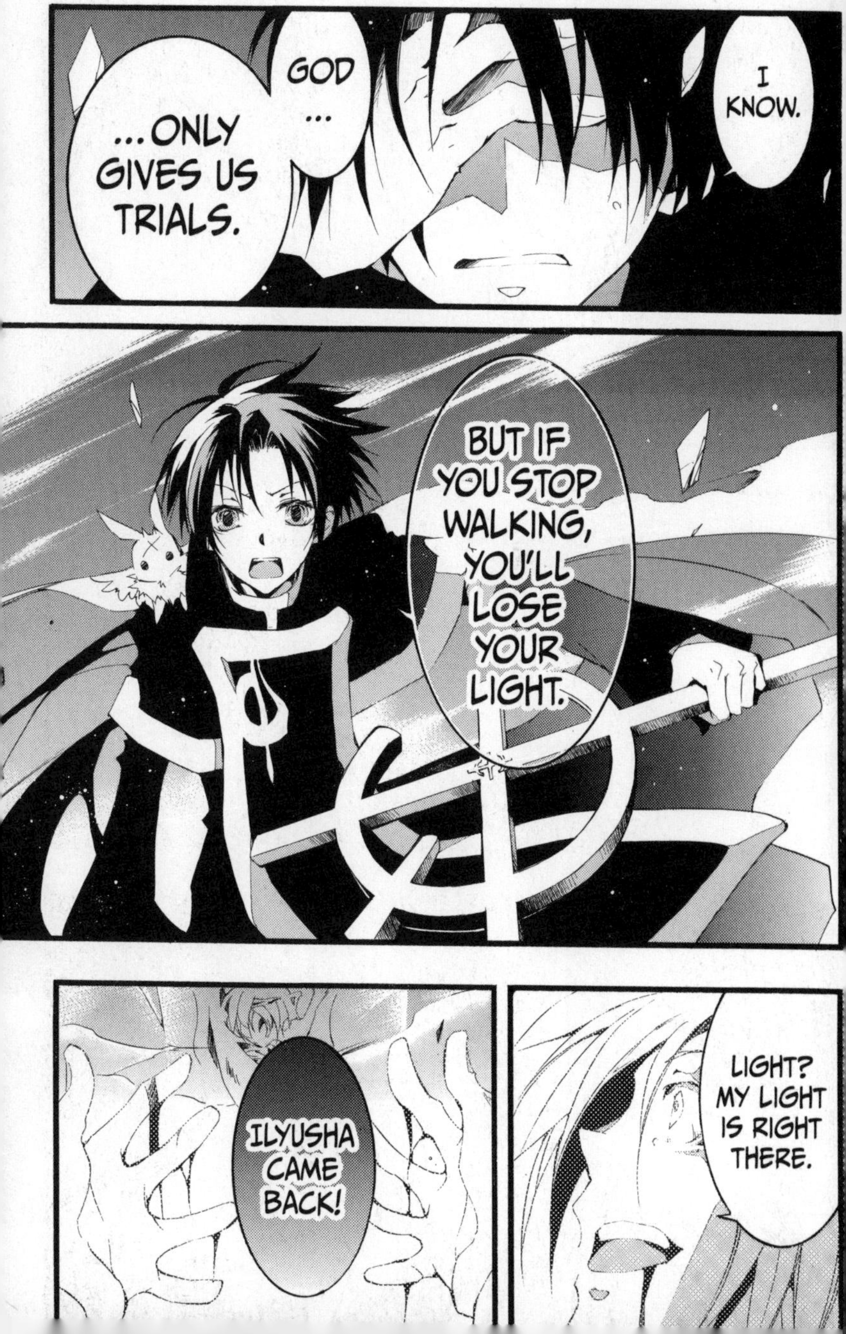
I KNOW.
GOD ...
...ONLY GIVES US TRIALS.
BUT IF YOU STOP WALKING, YOU'LL LOSE YOUR LIGHT.
LIGHT? MY LIGHT IS RIGHT THERE.
ILYUSHA CAME BACK!

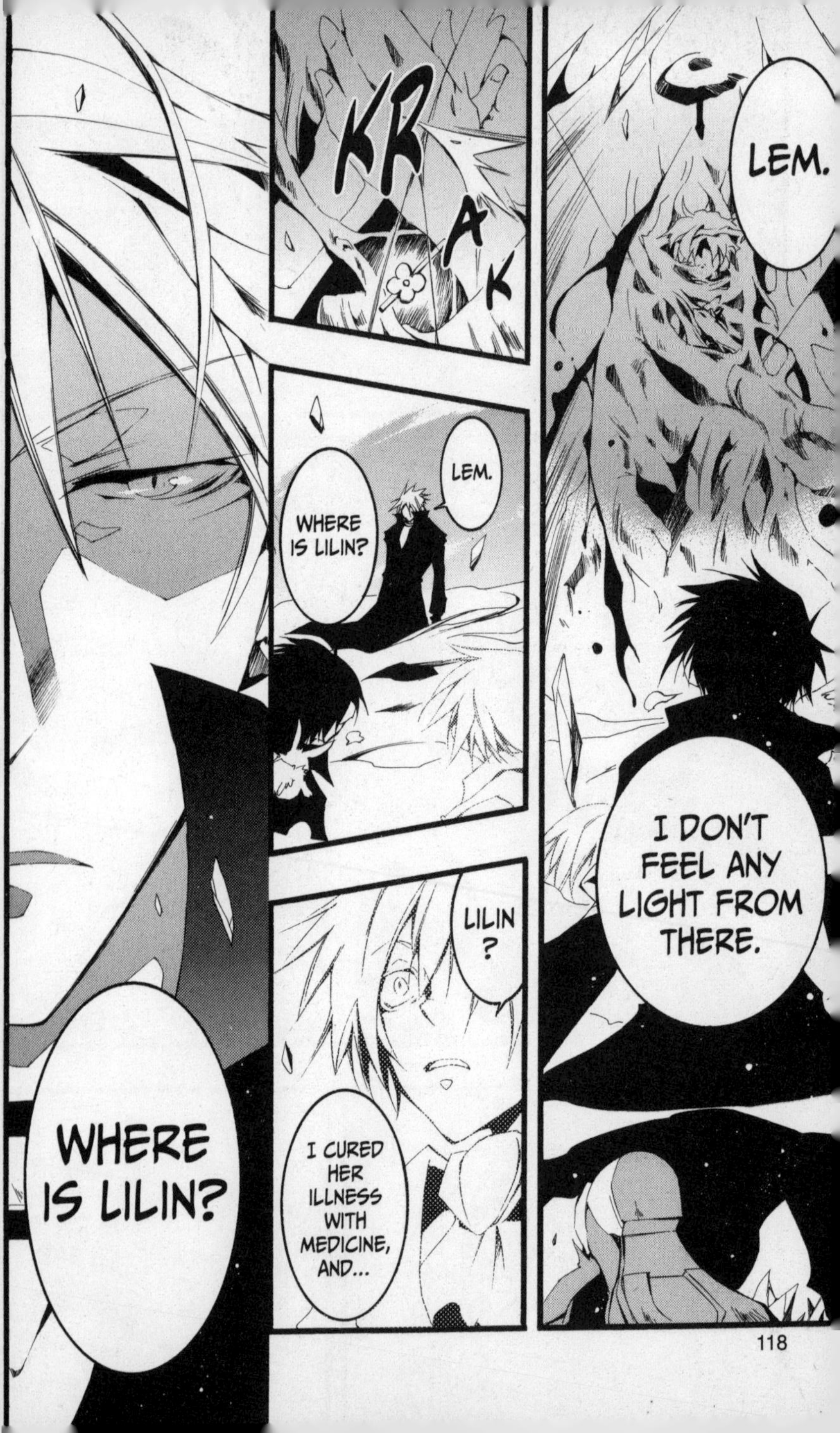
LEM.
I DON'T FEEL ANY LIGHT FROM THERE.
KRAK
LEM.
WHERE IS LILIN?
LILIN?
I CURED HER ILLNESS WITH MEDICINE, AND...
WHERE IS LILIN?

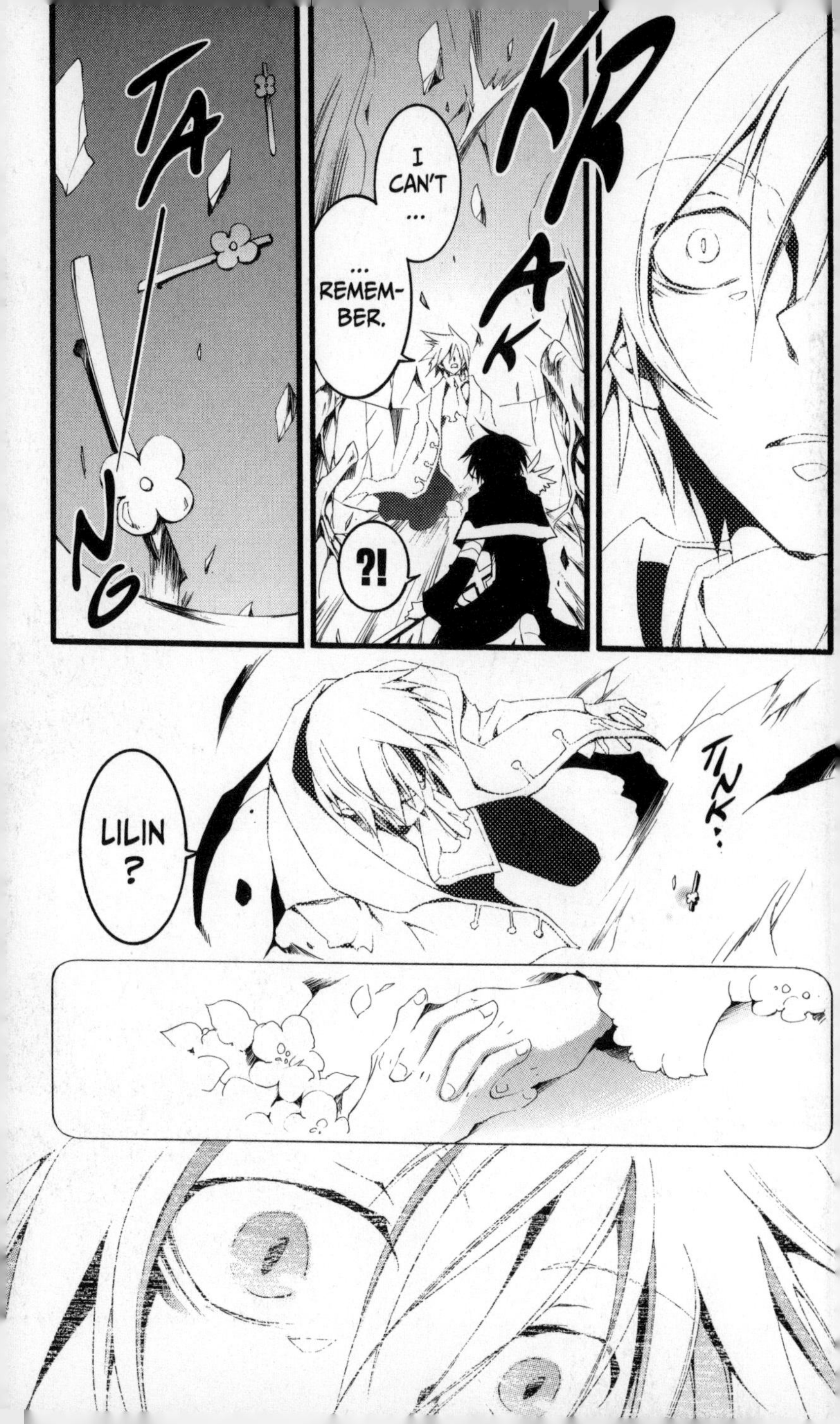
KRAK
I CAN'T ...
... REMEMBER.
?!
TANG
TINK...
LILIN?

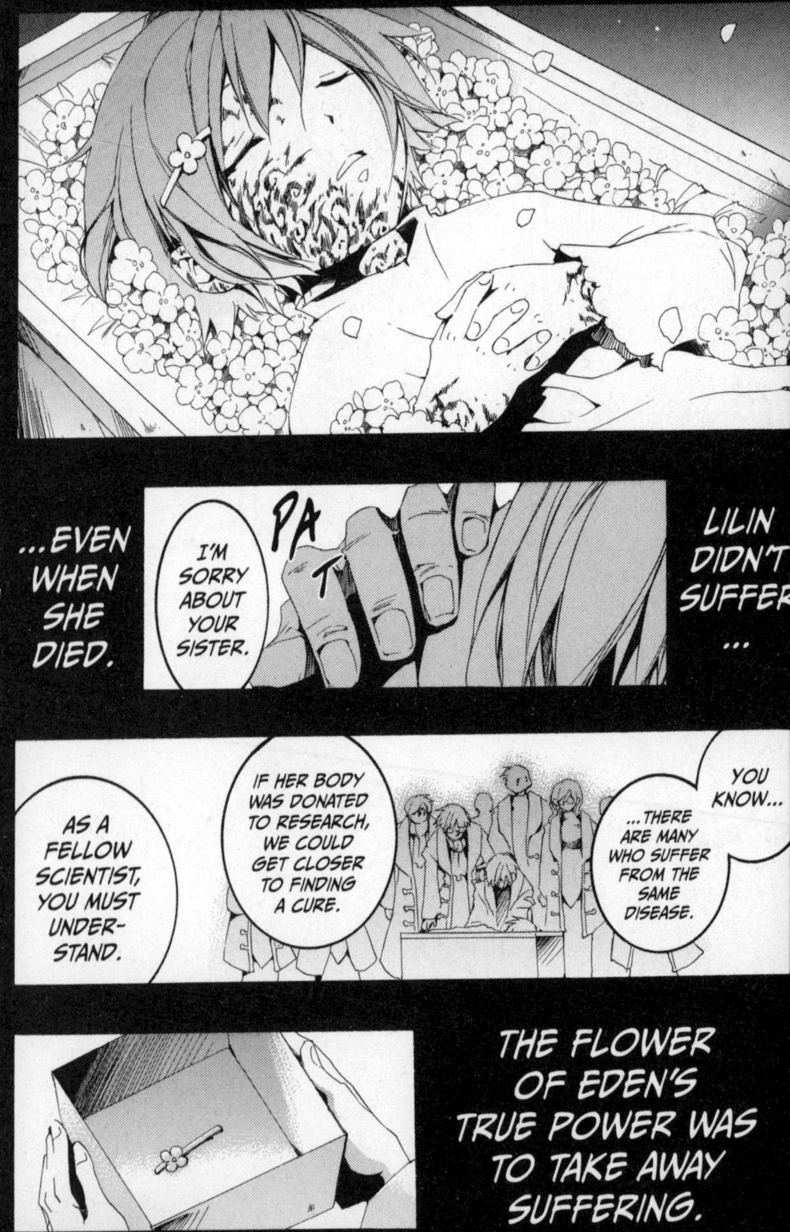
LILIN DIDN'T SUFFER...
PAT
I'M SORRY ABOUT YOUR SISTER.
...EVEN WHEN SHE DIED.
YOU KNOW...
...THERE ARE MANY WHO SUFFER FROM THE SAME DISEASE.
IF HER BODY WAS DONATED TO RESEARCH, WE COULD GET CLOSER TO FINDING A CURE.
AS A FELLOW SCIENTIST, YOU MUST UNDER-STAND.
THE FLOWER OF EDEN'S TRUE POWER WAS TO TAKE AWAY SUFFERING.

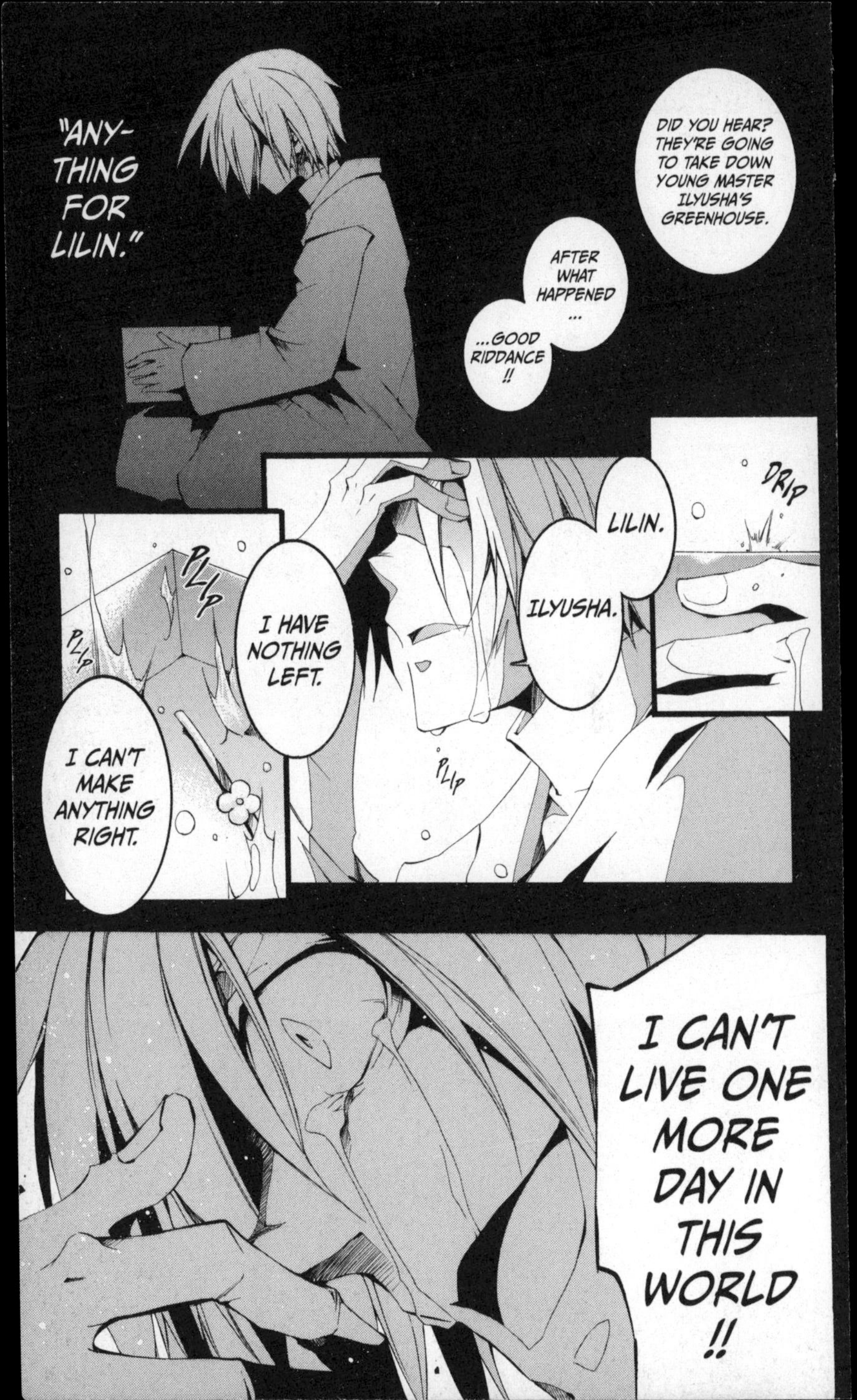
DID YOU HEAR? THEY'RE GOING TO TAKE DOWN YOUNG MASTER ILYUSHA'S GREENHOUSE.
AFTER WHAT HAPPENED ...
...GOOD RIDDANCE !!
"ANY-THING FOR LILIN."
DRIP
LILIN.
ILYUSHA.
I HAVE NOTHING LEFT.
PLIP
PLIP
PLIP
I CAN'T MAKE ANYTHING RIGHT.
I CAN'T LIVE ONE MORE DAY IN THIS WORLD !!

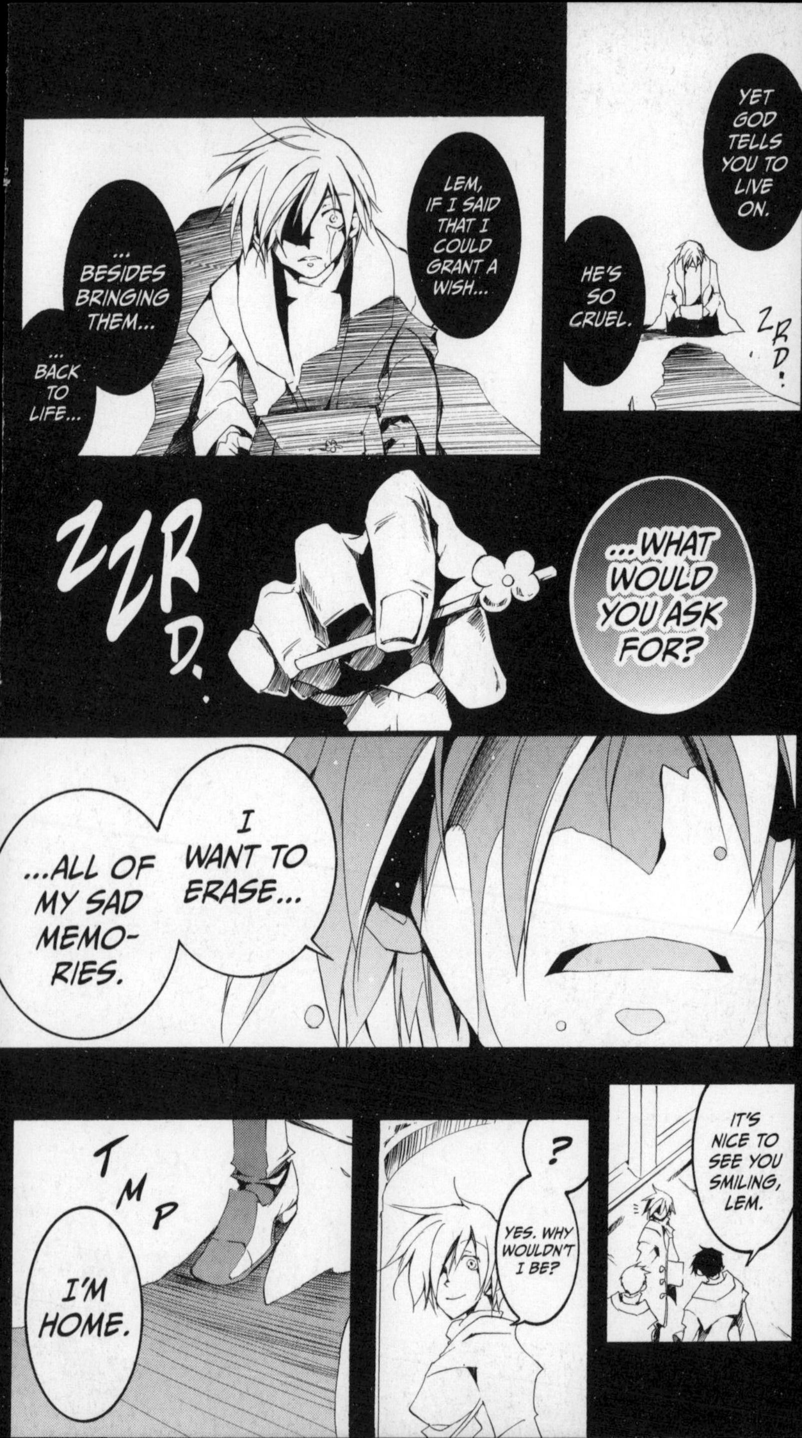
YET GOD TELLS YOU TO LIVE ON.
HE'S SO CRUEL.
ZRD!
LEM, IF I SAID THAT I COULD GRANT A WISH...
...BESIDES BRINGING THEM...
...BACK TO LIFE...
...WHAT WOULD YOU ASK FOR?
ZZRD.
I WANT TO ERASE...
...ALL OF MY SAD MEMORIES.
IT'S NICE TO SEE YOU SMILING, LEM.
?
YES. WHY WOULDN'T I BE?
TMP
I'M HOME.

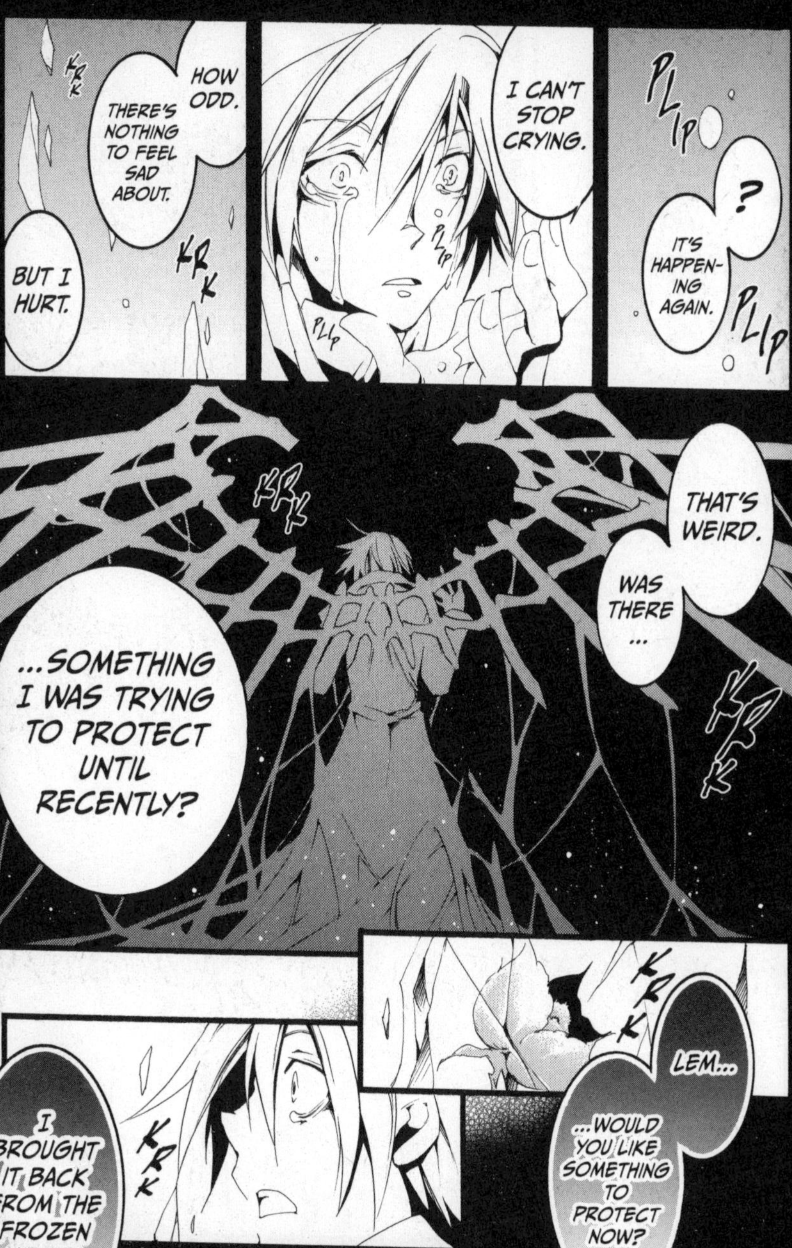
PLIP
?
IT'S HAPPEN-ING AGAIN.
PLIP
I CAN'T STOP CRYING.
PLIP
PLIP
KRK
HOW ODD.
THERE'S NOTHING TO FEEL SAD ABOUT.
KRK
BUT I HURT.
THAT'S WEIRD.
WAS THERE...
KRK
KRK
...SOMETHING I WAS TRYING TO PROTECT UNTIL RECENTLY?
KRK
LEM...
...WOULD YOU LIKE SOMETHING TO PROTECT NOW?
KRK
I BROUGHT IT BACK FROM THE FROZEN NORTH.

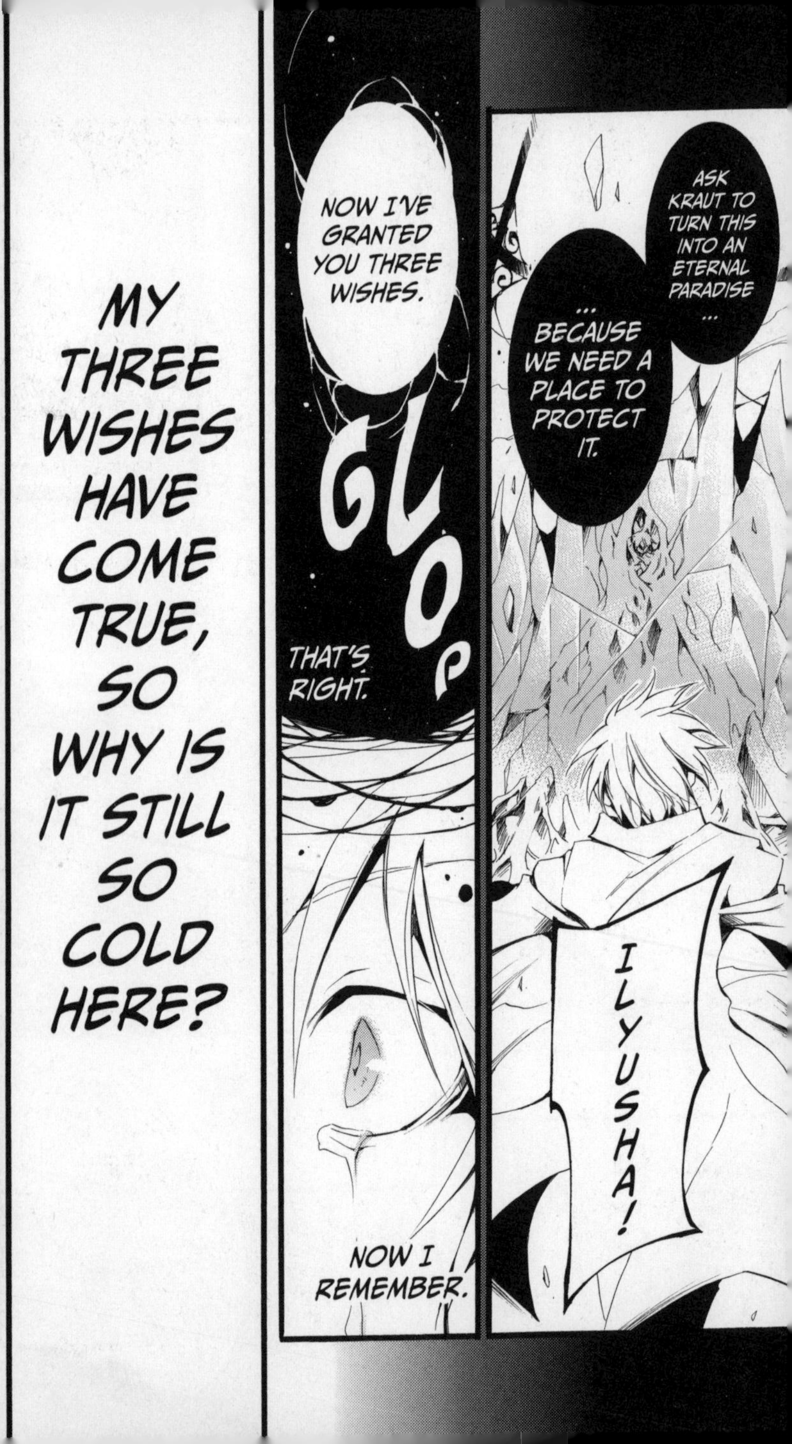
ASK KRAUT TO TURN THIS INTO AN ETERNAL PARADISE...
...BECAUSE WE NEED A PLACE TO PROTECT IT.
ILYUSHA!
NOW I'VE GRANTED YOU THREE WISHES.
GLOOP
THAT'S RIGHT.
NOW I REMEMBER.
MY THREE WISHES HAVE COME TRUE, SO WHY IS IT STILL SO COLD HERE?

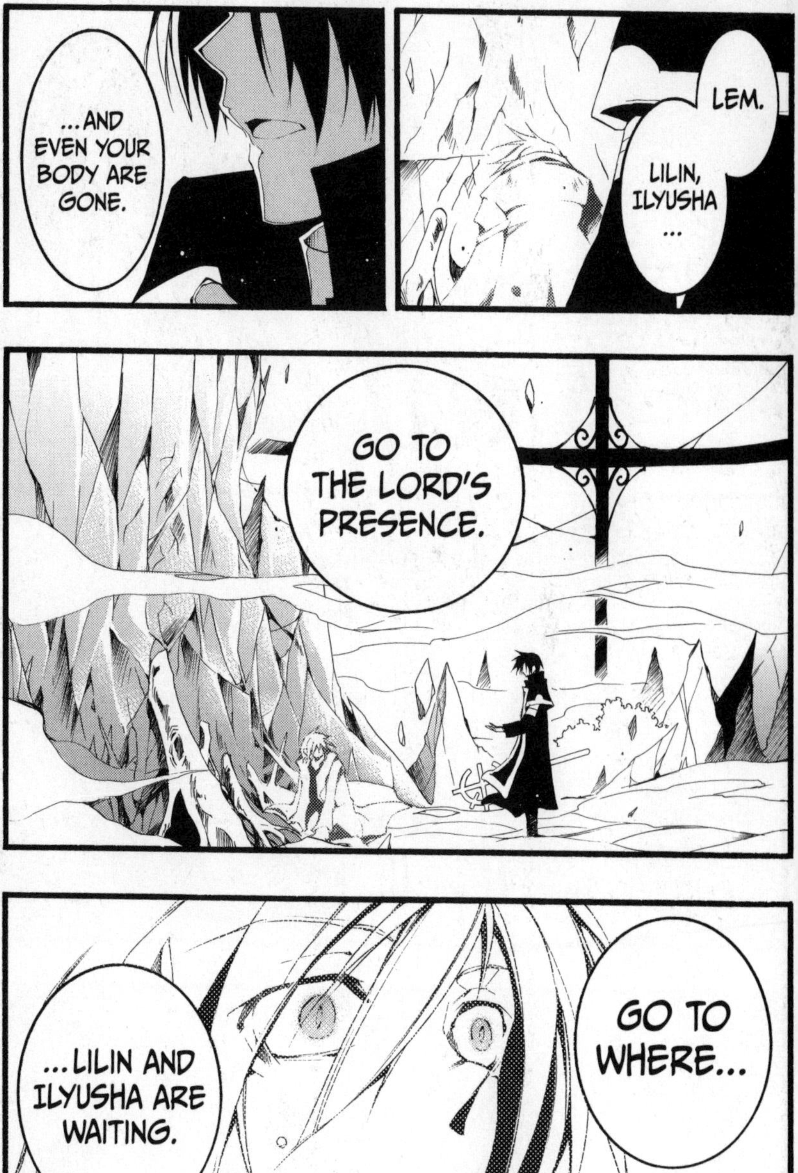
LEM.
LILIN, ILYUSHA ...
...AND EVEN YOUR BODY ARE GONE.
GO TO THE LORD'S PRESENCE.
GO TO WHERE...
...LILIN AND ILYUSHA ARE WAITING.

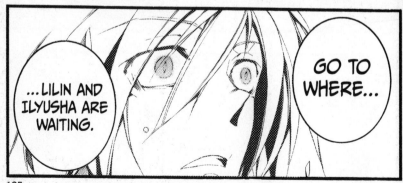

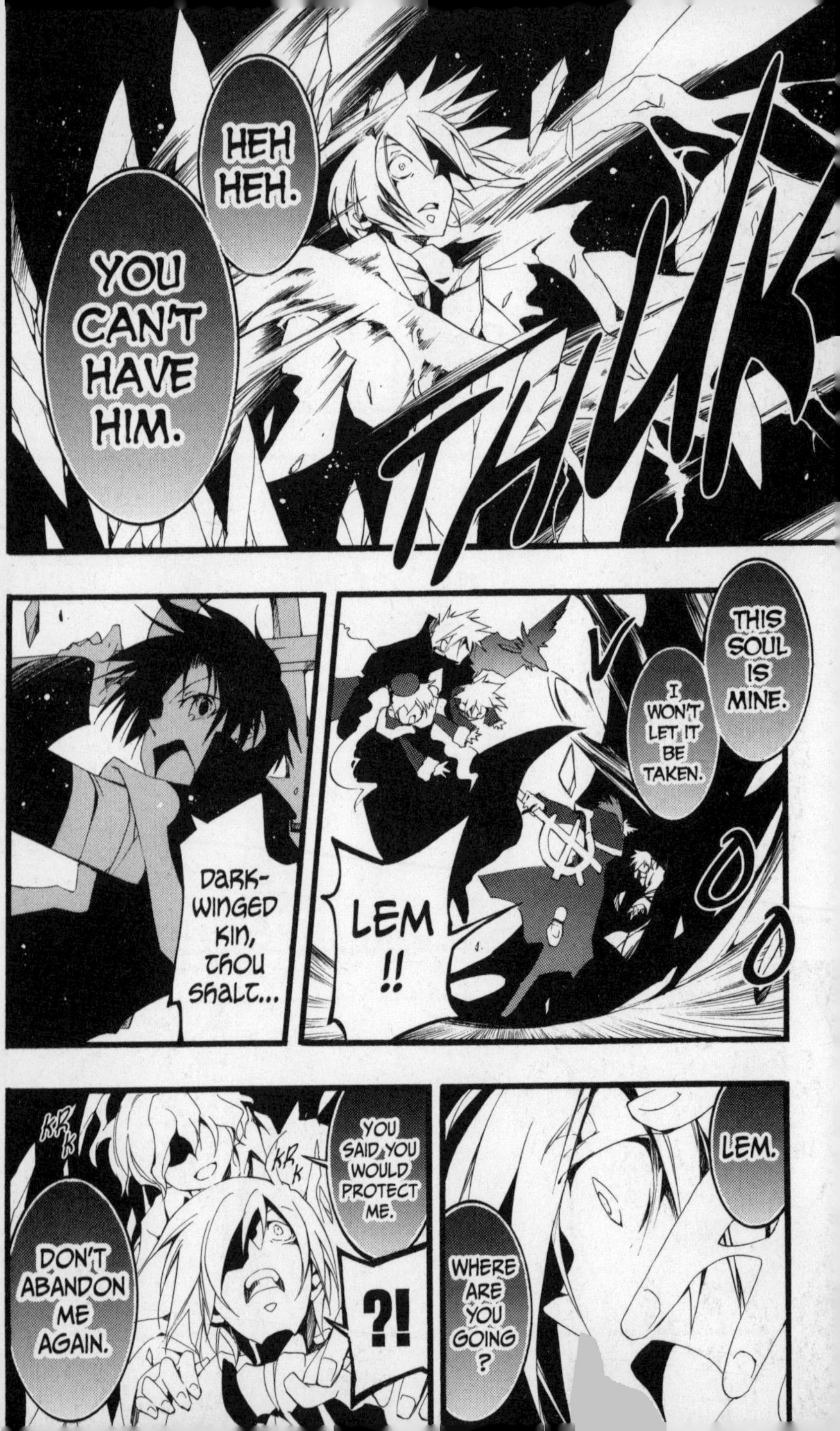
HEH HEH.
YOU CAN'T HAVE HIM.
THUK
THIS SOUL IS MINE.
I WON'T LET IT BE TAKEN.
LEM !!
DARK-WINGED KIN, THOU SHALT...
LEM.
WHERE ARE YOU GOING?
YOU SAID YOU WOULD PROTECT ME.
KRK
?!
DON'T ABANDON ME AGAIN.
KRK

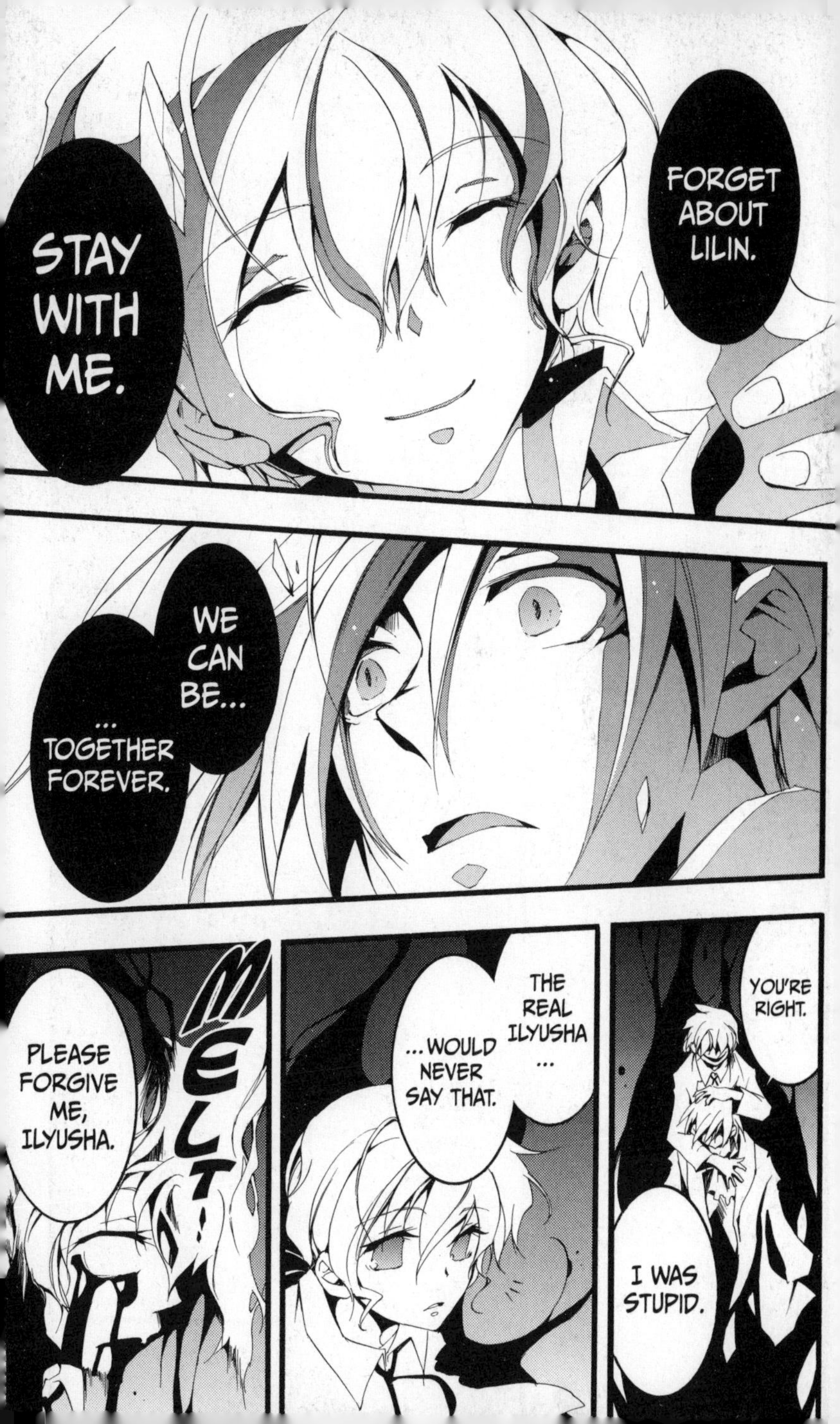
FORGET ABOUT LILIN.
STAY WITH ME.
WE CAN BE...
...TOGETHER FOREVER.
YOU'RE RIGHT.
I WAS STUPID.
THE REAL ILYUSHA ...
...WOULD NEVER SAY THAT.
PLEASE FORGIVE ME, ILYUSHA.
MELT!

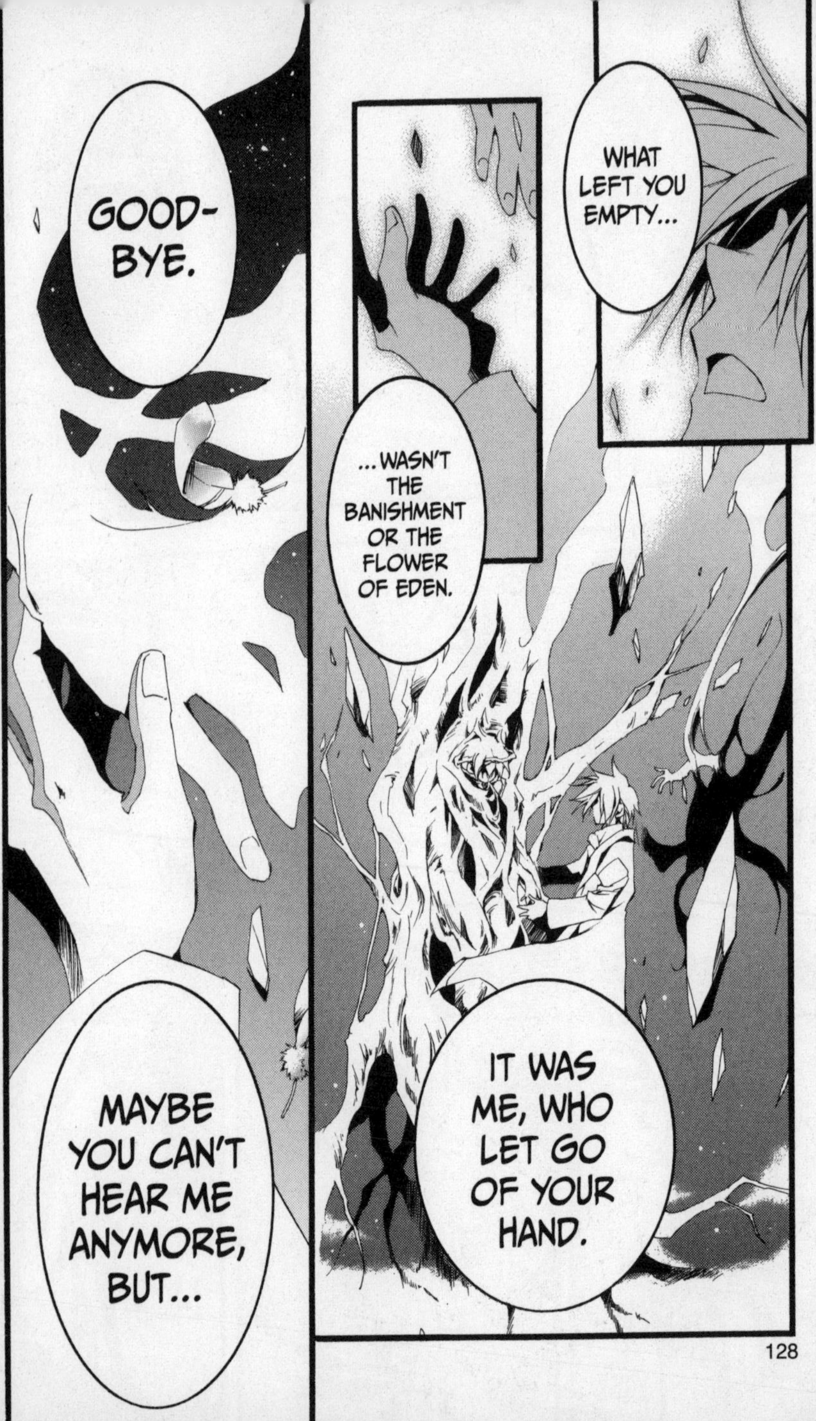
WHAT LEFT YOU EMPTY...
...WASN'T THE BANISHMENT OR THE FLOWER OF EDEN.
IT WAS ME, WHO LET GO OF YOUR HAND.
GOOD-BYE.
MAYBE YOU CAN'T HEAR ME ANYMORE, BUT...

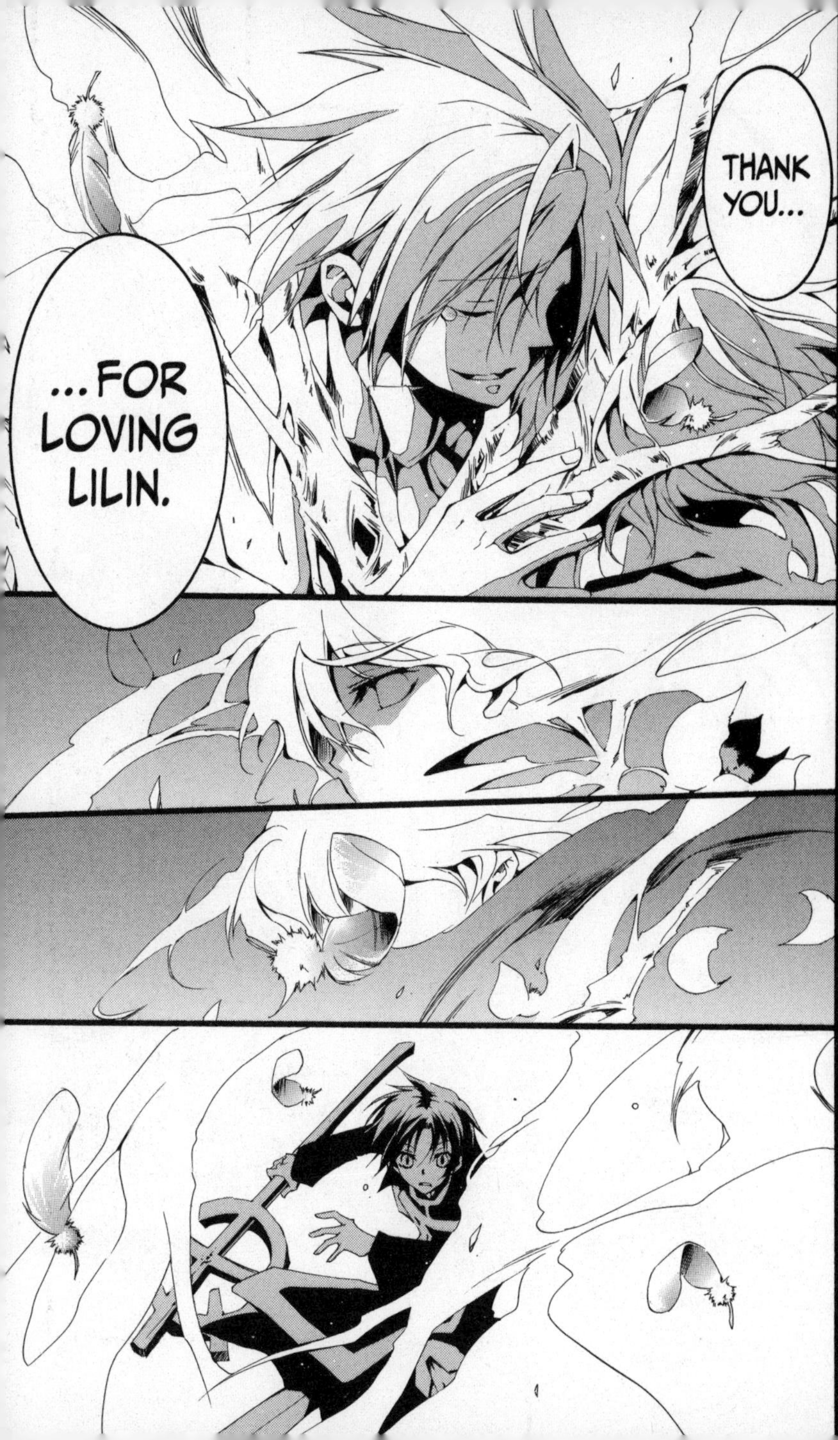
THANK YOU...
...FOR LOVING LILIN.

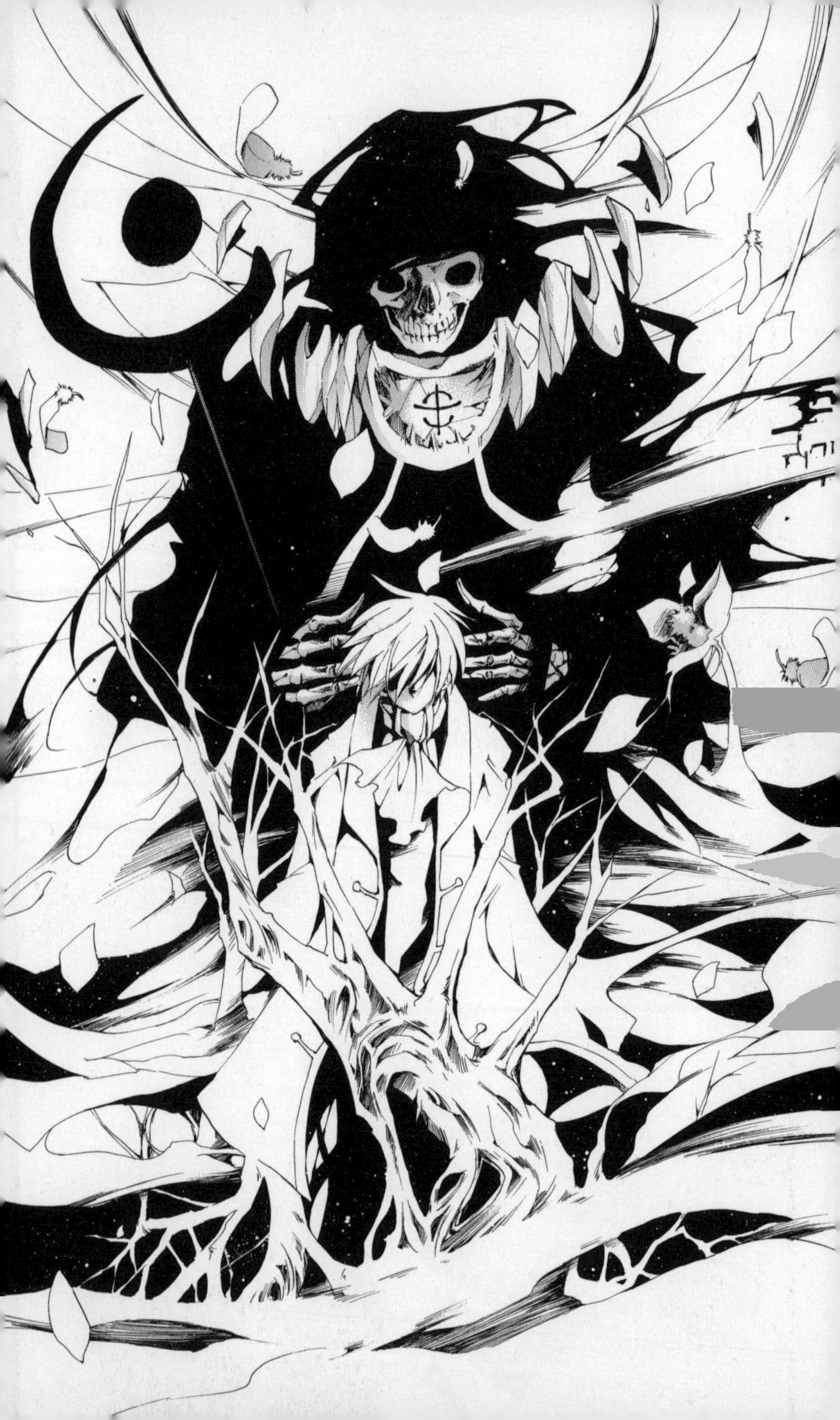

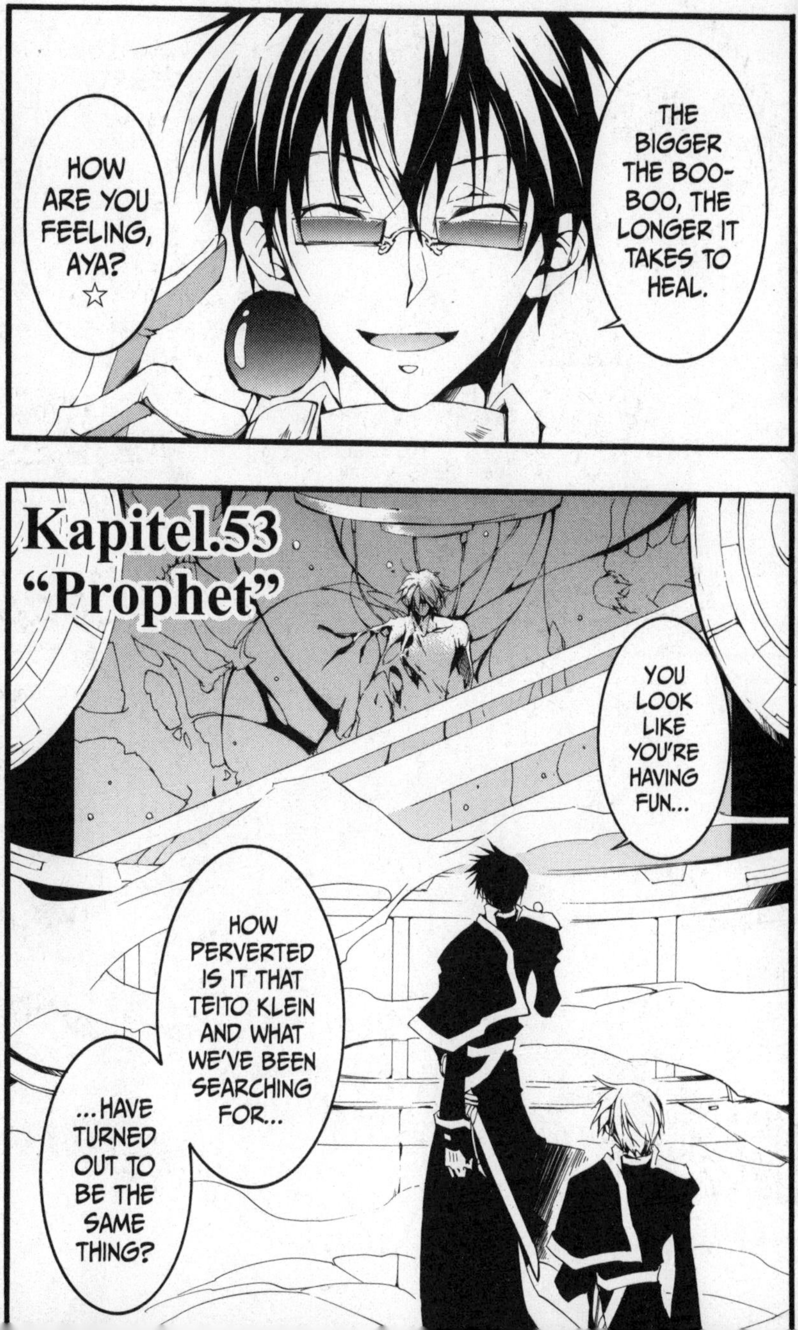
THE BIGGER THE BOO-BOO, THE LONGER IT TAKES TO HEAL.
HOW ARE YOU FEELING, AYA? ☆
Kapitel.53 “Prophet”
YOU LOOK LIKE YOU'RE HAVING FUN...
HOW PERVERTED IS IT THAT TEITO KLEIN AND WHAT WE'VE BEEN SEARCHING FOR...
...HAVE TURNED OUT TO BE THE SAME THING?

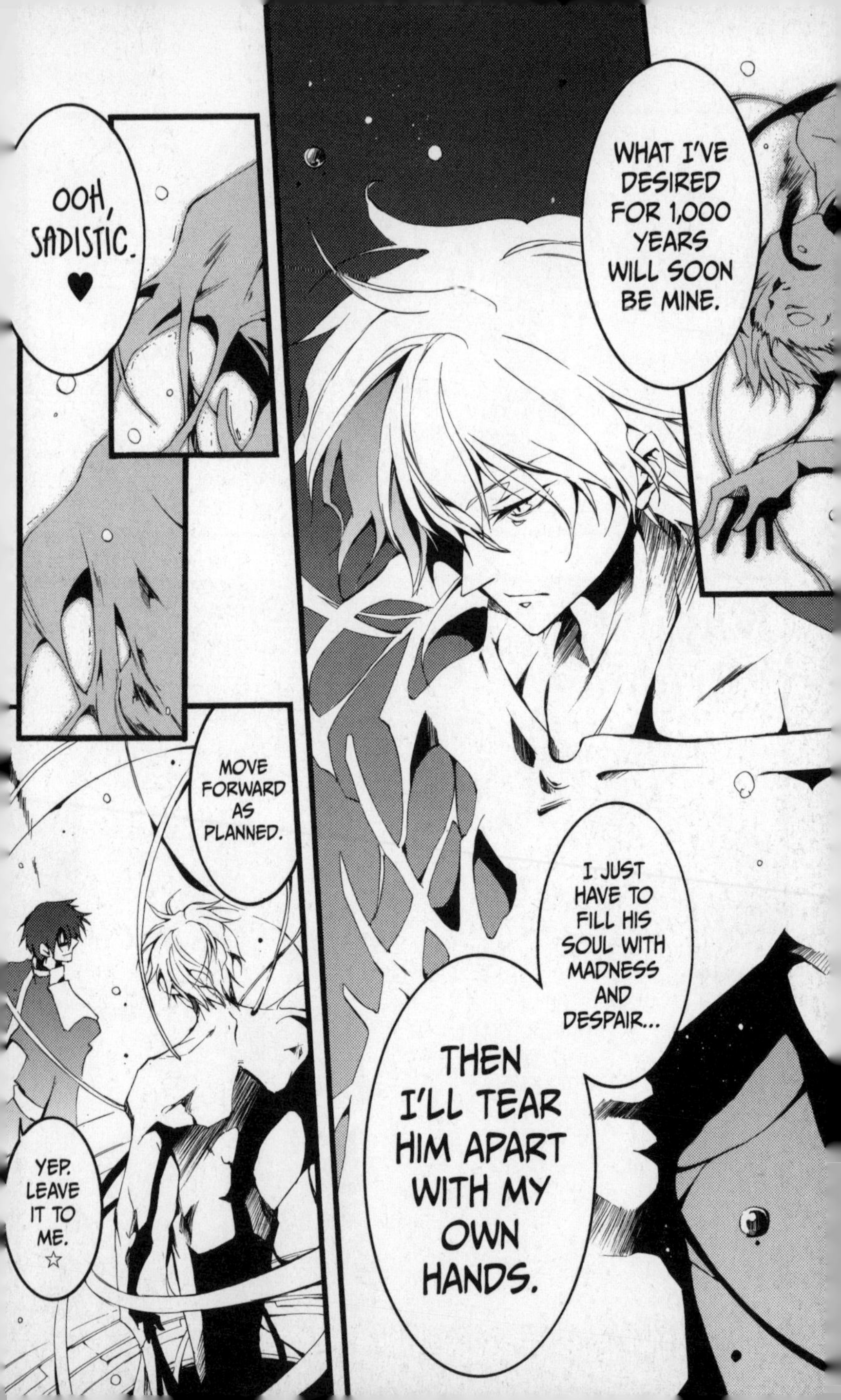
WHAT I'VE DESIRED FOR 1,000 YEARS WILL SOON BE MINE.
I JUST HAVE TO FILL HIS SOUL WITH MADNESS AND DESPAIR...
THEN I'LL TEAR HIM APART WITH MY OWN HANDS.
OOH, SADISTIC. ♥
MOVE FORWARD AS PLANNED.
YEP. LEAVE IT TO ME. ☆

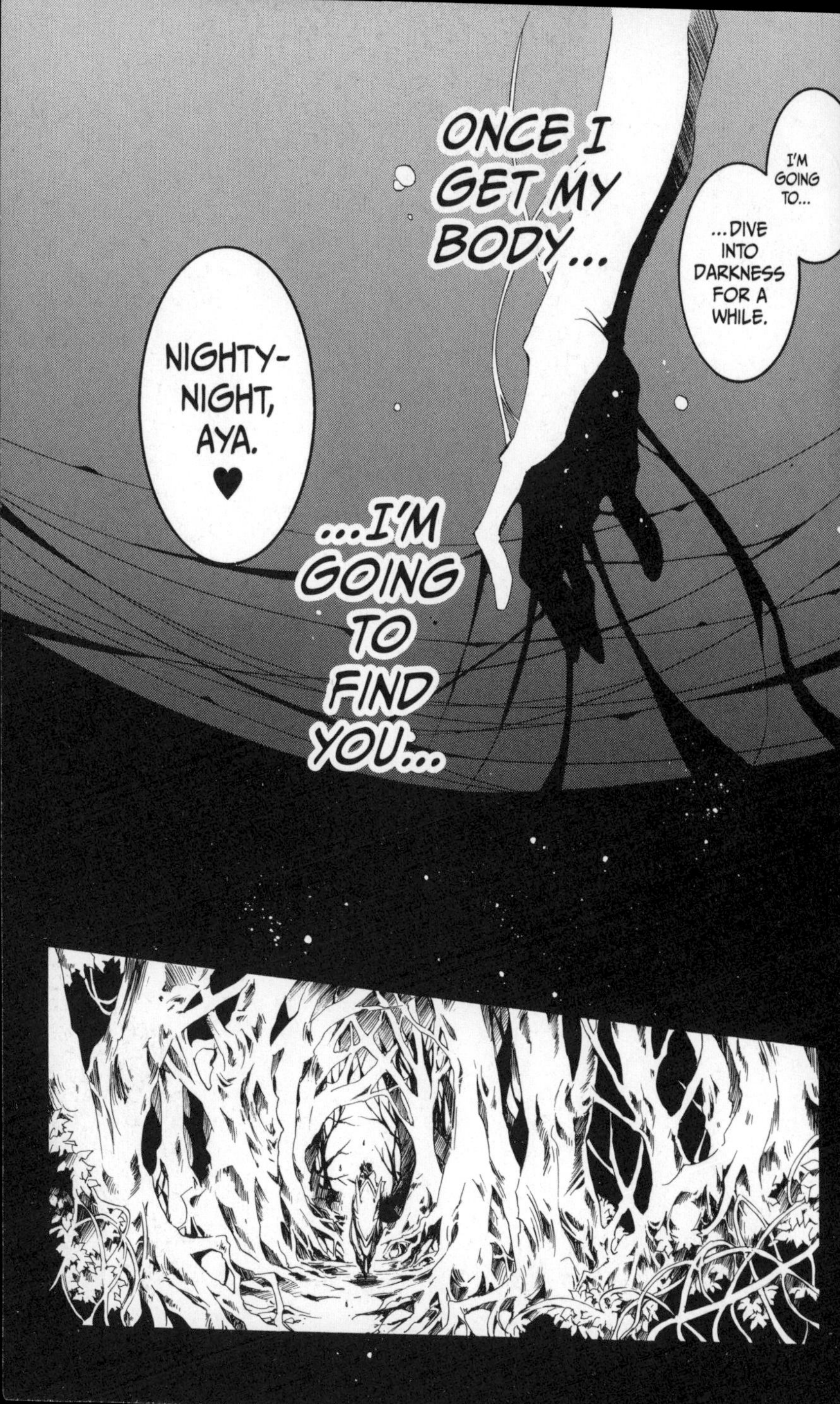
I'M GOING TO...
...DIVE INTO DARKNESS FOR A WHILE.
ONCE I GET MY BODY...
NIGHTY-NIGHT, AYA. ♥
...I'M GOING TO FIND YOU...

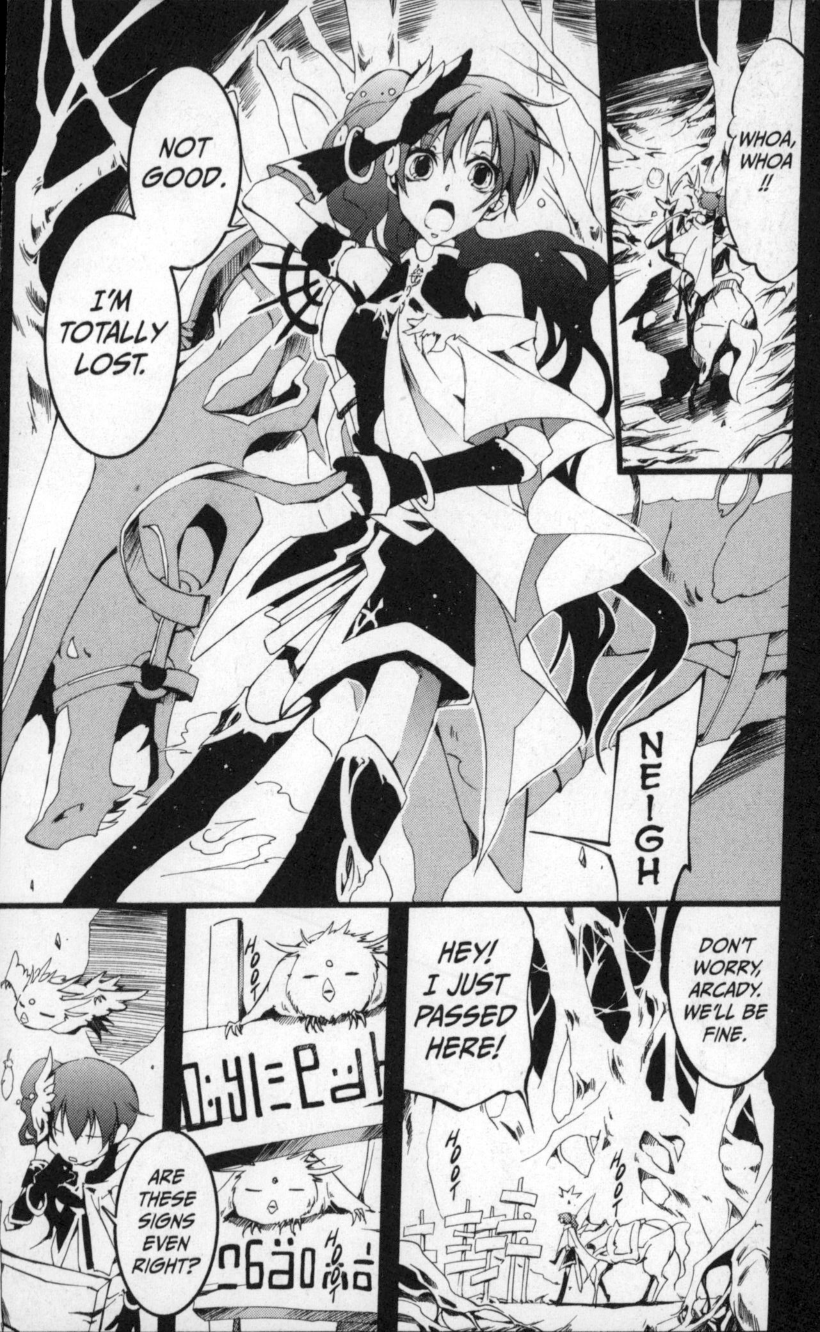
WHOA, WHOA!!
NOT GOOD.
I'M TOTALLY LOST.
NEIGH
DON'T WORRY, ARCADY. WE'LL BE FINE.
HEY! I JUST PASSED HERE!
HOOT
HOOT
HOOT
ARE THESE SIGNS EVEN RIGHT?
HOOT

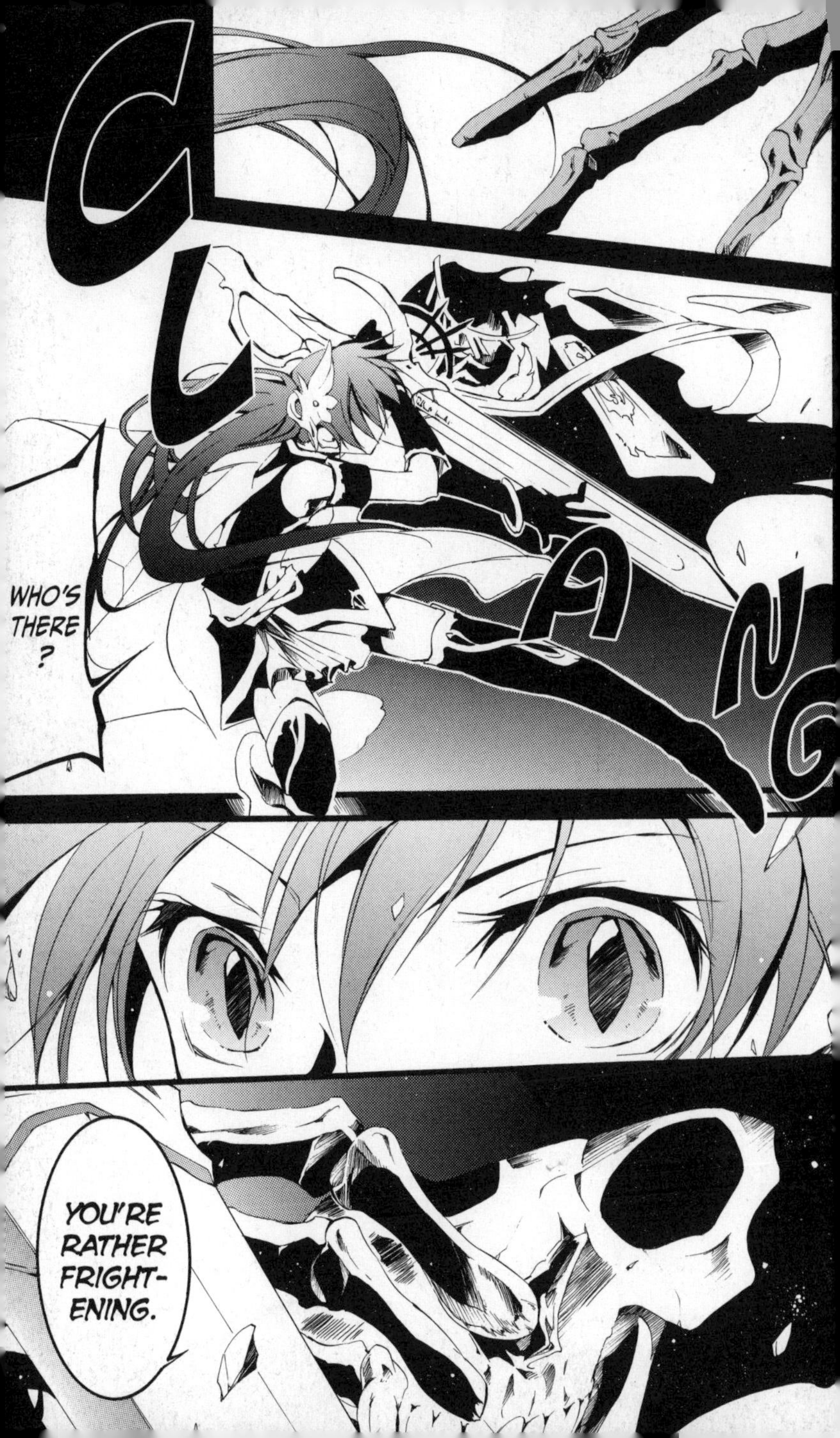
CLANG
WHO'S THERE?
YOU'RE RATHER FRIGHT-ENING.

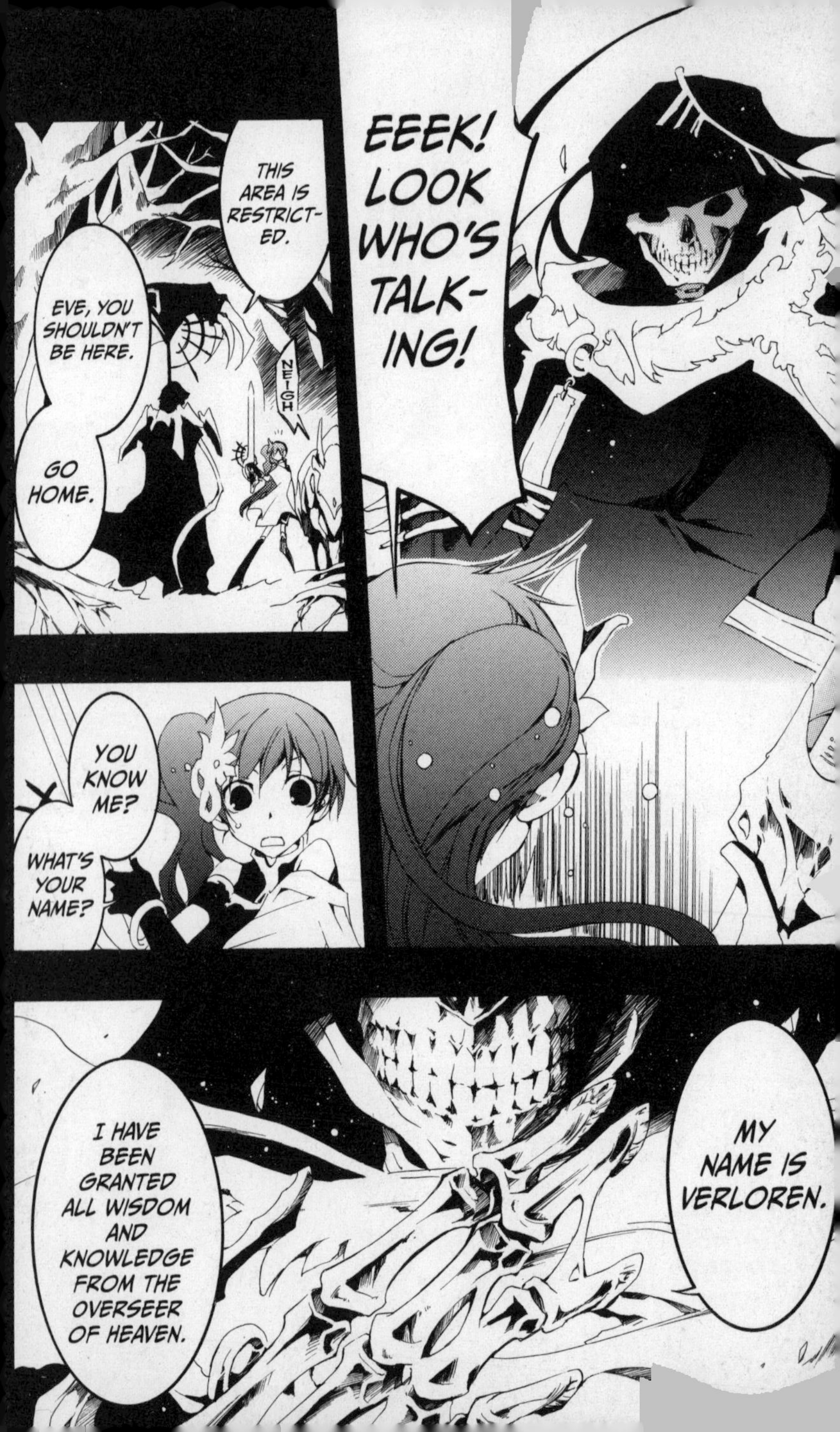
EEEK! LOOK WHO'S TALK-ING!
THIS AREA IS RESTRICT-ED.
EVE, YOU SHOULDN'T BE HERE.
NEIGH
GO HOME.
YOU KNOW ME?
WHAT'S YOUR NAME?
MY NAME IS VERLOREN.
I HAVE BEEN GRANTED ALL WISDOM AND KNOWLEDGE FROM THE OVERSEER OF HEAVEN.

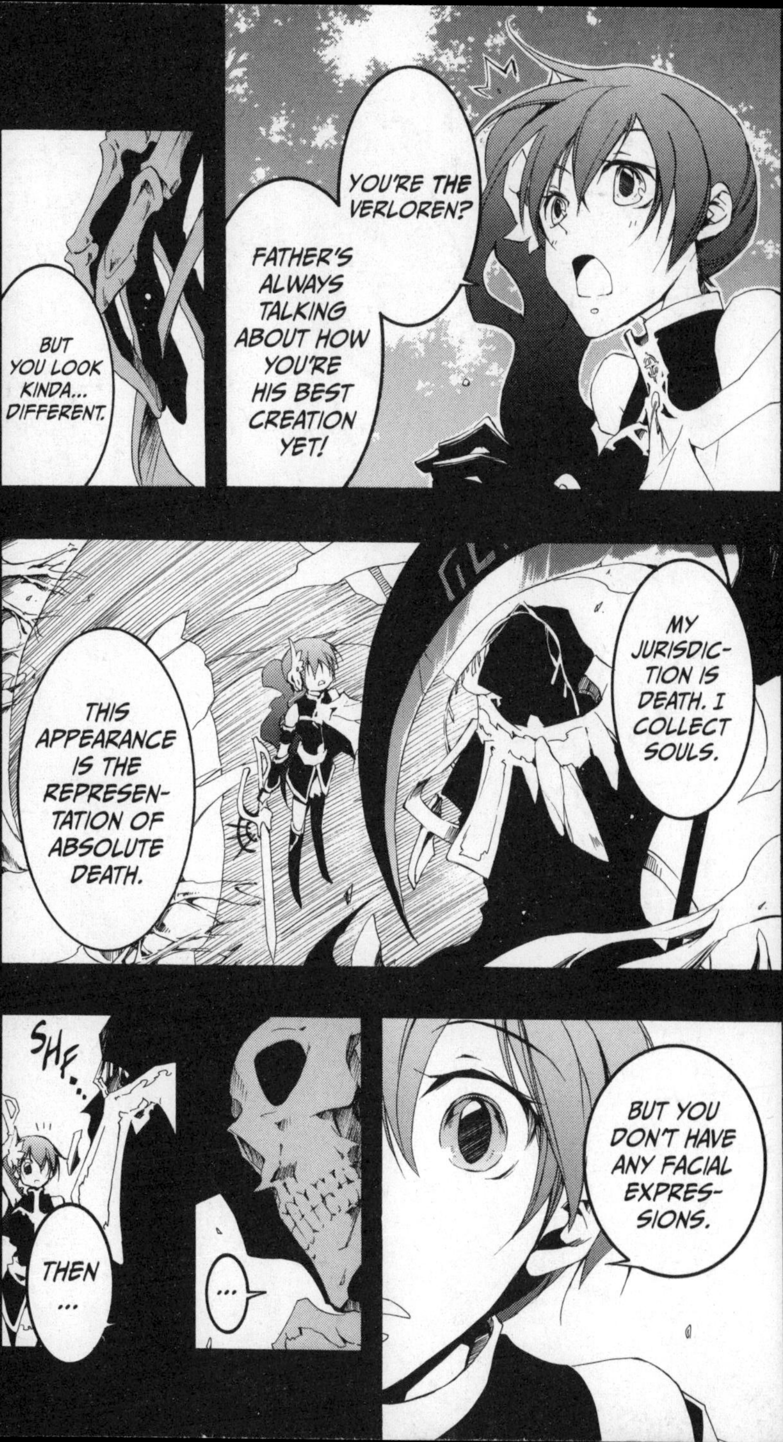
YOU'RE THE VERLOREN?
FATHER'S ALWAYS TALKING ABOUT HOW YOU'RE HIS BEST CREATION YET!
BUT YOU LOOK KINDA... DIFFERENT.
MY JURISDICTION IS DEATH. I COLLECT SOULS.
THIS APPEARANCE IS THE REPRESENTATION OF ABSOLUTE DEATH.
BUT YOU DON'T HAVE ANY FACIAL EXPRESSIONS.
...
SHF...
THEN...

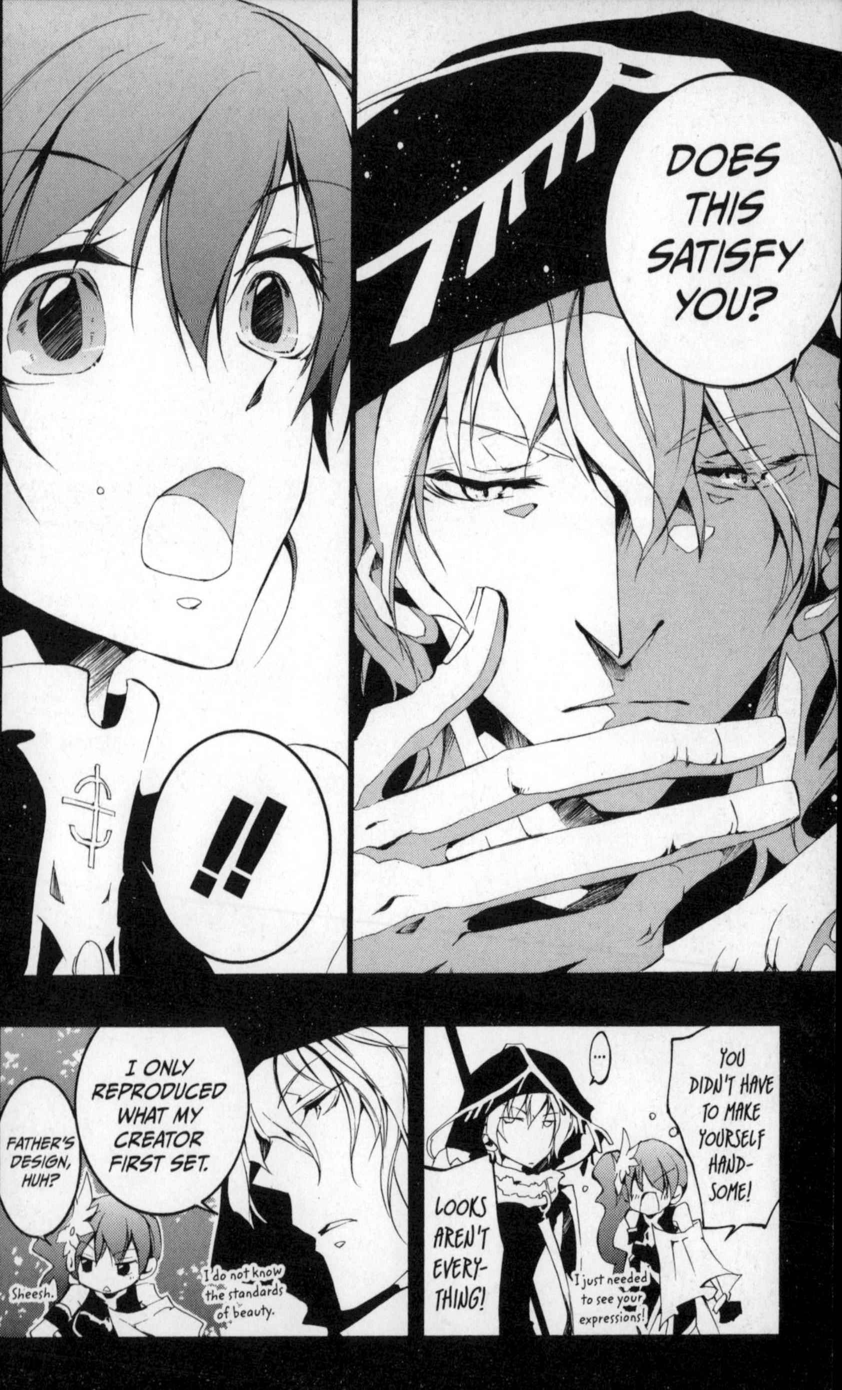
DOES THIS SATISFY YOU?
!!
YOU DIDN'T HAVE TO MAKE YOURSELF HAND-SOME!
...
LOOKS AREN'T EVERY-THING!
I just needed to see your expressions!
I ONLY REPRODUCED WHAT MY CREATOR FIRST SET.
FATHER'S DESIGN, HUH?
I do not know the standards of beauty.
Sheesh.

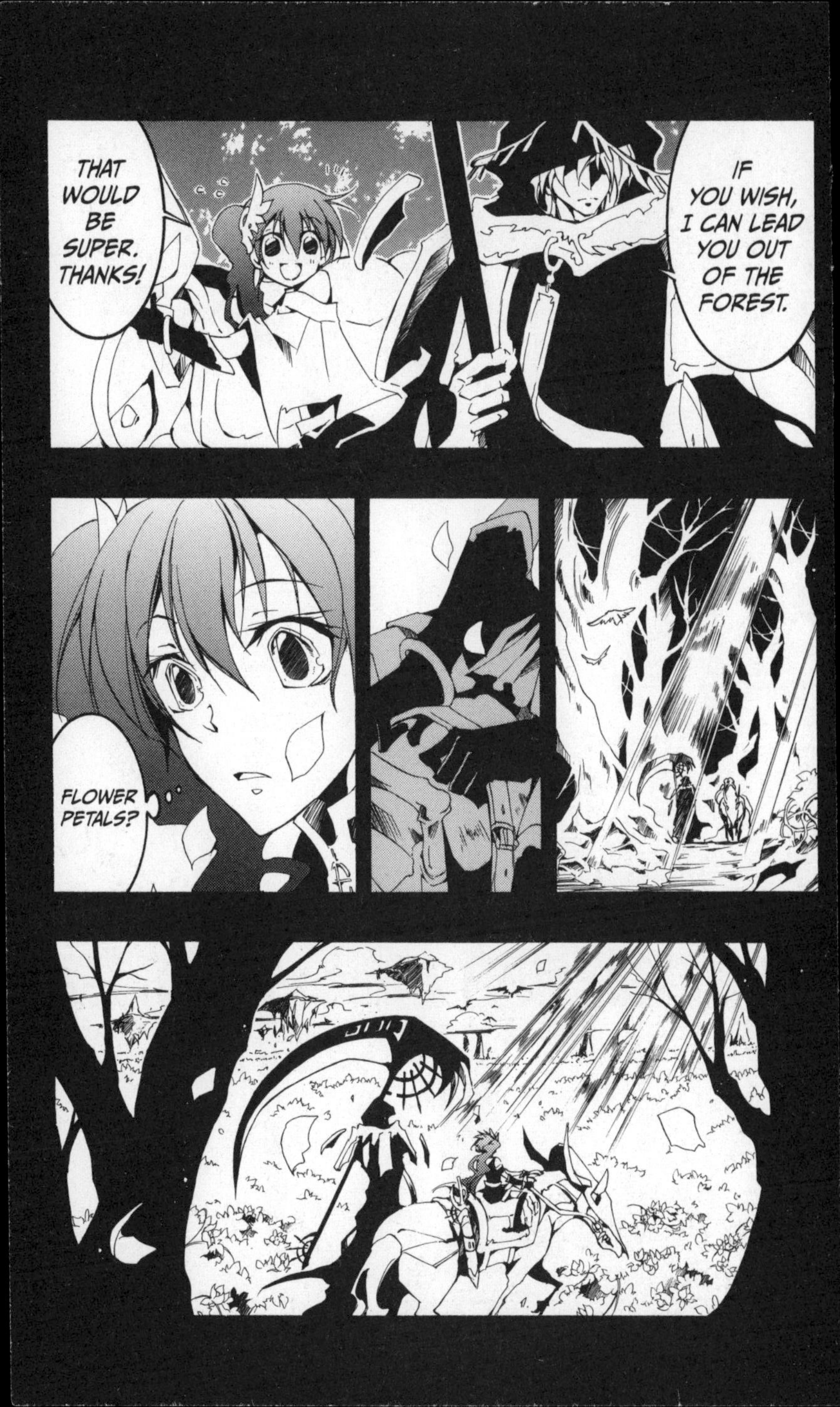
IF YOU WISH, I CAN LEAD YOU OUT OF THE FOREST.
THAT WOULD BE SUPER. THANKS!
FLOWER PETALS?

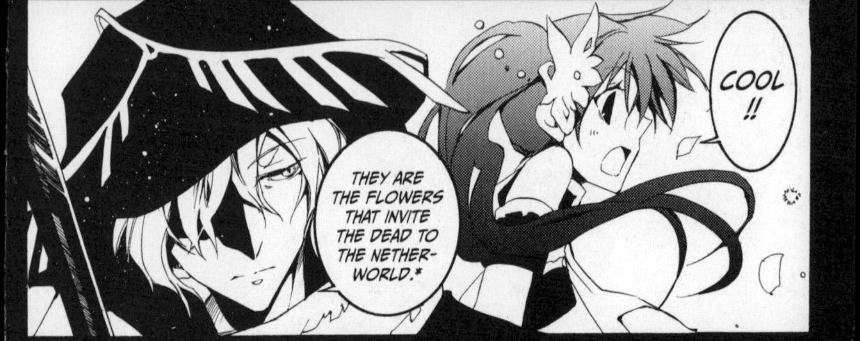
COOL !!
THEY ARE THE FLOWERS THAT INVITE THE DEAD TO THE NETHER-WORLD.*

*A place where the dead await the judgment of the Overseer of Heaven.

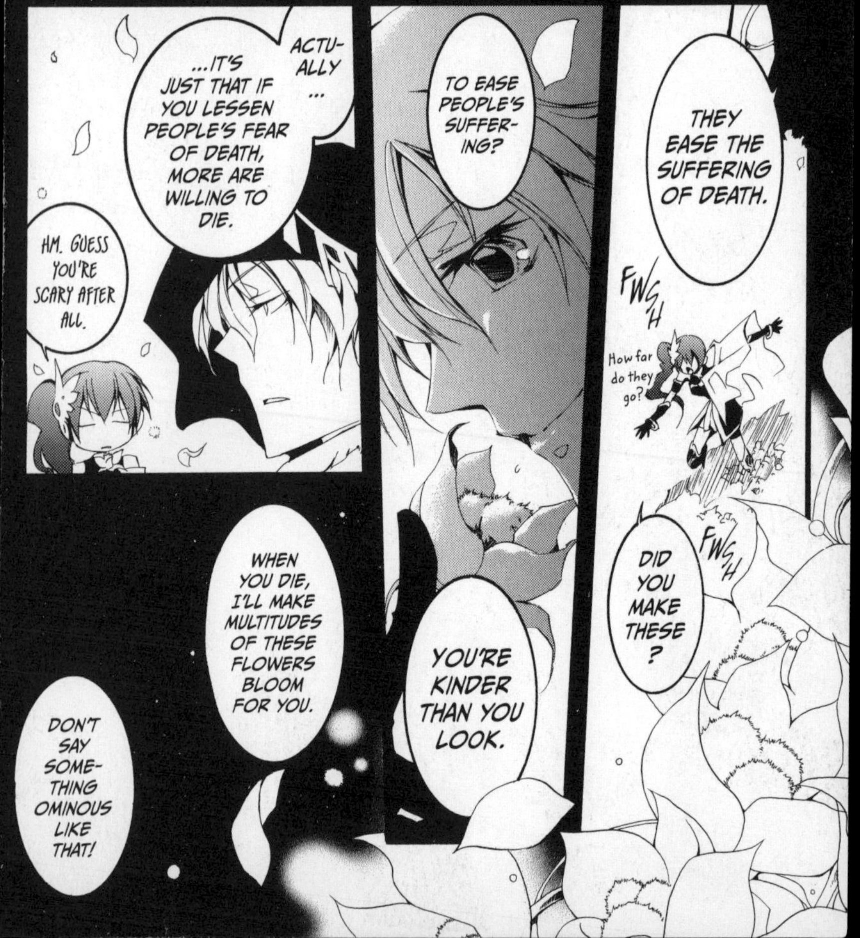
THEY EASE THE SUFFERING OF DEATH.
FWSH
How far do they go?
FWSH
DID YOU MAKE THESE ?
TO EASE PEOPLE'S SUFFER-ING?
YOU'RE KINDER THAN YOU LOOK.
ACTU-ALLY ...
...IT'S JUST THAT IF YOU LESSEN PEOPLE'S FEAR OF DEATH, MORE ARE WILLING TO DIE.
HM. GUESS YOU'RE SCARY AFTER ALL.
WHEN YOU DIE, I'LL MAKE MULTITUDES OF THESE FLOWERS BLOOM FOR YOU.
DON'T SAY SOME-THING OMINOUS LIKE THAT!

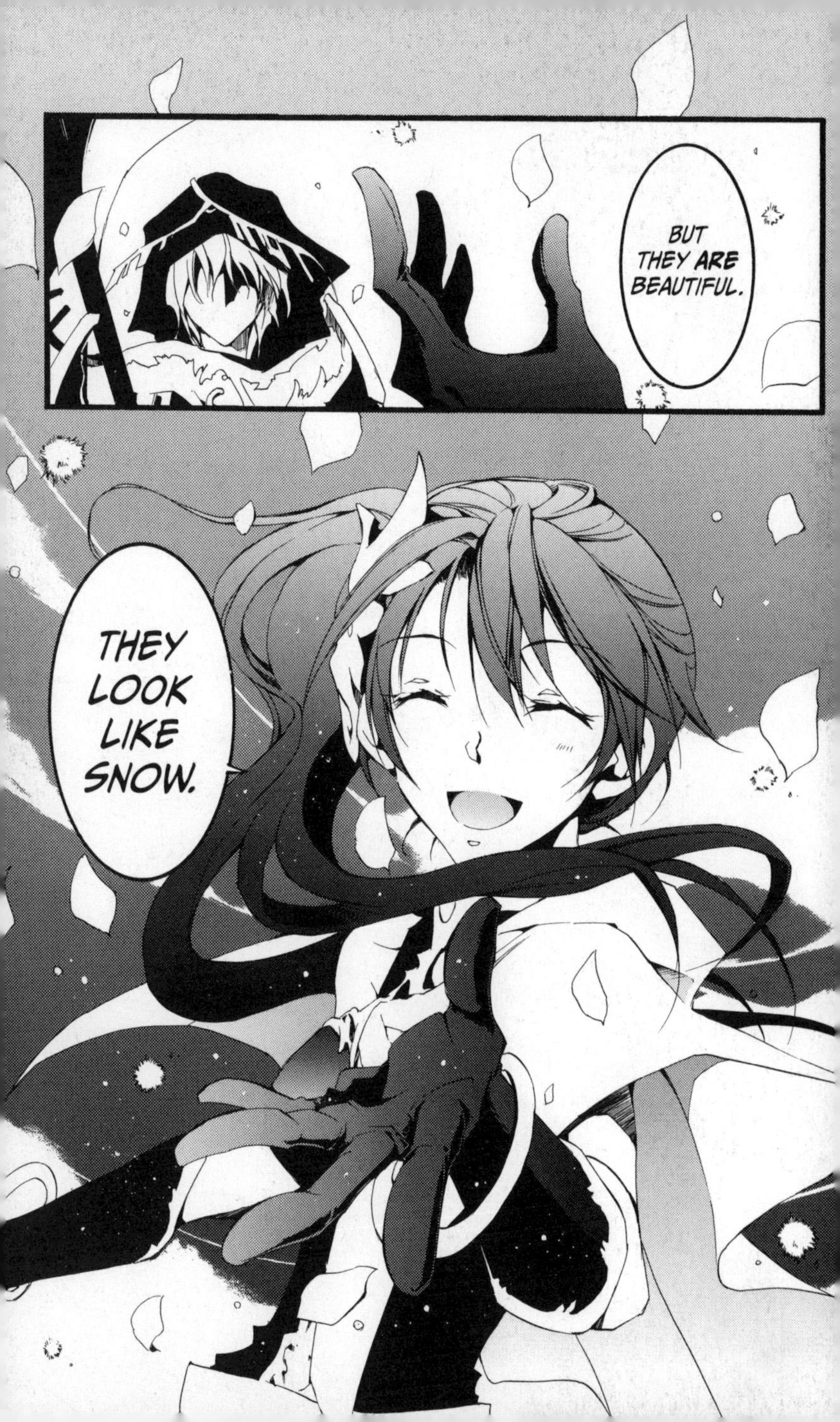
BUT THEY ARE BEAUTIFUL.
THEY LOOK LIKE SNOW.

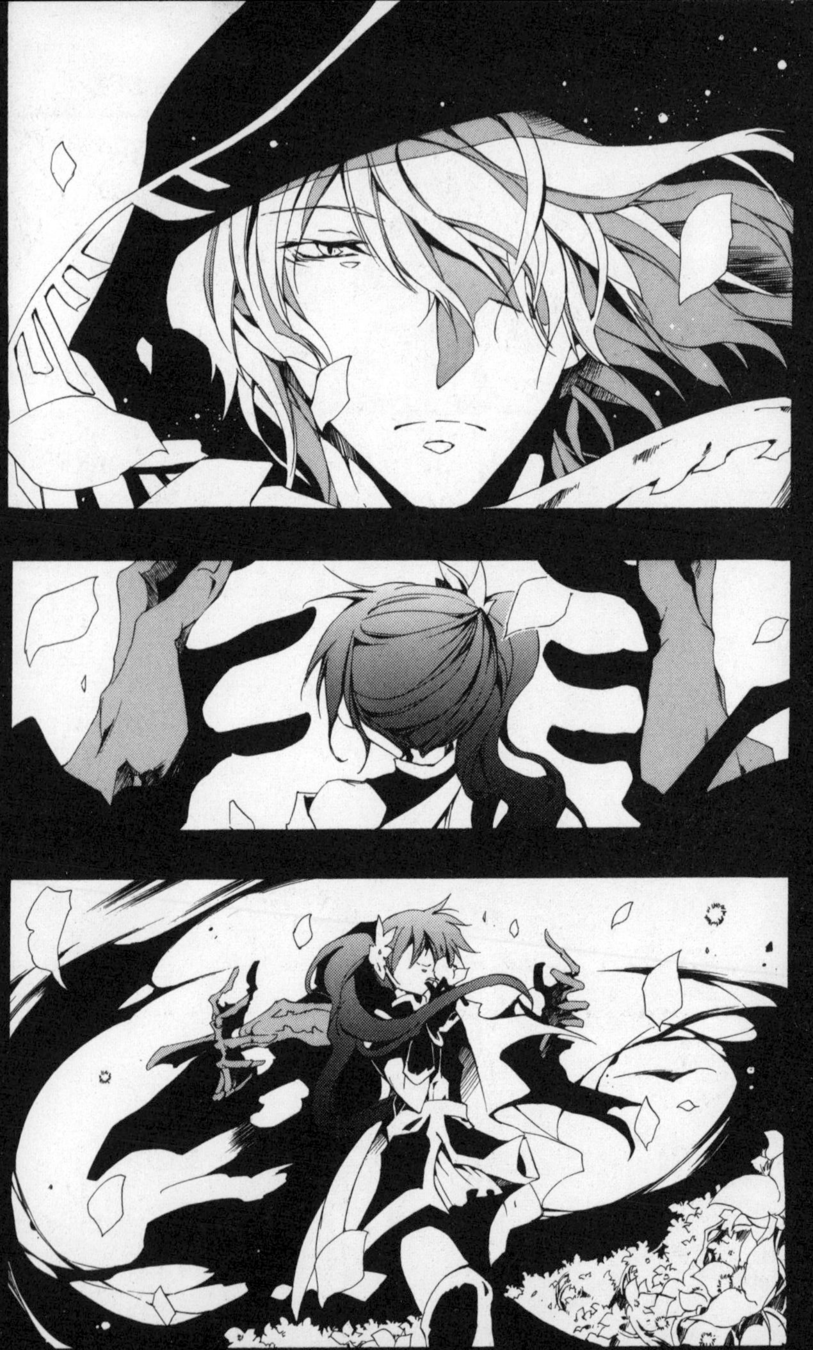

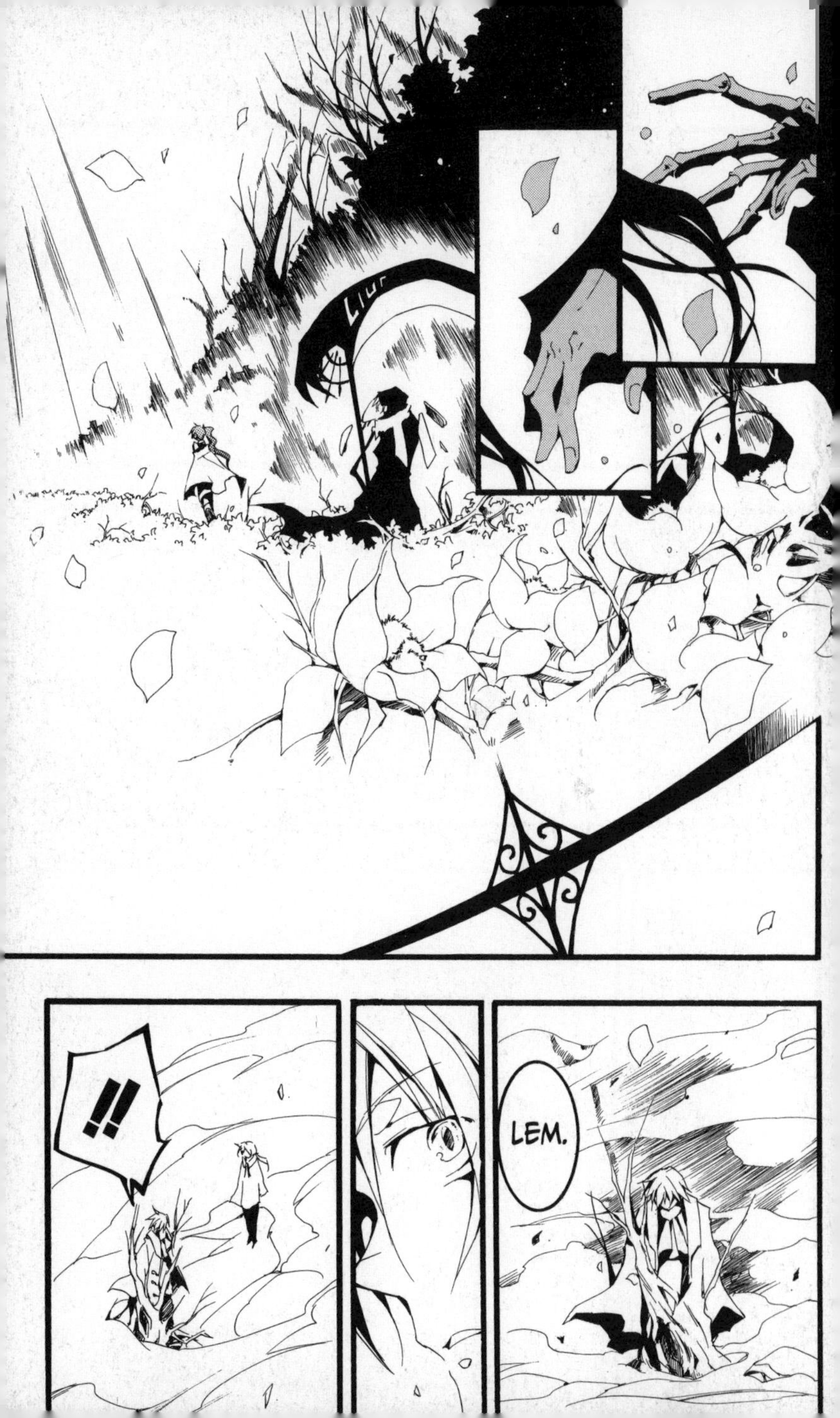
LEM.
!!

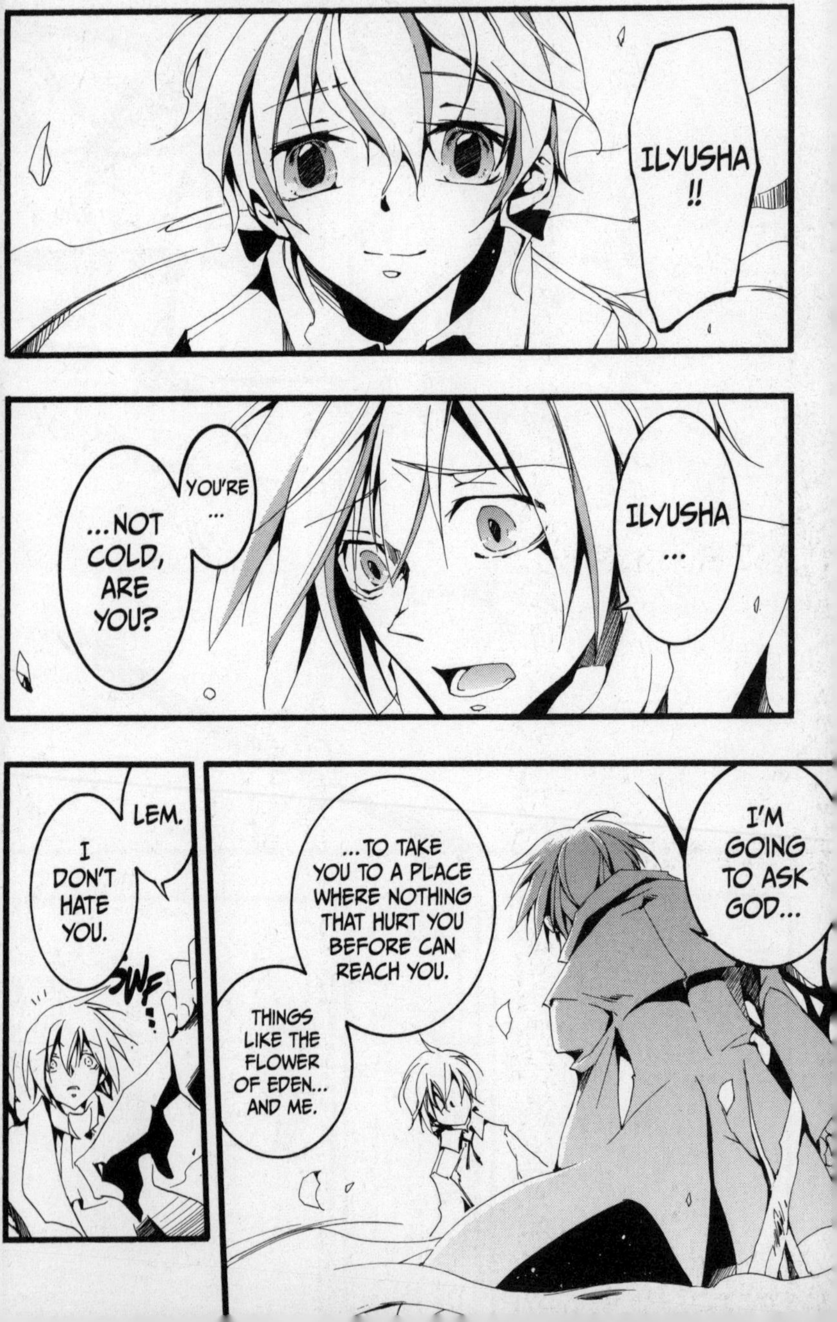
ILYUSHA!!
ILYUSHA...
YOU'RE...
...NOT COLD, ARE YOU?
I'M GOING TO ASK GOD...
...TO TAKE YOU TO A PLACE WHERE NOTHING THAT HURT YOU BEFORE CAN REACH YOU.
THINGS LIKE THE FLOWER OF EDEN... AND ME.
LEM.
I DON'T HATE YOU.
SWF

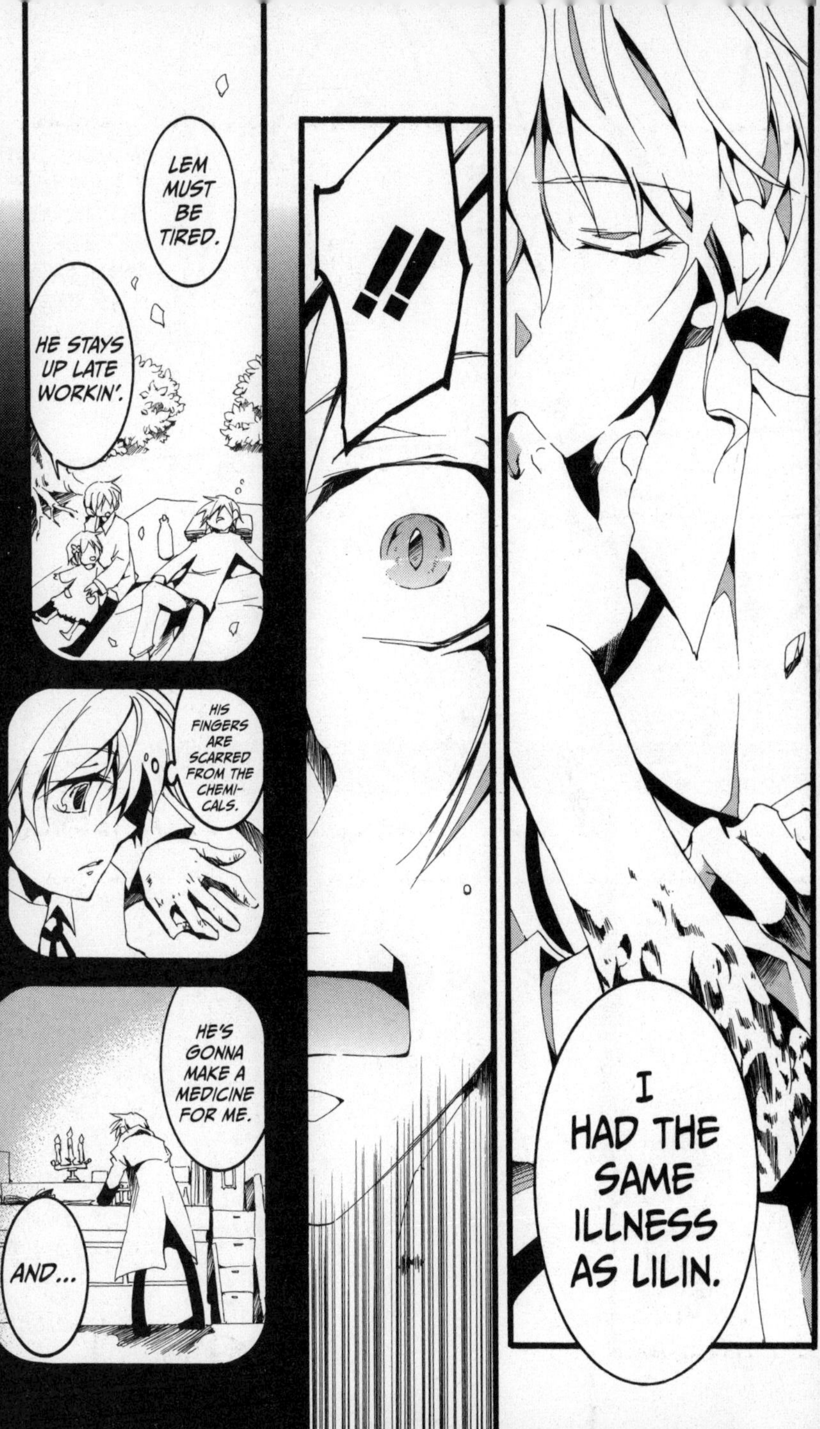
I HAD THE SAME ILLNESS AS LILIN.
!!
LEM MUST BE TIRED.
HE STAYS UP LATE WORKIN'.
HIS FINGERS ARE SCARRED FROM THE CHEMI-CALS.
HE'S GONNA MAKE A MEDICINE FOR ME.
AND...

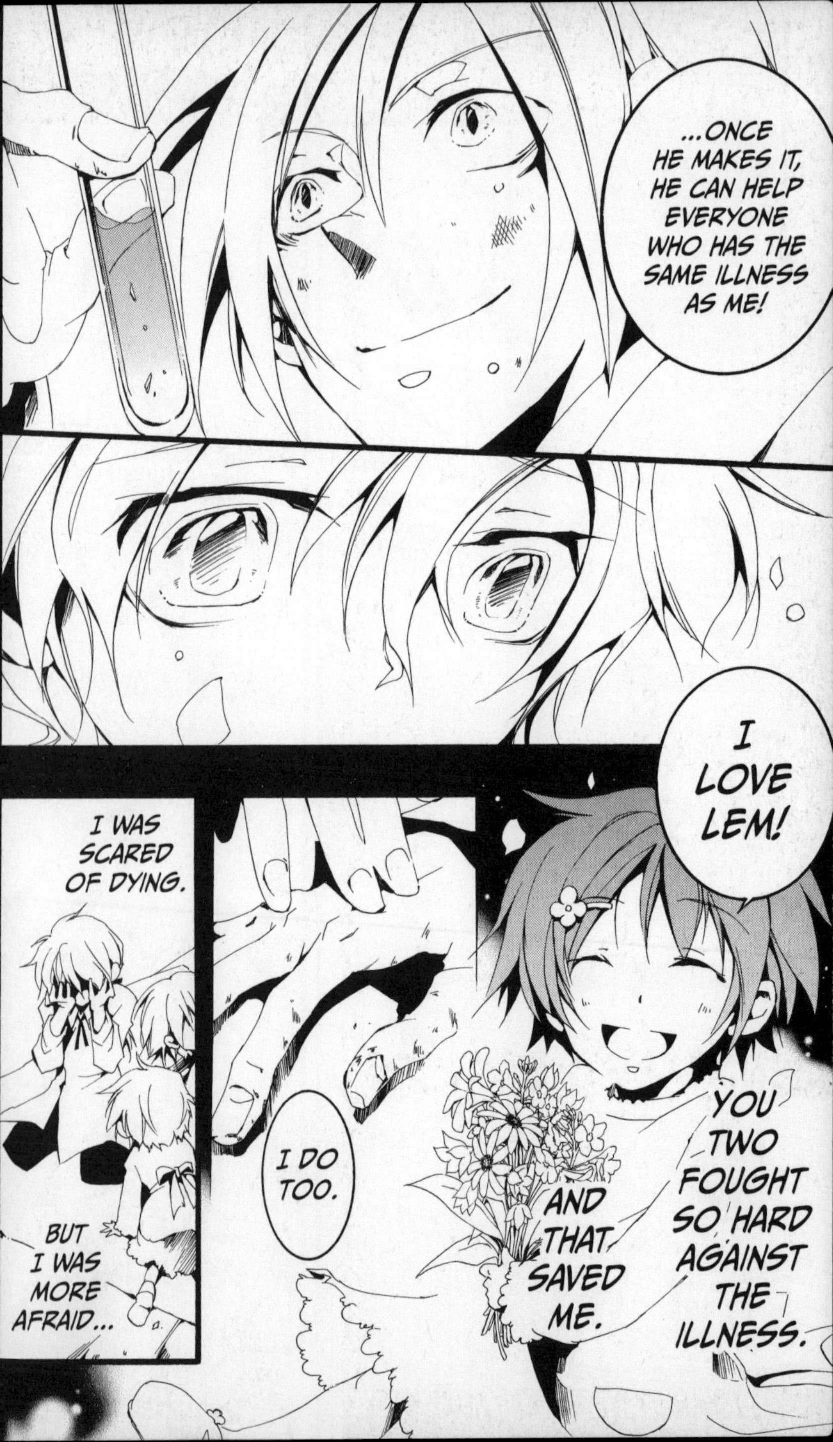
...ONCE HE MAKES IT, HE CAN HELP EVERYONE WHO HAS THE SAME ILLNESS AS ME!
I LOVE LEM!
YOU TWO FOUGHT SO HARD AGAINST THE ILLNESS.
AND THAT SAVED ME.
I DO TOO.
I WAS SCARED OF DYING.
BUT I WAS MORE AFRAID...

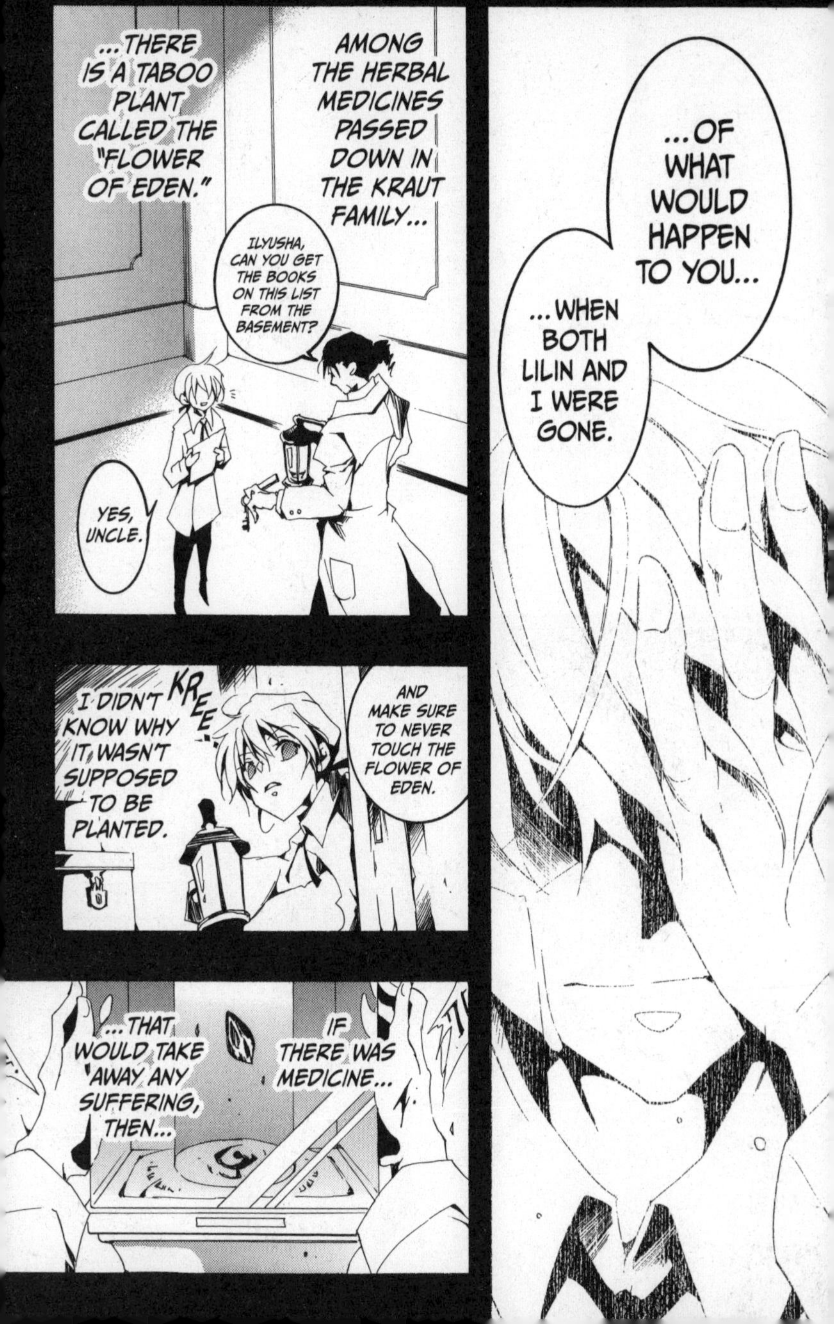
...OF WHAT WOULD HAPPEN TO YOU...
...WHEN BOTH LILIN AND I WERE GONE.
AMONG THE HERBAL MEDICINES PASSED DOWN IN THE KRAUT FAMILY...
...THERE IS A TABOO PLANT CALLED THE "FLOWER OF EDEN."
ILYUSHA, CAN YOU GET THE BOOKS ON THIS LIST FROM THE BASEMENT?
YES, UNCLE.
AND MAKE SURE TO NEVER TOUCH THE FLOWER OF EDEN.
KREE
I DIDN'T KNOW WHY IT WASN'T SUPPOSED TO BE PLANTED.
IF THERE WAS MEDICINE...
...THAT WOULD TAKE AWAY ANY SUFFERING, THEN...

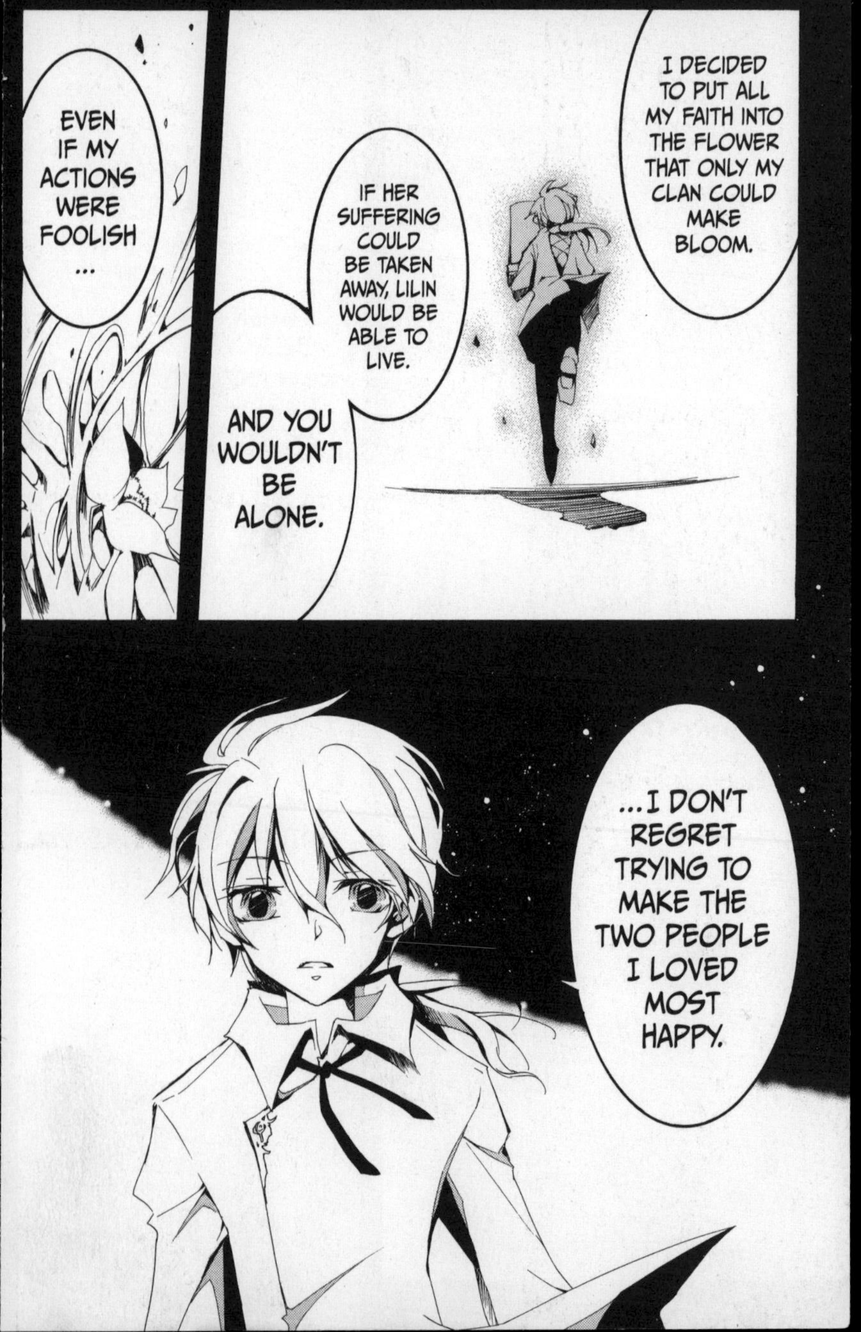
I DECIDED TO PUT ALL MY FAITH INTO THE FLOWER THAT ONLY MY CLAN COULD MAKE BLOOM.
IF HER SUFFERING COULD BE TAKEN AWAY, LILIN WOULD BE ABLE TO LIVE.
AND YOU WOULDN'T BE ALONE.
EVEN IF MY ACTIONS WERE FOOLISH ...
...I DON'T REGRET TRYING TO MAKE THE TWO PEOPLE I LOVED MOST HAPPY.

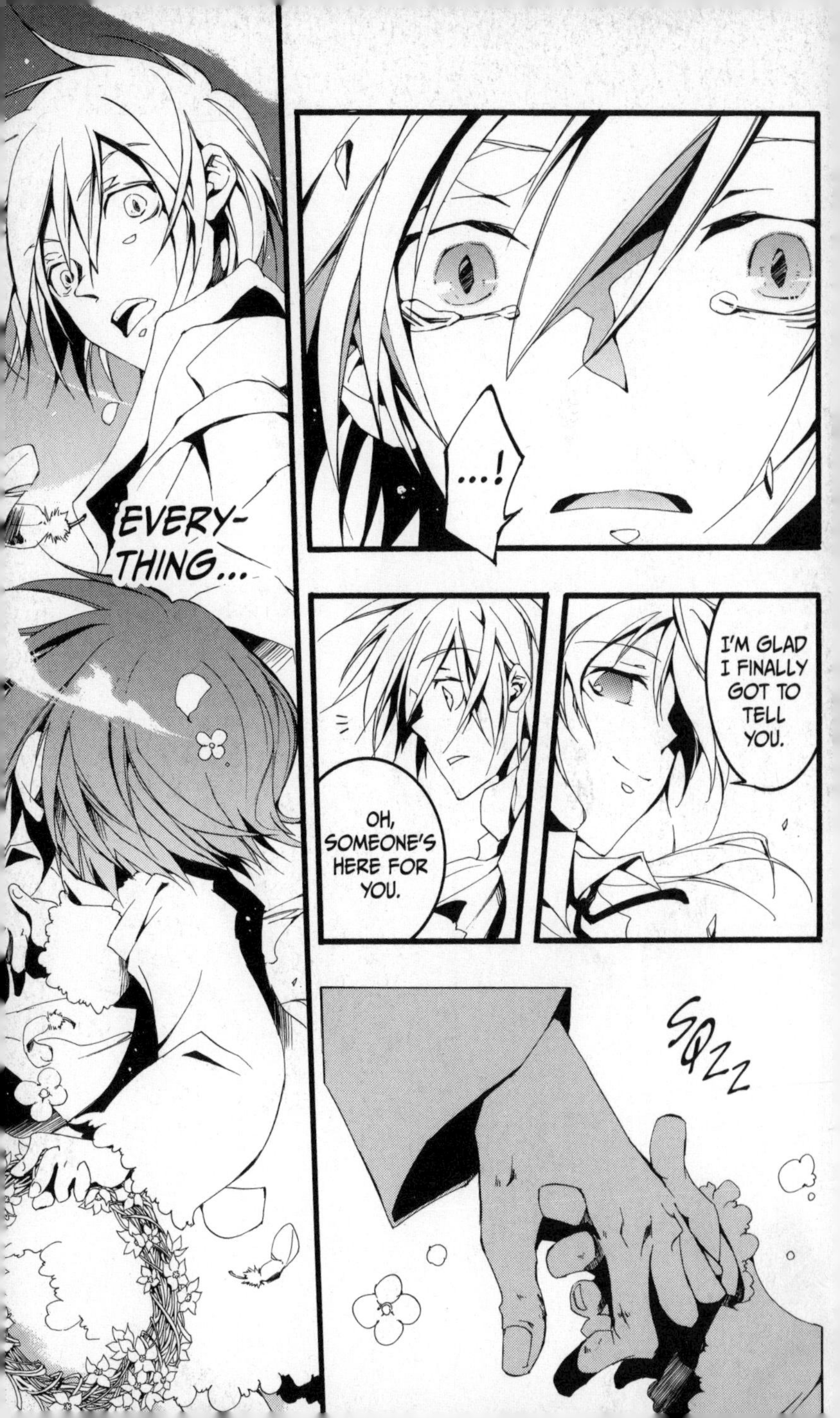
...!
I'M GLAD I FINALLY GOT TO TELL YOU.
OH, SOMEONE'S HERE FOR YOU.
SQZZ
EVERY-THING...

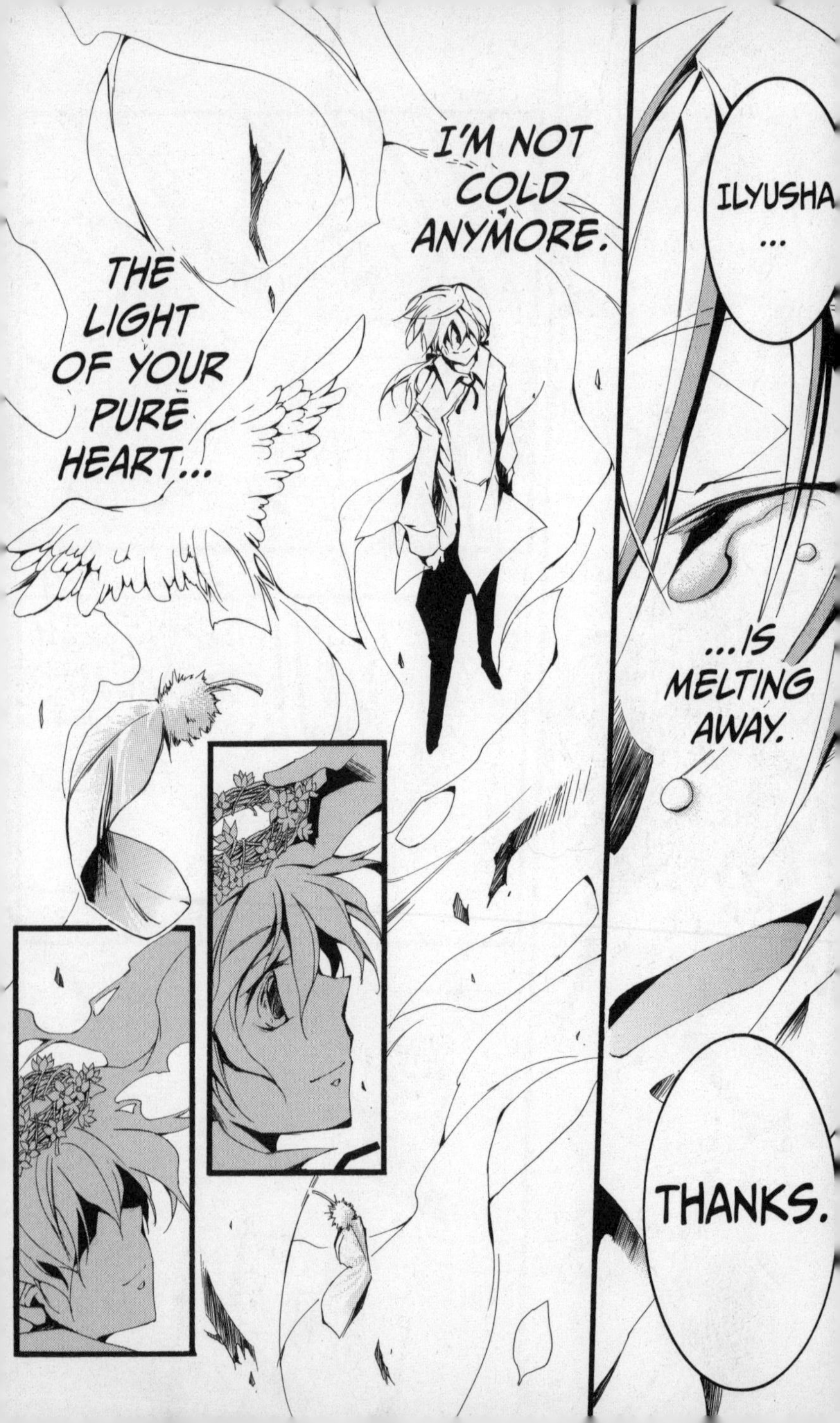
ILYUSHA ...
...IS MELTING AWAY.
THANKS.
I'M NOT COLD ANYMORE.
THE LIGHT OF YOUR PURE HEART...

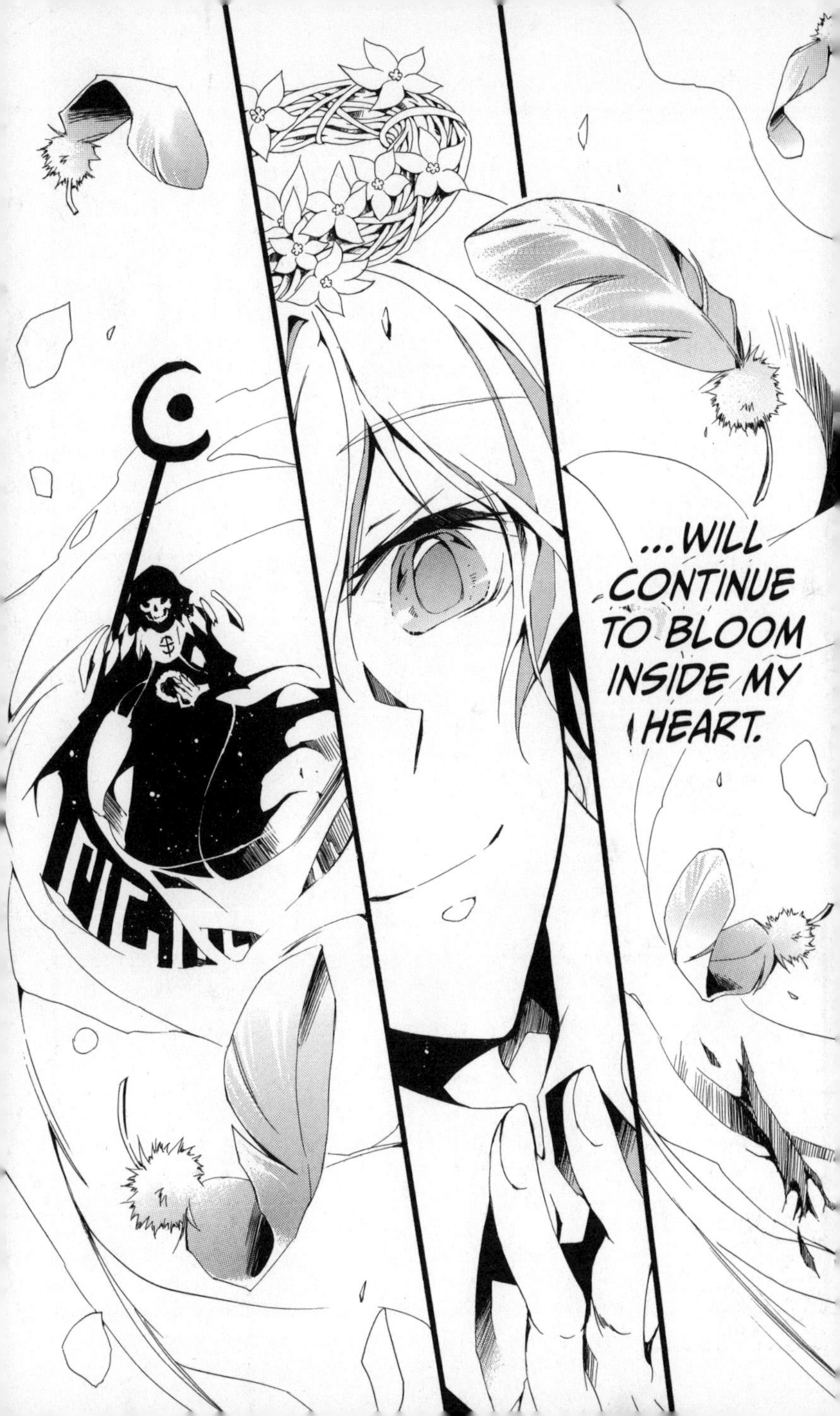
...WILL CONTINUE TO BLOOM INSIDE MY HEART.

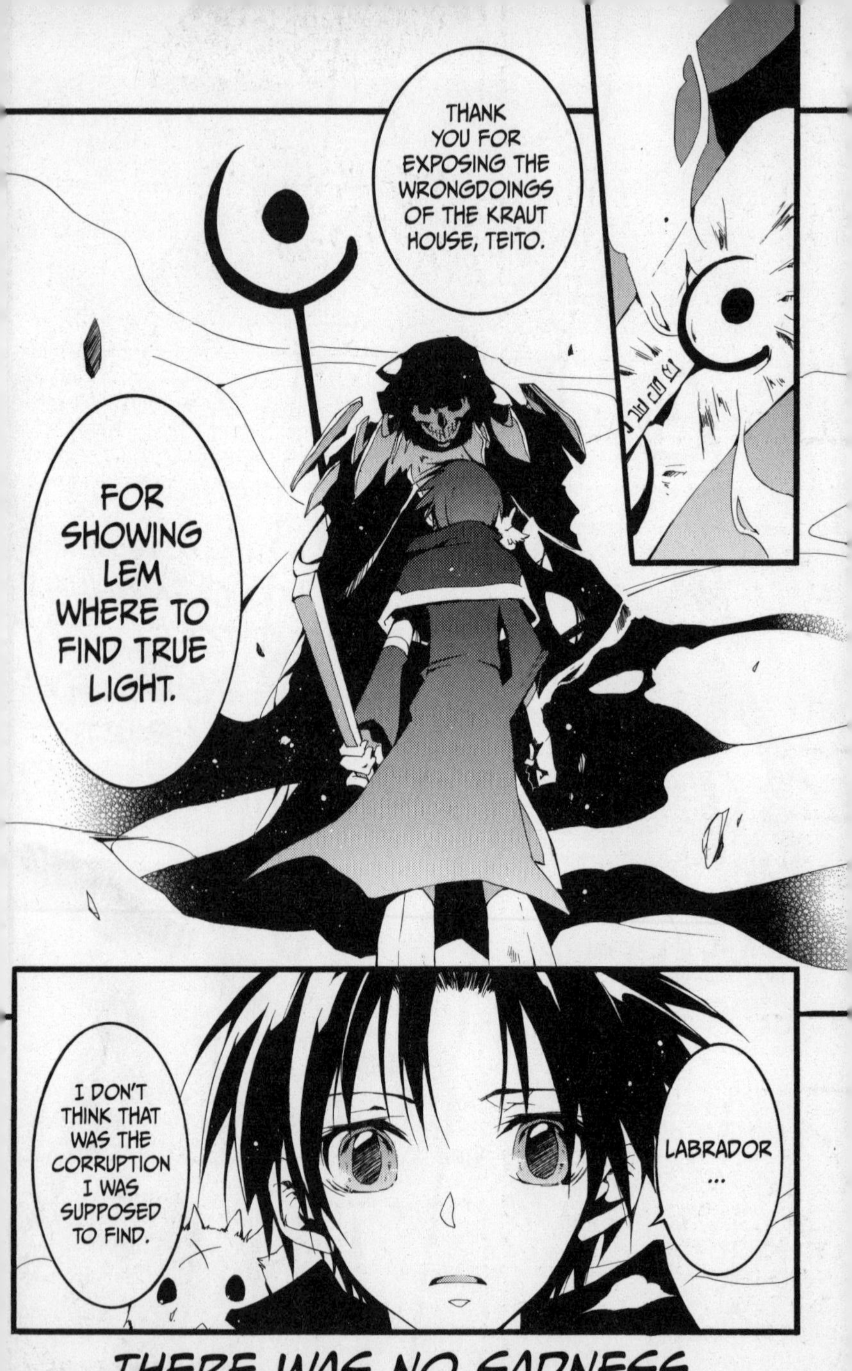
THANK YOU FOR EXPOSING THE WRONGDOINGS OF THE KRAUT HOUSE, TEITO.
FOR SHOWING LEM WHERE TO FIND TRUE LIGHT.
LABRADOR ...
I DON'T THINK THAT WAS THE CORRUPTION I WAS SUPPOSED TO FIND.

THERE WAS NO SADNESS.

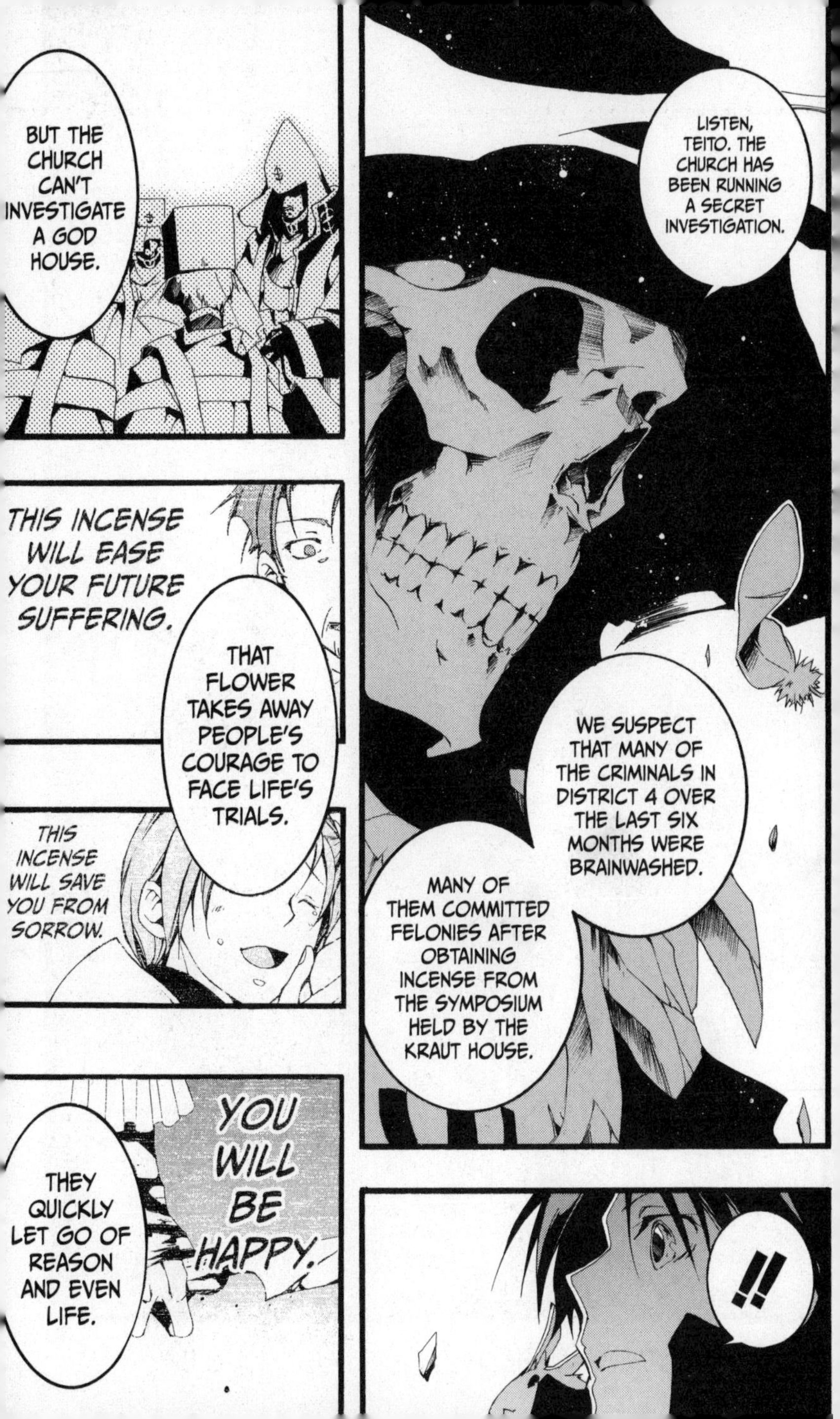

LISTEN, TEITO. THE CHURCH HAS BEEN RUNNING A SECRET INVESTIGATION.
WE SUSPECT THAT MANY OF THE CRIMINALS IN DISTRICT 4 OVER THE LAST SIX MONTHS WERE BRAINWASHED.
MANY OF THEM COMMITTED FELONIES AFTER OBTAINING INCENSE FROM THE SYMPOSIUM HELD BY THE KRAUT HOUSE.
!!
BUT THE CHURCH CAN'T INVESTIGATE A GOD HOUSE.
THIS INCENSE WILL EASE YOUR FUTURE SUFFERING.
THAT FLOWER TAKES AWAY PEOPLE'S COURAGE TO FACE LIFE'S TRIALS.
THIS INCENSE WILL SAVE YOU FROM SORROW.
YOU WILL BE HAPPY.
THEY QUICKLY LET GO OF REASON AND EVEN LIFE.

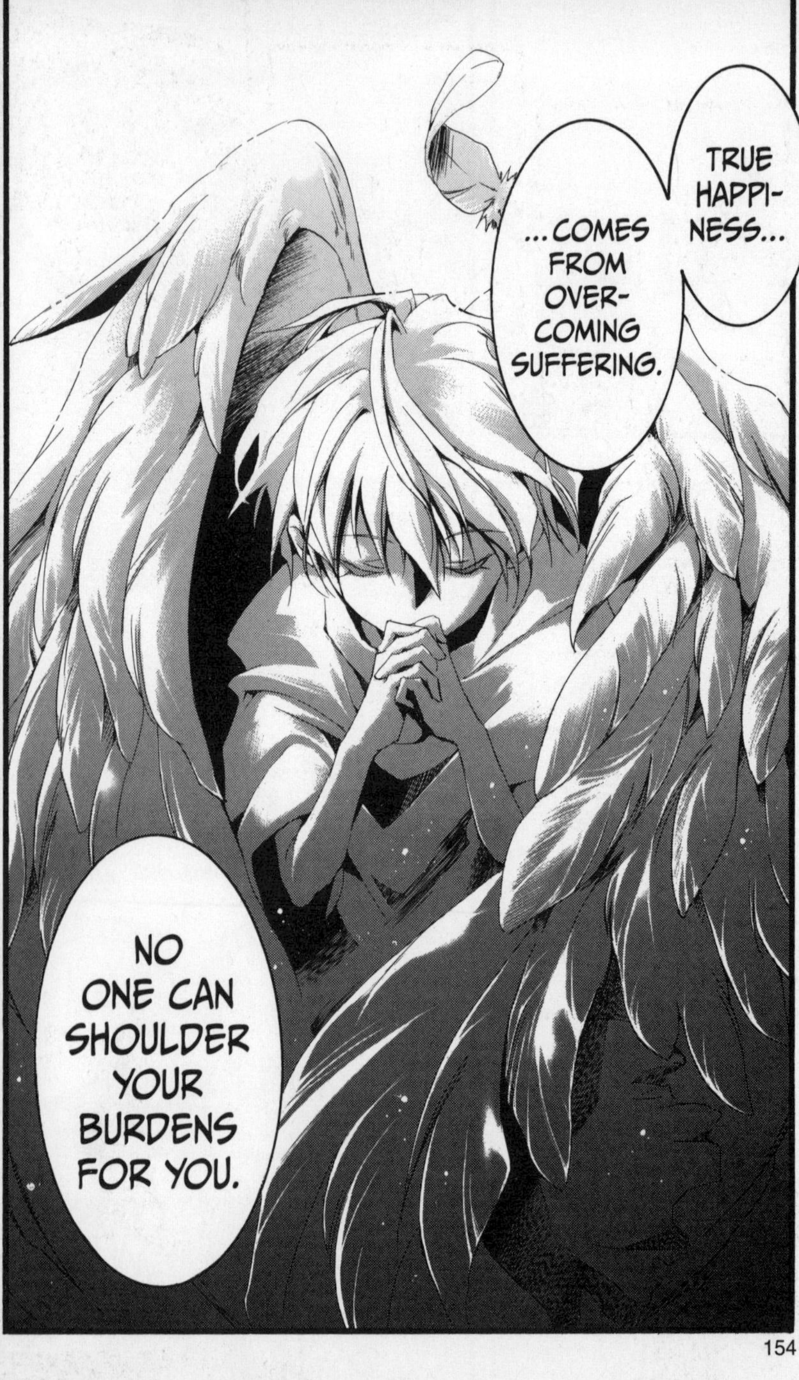
TRUE HAPPINESS...
...COMES FROM OVERCOMING SUFFERING.
NO ONE CAN SHOULDER YOUR BURDENS FOR YOU.

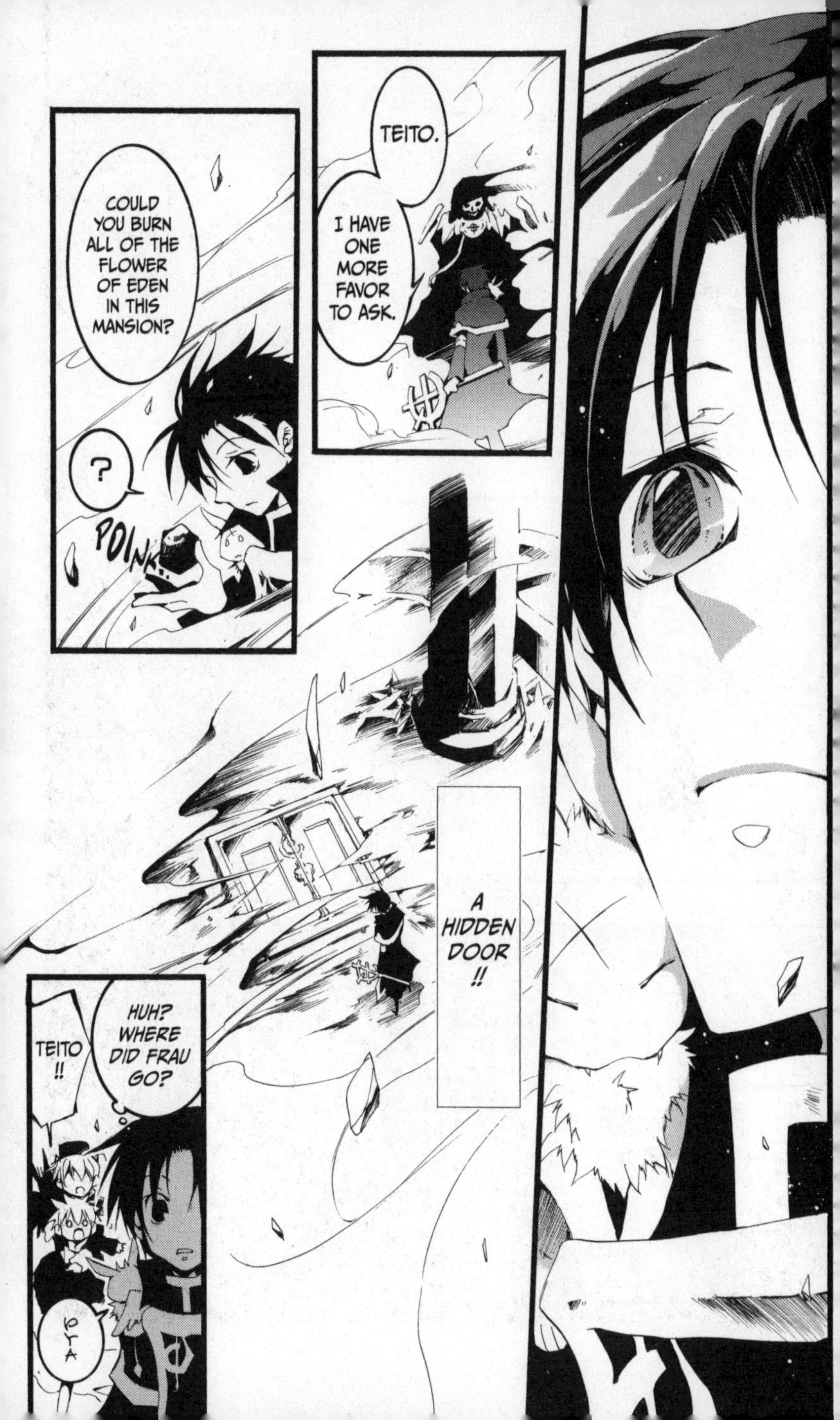
TEITO.
I HAVE ONE MORE FAVOR TO ASK.
COULD YOU BURN ALL OF THE FLOWER OF EDEN IN THIS MANSION?
?
POINK...
A HIDDEN DOOR!!
HUH? WHERE DID FRAU GO?
TEITO!!
PYA

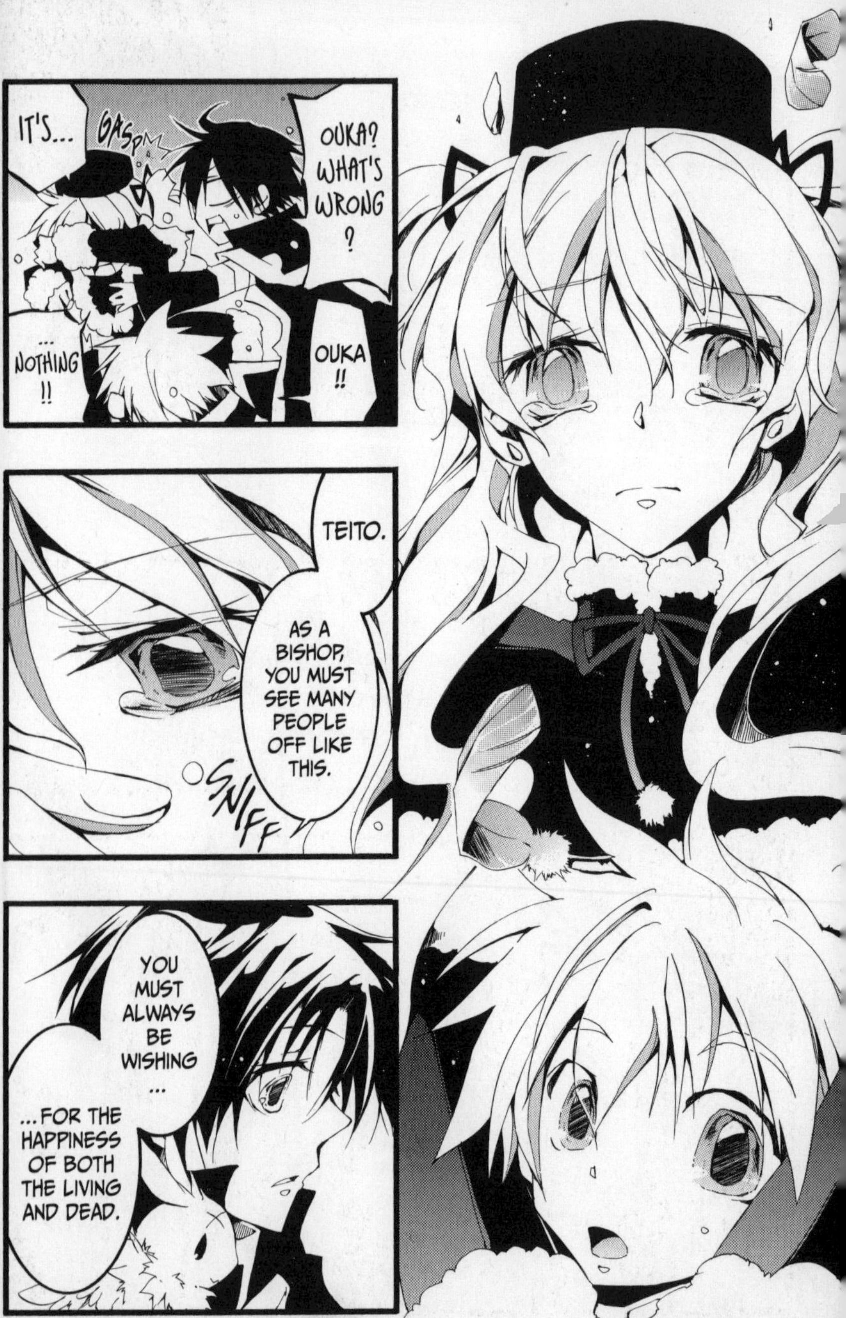
OUKA? WHAT'S WRONG?
GASP
IT'S...
OUKA!!
...NOTHING!!
TEITO.
AS A BISHOP, YOU MUST SEE MANY PEOPLE OFF LIKE THIS.
SNIFF
YOU MUST ALWAYS BE WISHING...
...FOR THE HAPPINESS OF BOTH THE LIVING AND DEAD.

TAK

HUFF

HUFF

TAK

?!!

LEM! WHAT WAS THAT EXPLO-SION?

HOW MANY TIMES HAVE I TOLD YOU TO BE CAREFUL!

KREE

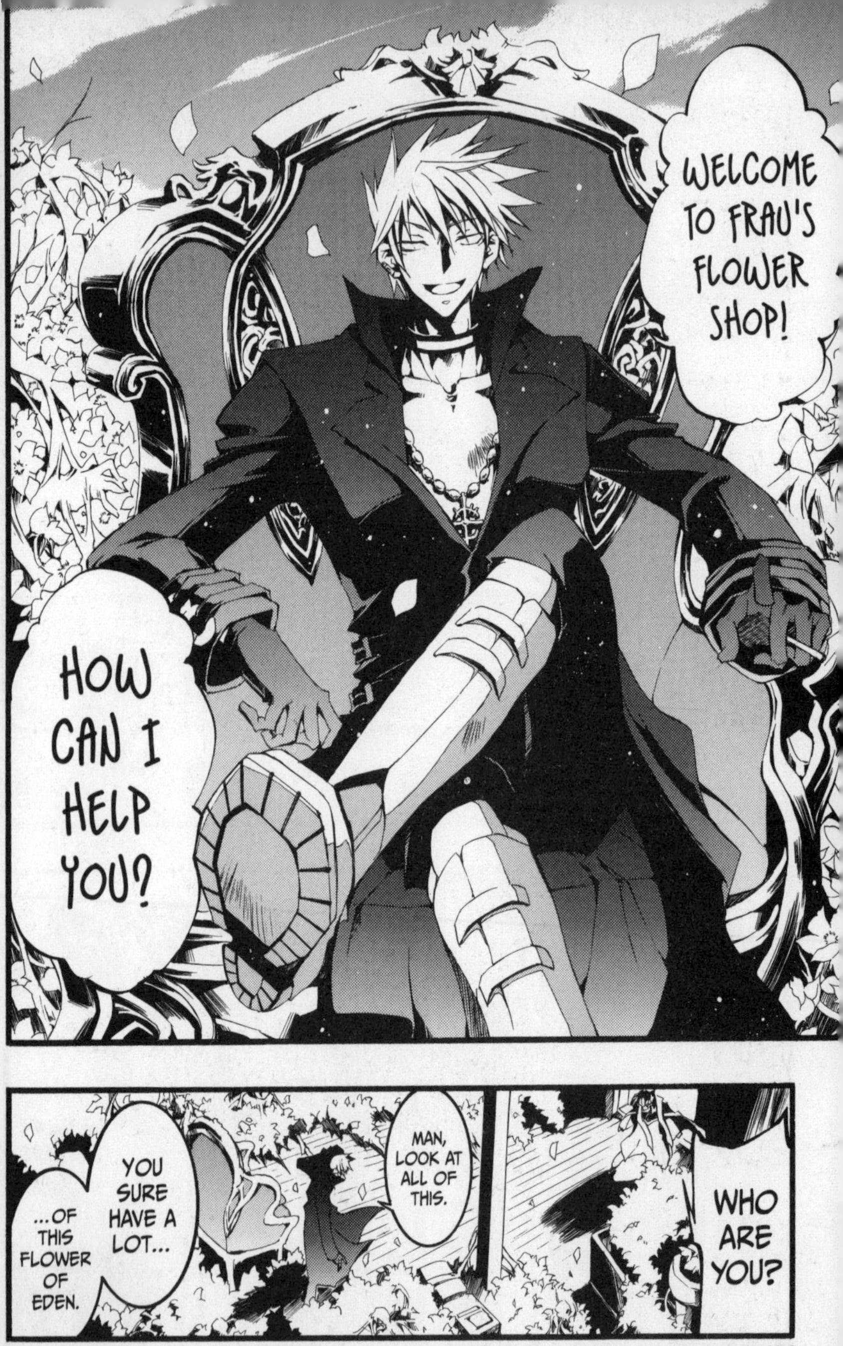
WELCOME TO FRAU'S FLOWER SHOP!
HOW CAN I HELP YOU?
WHO ARE YOU?
MAN, LOOK AT ALL OF THIS.
YOU SURE HAVE A LOT...
...OF THIS FLOWER OF EDEN.

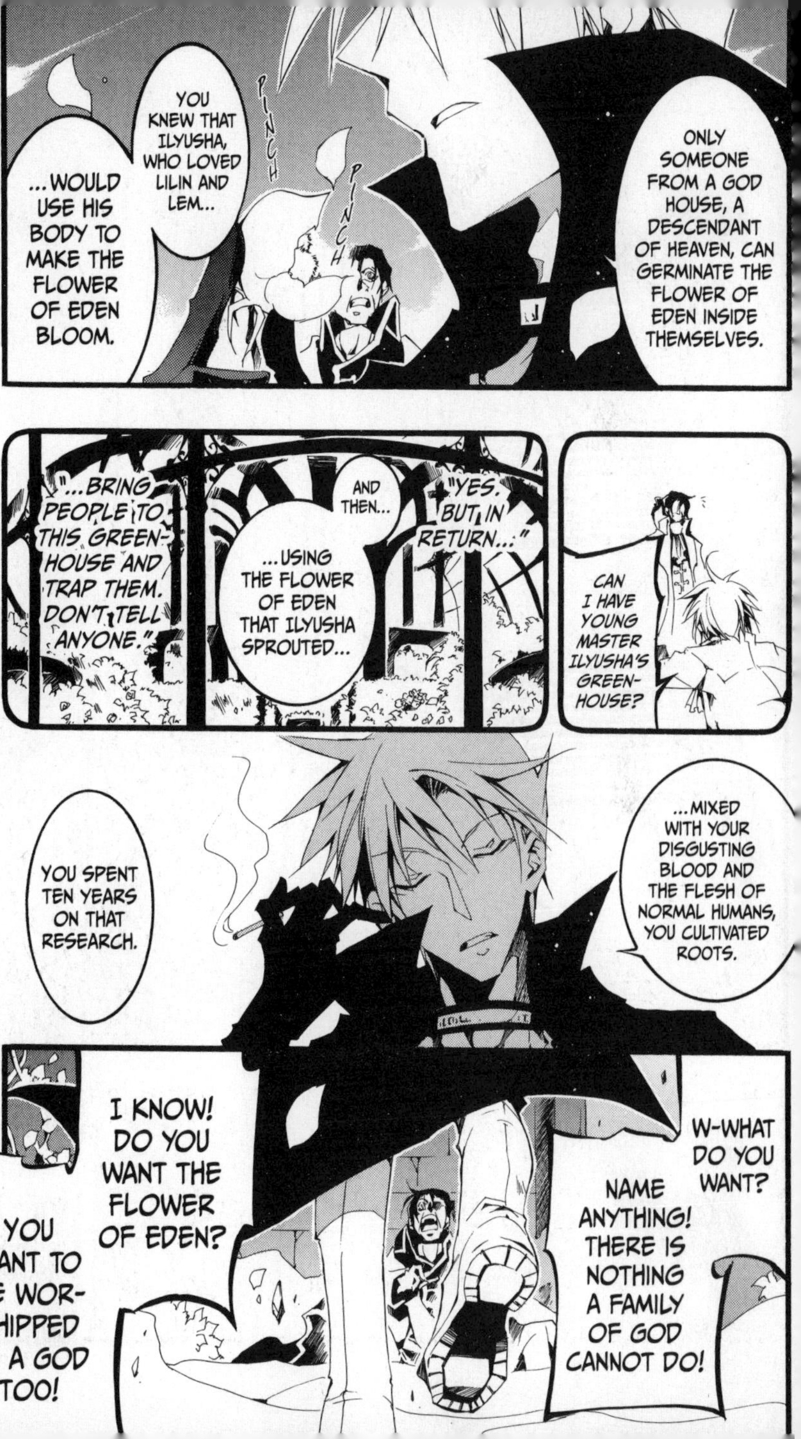
ONLY SOMEONE FROM A GOD HOUSE, A DESCENDANT OF HEAVEN, CAN GERMINATE THE FLOWER OF EDEN INSIDE THEMSELVES.
PINCH
PINCH
YOU KNEW THAT ILYUSHA, WHO LOVED LILIN AND LEM...
...WOULD USE HIS BODY TO MAKE THE FLOWER OF EDEN BLOOM.
CAN I HAVE YOUNG MASTER ILYUSHA'S GREEN-HOUSE?
"YES. BUT IN RETURN..."
"...BRING PEOPLE TO THIS GREEN-HOUSE AND TRAP THEM. DON'T TELL ANYONE."
AND THEN...
...USING THE FLOWER OF EDEN THAT ILYUSHA SPROUTED...
...MIXED WITH YOUR DISGUSTING BLOOD AND THE FLESH OF NORMAL HUMANS, YOU CULTIVATED ROOTS.
YOU SPENT TEN YEARS ON THAT RESEARCH.
W-WHAT DO YOU WANT?
NAME ANYTHING! THERE IS NOTHING A FAMILY OF GOD CANNOT DO!
I KNOW! DO YOU WANT THE FLOWER OF EDEN?
YOU WANT TO BE WOR-SHIPPED AS A GOD TOO!

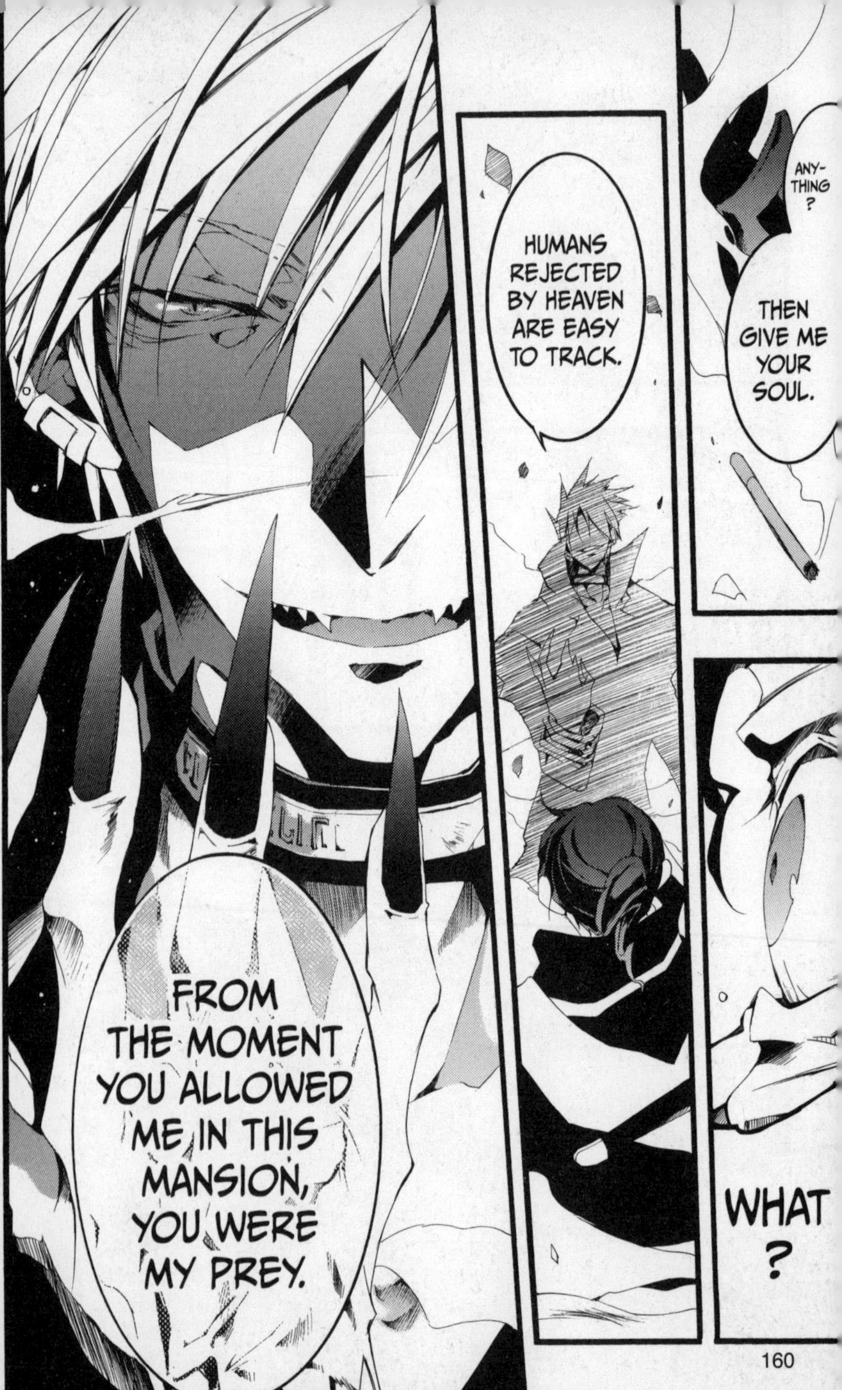
ANY-THING?
THEN GIVE ME YOUR SOUL.
WHAT?
HUMANS REJECTED BY HEAVEN ARE EASY TO TRACK.
FROM THE MOMENT YOU ALLOWED ME IN THIS MANSION, YOU WERE MY PREY.

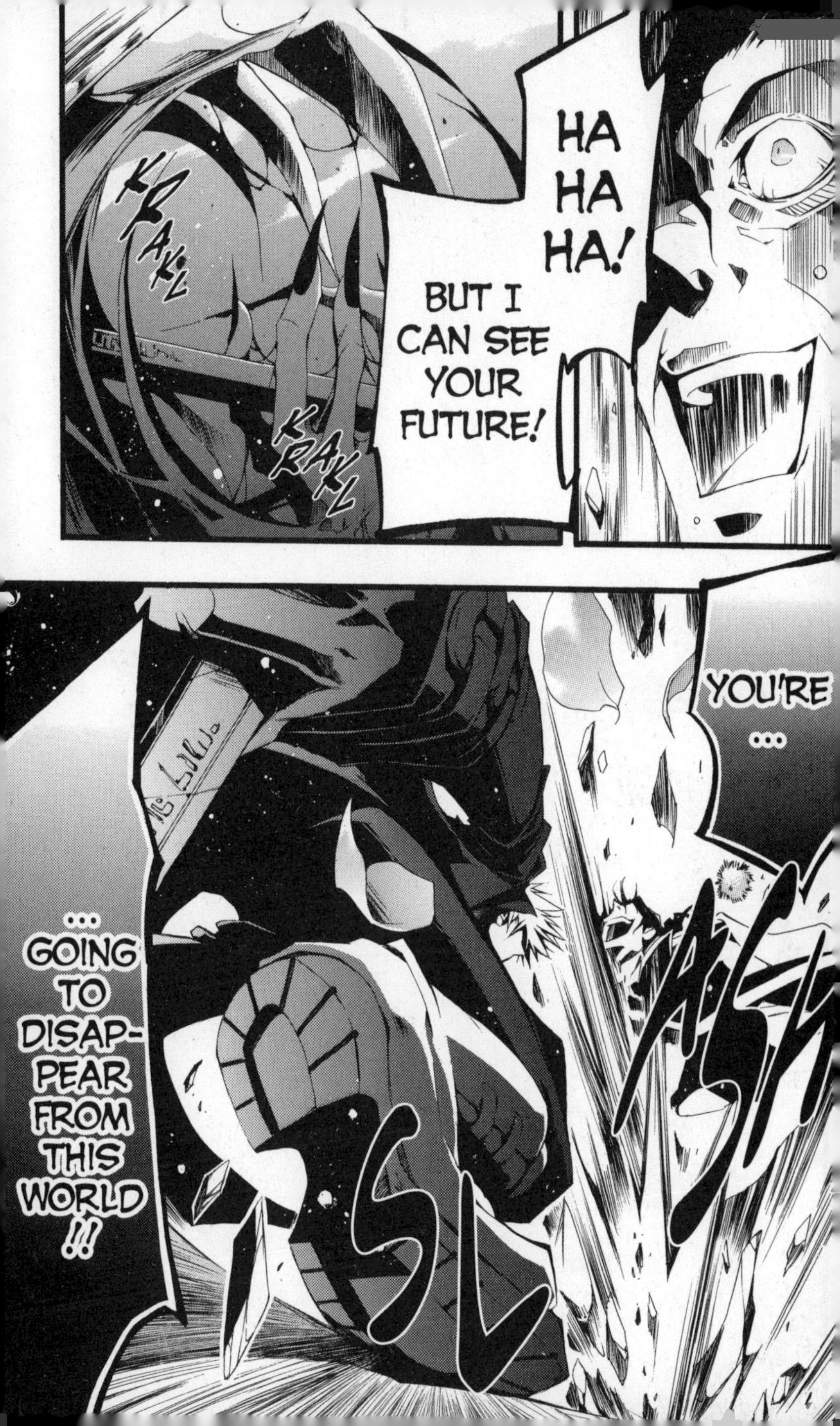
HA HA HA!
BUT I CAN SEE YOUR FUTURE!
KRAKL
KRAKL
YOU'RE ...
... GOING TO DISAPPEAR FROM THIS WORLD!!
SLASH

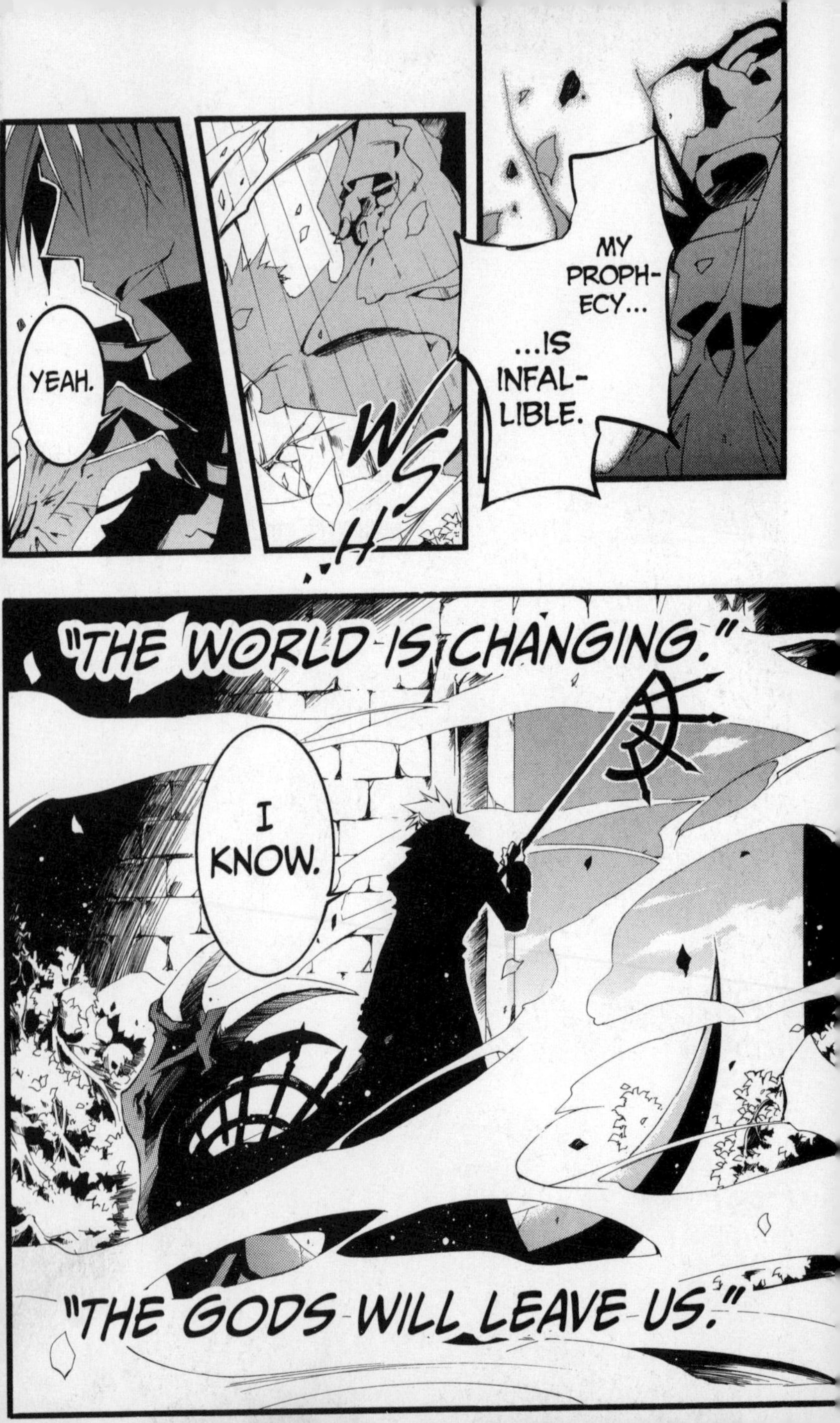
MY PROPHECY...
...IS INFALLIBLE.
WSH...
YEAH.
"THE WORLD IS CHANGING."
I KNOW.
"THE GODS WILL LEAVE US."

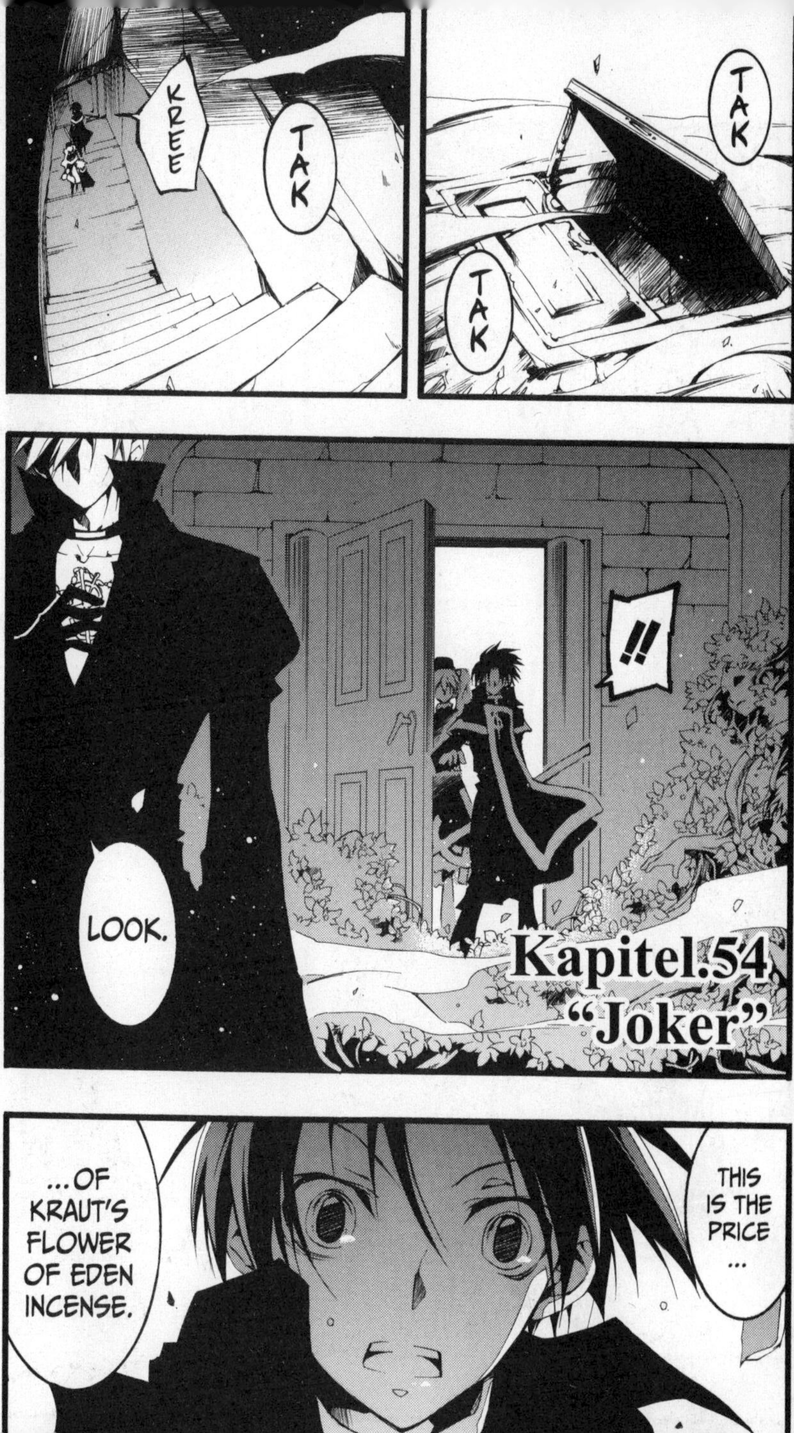
TAK
TAK
TAK
KREE
!!
LOOK.
Kapitel.54
"Joker"
THIS IS THE PRICE ...
...OF KRAUT'S FLOWER OF EDEN INCENSE.

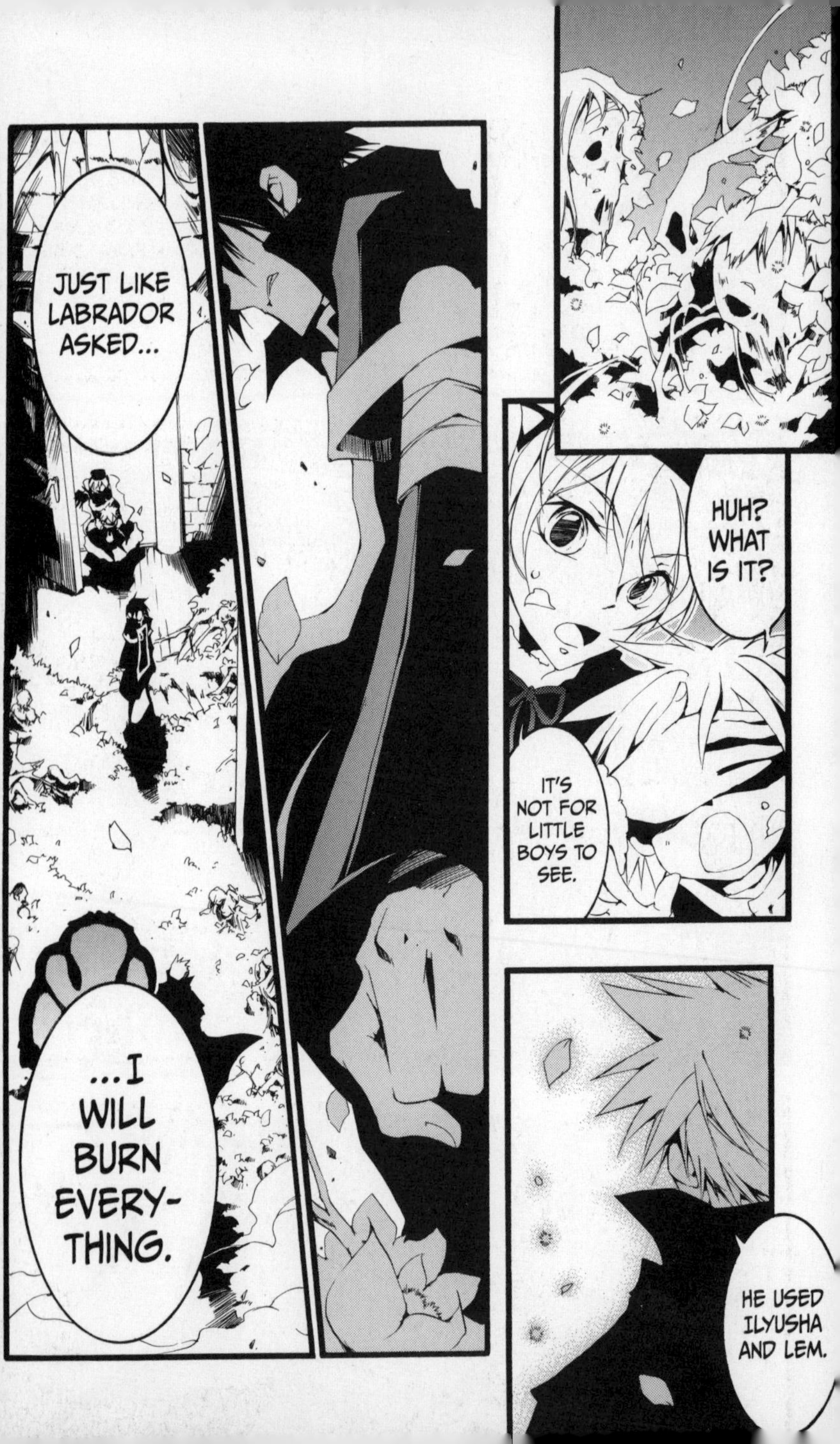
HUH? WHAT IS IT?
IT'S NOT FOR LITTLE BOYS TO SEE.
HE USED ILYUSHA AND LEM.
JUST LIKE LABRADOR ASKED...
...I WILL BURN EVERYTHING.

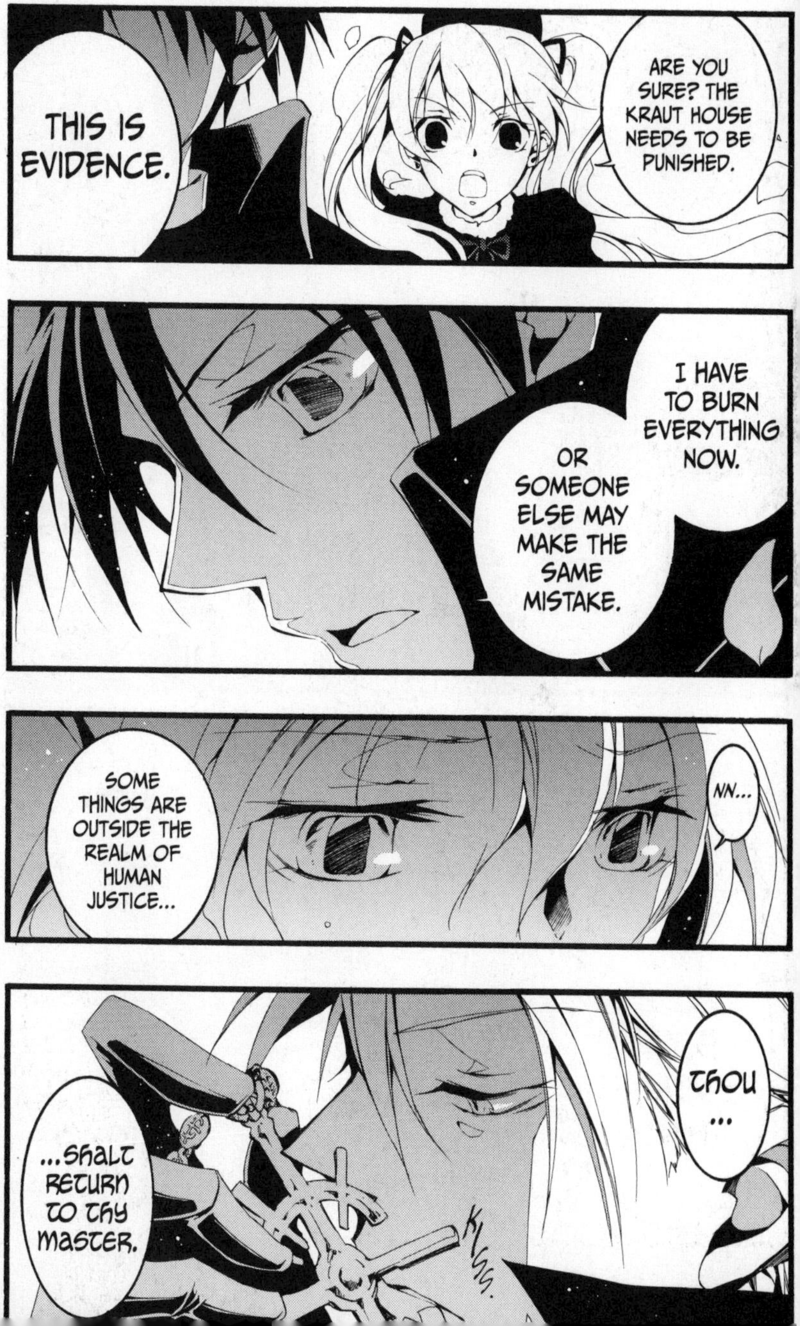
ARE YOU SURE? THE KRAUT HOUSE NEEDS TO BE PUNISHED.
THIS IS EVIDENCE.
I HAVE TO BURN EVERYTHING NOW.
OR SOMEONE ELSE MAY MAKE THE SAME MISTAKE.
NN...
SOME THINGS ARE OUTSIDE THE REALM OF HUMAN JUSTICE...
THOU...
...SHALT RETURN TO THY MASTER.
KISS

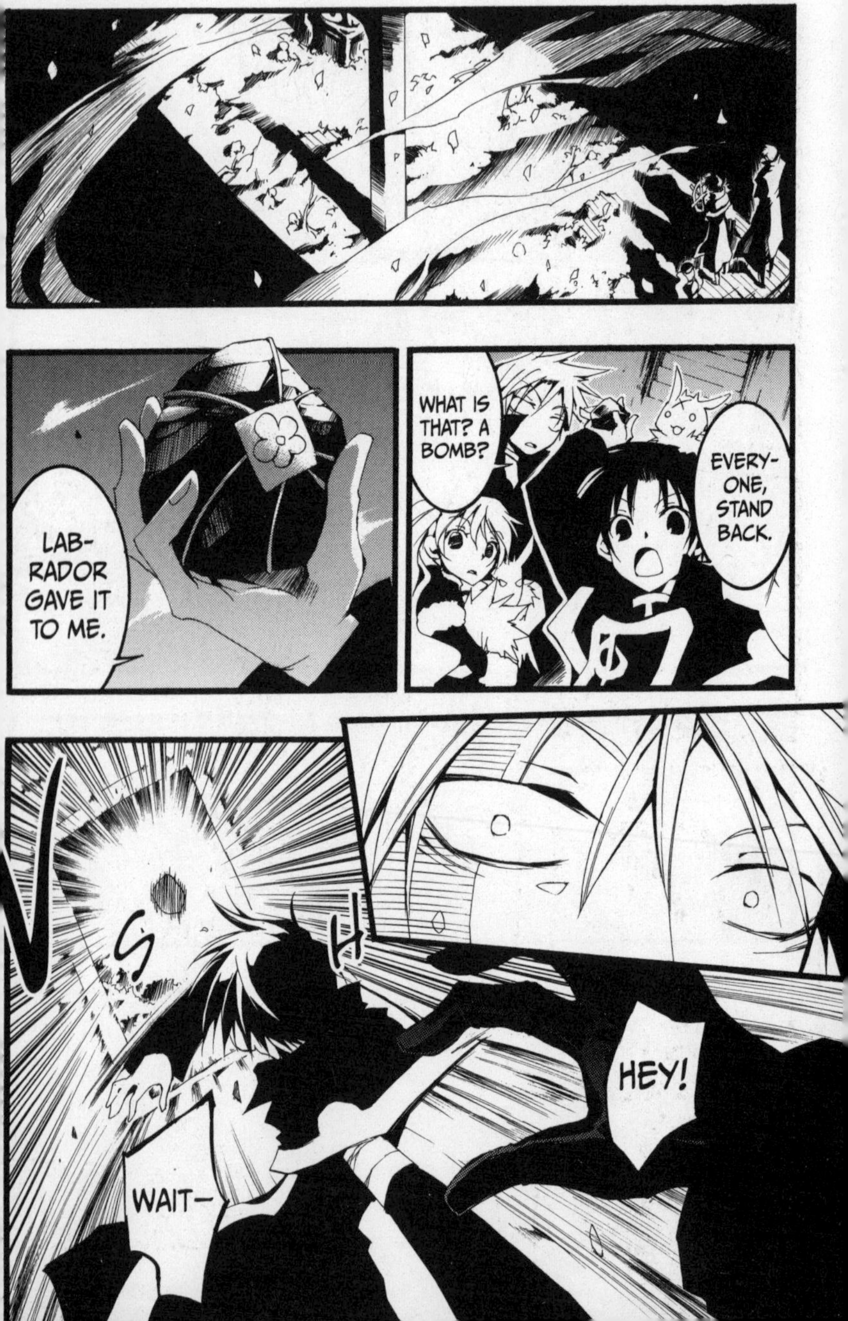
WHAT IS THAT? A BOMB?
EVERY-ONE, STAND BACK.
LAB-RADOR GAVE IT TO ME.
HEY!
WAIT–

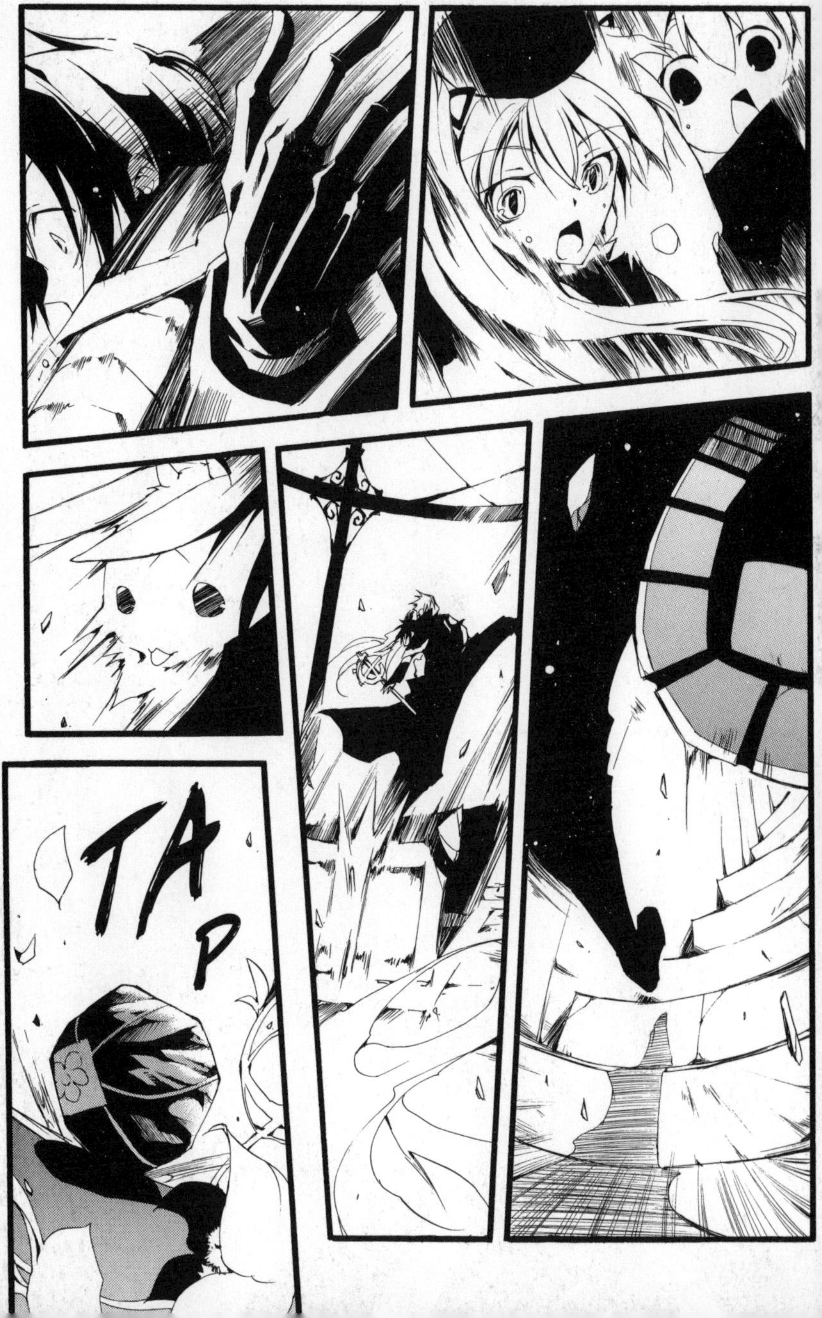
TAP

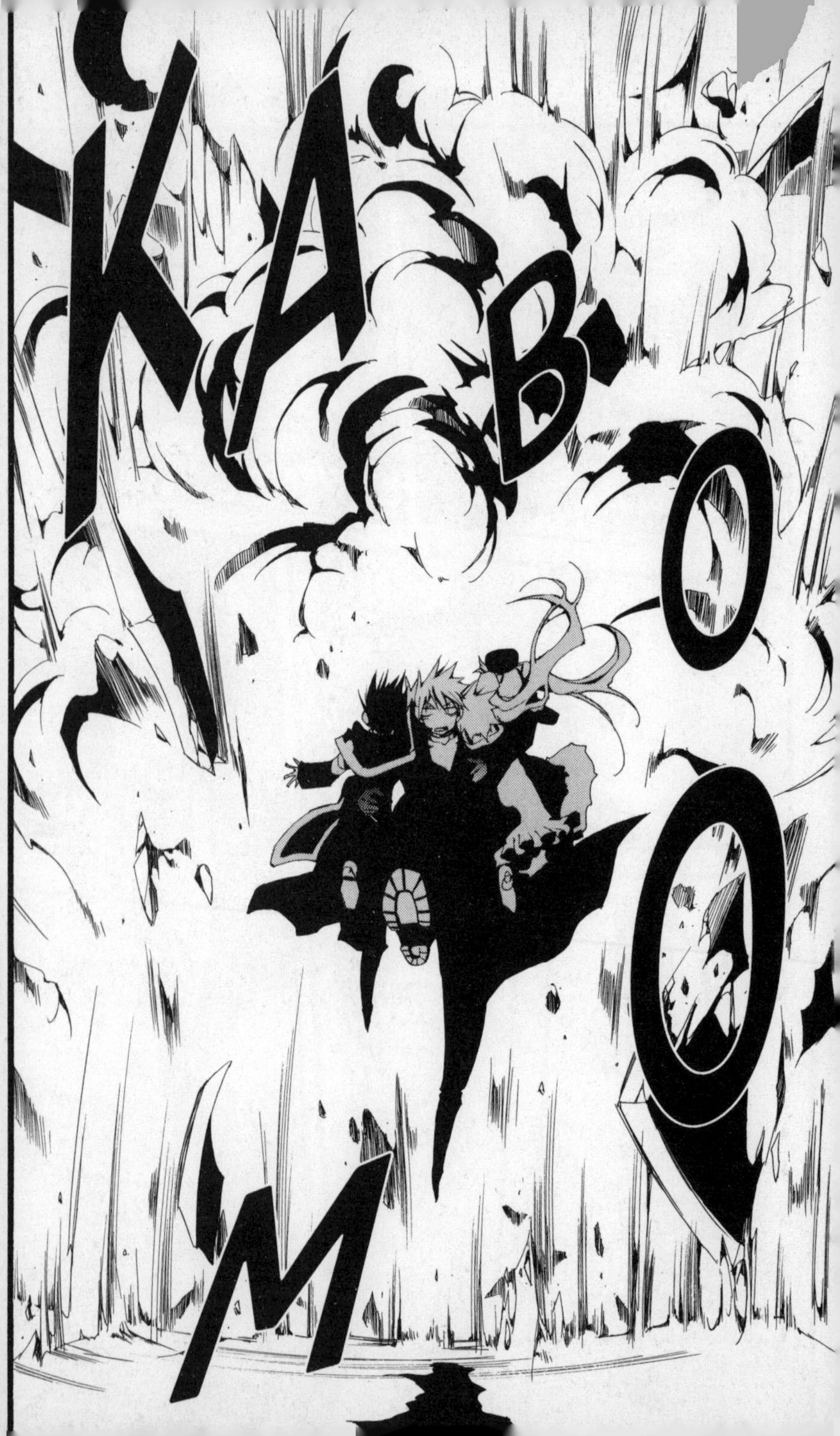
KABOOM

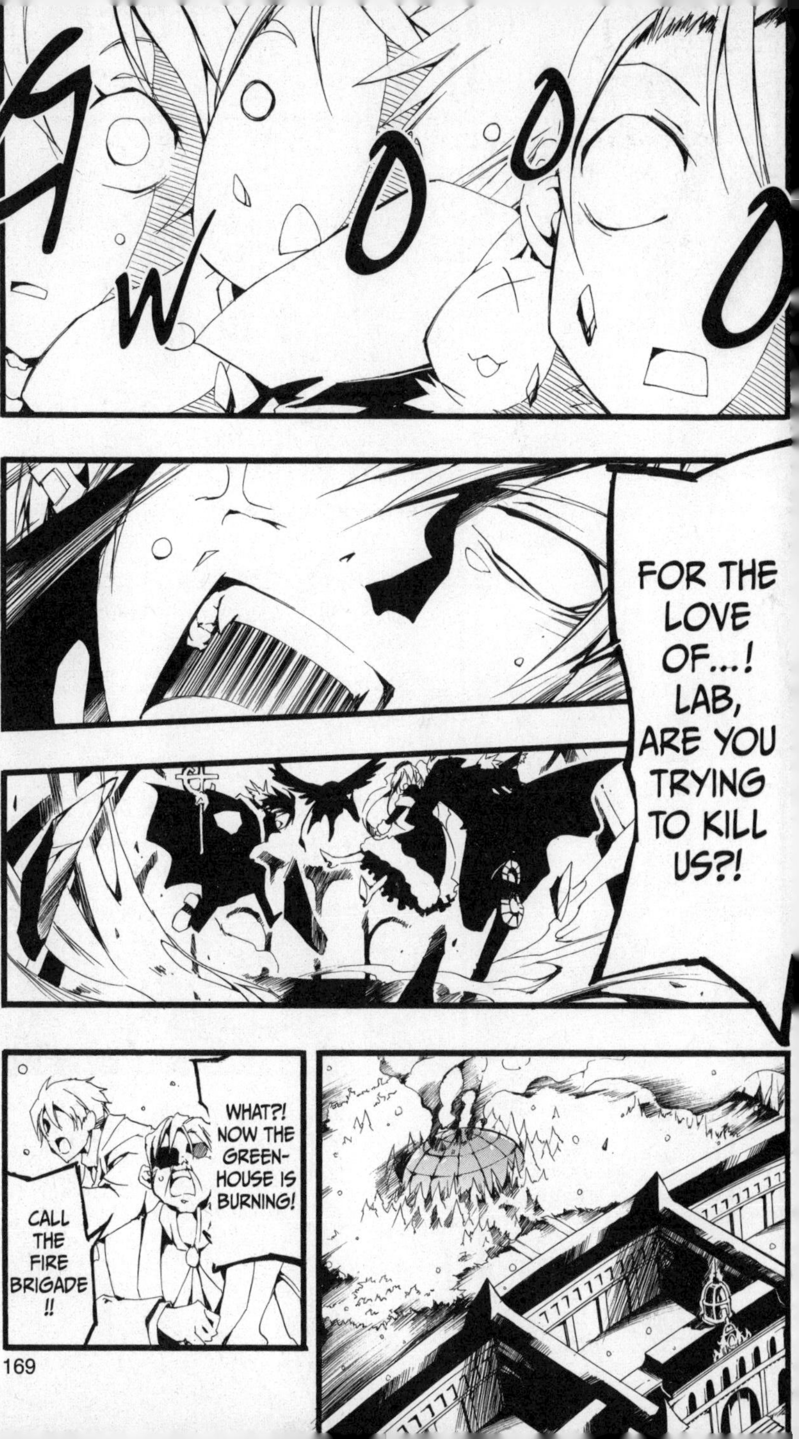
GWOOOO
FOR THE LOVE OF...! LAB, ARE YOU TRYING TO KILL US?!
WHAT?! NOW THE GREEN-HOUSE IS BURNING!
CALL THE FIRE BRIGADE!!

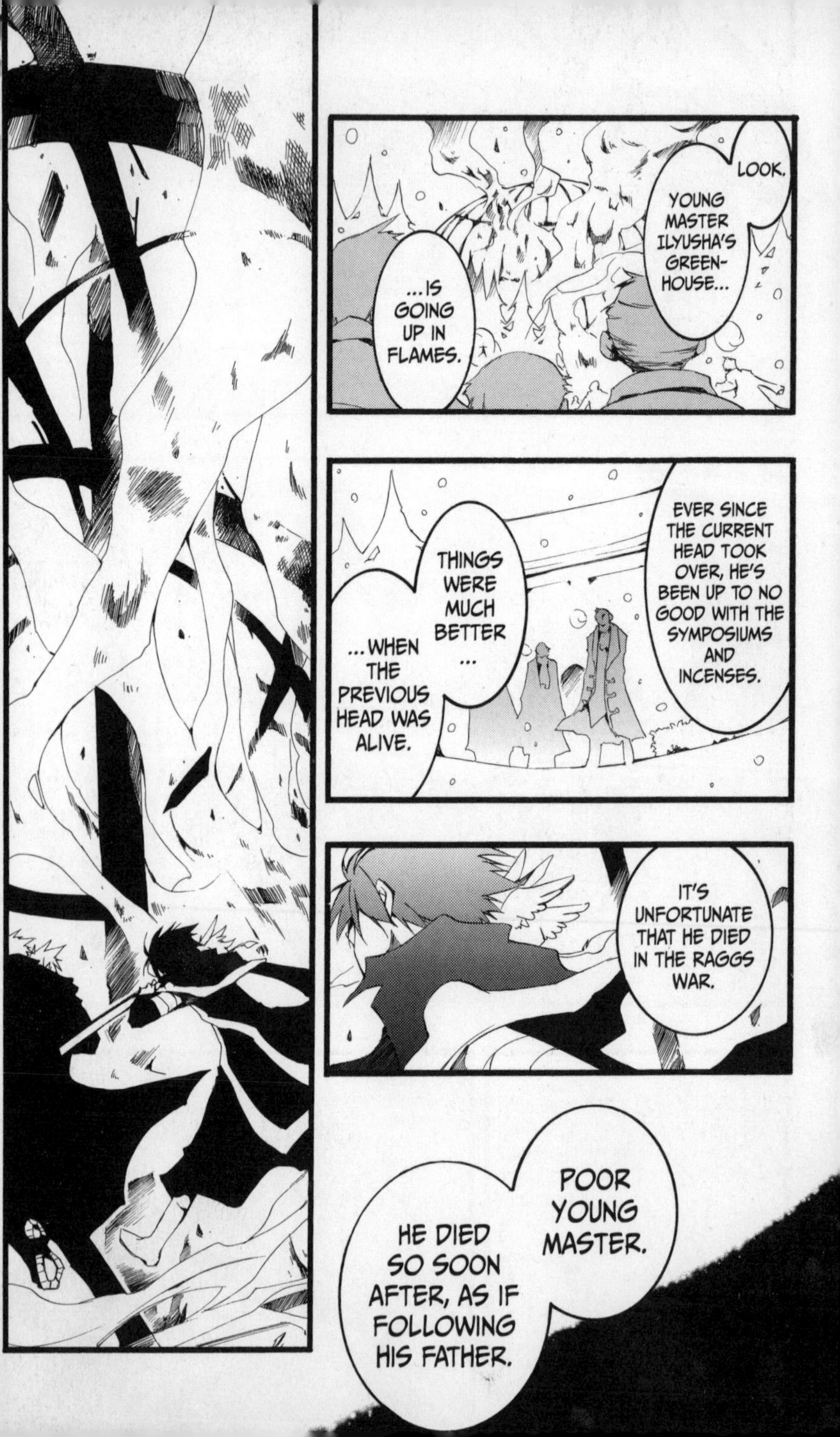
LOOK.
YOUNG MASTER ILYUSHA'S GREEN-HOUSE...
...IS GOING UP IN FLAMES.
EVER SINCE THE CURRENT HEAD TOOK OVER, HE'S BEEN UP TO NO GOOD WITH THE SYMPOSIUMS AND INCENSES.
THINGS WERE MUCH BETTER...
...WHEN THE PREVIOUS HEAD WAS ALIVE.
IT'S UNFORTUNATE THAT HE DIED IN THE RAGGS WAR.
POOR YOUNG MASTER.
HE DIED SO SOON AFTER, AS IF FOLLOWING HIS FATHER.

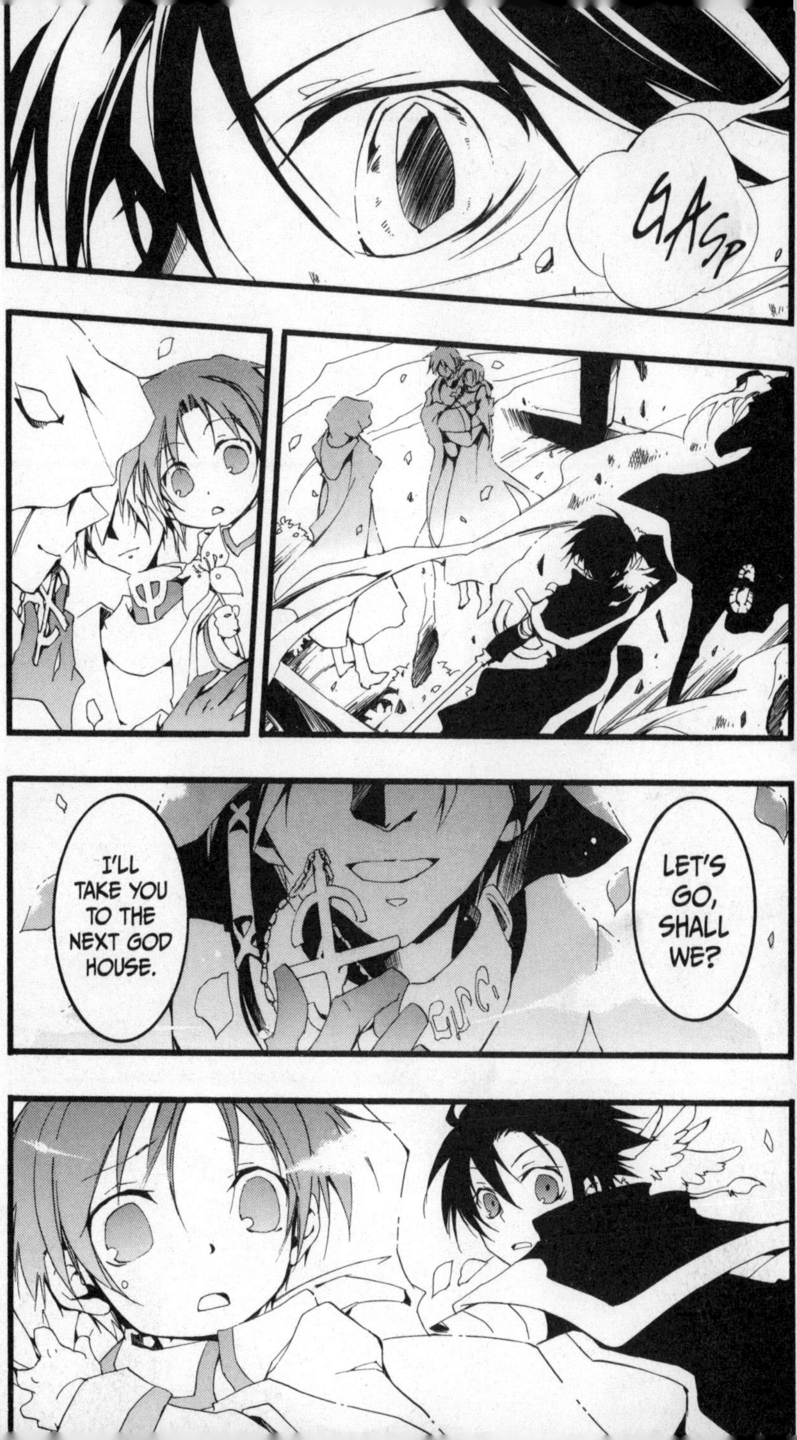
GASP
LET'S GO, SHALL WE?
I'LL TAKE YOU TO THE NEXT GOD HOUSE.

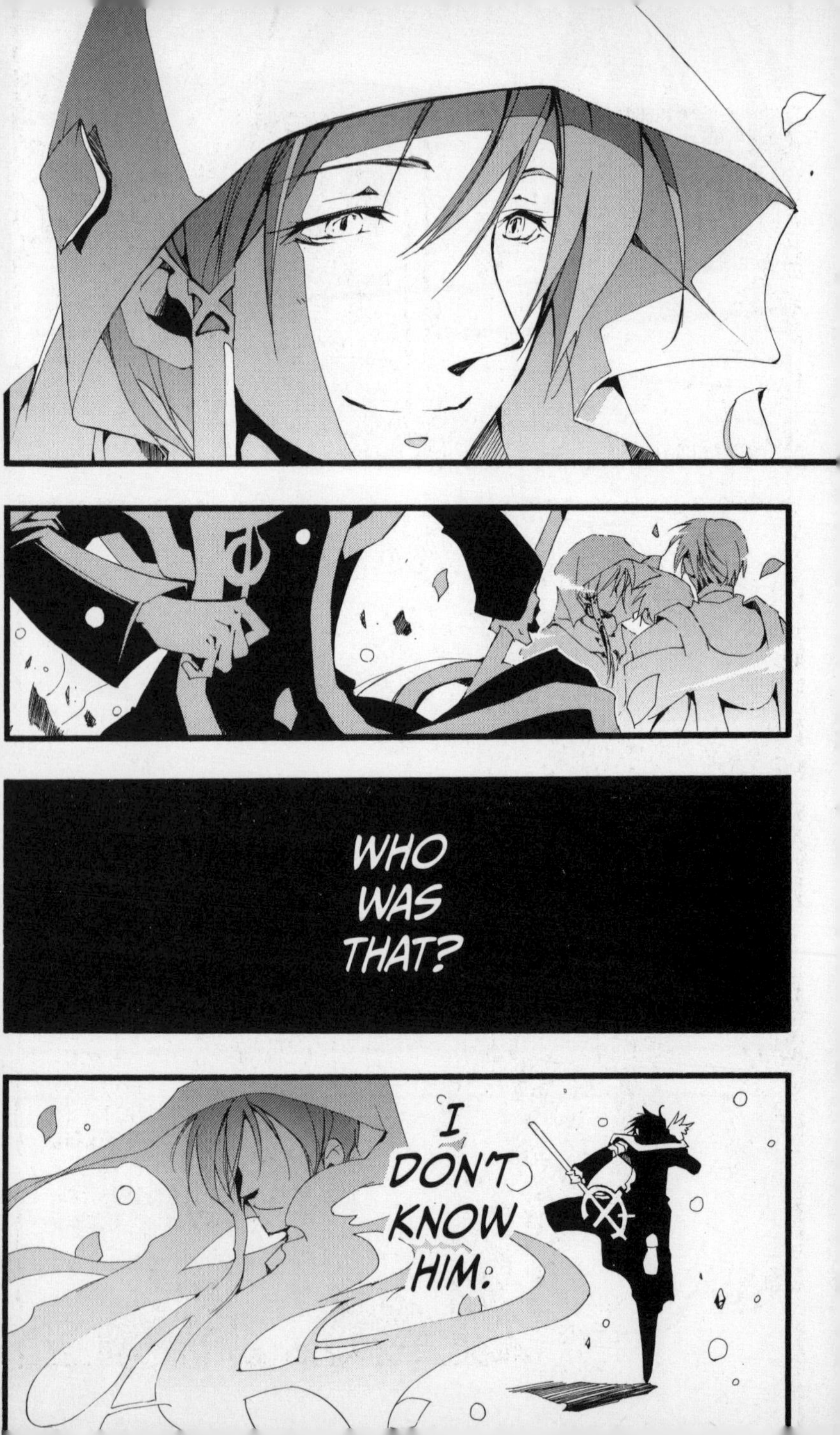
WHO WAS THAT?
I DON'T KNOW HIM.

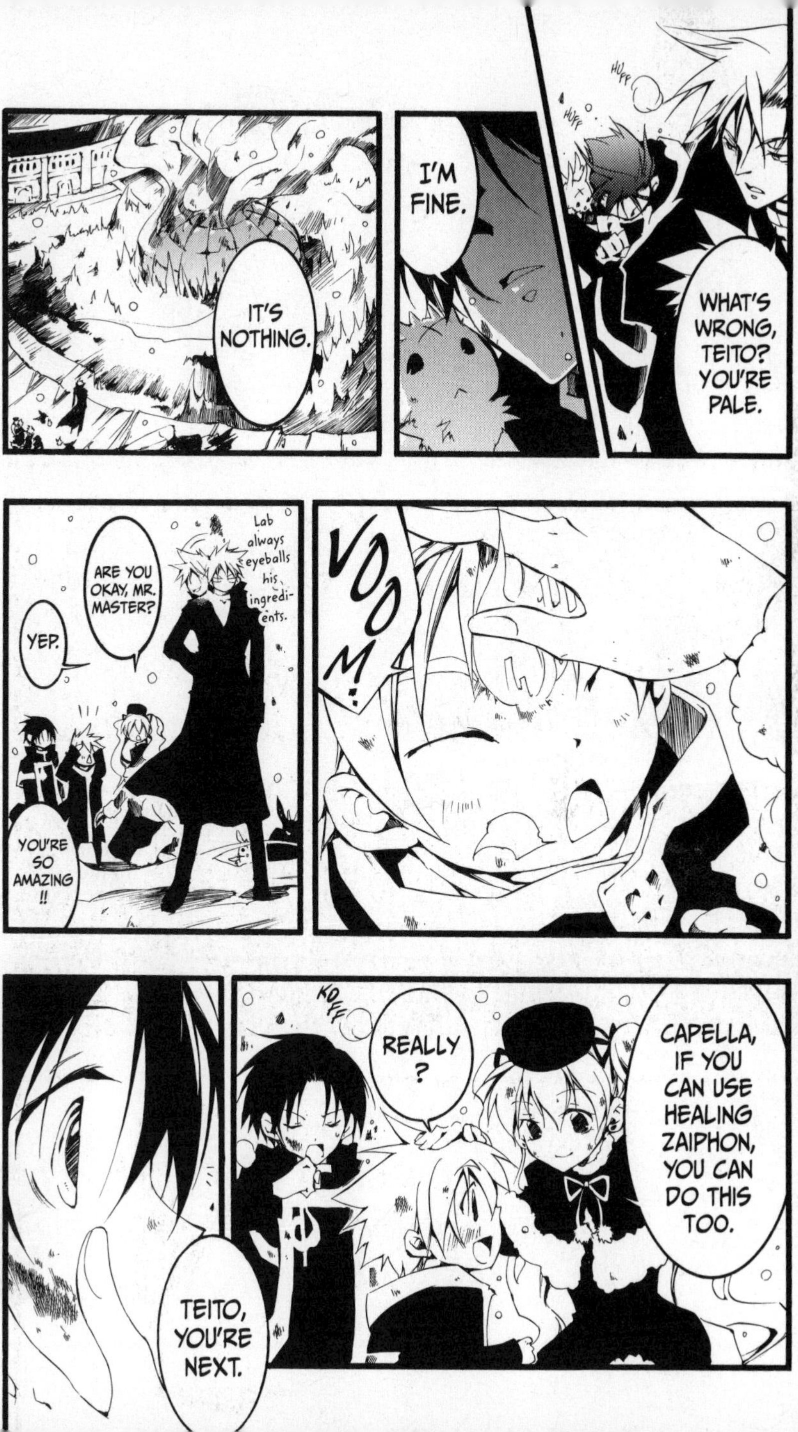
HUFF
HUFF
WHAT'S WRONG, TEITO? YOU'RE PALE.
I'M FINE.
IT'S NOTHING.
VOOM!
Lab always eyeballs his ingredients.
ARE YOU OKAY, MR. MASTER?
YEP.
YOU'RE SO AMAZING!!
CAPELLA, IF YOU CAN USE HEALING ZAIPHON, YOU CAN DO THIS TOO.
KOFF
REALLY?
TEITO, YOU'RE NEXT.

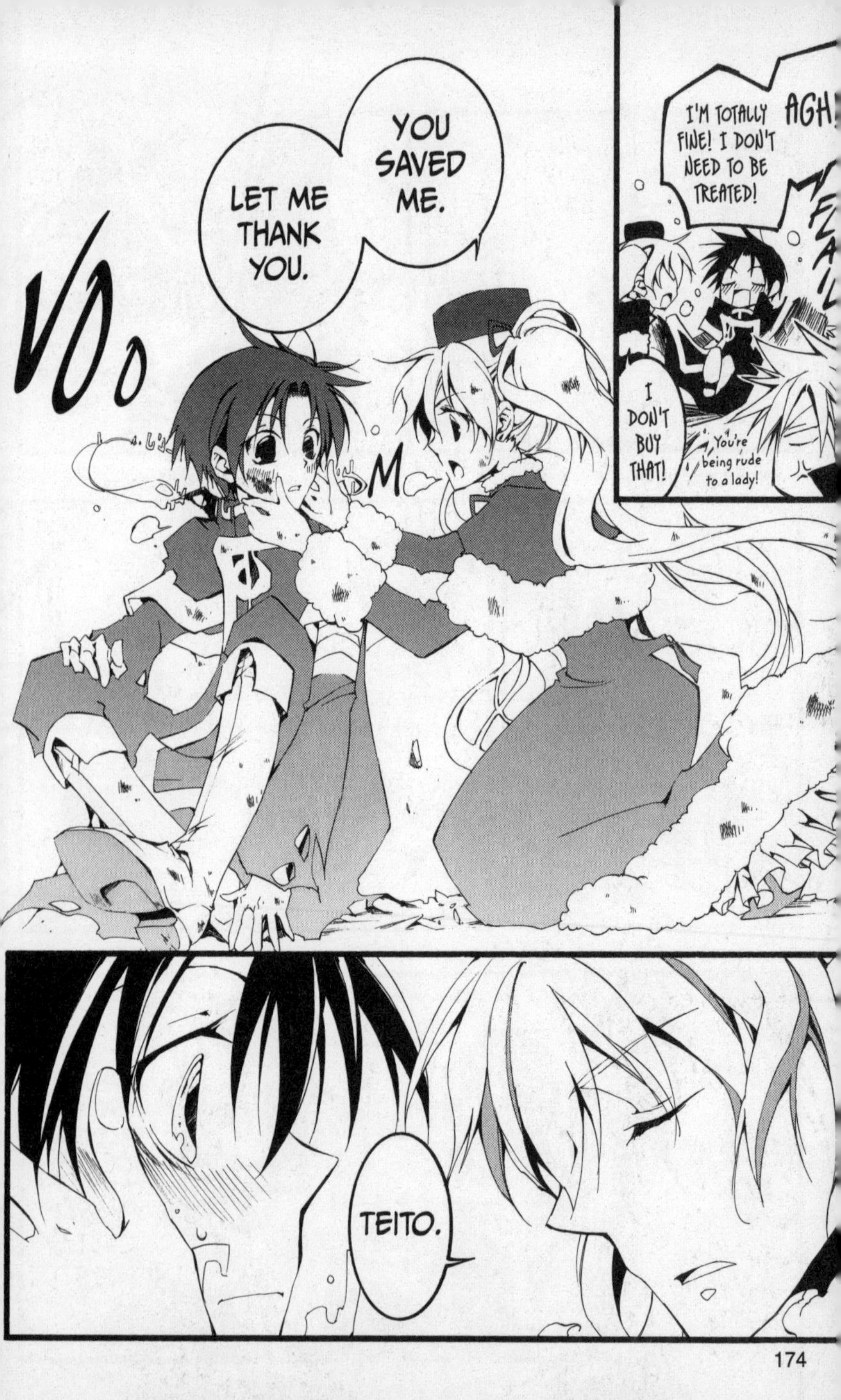
AGH!
FLAIL
I'M TOTALLY FINE! I DON'T NEED TO BE TREATED!
I DON'T BUY THAT!
You're being rude to a lady!
YOU SAVED ME.
LET ME THANK YOU.
TEITO.

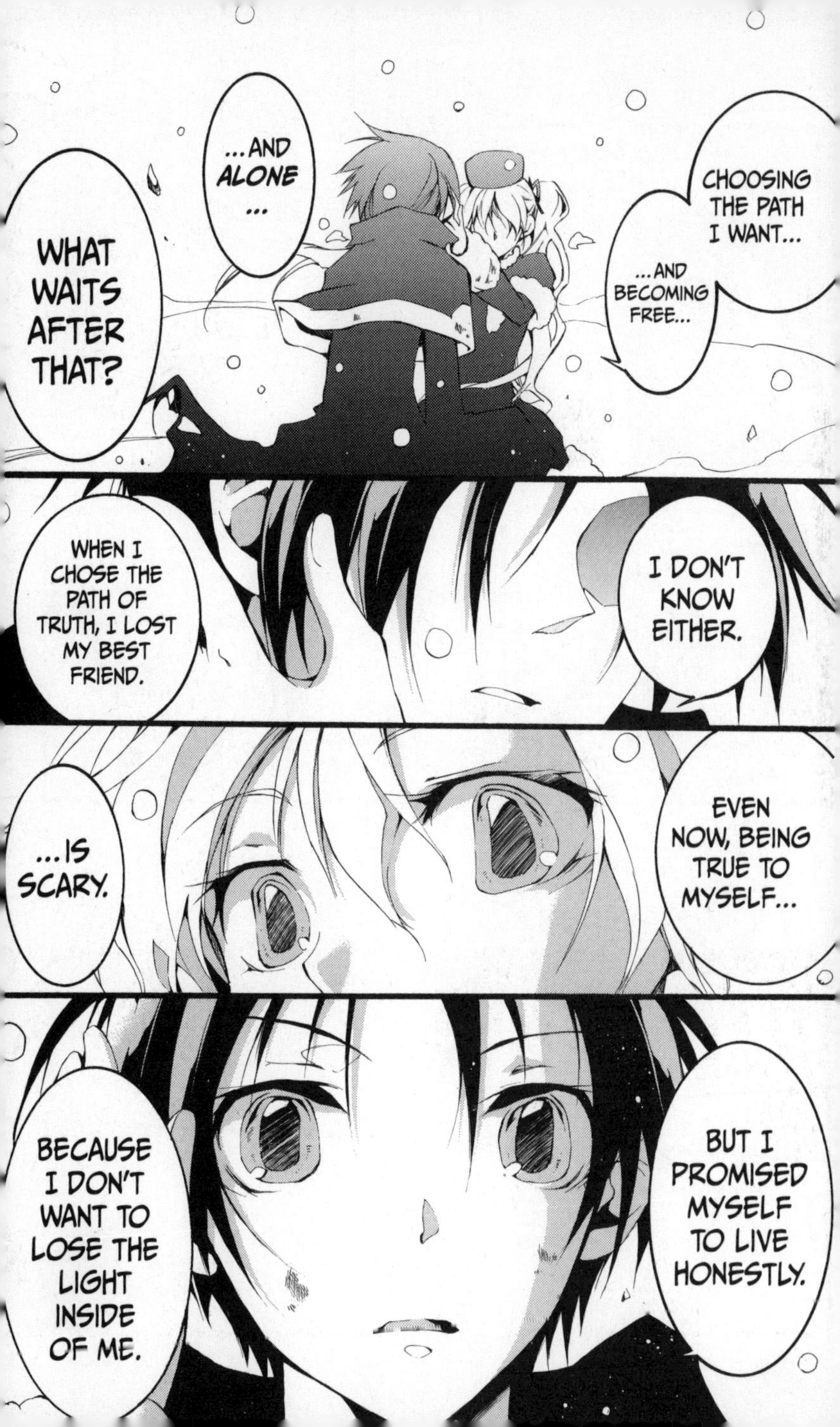
CHOOSING THE PATH I WANT...
...AND BECOMING FREE...
...AND ALONE ...
WHAT WAITS AFTER THAT?
I DON'T KNOW EITHER.
WHEN I CHOSE THE PATH OF TRUTH, I LOST MY BEST FRIEND.
EVEN NOW, BEING TRUE TO MYSELF...
...IS SCARY.
BUT I PROMISED MYSELF TO LIVE HONESTLY.
BECAUSE I DON'T WANT TO LOSE THE LIGHT INSIDE OF ME.

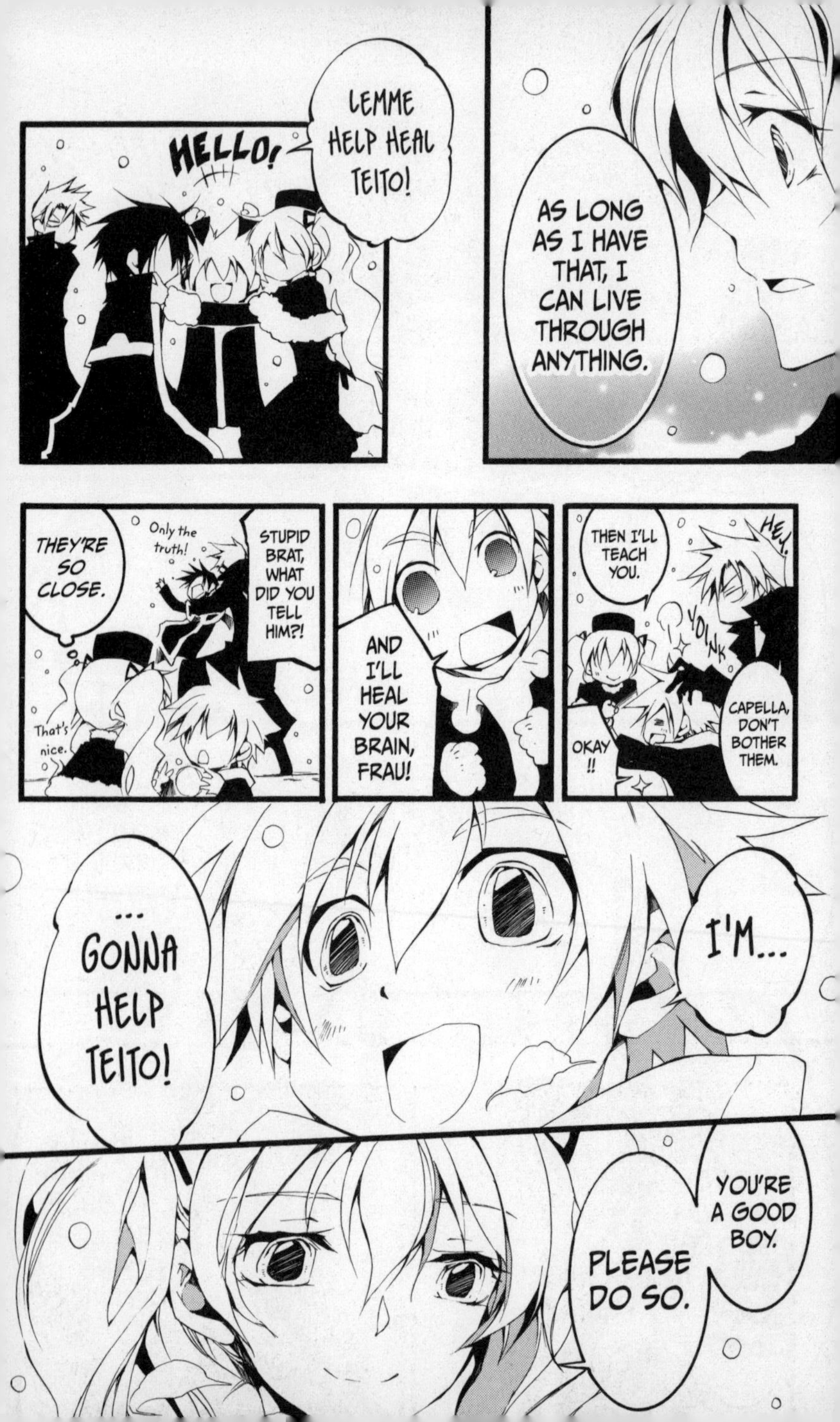
AS LONG AS I HAVE THAT, I CAN LIVE THROUGH ANYTHING.
LEMME HELP HEAL TEITO!
HELLO!
HEY.
THEN I'LL TEACH YOU.
YOINK
CAPELLA, DON'T BOTHER THEM.
OKAY!!
AND I'LL HEAL YOUR BRAIN, FRAU!
STUPID BRAT, WHAT DID YOU TELL HIM?!
Only the truth!
THEY'RE SO CLOSE.
That's nice.
I'M...
...GONNA HELP TEITO!
YOU'RE A GOOD BOY.
PLEASE DO SO.

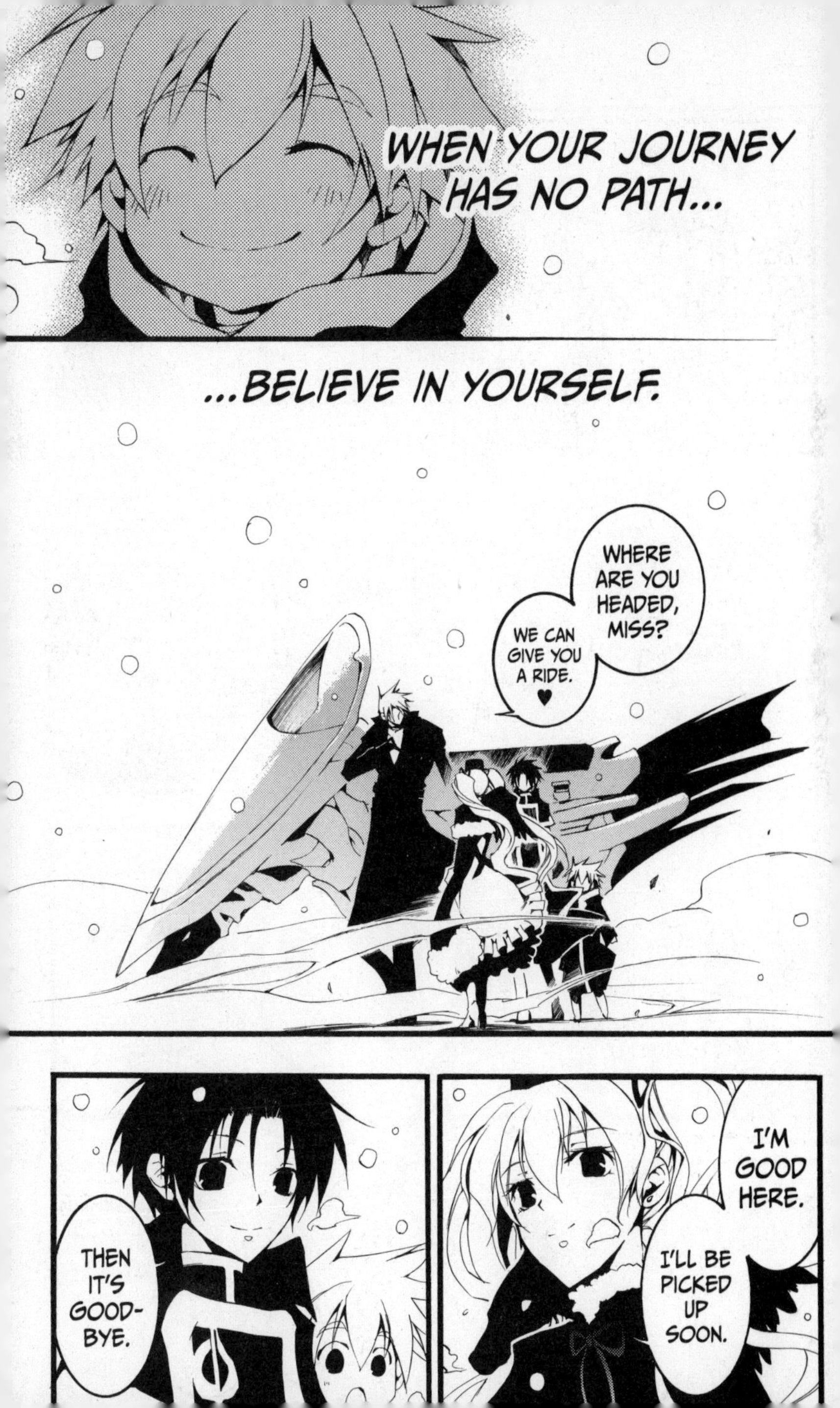
WHEN YOUR JOURNEY HAS NO PATH...
...BELIEVE IN YOURSELF.
WHERE ARE YOU HEADED, MISS?
WE CAN GIVE YOU A RIDE. ♥
I'M GOOD HERE.
I'LL BE PICKED UP SOON.
THEN IT'S GOOD-BYE.

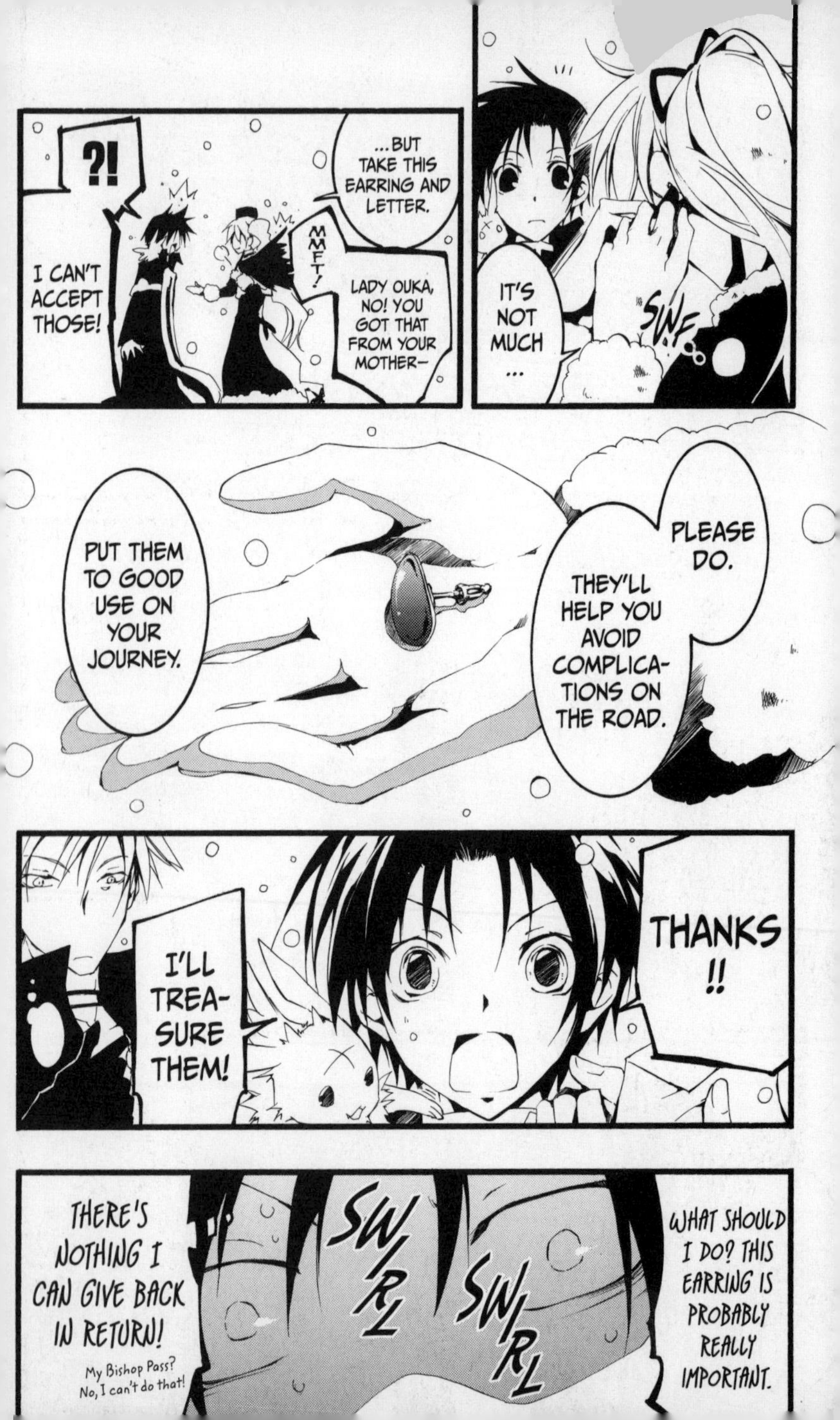
IT'S NOT MUCH ...
SWF
...BUT TAKE THIS EARRING AND LETTER.
MMFT!
LADY OUKA, NO! YOU GOT THAT FROM YOUR MOTHER—
?!
I CAN'T ACCEPT THOSE!
PLEASE DO.
THEY'LL HELP YOU AVOID COMPLICATIONS ON THE ROAD.
PUT THEM TO GOOD USE ON YOUR JOURNEY.
THANKS !!
I'LL TREASURE THEM!
WHAT SHOULD I DO? THIS EARRING IS PROBABLY REALLY IMPORTANT.
SWIRL
SWIRL
THERE'S NOTHING I CAN GIVE BACK IN RETURN!
My Bishop Pass? No, I can't do that!

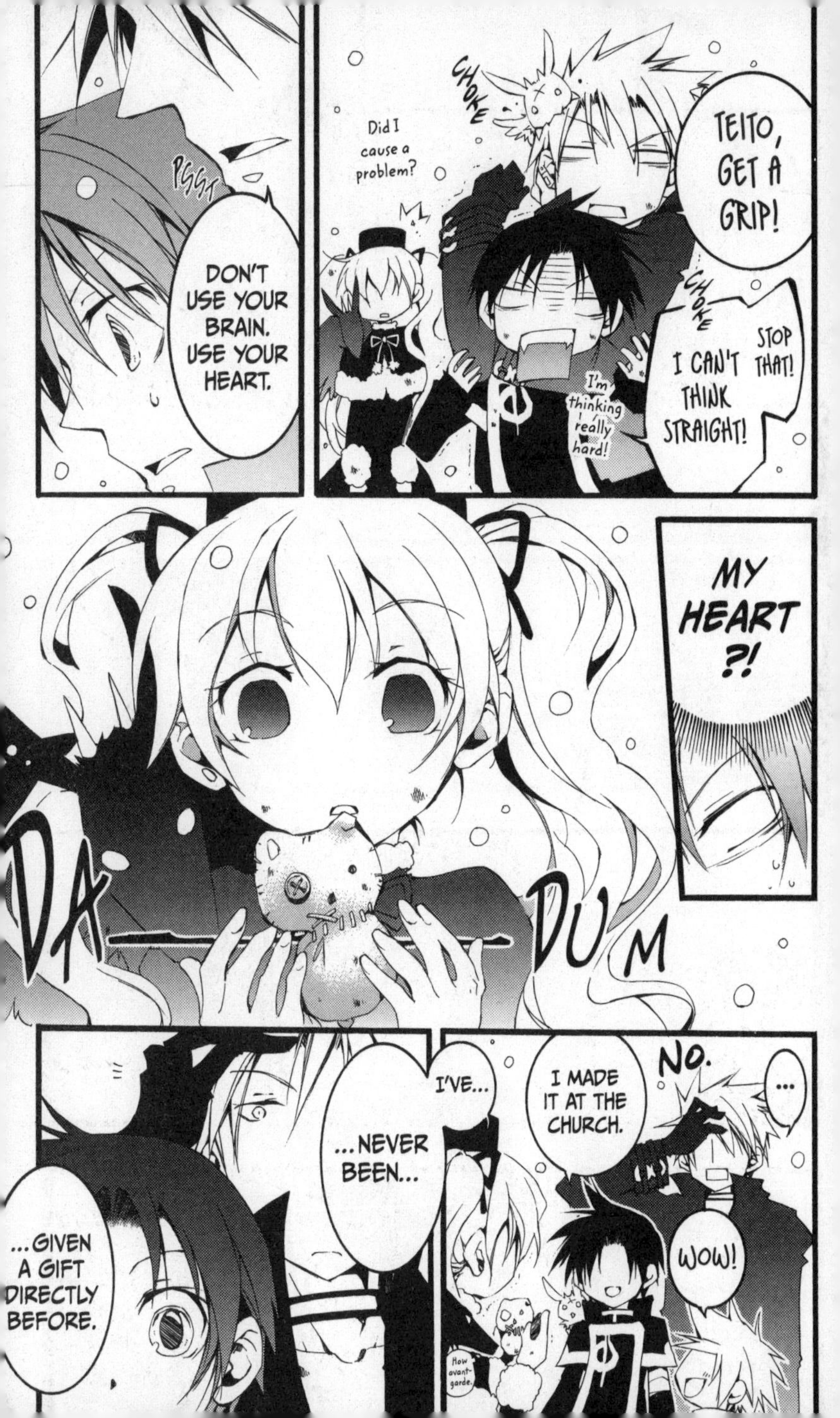
TEITO, GET A GRIP!
CHOKE
Did I cause a problem?
CHOKE
STOP THAT!
I CAN'T THINK STRAIGHT!
I'm thinking really hard!
PSST
DON'T USE YOUR BRAIN. USE YOUR HEART.
MY HEART?!
DA DUM
...
NO.
I MADE IT AT THE CHURCH.
WOW!
How avant-garde.
I'VE...
...NEVER BEEN...
...GIVEN A GIFT DIRECTLY BEFORE.

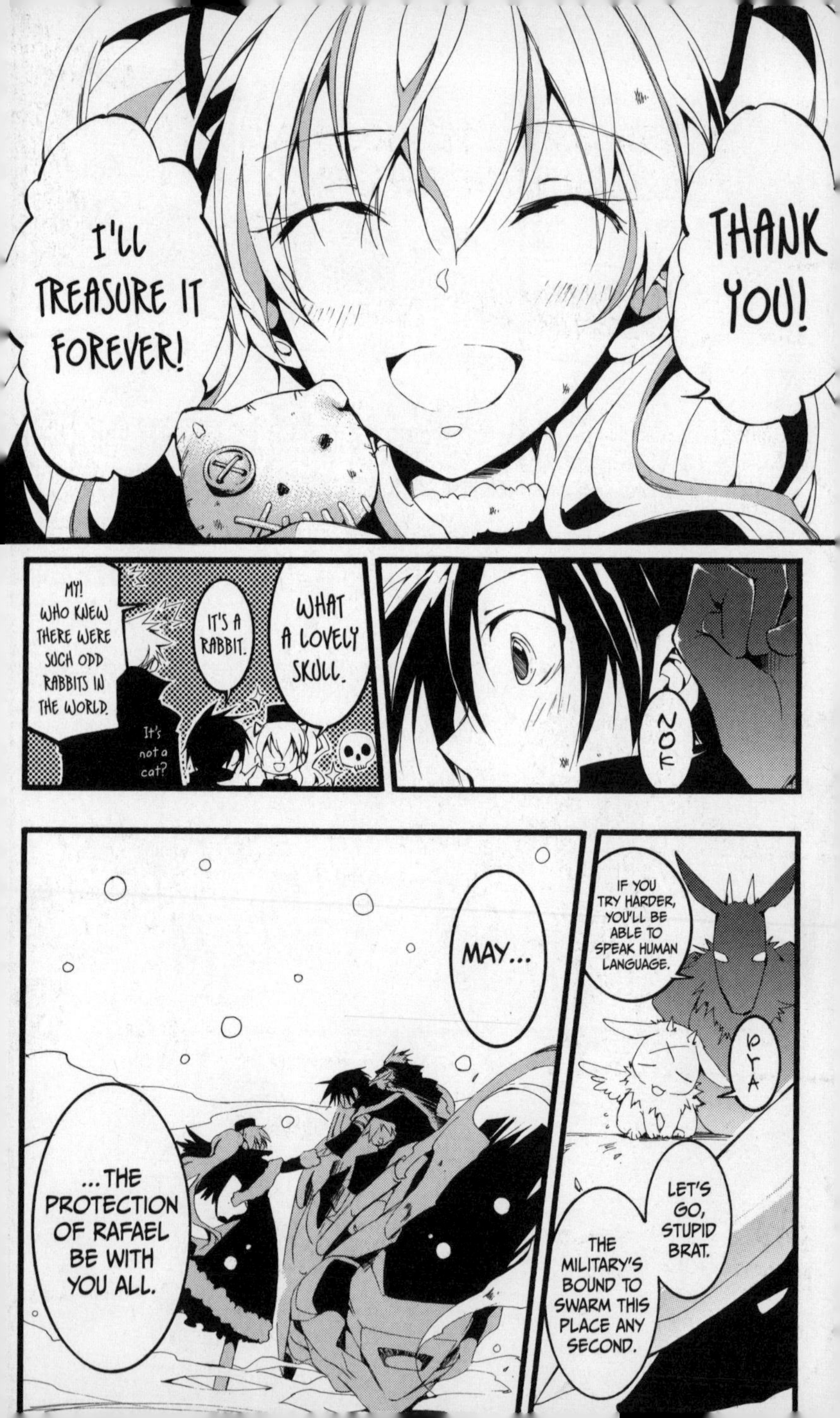
THANK YOU!
I'LL TREASURE IT FOREVER!
NO!
WHAT A LOVELY SKULL.
IT'S A RABBIT.
MY! WHO KNEW THERE WERE SUCH ODD RABBITS IN THE WORLD.
It's not a cat?
IF YOU TRY HARDER, YOU'LL BE ABLE TO SPEAK HUMAN LANGUAGE.
PYA
LET'S GO, STUPID BRAT.
THE MILITARY'S BOUND TO SWARM THIS PLACE ANY SECOND.
MAY...
...THE PROTECTION OF RAFAEL BE WITH YOU ALL.

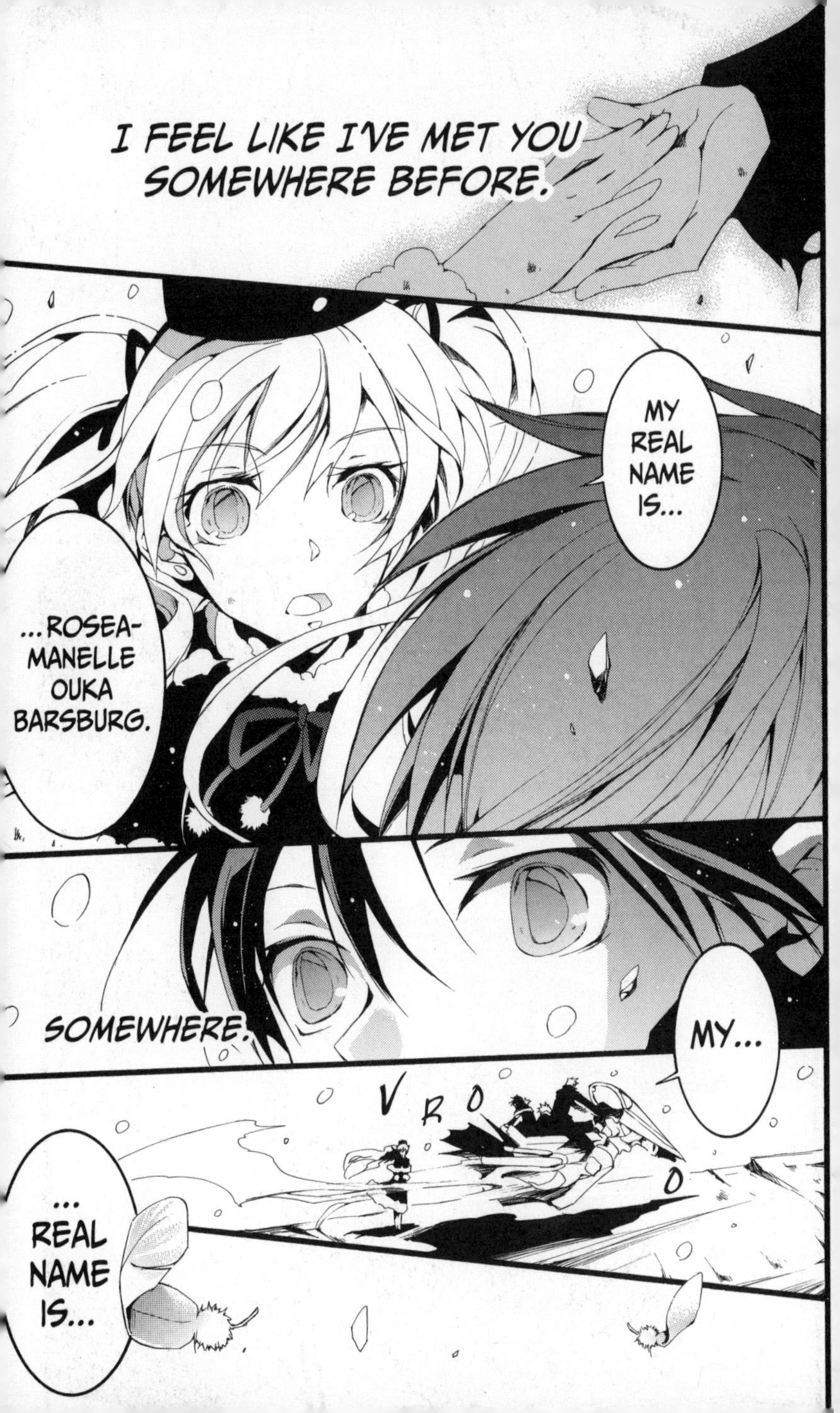
I FEEL LIKE I'VE MET YOU SOMEWHERE BEFORE.
MY REAL NAME IS...
...ROSEA-MANELLE OUKA BARSBURG.
SOMEWHERE.
MY...
V R O O
... REAL NAME IS...

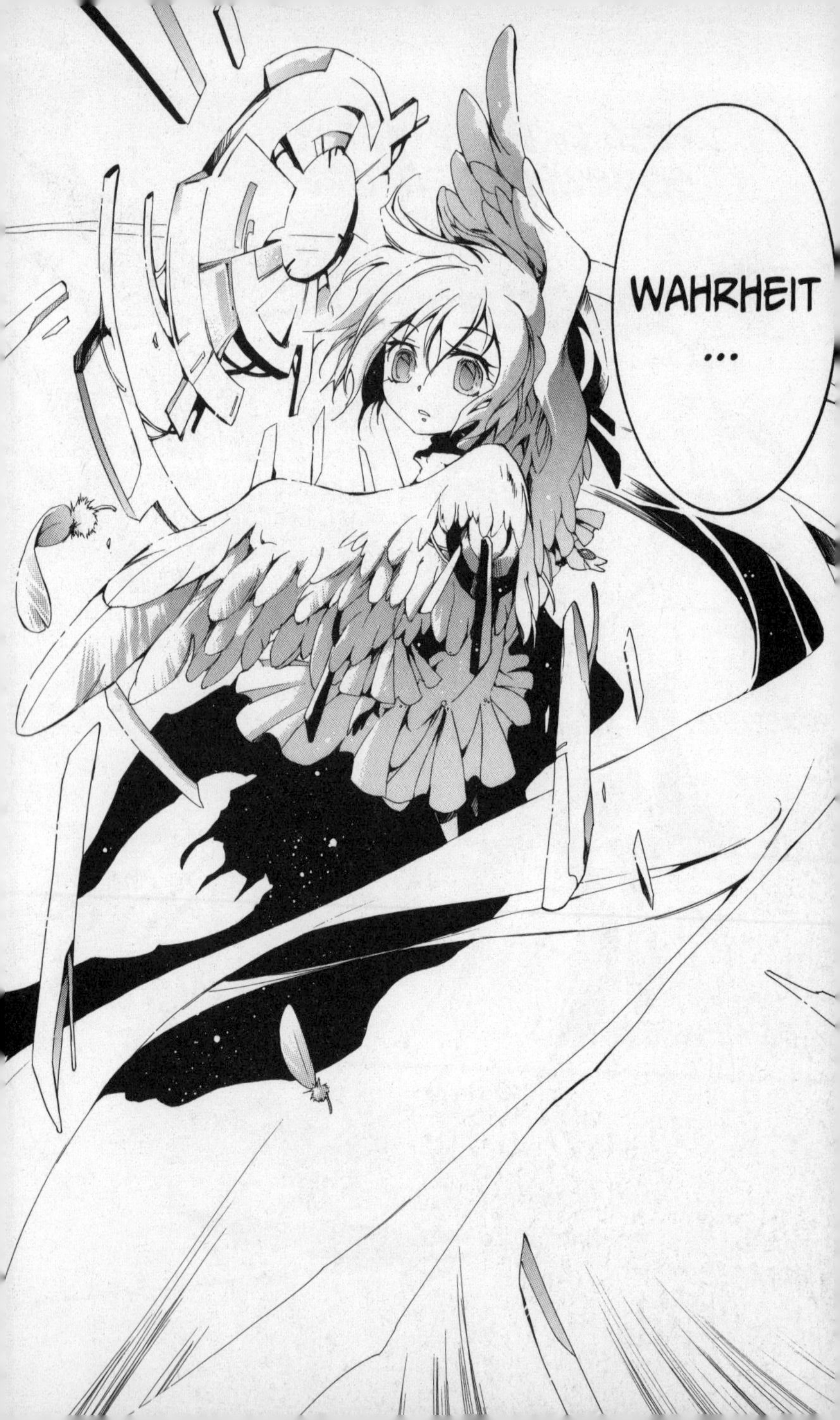
WAHRHEIT ...

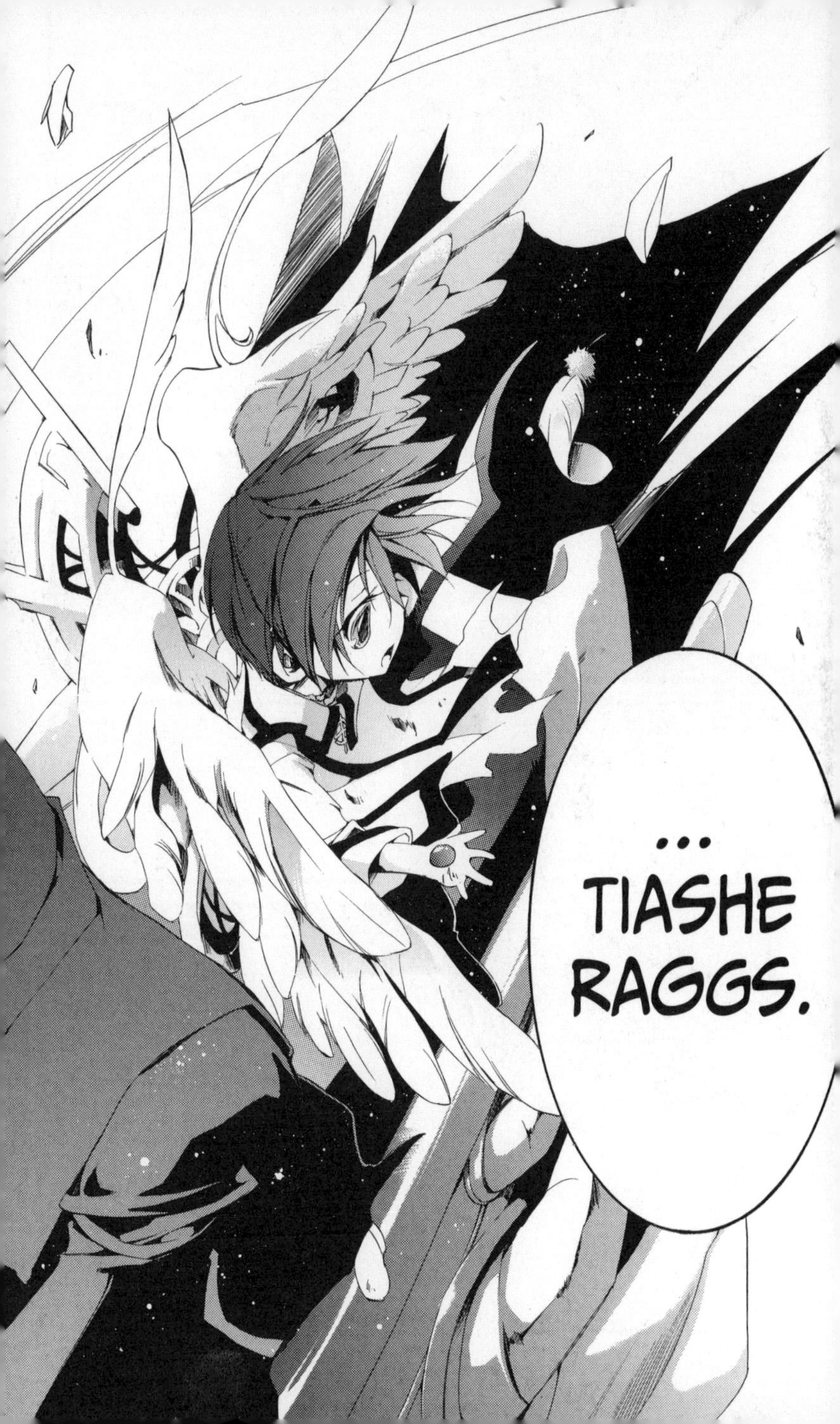
... TIASHE RAGGS.

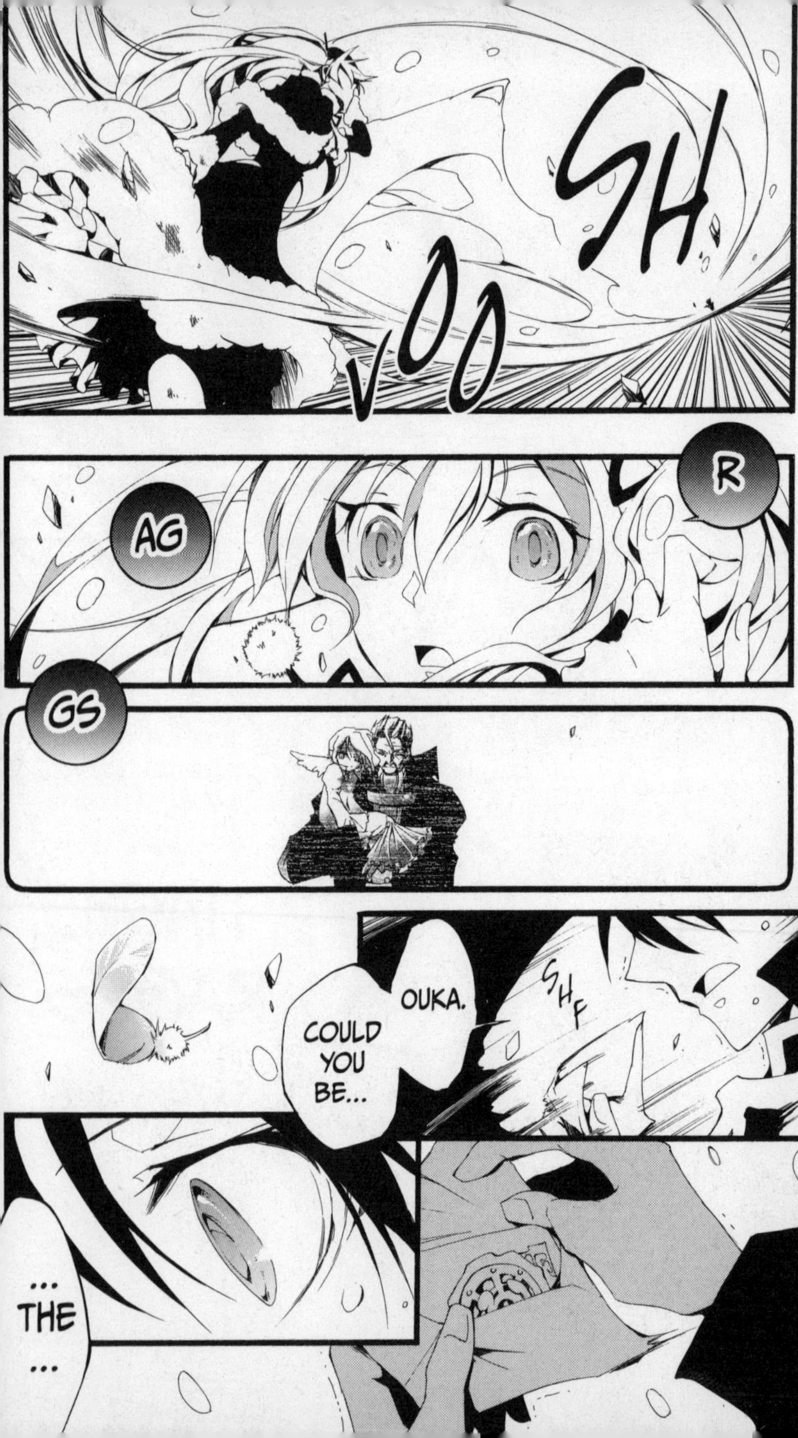
VOOSH
R
AG
GS
OUKA.
COULD YOU BE...
SHF
...THE...

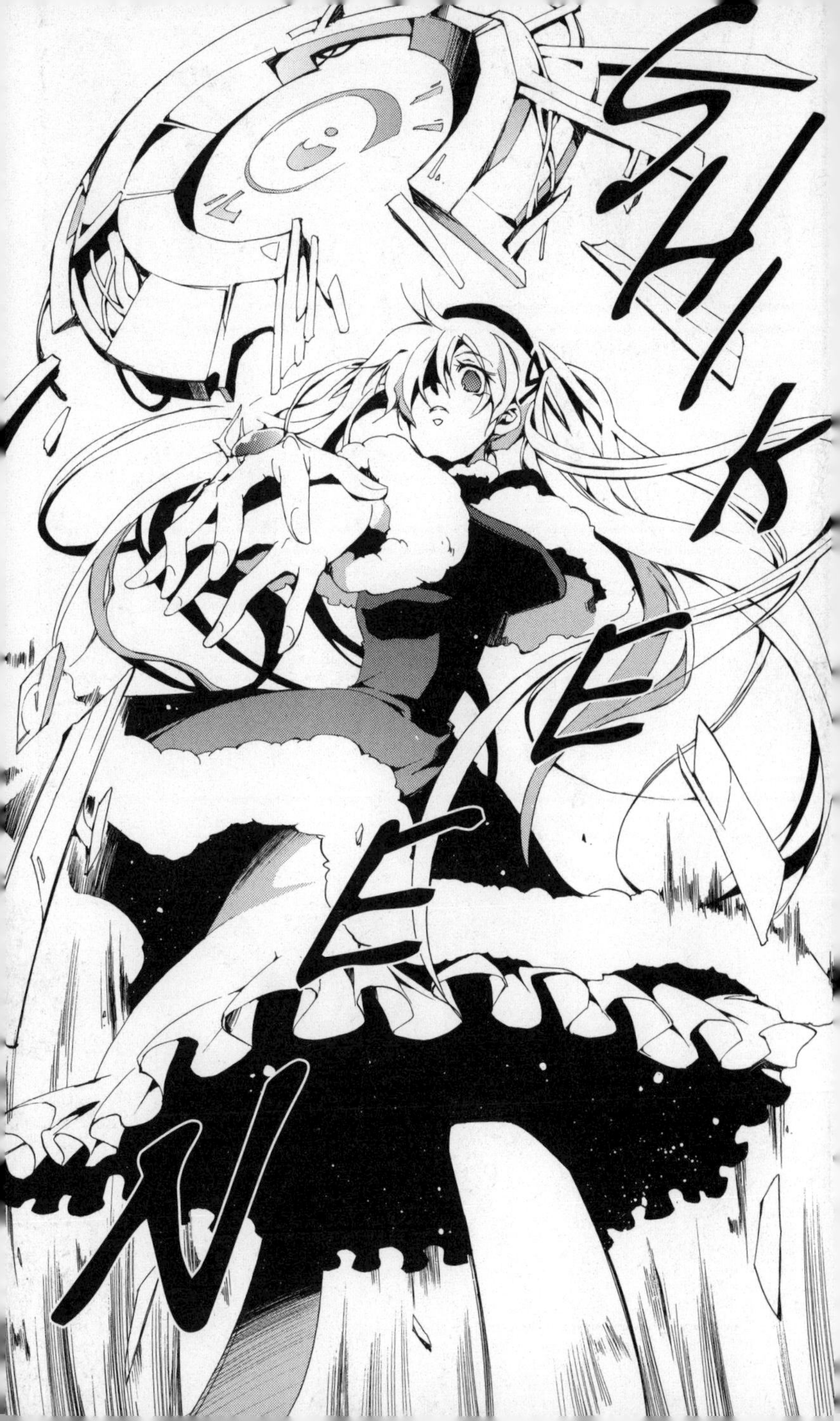
SHIKEEN

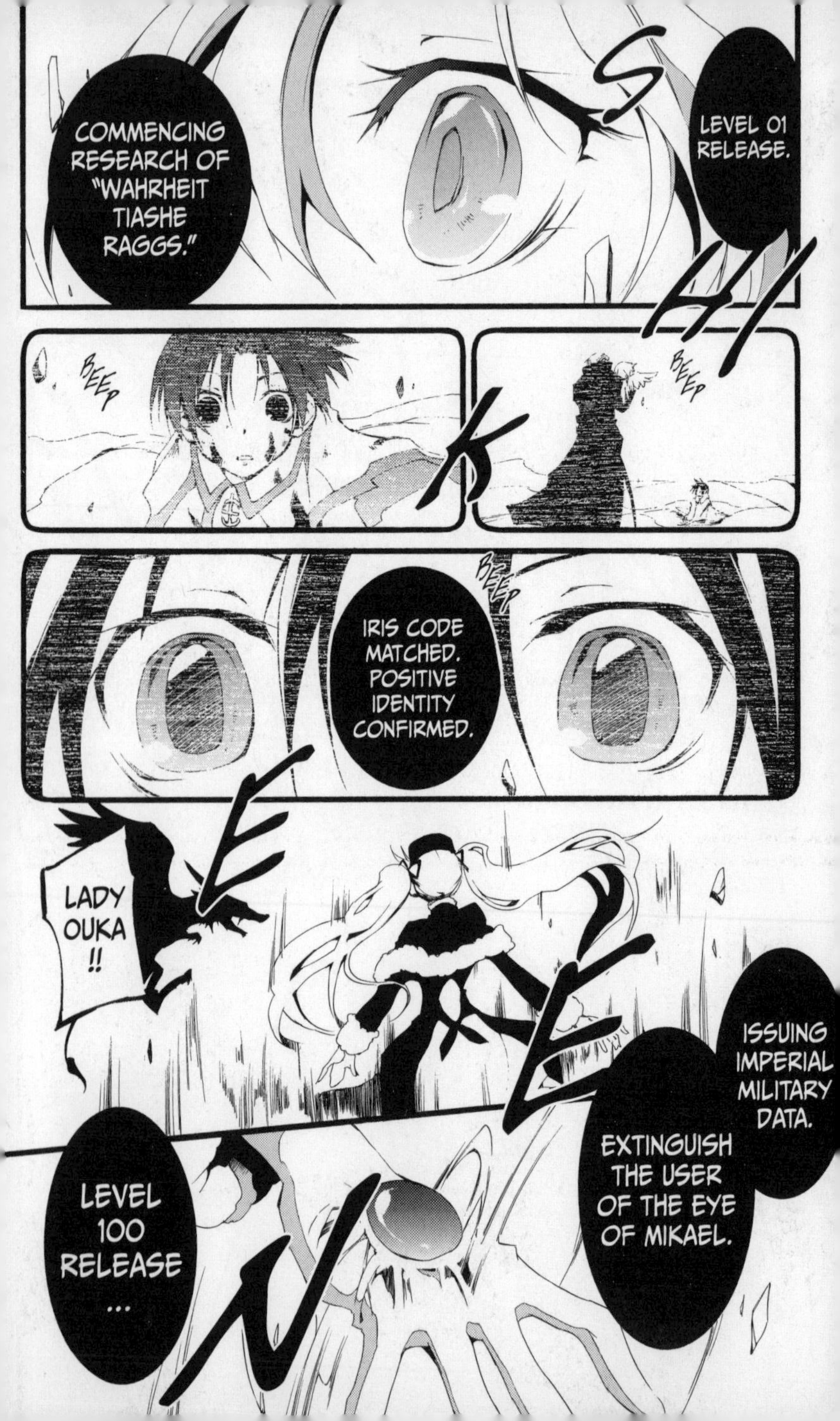
LEVEL 01 RELEASE.
COMMENCING RESEARCH OF "WAHRHEIT TIASHE RAGGS."
BEEP
BEEP
BEEP
IRIS CODE MATCHED. POSITIVE IDENTITY CONFIRMED.
ISSUING IMPERIAL MILITARY DATA.
LADY OUKA !!
EXTINGUISH THE USER OF THE EYE OF MIKAEL.
LEVEL 100 RELEASE ...

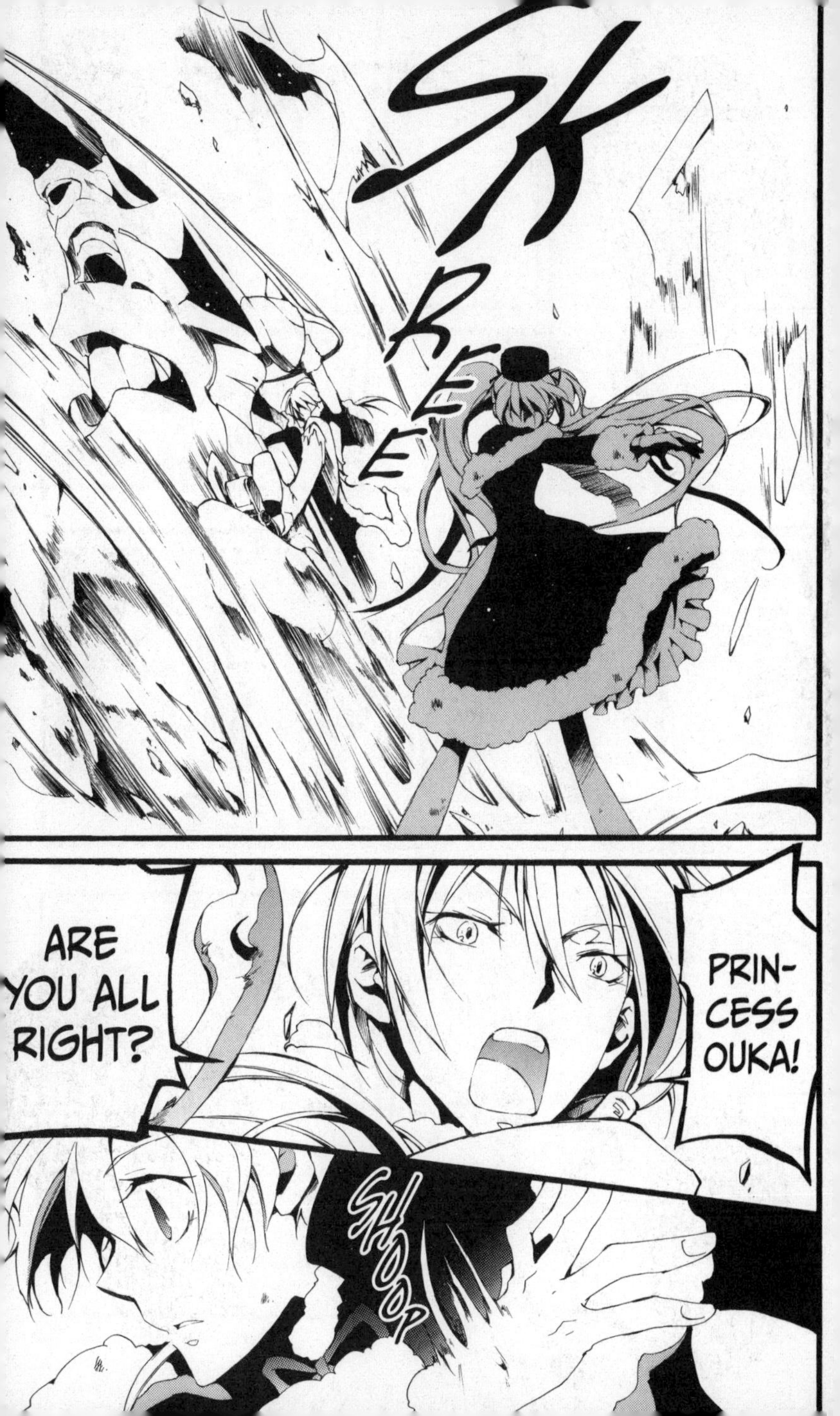
SKREEE
PRIN-CESS OUKA!
ARE YOU ALL RIGHT?
SHOOOP

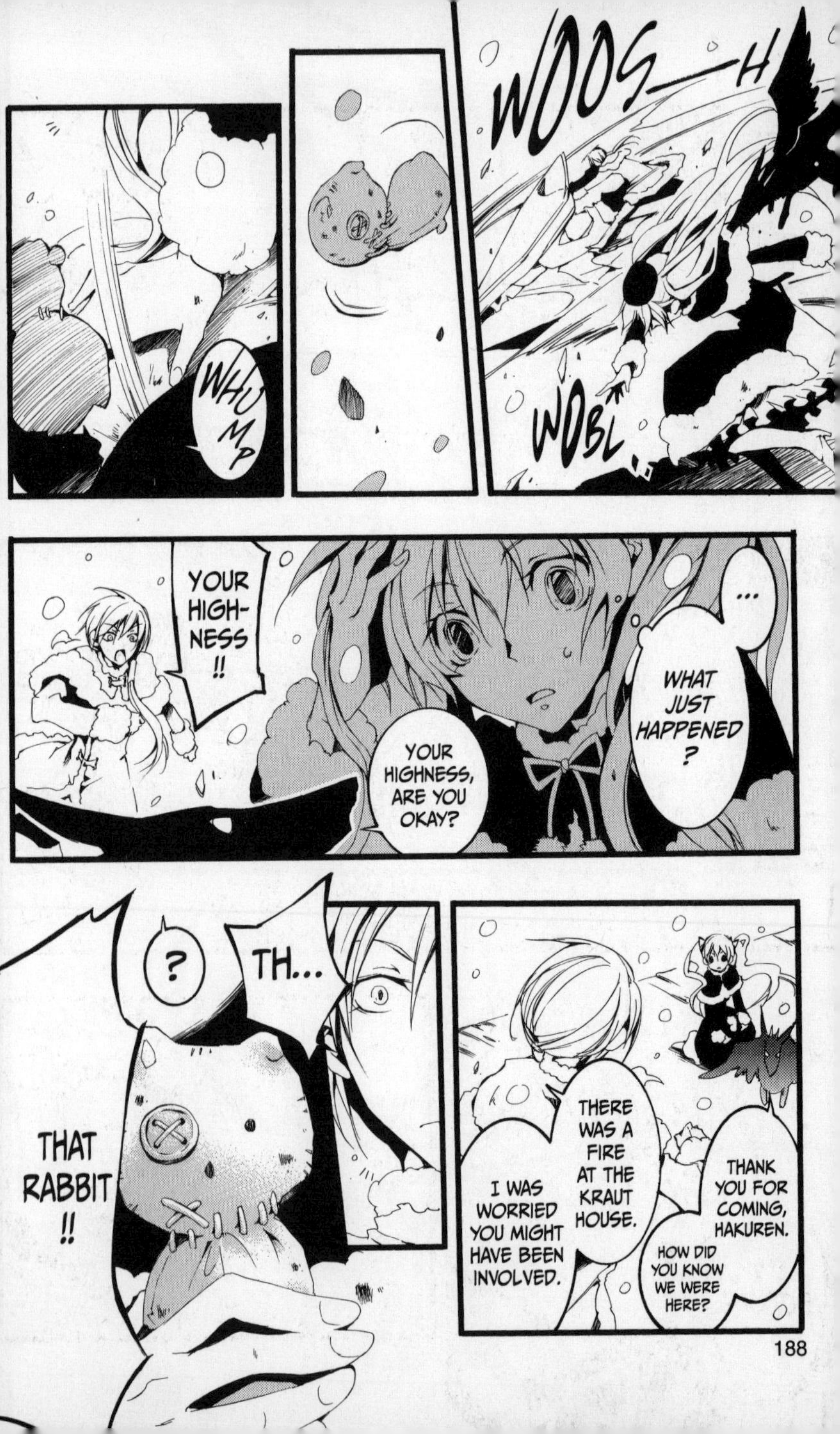
WOOS—H
WOBL
WHUMP
...
WHAT JUST HAPPENED?
YOUR HIGHNESS, ARE YOU OKAY?
YOUR HIGHNESS!!
THANK YOU FOR COMING, HAKUREN.
HOW DID YOU KNOW WE WERE HERE?
THERE WAS A FIRE AT THE KRAUT HOUSE.
I WAS WORRIED YOU MIGHT HAVE BEEN INVOLVED.
TH...
?
THAT RABBIT!!

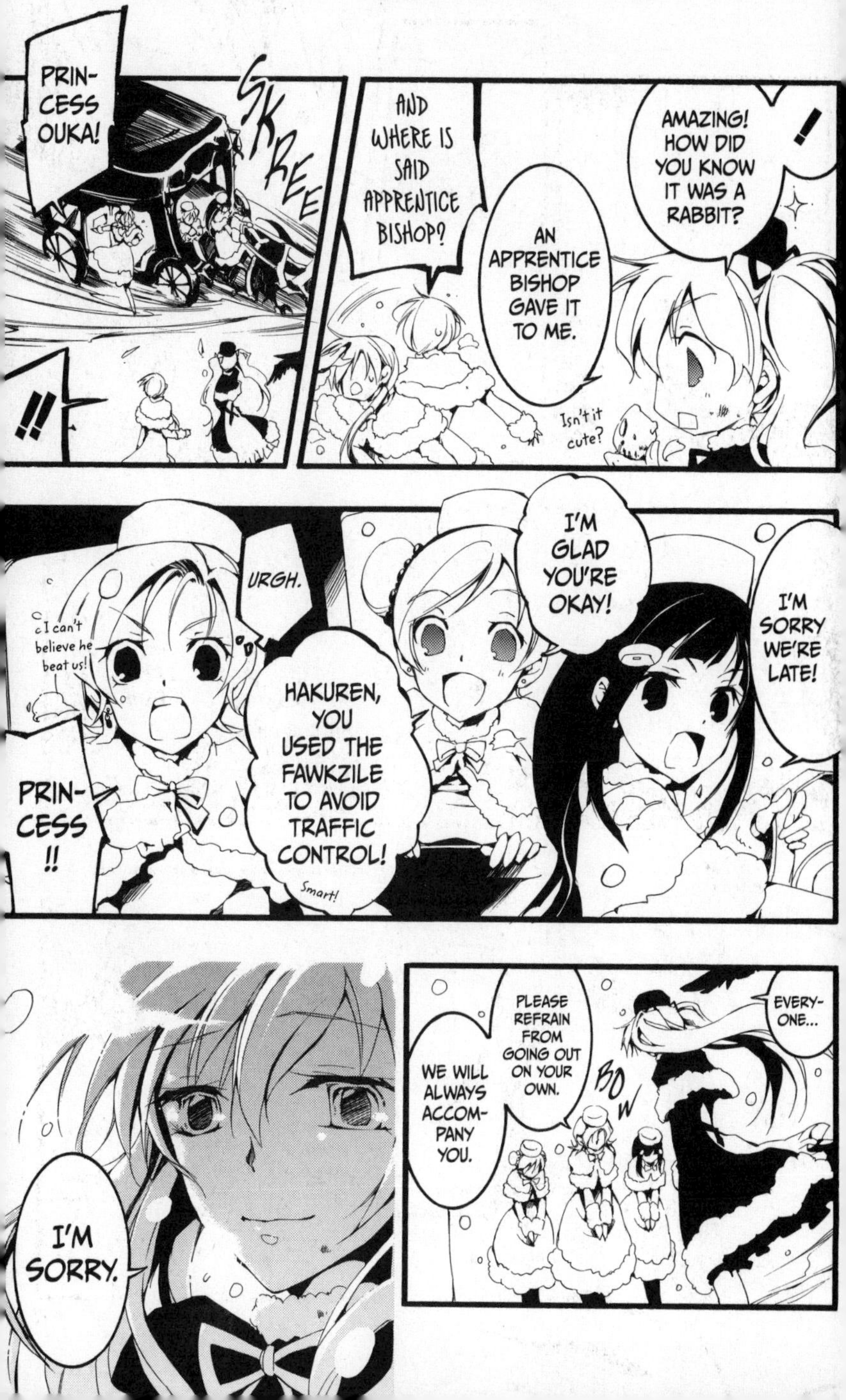
!
AMAZING! HOW DID YOU KNOW IT WAS A RABBIT?
AN APPRENTICE BISHOP GAVE IT TO ME.
Isn't it cute?
AND WHERE IS SAID APPRENTICE BISHOP?
PRIN-CESS OUKA!
SKREEE
!!
I'M SORRY WE'RE LATE!
I'M GLAD YOU'RE OKAY!
HAKUREN, YOU USED THE FAWKZILE TO AVOID TRAFFIC CONTROL!
Smart!
URGH.
I can't believe he beat us!
PRIN-CESS !!
EVERY-ONE...
BOW
PLEASE REFRAIN FROM GOING OUT ON YOUR OWN.
WE WILL ALWAYS ACCOM-PANY YOU.
I'M SORRY.

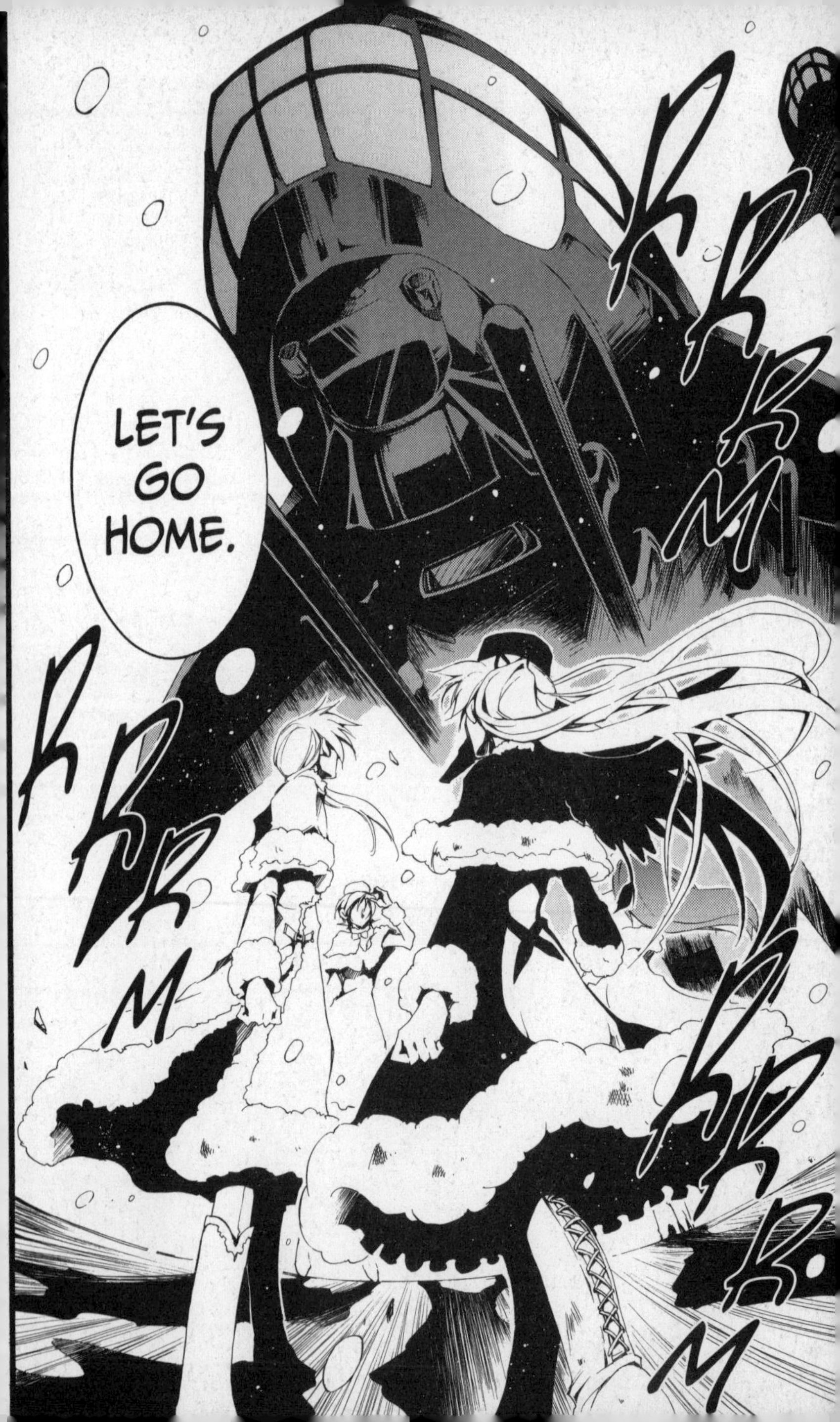
LET'S GO HOME.
KRRRM

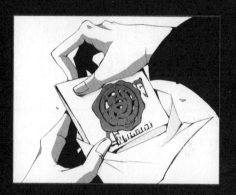

The Royal Family cordially invites

Zeito

by order of His Majesty to the birthday party of
Her Highness and First Princess Roseamanelle
Ouka Barsburg at the Barsburg palace on XXth
day of XX year at three o'clock in the afternoon.
Formal attire is required.

Bonus

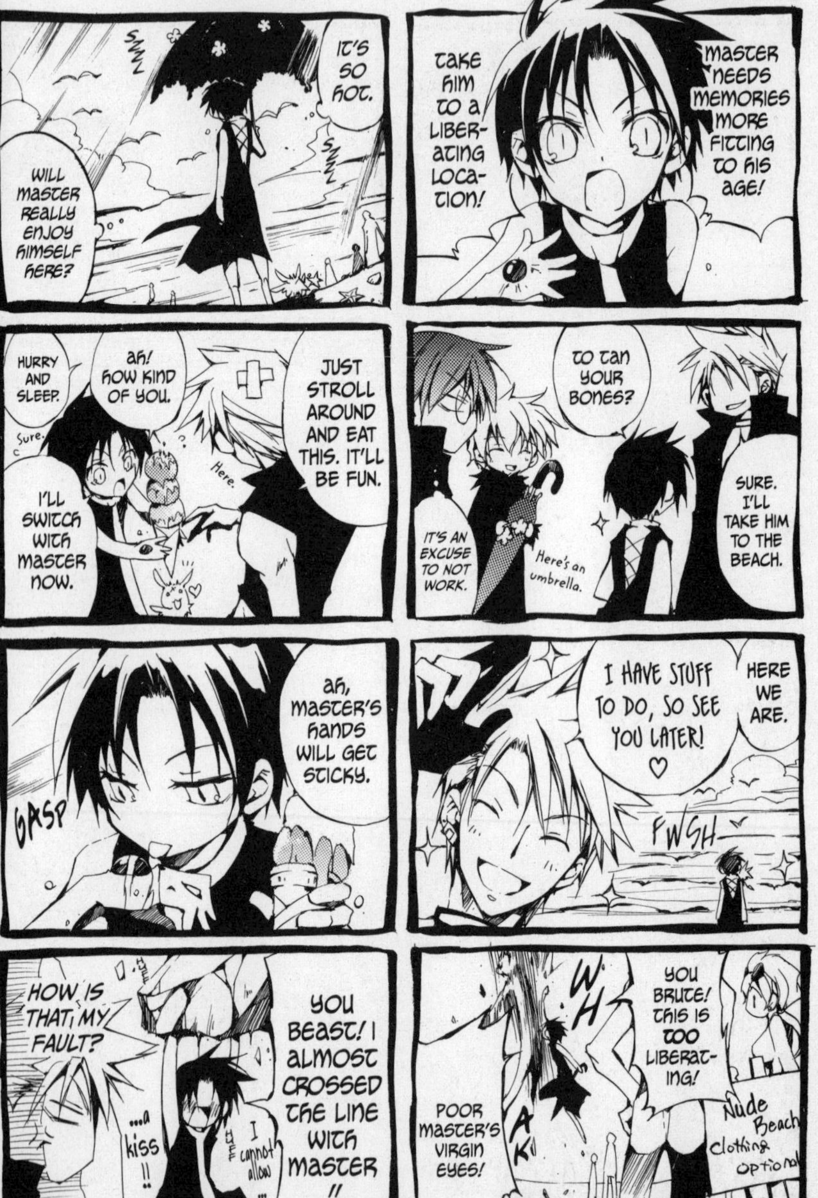
Master needs memories more fitting to his age!
Take him to a liberating location!
It's so hot.
SZZZ
SZZZ
Will master really enjoy himself here?
To tan your bones?
Sure. I'll take him to the beach.
Here's an umbrella.
It's an excuse to not work.
Just stroll around and eat this. It'll be fun.
Here.
Ah! How kind of you.
Hurry and sleep.
Sure.
I'll switch with master now.
Here we are.
I have stuff to do, so see you later! ♡
FWSH
Ah, master's hands will get sticky.
GASP
You brute! This is too liberating!
Nude Beach
Clothing optional
WHAK
Poor master's virgin eyes!
You beast! I almost crossed the line with master!!
I cannot allow...
...a kiss!!
How is that my fault?

Mikael's real form →

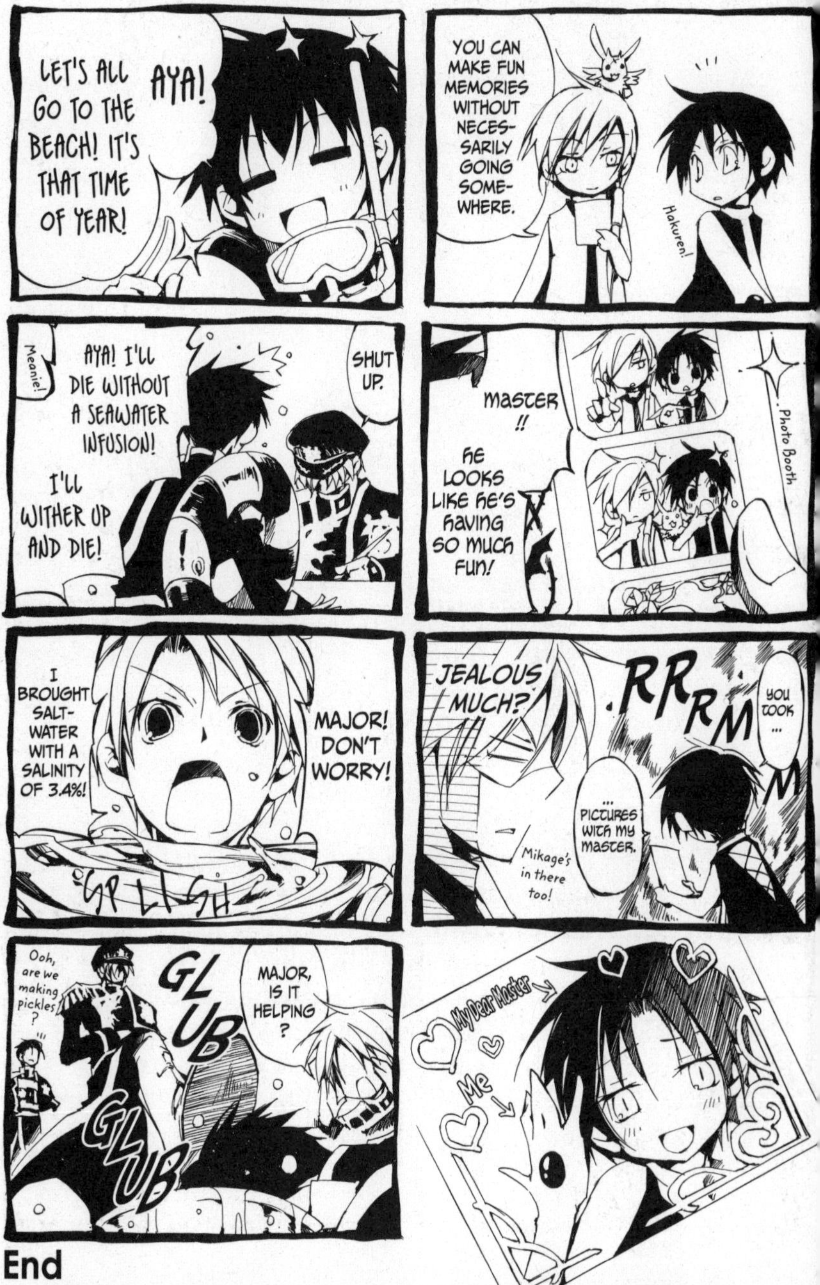
YOU CAN MAKE FUN MEMORIES WITHOUT NECES-SARILY GOING SOME-WHERE.
Hakuren!
AYA!
LET'S ALL GO TO THE BEACH! IT'S THAT TIME OF YEAR!
Photo Booth
MASTER!!
HE LOOKS LIKE HE'S HAVING SO MUCH FUN!
SHUT UP.
AYA! I'LL DIE WITHOUT A SEAWATER INFUSION!
Meanie!
I'LL WITHER UP AND DIE!
YOU TOOK ...
RRRMMM
JEALOUS MUCH?
... PICTURES WITH MY MASTER.
Mikage's in there too!
MAJOR! DON'T WORRY!
I BROUGHT SALT-WATER WITH A SALINITY OF 3.4%!
SPLISH
My Dear Master
Me
MAJOR, IS IT HELPING?
GLUB
GLUB
Ooh, are we making pickles?

End

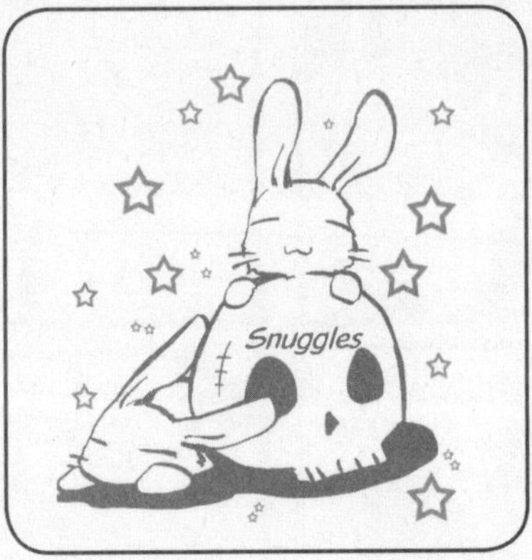
Snuggles

A stray cat has been coming to our place for four months. Finally it has opened up to us enough to sleep on our laps. (*Yay!*)

—Yuki Amemiya & Yukino Ichihara, 2009

Yuki Amemiya was born in Miyagi, Japan, on March 25. Yukino Ichihara was born in Fukushima, Japan, on November 24. Together they write and illustrate *07-Ghost*, the duo's first series. Since its debut in 2005, *07-Ghost* has been translated into a dozen languages, and in 2009 it was adapted into a TV anime series.

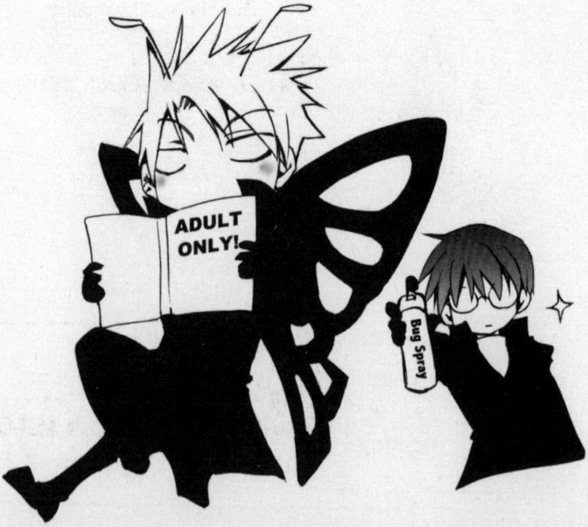
ADULT ONLY!
Bug Spray

07-GHOST

Volume 9

STORY AND ART BY
YUKI AMEMIYA and YUKINO ICHIHARA

Translation/Satsuki Yamashita
Touch-up Art & Lettering/Vanessa Satone
Design/Yukiko Whitley
Editor/Hope Donovan

07-GHOST © 2009
by Yuki Amemiya/Yukino Ichihara
All rights reserved.
Original Japanese edition published by
ICHIJINSHA, INC., Tokyo.
English translation rights arranged with
ICHIJINSHA, INC.

Printed in Canada

Published by VIZ Media, LLC
P.O. Box 77010
San Francisco, CA 94107

10 9 8 7 6 5 4 3 2 1
First printing, March 2014

www.viz.com

Hey! You're Reading in the Wrong Direction!

This is the end of this graphic novel!

To properly enjoy this VIZ graphic novel, please turn it around and begin reading from right to left. Unlike English, Japanese is read right to left, so Japanese comics are read in reverse order from the way English comics are typically read.

This book has been printed in the original Japanese format in order to preserve the orientation of the original artwork. Have fun with it!

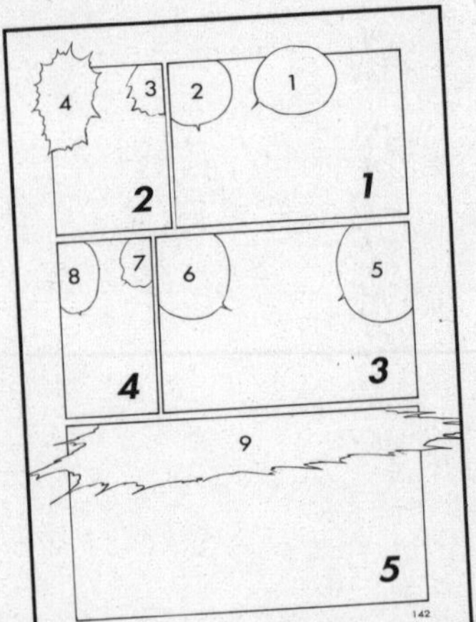
1
2
1
3
4
2
5
6
3
7
8
4
9
5
142

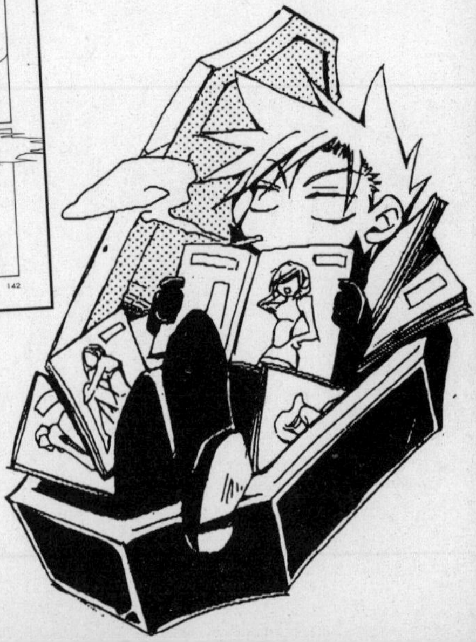